THE INDIGENOUS WORLD 2000/2001

IWGIA
Copenhagen 2001

THE INDIGENOUS WORLD 2000/2001

Compilation and editing of this edition of The Indigenous World has been coordinated by Anette Molbech.

Cover and Typesetting: Jorge Monrás

Spanish translation: Mario Di Lucci

Spanish proofreading: Janet Ferrari

English translation: Elaine Bolton

English proofreading: Elaine Bolton & Birgit Stephenson

Regional editors:
>   *The Arctic & North America:* Kathrin Wessendorf
>   *South America; Mexico & Central America;*
>   *The Pacific & Australia:* Diana Vinding
>   *Asia:* Christian Erni
>   *Africa:* Marianne Jensen
>   *Indigenous Rights:* Lola García-Alix

Prepress and Print: Eks-Skolens Trykkeri, Copenhagen, Denmark

ISSN: 0105-4503 - **ISBN:** 87-90730-48-8

Cover Photo: By Arthur Krasilnikoff, Female Bushman with child,
                 Botswana, Africa.

**INTERNATIONAL WORK
GROUP FOR INDIGENOUS AFFAIRS**
Classensgade 11 E, DK 2100 - Copenhagen, Denmark
Tel: (+45) 35 27 05 00 - Fax: (+45) 35 27 05 07
E-mail: iwgia@iwgia.org - www.iwgia.org

This book has been produced
with financial support from the
Danish Ministry of Foreign Affairs and from
the Norwegian Agency for Development Cooperation

CONTENTS

PREFACE

The intention of *The Indigenous World 2000/2001* has been to try to reflect the most crucial developments that have affected indigenous peoples in the different regions of the world in the last year or so.

Therefore we are extremely grateful for the contributions we have received. Without these this book could not have been published and our intention of mirroring the progress and setbacks of the indigenous world would have been impossible to get even close to.

To report on the world comprehensively is an ambitious task – and we are well aware that this issue of *The Indigenous World* has its omissions and insufficiencies in terms of covering issues, peoples and countries. Also, the articles naturally reflect the different points of departure that the authors have taken when writing about a specific area. We have decided to keep the articles that way as we find it important to maintain the authenticity of the reports published in this book. This may lead some readers to conclude that *The Indigenous World* is an *insider's* book that requires more than a minimum of knowledge about specific areas and peoples. However, the intention of the book is to reflect what happened or led up to the situation that a given area has found itself in during the past year – since the last edition of the book was published.

A detailed book on the indigenous world would be wonderful, but nevertheless a task that would require research resources which we do not have the capacity to meet. The contributions have been written on an entirely voluntary basis by a large number of indigenous and non-indigenous authors. We appreciate that it is at all possible to involve so many people in this book, people who use their scarce spare time to contribute to this "mosaic" of reflections on the indigenous world.

This year, we are very content to be able to cover developments in China and North America, Laos, Vietnam, New Zealand and a number of Pacific Islands which were not included last year. We would have liked to bring more detailed information about the crucial situation in Burma, however, but this proved impossible since we had very limited time to do so. We are also happy to be able to cover Ethiopia again, although the article focuses on a specific part of the country and there are other peoples and parts of the country which might have been included.

Even though we will always strive to achieve as complete a book as possible, our limited capacity does not allow us to cover the world the way it is – in all aspects. The book should be read as a dedicated effort to provide and assemble bits and pieces of a highly complex world. We would therefore appreciate your comments, suggestions and if possible your concrete contributions to next year's issue, which we hope to make ever more complete.

Anette Molbech
Coordinating editor

CONTRIBUTIONS

CONTRIBUTIONS

IWGIA would like to extend warm thanks to the following people and organisations for having contributed to *The Indigenous World 2000/2001*. We would also like to thank the authors who wished to remain anonymous and therefore are not mentioned below. Without their contributions this book would not have been published.

PART I

THE ARCTIC & NORTH AMERICA

This section has been compiled and edited by Kathrin Wessendorf, IWGIA Arctic Program Coordinator.

Marianne Lykke Thomsen has been associated with IWGIA for many years. She has worked for the Inuit Circumpolar Conference, the Greenland Home Rule, The Office of International Relations. Marianne Lykke Thomsen is the Greenland Home Rule representative in Ottawa *(The Arctic Council).*

Mattias Åhrén is a Saami, working as an associate at Danowsky & Partners lawfirm in Stockholm. He also works for the Saami Council *(Sápmi,* Sweden).

Leif Rantala is a teacher of Saami language and culture at the University of Lapland (in Rovaniemi, Finland). Leif Rantala has specialized on the Russian Saami *(Russia and Finland).*

Olga Murashko is an anthropologist, co-founder of the IWGIA local group in Russia and presently a member of IWGIA's board *(Russia – Indigenous Peoples in Russia).*

Helle Høgh is a Ph.D. student at the Department of Ethnography and Social Anthropology, University of Aarhus, Denmark. Helle Høgh conducted fieldwork in Nunavut in 1996 and 1999 *(Nunavut).*

Michael Posluns maintains a watching brief on discussions of First Nations matters in the Canadian Parliament. He is presently completing a doctoral dissertation on First Nations testimony before Canadian Parliamentary committees in the 1970s entitled *The Public Emergence of the Vocabulary of First Nations' Self-Government (Canada: First Nations Relations at the End of the Second Millenium)*.

Russel Diabo is a member of the Mohawk Nation at Kahnawake in Quebec. He holds a B.A. in Native Studies from Laurentian University in Canada, and has undertaken graduate studies towards an M.A. at the University of Arizona and Carleton University in Ottawa. Mr. Diabo was the Coordinator on Indian Act Amendments for the Assembly of First Nations during 1996-97. He is presently an advisor to the Interior Alliance of Indigenous Nations in British Columbia, Canada (*Canada: First Nations Governance Act and First Nations Financial Institutions Act*).

Jim Edmonson has worked for aboriginal organizations at the national, regional and commmunity levels since 1985. He has spent much of this time as an advisor and negotiator in talks with the federal and territorial governments on land claims and self-government (*Northwest Territories*).

Georg Henriksen is an anthropologist and a professor at the Department of Social Anthropology, University of Bergen, Norway. Georg Henriksen is the Chairman of IWGIA's international board. He has worked extensively with the Innu (*The Innu Nation*).

Martha McCollough is a cultural anthropologist in the Anthropology and Ethnic Studies Department at the University of Nebraska. Her research interests include the relationships between states and nonstate societies. She is currently working on a book that explores terrorism prior to the reservation era in the United States (*USA*).

MEXICO, CENTRAL AND SOUTH AMERICA

This section has been compiled and edited by Diana Vinding, IWGIA Latin America & Pacific Program Coordinator.

Araceli Burguete Cal y Mayor is a sociologist and researcher at the Centre for Research and Higher Studies in Social Anthropology (CIESAS) and advisor to the indigenous organisation ANIPA (*Mexico*).

13

Kajkoj Máximo Abrahan Ba Tiul is a Poqomchi Maya philosopher and anthropologist. He has worked for the Coordinating Body of NGOs and Cooperatives – CONGCOOP – and has been a member of Nukuj Ajpop and COPMAGUA. He is currently Director of the Civil Society Dissemination Programme of the International Committee of the Red Cross and a columnist for *El Periódico (Guatemala)*.

Margarita Antonio is a Miskita journalist from the Nicaraguan North Atlantic Coast and currently the Director of the Communication Programme of the University of the Autonomous Regions of the Nicaraguan Caribbean Coast, URACCAN, and editor of the newspaper *Autonomía* (Autonomy). She is the Nicaraguan representative of the International Association of Community Radio, AMARC *(Nicaragua)*.

Gilbert González Maroto is an indigenous Brunca and runs the Centre for Indigenous Development (CEDIN S.A.) in Puntarenas, Costa Rica. You can visit the Centre at: http://www.cedin.iwarp.com *(Costa Rica)*.

Atencio López is an indigenous Kuna and lawyer. He is President of the NGO "Napguana" *(Panama)*.

Luis Jesús Bello is a lawyer, Ombudsman for the State of Amazonas and Member of the Human Rights Office of the Vicariate of Puerto Ayacucho. He is also consultant to the Regional Organisation of Indigenous Peoples of the Amazon (ORPIA) and the Permanent Commission of Indigenous Peoples of the Venezuelan National Assembly *(Venezuela)*.

Alberto Achito Lubia is an indigenous Embera from Juradó (Chocó) and a distinguished leader from the Colombian Pacific. He was a founder member of OREWA, and was also its President. He is currently coordinator for environmental issues with the National Indigenous Organisation of Colombia (ONIC) and a member of the Indigenous Coordinating Body of the Pacific. His article on Colombia is dedicated to his brother, Armando Achito Lubiaza, an Embera leader murdered by paramilitaries in December 2000 *(Colombia)*.

Carlos Viteri is an Amazonian Quechua from Ecuador, an anthropologist and adviser to the Quechua deputy Nina Pacari Vega *(Ecuador)*.

Pedro García Hierro, a lawyer, is President of the NGO "Racimos de Ungurahui" based in Lima, Peru. He is author of the IWGIA Document *Territorios Indígenas y la Nueva Legislación Agraria en el Perú* (Indigenous Territories and the New Agrarian Legislation in Peru) *(Peru)*.

Leonardo Tamburini and *Ana Cecilia Betancour* are both lawyers working for the Centre for Legal Studies and Social Research – CEJIS – in Santa Cruz, Bolivia. The former is Coordinator of the Indigenous Programme and the latter a volunteer from the Dutch Development Cooperation Service. The information has been provided by the CEJIS offices in Santa Cruz, Trinidad, Riberalta and Cochabamba, regions in which the institute advises indigenous and peasant organisations on issues of land titling processes and defence of their rights *(Bolivia)*.

Rodrigo Villagra is an anthropologist and lawyer. He has worked for TIERRAVIVA, a Paraguayan NGO, since 1994 *(Paraguay)*.

Christian Groes-Green is a student of anthropology at the University of Copenhagen. He is currently in Manaus, Brazil, doing field work among the Satere Mawe people *(Brazil)*.

Morita Carrasco is an anthropologist and lecturer at the University of Buenos Aires, Argentina. She is the author of the IWGIA Document *La Tierra que Nos Quitaron* (The Land they Took from Us), which considers the conditions of indigenous peoples in Argentina *(Argentina)*.

Dorthe Kristensen, M. Sc. in Anthropology from the University of London, was for many years a member of the National Group of IWGIA in Denmark. In 1999-2000 she carried out field research in Chile concerning issues of identity and politics as related to traditional medicine and religion *(Chile)*.

AUSTRALIA AND THE PACIFIC

This section has been compiled and edited by Diana Vinding, IWGIA Latin America & Pacific Program Coordinator.

Peter Jull and *Kathryn Bennett* research and write on indigenous politics in international contexts at the School of Political Science and International Studies, University of Queensland, Brisbane, Australia *(Australia)*.

Taki Anaru is a barrister and solicitor from Aotearoa/New Zealand. Until recently he was the Senior Solicitor with the Maori Legal Service. He now lives and works in the Cook Islands (*New Zealand*).

Jimmy Nâunââ is the Assistant Director - Decolonisation and Indigenous Rights at the Pacific Concerns Resource Centre (PCRC) in Suva, Fiji Islands. He compiled and edited the report on the Pacific, which also draws on contributions by the PCRC Director and colleague - Assistant Directors in their specific areas of expertise (*The Pacific Islands*).

AFRICA

This section has been compiled and edited by Marianne Jensen, IWGIA Africa Program Coordinator.

North Africa

Hassan Idbalkassm is an Amazigh from Morocco. He is a lawyer and President of the Amazigh association "Tamaynut", which he founded in 1978. He is also the Vice-President of the "Congrés Mondial Amazigh", which has a membership of more than 70 Amazigh associations in North Africa and Europe (*North Africa: The Situation of the Amazigh Peoples*).

East Africa

Nyikaw Abula Ochalla is an indigenous Anuak from the Gambela National State. He holds a degree in management and public administration from the university of Addis Ababa, Ethiopia. After his graduation he worked for both the federal and local government. He currently lives in the UK where he applied for political asylum in 1999 due to the widely reported human rights abuses and the persecution carried out by the Ethiopian government. He is a founder of the non-violent political organisation, the "Gambela Peoples Democratic Congress" and the indigenous "Anywaa Survival Organisation" which advocate the rights of the indigenous people of the Gambela Nation within Ethiopia and Sudan (*Ethiopia*).

Naomi Kipuri is a Maasai from the Kajiado district of Kenya. She is an anthropologist by training. Naomi Kipuri taught at the University of Nairobi and is now a development consultant. She does research and development and is interested in development concerns and issues relating to human rights and the rights of indigenous peoples *(Kenya)*.

Benedict Ole Nangoro is a Maasai from Kiteto in Tanzania. He holds a M. Phil. in Development Studies from the Institute of Development Studies of the University of Sussex, UK. He is currently working with CORDS, a local NGO involved with indigenous pastoral Maasai communities on issues of land demarcation, mapping, registration and collective titling *(Tanzania)*.

Central Africa

Dorothy Jackson is the Africa Programme Coordinator for the Forest Peoples Programme. ***Justin Kenrick*** is an anthropologist at the University of Edinburgh and Uganda project officer with the Forest Peoples Programme *(The Great Lakes Region and Cameroon)*.

Southern Africa

Magdalena Brörmann is an educationalist who has served as a development worker in the fields of early childhood development, in-service teacher training and adult education in various African countries for over two decades. She is currently working as a mentor for young San trainees at the WIMSA regional office in Windhoek, Namibia *(Namibia)*.

Robert K. Hitchcock is Professor of Anthropology and Geography and the Coordinator of African Studies at the University of Nebraska-Lincoln, Lincoln, Nebraska, USA. He is also the coordinator of the Human Rights and Human Diversity Initiative, a program funded by the UNL College of Arts and Sciences and the Ford Foundation. Hitchcock has spent much of the past two and a half decades working among the San of southern Africa, where he has concentrated on issues relating to development, human rights, and empowerment. Hitchcock is the author of *Kalahari Communities: Bushmen and the Politics of the Environment in Southern Africa* (Copenhagen: IWGIA, 1996) and is a co-editor of *Hunters and Gatherers in the Modern World: Conflict, Resistance, and Self-Determination* (New York: Berghahn Books, 2000) *(Botswana)*.

Nigel Crawhall is an activist for indigenous peoples rights. He has worked with the Indigenous Peoples of Africa Co-ordinating Committee (IPACC), and is project manager on an indigenous knowledge and cultural resources management and training project with the South African San Institute (SASI) *(South Africa).*

ASIA

This section has been compiled, edited and partially written by Christian Erni, Asia Program Coordinator at IWGIA.

South Asia

Parshu Ram Tamang is a Senior Lecturer in Economics at Sarawati Multiple Campus, Tribhuvan University, Kathmandu, Nepal. He is a founding member, until recently General Secretary and currently advisor to the Nepal Federation of Nationalities (NEFEN). He is also the President of Nepal Tamang Ghedung (NTG) *(Nepal).*

C. R. Bijoy is a human rights activist. During the last sixteen years he has been involved and associated with indigenous issues and organisations in India and has written about these and related matters. *Walter Fernandes* has been working on tribal issues in India for two decades. He is the former director of the Indian Social Institute, New Delhi, and editor of Social Action. At present he is director of the North Eastern Social Research Centre. *Samar Bosu Mullick* is a political activist, teacher and researcher who has been working in solidarity with the indigenous peoples of Jharkhand for the last quarter of a century. He was one of the front line people in the Jharkhand movement for a separate state *(India).*

Wiveca Stegeborn is a Cultural Anthropologist (M.A. from Washington State University) attached to the University of Tromsoe, Norway, where she will submit her Ph.D dissertation. She has been conducting research among the Wanniyala-Aetto of Sri Lanka since 1977 *(Sri Lanka).*

East and Southeast Asia

Masaharu Konaka has worked for the Buraku Liberation League, Tokyo, as a secretary for several years. Since his return to Sapporo, he has been engaged in translation work for the activities of the Ainu people. *Robert E. Gettings*, an Associate Professor of Hokusei Women's Junior College, kindly checked and corrected the English. He was born in Boston in 1952 and has a keen interest in indigenous movements *(Japan)*.

Harald Bøckman, a sinologist, is Research Fellow at the International Institute of Peace Research in Oslo, Norway. His main field of research is the historical emergence of Chineseness and the relationship between China and her neighbours from an historical perspective *(China)*.

The *Association for Taiwan Indigenous People's Policies (ATIPP)* is an NGO established and administered by Taiwanese indigenous activists. ATIPP is working for the empowerment of Taiwan's indigenous peoples and, as a research and advocacy group, ATIPP seeks to promote the rights of Taiwan's indigenous peoples through policy-making, bill-lobbying and other means *(Taiwan)*.

AnthroWatch is a Manila-based research and advocacy group working closely with indigenous peoples in the Philippines. *Joan Carling* is Secretary General of the Cordillera Peoples Alliance (CPA) based in Baguio in the Cordilleras of Northern Luzon in the Philippines. *Jimid Mansayagan* is an Erumanen Ne Menuvu of Central Mindanao. He has been the Secretary General of Lumad Mindanaw (Peoples Federation) for eleven years and is currently involved in a village-based indigenous movement called Kebager te Ked-Inged. *Michael P. Lacson* is the national secretary of Bangsa Palawan (Indigenous Alliance for Equity and Well-Being). *Dario Novellino* is international advisor to the same organization. He is presently affiliated with the Department of Anthropology at the University of Kent in Canterbury (UK), as well as with the Institute of the Philippine Culture, Ateneo de Manila University *(Philippines)*.

Torben Retbøll teaches history and Latin at Aarhus Katedralskole, a senior college in Aarhus, Denmark. He has written and edited several books on mass media and international affairs, including three IWGIA documents about East Timor, published in 1980, 1984 and 1998 *(East Timor)*.

Danilo Geiger is a Social Anthropologist currently working at the Department of Social Anthropology of the University of Zurich,

Switzerland. He was one of the founding members of the Swiss National Group of IWGIA and has lived and worked extensively with indigenous peoples in the Philippines and Indonesia. *Emilianus Ola Kleden* is the Information and Communication Manager of the Secretarial Office of the Indonesian national indigenous peoples' umbrella organisation, AMAN (Alyansi Masyarakat Adat Nusantara) *(Indonesia)*.

Colin Nicolas is the coordinator for the Center for Orang Asli Concerns (COAC), Kuala Lumpur, Malaysia *(Malaysia)*.

Wiwat Tamee, a Lisu, has assumed a growing role in advocacy relating to indigenous rights and issues in his native country, Thailand. He is currently the director of the Centre for Coordination of Non-Governmental Tribal Development Organizations in Chiang Mai, Thailand *(Thailand)*.

Hanneke Meijers is a gender and natural resources consultant. She has worked in Asia, Africa and South East Asia. Since 1990 she has been living and working in Cambodia *(Cambodia)*.

Luingam Luithui, a Tangkhul Naga, is a human rights advocate. For twenty-five years he has been actively involved in local and regional networking among indigenous peoples and alliance building with NGOs *(Nagalim)*.

PART II

INDIGENOUS RIGHTS

This section has been compiled and edited by Lola García-Alix, IWGIA Human Rights Program Coordinator.

Dr. Sarah Pritchard is an Australian barrister and academic at the Faculty of Law, the University of New South Wales. She has worked with Aboriginal organisations in Australia and at the United Nations for a number of years. Sarah Pritchard has provided legal assistance via IWIGA concerning the Draft Declaration on Indigenous Peoples *(The United Nations: The 6th Session of the Commission on Human Rights Working Group on the Declaration on the Rights of Indigenous Peoples)*.

Lola García-Alix is the Coordinator of Human Rights Activities at IWGIA *(The United Nations: The Permanent Forum on Indigenous Peoples).*

Dr. Carlyle Corbin is Minister of State for External Affairs for the U.S. Virgin Islands. He serves as the Secretary General of the Offshore Governor's Forum comprised of the elected governments of Guam, American Samoa, the Commonwealth of the Northern Mariana Islands and the U.S. Virgin Islands. He has participated in the proceedings of the United Nations' Special Committee on Decolonization since 1982 *(United Nations: Towards the Integration of Non-Independent Countries in the Unites Nations System).*

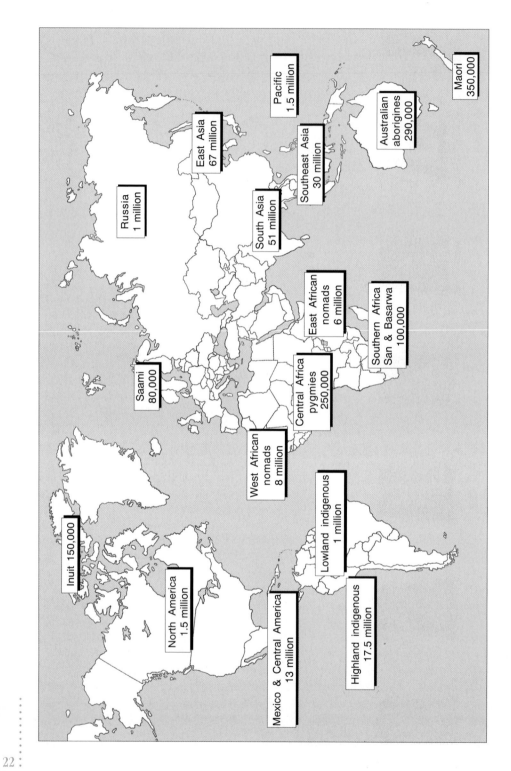

Maori 350,000

Pacific 1.5 million

Australian aborigines 290,000

East Asia 67 million

Southeast Asia 30 million

Russia 1 million

South Asia 51 million

East African nomads 6 million

Southern Africa San & Basarwa 100,000

Saami 80,000

Central Africa pygmies 250,000

West African nomads 8 million

Lowland indigenous 1 million

Inuit 150,000

North America 1.5 million

Mexico & Central America 13 million

Highland indigenous 17.5 million

PART I

THE INDIGENOUS WORLD
BY REGIONS & COUNTRIES

THE ARCTIC

THE ARCTIC

THE ARCTIC COUNCIL

The second Arctic Council Ministerial meeting was held in Barrow, Alaska in October last year. The towns of Barrow and North Slope Borough - known for their great hospitality - were hosting the meeting, which took place in the middle of the bowhead hunt and thus provided the best of food and excitement for the international gathering.

The Arctic Council welcomed two new members as Permanent Participants, namely Gwich'in Council International and Arctic Athabaskan Council. The two organizations represent Gwich'in and Athabaskan-speaking peoples from both Canada and Alaska.

The Premier of Greenland, Jonathan Motzfeldt, who was heading the joint Danish, Faroese and Greenland Delegation for the Kingdom of Denmark, made it clear in his opening speech that it is important that the Arctic Council should develop into a forum that is accessible and of interest to the peoples actually living in the Arctic. The Premier noted with satisfaction that the Greenland initiative to conduct a circumpolar survey of the living conditions of the peoples of the Arctic was adopted by the Council.

Another major achievement during the Ministerial meeting was the adoption of a strategy for sustainable development in the form of a so-called framework document, which establishes some important guiding principles for the future work of the Council and the Sustainable Development Working Group (SDWG).

The Arctic Council Action Plan (ACAP) was endorsed by the Arctic Council as an umbrella strategy to reduce and eliminate pollution of the Arctic environment. Finally, it was decided to go ahead with the Arctic Climate Impact Assessment (ACIA), which is intended to become a comprehensive study of the environmental, health, social and economic impact of climate change in the Arctic.

The Arctic Council Ministerial meeting concluded with the signing of the Barrow Declaration - the workplan for the next two years under a Finnish Chairmanship. The Finnish Chairmanship this year features the 10-year Anniversary of the Rovaniemi Declaration of the so-called Finnish Initiative declaring the development and implementation of an Arctic Environmental Protection Strategy (AEPS). The AEPS, which is now incorporated into the Arctic Council, has proven to be a very successful environmental strategy.

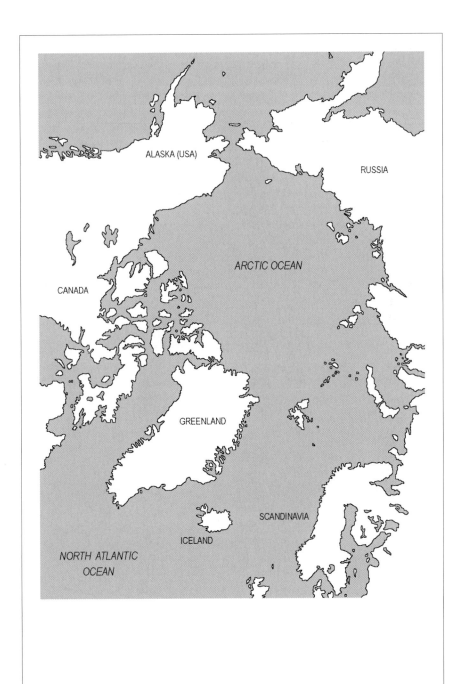

THE ARCTIC

GREENLAND

The National Missile Defense

I n the foreign policy area, a great deal of the discussion throughout the year was centred on a deity – everybody talks about it but nobody has seen it: the National Missile Defense (NMD) with which the USA wants to shield itself against missile attacks from rogue states such as North Korea and Iraq. The remaining American military base in Greenland, Thule Air Base, has been included in the plans, and is to be used as a tracking station for incoming missiles. Both the Danish and the Greenlandic governments have refused to take a stand on the issue, claiming they have not yet received an official enquiry from the United States. The establishment in the USA seems to be all for going ahead with the plans, especially the new administration, but all the tests that have been conducted so far have failed. The plans to develop a NMD have received criticism from the European allies, but Denmark has remained uncommitted. Nevertheless, if one were to analyse the Danish government's silence, it seems more like a silent acceptance, for historically Denmark has always wanted to please "Big Brother", as the different cases of forced relocation of the local population in 1953, deployment of nuclear arsenals in Greenland against the official policy of a non-nuclear Danish Kingdom and environmental pollution from abandoned American bases show, at the expense of Greenlandic interests. The official Greenlandic government's opinion has been that the NMD should not jeopardise nuclear proliferation, and that the USA should come to terms with Russia regarding compatibility of the 1972 ABM Treaty. The last, and also most important, demand is that Greenland should sit at the table when the issue is discussed with the USA.

The issue has the potential of creating a split between the Greenland coalition government of Siumut and Inuit Ataqatigiit. The party of Social Democratic observance, Siumut, has been more cautious about stating a clear opinion, citing the above-mentioned conditions, while the Socialist Inuit Ataqatigiit has loudly rejected the idea of creating the NMD and far less involving the Thule Air Base in it. But besides being a politically hot issue, it has far more fundamental importance for the increasing need to develop a foreign policy capacity, as Greenland has demanded to be included in the decision-making process, instead of Denmark alone taking action on behalf of Greenland. In the sphere of security-policy in particular, Denmark has in the past been quite reluctant to share its decision-making with

Greenland, not least since Denmark has benefited from the American presence in Greenland in relation to NATO over the years. But, as the autonomy of Greenland is evolving in the foreign policy area, Denmark can no longer ignore the opinion of the Greenlanders and it will create a political crisis between the two countries if Denmark goes against the opinion of Greenland on this issue. The Danish feelings of guilt at hiding information from the Greenlanders about the deployment of nuclear missiles throughout the 1950s and 1960s, together with the forced relocation of the local population in 1953 when the base was being expanded, as well as the crash of a B-52 bomber in 1968 with four hydrogen bombs and the environmental consequences, are all too historically vivid for the Danes to deny the Greenlandic people a say in this matter – whatever the outcome might be.

The Integration of Danes into Society

The language debate continued to create controversy, coupled with the issue of the integration into society of Danes living in Greenland. The vocal critics claim that the Danish language is too dominant in the sphere of public administration after 22 years of Home Rule and that Danish-speaking persons are promoted at the expense of qualified Greenlanders. The fact that many of the academic positions in public administration are filled by Danes, as there is a shortage of Greenlandic-speaking people with university degrees shows, according to the critics, that the government policy in the field of education has failed. Others say that it is an expression of continued colonialism. The critics go on to say that it should be a requirement, if one is to fulfil a position in Greenlandic society, to be able to speak Greenlandic. Many of the Danes who come to Greenland to work stay only 2 or 3 years and have no chance to learn the language since there is no policy or established programme to integrate them into society and offer them intensive language lessons. However, it is also often stressed that the educational system should be blamed for not giving the Greenlanders the necessary skills in foreign languages to be able to acquire a higher education. The issue can thus be characterised as a frustration that, after 22 years of being in charge of planning and executing policies, Greenland has not been able to educate as many people as it would like to fulfil those positions that require a lengthy and strenuous university degree in all the different fields. Greenland has invested heavily in education and has given its young people beneficial opportunities to obtaining an education. There were great hopes of overturning the historical dominance of the Danes in management positions when Greenland attained home rule in 1979. But, although there has been an increased number of Greenlanders in management positions and among academics, the fact that Greenland has gone from a traditional hunting society to a modern industrial society shows that it takes a long time to create a well-educated populace in which there has been no tradition of acquiring an academic education. On top of this, a recent study among university students taking their degrees in Denmark showed that they were more likely than not to be from a mixed family in which one parent is Danish and the other Greenlandic.

The study mentioned also showed that students who lack Greenlandic language skills are often prejudiced against and feel inferior to the rest of society in Greenland, as they cannot speak their mother tongue so well. This might in part explain why a large number of Greenlanders with a higher education remain in Denmark upon finishing their studies. Thus, even though only a few Greenlanders have been educated as engineers, and in spite of the many opportunities at home, most of them settle in Denmark.

Although the two groups function well together in general, the language issue is often used for political purposes. However, whatever viewpoints exist, it seems to be generally agreed that significant investments have to be made in the educational system, first of all in the area of primary education but also as regards the education of Greenlandic teachers. Many teachers in Greenland speak only Danish but the real challenge to the Home Rule authorities is the education of Greenlandic teachers.

The Greenland Self-government Commission

In late 1999, the Greenland Premier, Jonathan Motzfeldt, presented a Self-government Commission to look into Greenland's future position as part of the Danish realm (see *The Indigenous World 1999-2000*). The members of the Commission are all prominent Greenlandic politicians. Working Groups have been established by the Commission and, in early 2001, a conference was called in Nuuk to discuss security and defence issues.

All political parties in Greenland have increased the emphasis on self-governance as an issue on the political agenda. More than 20 years of Home Rule has revealed a need to reconsider the existing division of responsibilities between Denmark and Greenland, including foreign relations. While some politicians talk of revising the current arrangement, others are in favour of a completely new agreement based on an equal partnership. Independence is not included in the Self-government Commission's terms of reference, but the vision for the future - shared by most Greenlanders - seems to be a Greenland in control of its own economy and being able to deal with other nations at its own discretion.

No Oil in the First Drilling

The year 2000 also saw the results of the long-awaited oil-drilling 150 km west of Nuuk in Fyllas Banke. The Norwegian oil company, Norsk Hydro, together with other international oil companies, obtained the concession to drill for oil in the geologically interesting field west of Nuuk. There were high expectations among Greenlanders that finding oil would be a way of forging a path towards greater economic independence from Denmark. The block grant from Denmark accounts for 54.5 per cent of Home Rule revenue and 38.7 per cent of total public revenue. But the first exploration did not result in any oil flowing from under Greenland. However, statistics show that the probability of finding oil on the first drilling is extremely low and another consolation is that in an oil-producing country such as Norway, it took 13 drillings before they found oil. There was naturally disappointment in Greenland as the outlook for other trial drillings may be negatively affected. The decision to drill in other areas has not yet been taken.

The prospect of finding oil in massive quantities also brought up the issue of the economic and social consequences it will have on society as a whole. Calculations and studies have been undertaken in this regard, which show that the workforce in Greenland will have to be educated in a new field if it is to be actively involved in the oil adventure. The influx of foreign workers may disrupt the social fabric of the small Greenlandic communities; new service sectors and heavy investment in infrastructure in order to support the oil industry will also create a strain on the public sector budget. Not least, the demand for housing in a town like Nuuk - which already has a considerable shortage of housing - will require the import of workers and heavy investments that may lead to a spiralling economy, since the relatively small markets in Greenland will be hard pushed to absorb the large amounts of money that will rapidly flow in to meet the demands of the oil industry.

SÁPMI - SWEDEN

ILO Convention No. 169

S weden has not yet ratified ILO Convention No. 169 on Indigenous and Tribal People ("ILO Convention No. 169")[1]. In 1999,
an investigator appointed by the government to evaluate whether
Sweden should ratify ILO Convention No. 169 (the "ILO Investigation")[2], recommended that Sweden should do so. The recommendation was reiterated in August 2000 by the UN Committee on the
Elimination of Racial Discrimination (CERD), in its then submitted
Concluding Observations on Sweden (the "Concluding Observations
2000")[3]. The government responded by launching another investigation. The results of this investigation were initially supposed to be
presented in a writ before the Swedish parliament during autumn
2000. The date has been moved forward a couple of times. According
to the latest information from the government, the writ will be
presented to parliament sometime during autumn 2001.

Land Rights - Generally

Sweden's main obstacle to ratification of ILO Convention No. 169 is
Article 14, which states that indigenous peoples' ownership and possession of the lands that they traditionally occupy shall be recognised.
As the government hesitated ratifying ILO Convention No. 169, the
Saami people's land rights were further eroded during the year 2000.
    When regulating or otherwise dealing with the Saami people's right
to land, Swedish authorities have always presupposed that the Saami
people have no legal right to the land that they traditionally occupy.
    Disregarding the uncertainty over ownership, the Swedish public
power plant company *Vattenfall* has applied to be registered as the
owner of three separate land-areas within the traditional Saami territory. In all three cases, the *Sameby*[4] concerned has challenged the
application, arguing that Vattenfall cannot be registered as owner since
it has not been sufficiently demonstrated that the land belonged to the
state in the first place. Indeed, the Samebys regard themselves as owners
of the land under dispute. In the first of the three cases, the court of the
first instance decided in favour of the Sameby, stating that it was not
sufficiently clear that Vattenfall, claiming to derive its right from the state,
actually owned the land. The court of appeal reversed this in a decision
of June 22, 2000. The case is currently pending in the Supreme Court.
Should the Supreme Court agree with the court of appeal, the Sameby will

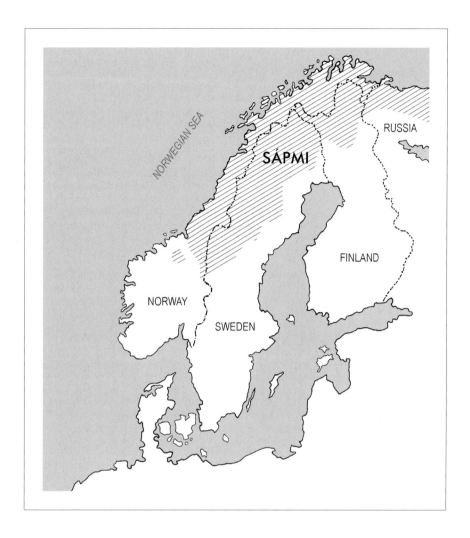

need to initiate full-scale court proceedings over the ownership of the land in question. If not, Vattenfall will be registered as owner of a part of the area that the Sameby traditionally occupies.

In addition, privatisation of previously publicly held forest and hydroelectric companies further eroded the Saami people's land rights during the year 2000. The transfer of land held by such entities into the private sector, without clarification of the legal status of the land, has resulted in the forest and hydroelectric companies expanding their businesses further into the Saami's summer and winter grazing areas.

As the ILO Investigation pointed out, there is no doubt that Sweden's attitude with regard to the Saami People's land rights is not compatible with ILO Convention No. 169. In its Concluding

Observations 2000, CERD too expressed concern over the Saami people's land rights, particularly highlighting the threats associated with the privatisation of land in the Saami territories. CERD recommended Sweden to enact legislation recognising the Saami people's land rights. Demonstrating considerable insight, CERD connected the Saami people's right to land with the Saami people's possibilities for pursuing their traditional way of life.

Land and Cultural Rights – Winter Grazing Areas

Reindeer husbandry is one of the main traditional livelihoods of the Saami people. Most Saami would agree that a living reindeer husbandry industry is paramount for the preservation of the Saami culture. Even if not recognised as owners of their traditional land, the Saami are - under Swedish legislation - allowed to carry out reindeer husbandry in areas that they have used "from time immemorial".[5] The legislation does not define, however, which, in the government's opinion, these areas are. The uncertainty has resulted in conflicts, particularly in the winter grazing areas, which the Saami nowadays to a large extent share with the non-Saami population. There are currently seven cases pending in the Swedish courts, where non-Saami claim compensation from different Samebys because of the reindeers grazing on land to which the non-Saami hold title but which, also, according to the Sameby, form part of their traditional winter grazing areas. Both sides have asked the government to intervene and assist in formulating a solution acceptable to both parties. In autumn 2000, in response to CERD's criticism in the Concluding Observations 2000, the minister of agriculture promised to appoint a commission with the task of investigating what areas the Saami people have used from time immemorial. Since the commission is to be financed from within the existing budget, however, it has not yet been constituted, due to lack of funding. Meanwhile, during the year 2000, a couple of the Samebys sued have announced that they can no longer afford to carry on the law-suits. Some other Samebys are negotiating with the landowners, trying to reach a settlement. If no settlement is reached, the court of appeal is expected to rule on the first of these cases within the next couple of months.

Having to pay compensation for using their winter grazing areas would be the end for many reindeer husbandry businesses. To add to the pressure on reindeer herders, there are predatory animals.

Cultural Rights – Predatory Animals

The four big predatory animals[6], together with the golden eagle, constitute perhaps the most severe threat to many reindeer herders. The number of predatory animals in some parts of the reindeer areas has increased dramatically in the last couple of years. There are reindeer herders who, in one year, have lost as many as 90 percent of their reindeer calves to predators. The Saami community has repeatedly pointed out that it is not feasible for about 1,000 reindeer husbandry businesses to carry the costs associated with preserving Sweden's predatory animals. The Saami argue that there must be a cap on how many killed reindeer each Sameby should have to sustain. Further, adequate compensation must be paid for each reindeer killed.

On December 21, 2000, the government submitted a bill to parliament, proposing a new policy with regard to predatory animals[7]. The bill does not contain any limitation on the number of killed reindeers each Sameby should have to sustain, and does not propose full compensation for the reindeers slain. The substantial financial loss caused by predatory animals results in many young Saami currently hesitating to become reindeer herders.

Land Rights - Hunting and Fishing Rights

In the Concluding Observations 2000, CERD particularly stressed its concern over the Saami people's hunting and fishing rights.

Responding to the criticism, the government has submitted the issue of the Saami people's hunting and fishing rights to a commission whose task is to undertake an overall review of topics relating to the Saami people in Sweden[8]. The commission has just announced, however, that it believes that the hunting and fishing rights are better investigated separately by a commission constituted for that particular task. This implies that there will be another couple of years before a proper evaluation is made of perhaps the most criticised regulation ever in Sweden relating to the Saami people.

Cultural Rights - the Saami Language Act

On April 1, 2000, new legislation allowing Saami to use the Saami language in legal and administrative proceedings came into force[9]. Commending the government for this particular legislation, in the

Concluding Observations 2000 CERD urged Sweden to broaden the scope of the act to cover the entire traditional Saami territory.

Notes

1   Finland and Russia have not ratified ILO Convention No. 169 either, while both Denmark and Norway have.
2   SOU 1999:25 – *Samerna ett ursprungsfolk i Sverige*
3   CERD/C57/CRP.3/Add. 2
4   A collective and well-defined social entity of individual Saami, accepted as a legal entity.
5   In Swedish *"urminnes hävd"*.
6   The predatory animals are: Wolf, wolverine, lynx and brown bear
7   Prop. 2000/01:57 *om en sammanhållen rovdjurspolitik*
8   *Rennäringspolitiska kommitten*
9   Lag (1999:1175) *om rätt att använda saamiska hos förvaltningsmyndigheter och domstolar.*

SÁPMI - RUSSIA

In Russia there exist two main Saami organizations: the Kola Saami Organization (AKS) and the Saami Public Organization of the Murmansk Region (OOSMO). The Nordic Saami Conference (held in September 2000 in Kiruna) adopted OOSMO as a new member of the Saami Council and OOSMO now has one seat on the Council. A seminar on land use in the Kola Peninsula was arranged with participants from the Scandinavian Saami. The seminar demanded that the federal level law "On the guarantee of the rights of the indigenous peoples" should be respected.

The cooperation between Lovozero and Karasjok, Norway, celebrated its 10 year anniversary. The Norwegian Saami have done a great deal to help the Lovozero region and particularly the Saami. The Norwegian religious organization has a permanent office in Lovozero with one person working primarily on humanitarian assistance programmes. Some Saami tried to visit their former home villages (Varzino), which they had been forced to leave in the 1960s but were forbidden to enter the area as it is now used by the military.

The Murmansk authorities gave 100,000 roubles for the publication of Saami textbooks. Nevertheless, the Saami language radio transmis-

The Northern Games, Russia. Sami preparing for the reindeer race. Photo: Leif Rantala

Chao Ke, Svein R. Nystö and Nina Afanasjeva, Utsjoki, Finland. Photo: Leif Rantala

sions were closed down due to lack of money. The freedom of the press is under more threat now than it was during the last years of the Soviet era. This is of concern to the local people, especially in Lovozero, the Saami capital of Russia. The authorities use economic methods to prevent the newspaper, Lovozerskaya Pravda, from printing critical articles on any topic, including the situation of the Saami people.

The situation in reindeer herding management is now a little better than before. The reindeer company's director has hired the OMON (special police) to fight against poachers. These measures to save the reindeer herds have been taken on the basis of a decree by the governor of October 12th 1998. Nevertheless, about 6,000 reindeer (out of 100,000) are being killed every year by poachers.

SÁPMI - FINLAND

Following the elections in the autumn of 1999, the new Saami Parliament began its work on the 1st January 2000. Pekka Aikio was re-elected as president of the Saami Parliament. At the opening ceremony in April, the president of Finland, Mrs. Tarja Halonen, made a speech stressing the importance of finding a solution to the land rights question in Saami areas and stating that she hoped the Saami would develop their cultural autonomy in co-operation with the Finnish decision-making bodies and authorities.

The quarrel over the definition of Saami continued throughout the year. During the year 2000, the relation between the Finns and the Saami continued to deteriorate. This development started some 6-7 years ago, when a group of Finns claimed that they, in fact, were Saami. When they did not succeed in making their claims heard and could not gain the right to vote in the Saami Parliament elections, they founded a clever movement declaring that the Saami and the Lapps (the old name for the Saami) were two different groups. The movement gained powerful support from some deputies of the Finnish Parliament and some Finnish journalists. This disinformation campaign has been very harmful to the Saami population in Finland. In 1999, there were some 650 persons whose applications to vote in the elections were denied by the supreme court. These people were Finns who declared themselves to be Saami.

Land Rights

A one-man committee comprised of judge Pekka Vihervuori had the task of researching what laws Finland should amend in order to be able to ratify ILO Convention 169. The issues in question are the Saami's right to land, water, national resources and traditional livelihood. Vihervuori suggested the establishment of a land rights council and a land rights fund to deal with practical issues on land rights and funding decisions. The Finnish state should pay 15 million Finnmarks per year into the fund. There were 77 bodies and organizations that responded to Mr. Vihervuori's suggestions.

After the report of Vihervuori's committee, a new committee was appointed, led by the governor of Lapland, Mrs. Pokka. It will continue to work on the same problem of land rights that Vihervuori had started to discuss. Half the members of this committee have been appointed by the Saami Parliament, the other half by various state and municipal bodies. Its work should be finished by November 2001.

The third committee is again a one-man committee comprised of judge Juhani Wirilander. His task is to investigate who should be considered land owners in the Saami area of Finland. His work should be finished by April 2001.

The fourth committee is a committee appointed by the Finnish Saami Parliament itself. It is also investigating issues of land ownership. Its work should be completed by July 2001.

In 2000, the researcher Kaisa Korpijaakko-Labba published a large investigation into what happened to the Saami land rights dating from before 1750. The study covers the period from 1750 up to 1917. In short, the results show that the forestry industry continuously rode roughshod over Saami land rights.

The New Finnish Constitution

Finland gained a new constitution on March 1 2000. Under the chapter "The right to one's language and culture (§ 17)" it states, "the Saami as indigenous people and the Romans and other minority groups have the right to maintain and develop their language and culture. The right of the Saami to use the Saami language in contacts with the authorities, is regulated by a special law." The constitution and a short explanation were also published in the Saami language.

THE INDIGENOUS PEOPLES OF RUSSIA

Changes in the National Legislation

In March, 2000, in accordance with Article 1 of the Federal Law *'On Guarantees of Rights of Indigenous Small Peoples of the Russian Federation"* (1999), a governmental enactment was adopted to extend *'The Unified List of Indigenous Small Peoples of the Russian Federation'* from 32 to 45 names, thereby including 11 new, officially recognized 'indigenous small peoples of the North' and 3 small peoples of the Caucasus (due to the fact that the authorities of the Republic of Dagestan were opposed to adding the Dagestani indigenous small peoples to the new List, whereas ethnographers estimated their number to be about 15).

The enactment was not supported by legislation that stated how to accomplish the rights of those peoples, which were included in the above List for the first time since their expulsion in 1926. During the years of Soviet power, the majority of these peoples' representatives had lost documentary proof confirming their membership of a specific people, since the column 'Nationality' in the passport could only be filled with the names of nationalities included in the official List of the USSR Peoples. The mechanism to restore within documents one's membership of one of the peoples newly included on the List is still unpublished. The body responsible for the elaboration of this mechanism is the Ministry for the Affairs of the Federation, National and Migration Policy.

The Federal Law *'On General Principles to Organize Communities of Indigenous Small Peoples of the North, Siberia and the Far East of the Russian Federation'* was passed on July 20, 2000 applying to peoples of the North, Siberia and the Far East only. The Law triggered contradictory responses from the Association of Indigenous Small Peoples (RAIPON).

The bottom line is that the said Federal Law, on the one hand, curtails the 'commercial' entrepreneurial activities of communities and, on the other, identifies in a very indistinct way the functions of communities as self-governmental agencies. At the same time, during the period of formulating this Federal legislation, which started in 1992, regional laws on community rights have been passed in approximately one third of the total number of 30 Northern regions. In some regions, Associations of Indigenous Peoples have succeeded in gaining more community rights than those guaranteed by the Federal Law. The Constitution of the Russian Federation stipulates streamlining of regional legislation in accordance with Federal. This could endanger indigenous peoples in regions with more democratic legislation on indigenous peoples' rights, losing some of the recently acquired rights as a result of such streamlining procedures. However, these regions are few, mainly the Khabarovsk Kray and the Koryak Autonomous Okrug. At the same time, there are over two dozen regions where the authorities never bothered to pass any regional legislation on indigenous peoples' rights before the Federal Laws came into effect; they only reflected the existence of indigenous peoples and their rights in high-sounding statements in the regional 'Charters' or in the temporary status of the indigenous peoples of their regions.

Since 1992, the State Duma has been in the process of elaborating a Federal Law on 'Territories of Traditional Nature Use'. It was adopted 'during the first reading' in 1998 and its new version is now being prepared for consideration. Its adoption may lead to similar consequences, entailing a split in the unity of the indigenous peoples' movement. To avoid this, the Russian Association of Indigenous Peoples of the North and IWGIA national group members are constantly monitoring the efforts to draw up the Law, making suggestions via their Deputies, publishing corresponding materials in their Journal, and trying to provide legal support to regional organizations of indigenous peoples in terms of protecting their rights.

The Government and Indigenous Peoples: Changes in the Structure of Executive Power

In May 2000, the State Committee for the North, which used to accumulate and channel budget funds into the regions, to be shared between programs of support for indigenous peoples of the North, Siberia and the Far East, was disbanded by Presidential ordinance. Despite the fact that its efforts were basically ineffective and that, over the last decade, two five-year state programs concerning the economic and social development of indigenous small peoples of the North failed to be fulfilled, this agency did, however, have a department available to which representatives of indigenous peoples of the North could appeal to. The most persistent among them had a chance of securing at least partial support for their regional projects. Now, the functions and budget funds of the State Committee for the North have been redirected to two reorganized Ministries: the Ministry of Economics of the Russian Federation and the Ministry for the Affairs of the Federation, National and Migration Policy. To date, both Ministries have been unable to form special structures for their dealings with the indigenous small peoples of the North. The problems facing indigenous small peoples are engulfed in the vastness of these Ministries' subject matters. Suffice to say that the Ministry for the Affairs of the Federation, National and Migration Policy is under constant criticism for its failure to cope with the migration activities in Chechnya, while the Ministry of Economics is criticized for its impotence in stopping the economic and fuel crisis in the Far East. The meeting of representatives of authorities held in Moscow on 27-28 November 2000 to probe into the problems of indigenous peoples of the North emphasized that the situation of the indigenous peoples was a matter of grave concern. It is worth noting that Governmental speakers interspersed their reports with data from the preceding year and even older demographic and social indicators of living standards.

Living Conditions of the Indigenous Peoples of Russia

According to RAIPON Vice-President, Dr. Larisa Abryutina, the main reason for the crisis in the situation of the indigenous peoples is the overwhelming state heritage of a policy of paternalism from the past, as well as the removal of children from their families to be educated in boarding schools, transforming the indigenous people into helpless personalities. These circumstances resulted in deficit in physical and emotional activities, which became the prerequisite for the deterioration in their health. The increase in cases of tuberculosis is statistically proven. Mortality due to this disease is as high as 40 cases per 100 persons in Khanty-Mansiisky autonomous region; in the Yamal-Nenets region this increases to 87 (in Russia the average is 10). The high rates of suicide in the North is mainly related to the alcohol addiction of some indigenous people. The mortality of indigenous peoples through suicide in the Chukotka comprised an average of 83.8 per 100,000 (in Russia this average is 30 per 100,000).

The average life expectancy of indigenous people of the North is 10-15 years less then that of the rest of Russia. In some regions, it is as low as 41-42 years among men. In most areas of Russia, the increase in the population is negative and falling. For example, the Itelmen in Kamchatka on average have had a negative population increase – minus 2.1 per thousand - for the last decade. According to data from the Institute of the Indigenous Peoples of the North (the Siberian Branch of the Russian Science Academy), in 1998 the Saami, Nganasan, Negidal, Aleut, Enets, Eskimo, Kumandins and Shor peoples' mortality rate was higher than their birth rate.

In comparison with 1990, the birth rate among the indigenous peoples of the North had decreased by 34%, while the mortality rate

A Nenets and a Saami participant at the IV Congress, Russia, April 2001. Photo: Kathrin Wessendorf

Sergey Haruchi, a Nenets from Siberia, re-elected president of RAIPON. Photo: Kathrin Wessendorf

had increased by 42%. The natural increase in the population of the indigenous peoples of the North had diminished 3-fold over that period.

Over the same period, the number of people in employment among the indigenous peoples of the North decreased in agriculture by 45%, in industry by 43%, in construction by 68%, and in commerce, communication and transport by 32%. The activity of these peoples continues to decrease in the traditional economies, and the level of unemployment in a number of indigenous settlements exceeds 60%. For example, in the Koryak autonomous region, in the small villages where Koryak people predominantly live, unemployment exceeds 85%. This fact, along with the critical state of the health and reproduction of indigenous peoples, is connected with the general social and economic crisis in the country and the degradation of the natural environment, provoked by the uncontrolled exploitation of natural resources.

Violations and Threats of Violations of the Rights of Indigenous Peoples

In the field of environmental protection, an increase in oil production in the subsistence areas of indigenous peoples, frequently without their consent or any ecological examination and without compensatory payment for damage, can be observed. The Sakhalin off-shore areas, the North of Western Siberia and the shelves of Taz and Ob Bays are particularly threatened by these economic ventures. The mining of minerals, on the other hand, affects the areas of Yakutia, Evenkia, Kamchatka, and Chukotka. Extensive felling of timber by timber companies can be detected in Karelia, Primorskiy and Khabarovsk Territories. And, in many regions, general environmental pollution is occurring caused by industrial and radioactive waste.

In the area of the right to land, education and healthcare, a campaign has commenced in some regions to take back land given to indigenous peoples as far back as 1992. The number of schools and teachers in the areas populated by indigenous people has been on the decrease ever since 1995, along with a shortage of textbooks, especially those needed to teach the native language. The reduction in the number of village hospitals and qualified medical staff, in accordance with the so-called plan for 'enlargement of village hospitals', which in actual fact means a reduction in their number (the Government is pursuing a policy of consolidating medical institutions into larger units), has been a fact of life since 1995 in the areas populated by indigenous peoples. A lack of food products is also constantly felt.

Conclusion

At the dawn of a new century, the socio-economic and legal position of indigenous peoples remains extremely complicated. The situation of the local groups residing in territories of traditional settlement and depending on traditional use of nature is considered - even by representatives of the authorities – to be disastrous. At the same time, there is no specialized department in Russia dealing with the problems of the indigenous peoples, there is no state agency responsible for this desperate situation. The task of improving the socio-economic position of indigenous peoples is not considered to be of overriding importance to the authorities. The problem facing indigenous peoples of not being able to exercise their right to land are not being solved since they are closely related to a solution of the general state problem concerning land and natural resource rights. Under such conditions, activities related to human rights concerns and information-oriented and practical efforts on the part of indigenous peoples' public organizations have developed at a pace. The recent increase in the RAIPON's activity, embracing 34 regional and ethnic organizations of indigenous peoples in Russia, has been most impressive. The expansion of its activities, the consolidation of its information interface with the regional communities, the publication of its own journal, an active position in relation to the state and regional authorities, its participation in international fora of indigenous peoples and higher international repute have all been gained through the multifarious activities organized by the current leadership of RAIPON elected in 1997, and re-elected in 2001, and through the support of RAIPON projects on the part of international organizations.

NUNAVUT

The year 2000 was not just the beginning of a new millennium but also the beginning of a great deal of hard work on the part of the new self-government in Nunavut, trying to improve conditions for Inuit-owned companies, and preparing and training government staff for decentralization of various government boards and departments, which are supposed to move to some of the major communities of Nunavut in order to create local jobs and development.

However, one of the most important debates in Nunavut in 2000 was the creation of a new indigenous policy based on Inuit Qaujimajatuqangit, in daily use referred to as IQ, which means "that which is long known by Inuit" in the local language Inuktitut. In English IQ is referred to as Inuit traditional knowledge. Inuit Qaujimajatuqangit is defined as Inuit values, world-views, language, social organization, knowledge, life skills, perceptions, etc., which have been passed on orally from one generation to another.

Guiding Principles for the Government of Nunavut

It is the vision of the Government of Nunavut that IQ should be integrated into all government policy and programs. Several hearings and workshops have been set up in Nunavut during the last 2-3 years to try to formulate IQ into a workable framework for Nunavut politicians. Drawing on elders' knowledge, experiences and expertise, which have traditionally guided and governed Inuit society, in 1999 the Nunavut Department of Sustainable Development defined six guiding principles for the Government of Nunavut's policy and program developments, based on the traditional society's model: 1)Pijitsirniq: the concept of serving, which lays out the relationships between the government and the people it serves, 2)Aajiiqatigiingniq: arriving at a decision through discussion/consensus decision-making, 3) Pilimmaksarniq: skills and knowledge acquisition through observation, and experience, 4) Piliriqatigiingniq: working together for a common purpose, 5)Avatimik Kammattiarniq: environmental stewardship, 6) Qanuqtuurunnarniq: being resourceful to solve problems by showing respect, tolerance towards each other and the environment.

The difficult part, of course, is to integrate these principles into a modern government structure. However, Nunavut Government's Inuit Qaujimajatuqangit Report, which was released in August 2000, has some very concrete recommendations.

Concrete Recommendations

The overall importance of implementing IQ is to apply Inuktitut as the working language of the government. Without the Inuktitut language, the Inuit traditional knowledge cannot thrive. The report states that the government should develop mandatory language lessons for non-Inuit staff, and that the government should

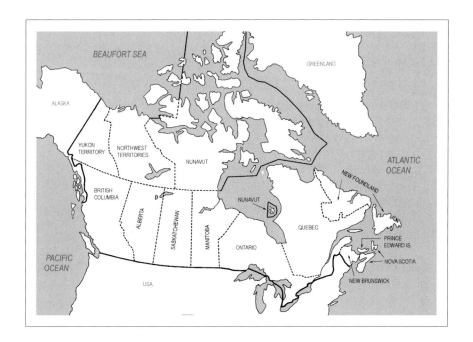

supply interpreters so that Inuit staff are not forced to speak English during internal meetings.

In order to increase its knowledge of traditional values and world-views, each government department should invite elders to run orientation sessions for non-Inuit staff and they should also be consulted on all policy, strategic planning, business planning and development sessions to ensure Inuit tradition and beliefs are respected during program and policy delivery. In the future, in Nunavut, there should be greater efforts made to research and record Inuit Qaujimajatuqangit-related topics for publication and mass distribution, to be used in creating Inuktitut teaching materials and to increase Inuit self-awareness.

Another important issue that has been suggested is to make government working hours more conducive to Inuit lifestyles. Government employees should get 'traditional leave' at certain times of the year to go caribou hunting, goose hunting, whale hunting, clam digging and berry picking.

The report finally states that a government Inuit Qaujimajatuqangit monitoring committee should be set up to examine the work conducted by agencies serving the Inuit. This task force was set up at the beginning of 2001 and it is supposed to monitor the work of the cabinet, the legislative assembly, the police and the Department of Justice in Nunavut (Nunatsiaq News 2001).

Women's Issues in Nunavut

Family violence has escalated over the last few years in Nunavut. The Status of Women Council, "Qulliit", and Nunavut Social Development Council (NSDC) have recommended that the Nunavut government adopt a Canadian national policy of "zero-tolerance" towards violence against women and children. NSDC suggests that a "community-wellness strategy" should be adopted, which means addressing violence through programs for batterers, counseling for both men and women and involvement of the broader community. In an interview, the president of the Nunavut Status of Women Council agrees to the community approach but she think there is also a need for caution. In the communities, some elders wants to address domestic violence via Inuit Qaujimajatuqanit but things are not the way they were before, especially due to alcohol and drug-related assaults, which are predominant in Nunavut (*Nunatsiaq News*:2000:Oct.13). This could be a potential problem for Inuit women in Nunavut with regard to the IQ policy.

References:

Department of Sustainable Development (1999): Inuit Qaujimajatuqangit Framework, Iqaluit

Arnakak Jaypetee (2000): "What is Inuit Qaujimajatuqangit?" *Nunatsiaq News*, August 25

***Nunatsiaq News* (2000):** " GN urged to adopt 'zero tolerance' resolution on family violence" October 13

***Nunatsiaq News* (2001):** "Nunavut's Inuit Qaujimajatuqangit group gets started" February 2

Report from the September Inuit Qaujimajatuqangit Workshop (2000) Niaqunngnut, Nunavut, September 29-30 Nunatsiaq News Iqaluit

NUNAVIK

The Nunavik Commission: Release of the Report in 2000

The Nunavik Commission, whose mandate is to propose a form of self-government for the Arctic territory of the Province of Quebec (Canada), should release its report in April 2001, after a little less than one and a half year of work.

Some 10,000 people inhabit Nunavik, a vast territory of 500,000 square kilometres, representing one third of the area of the Province of Quebec. The population is divided into 14 coastal villages. About 90% of the population is Inuit. The territory has a strong potential for economic development since it contains important mineral and wildlife resources. These resources are still exploited by the Inuit population, mainly as important food sources.

The Nunavik Commission was created in 1999 from a political agreement between the governments of Canada and Quebec, and the Inuit of Nunavik represented by the Makivik Corporation. The Commission is composed of 3 members appointed by the government of Quebec, 3 members by the Inuit, and 2 members by the government of Canada. It is headed by two commissioners, one appointed by the Inuit and the other by the government of Quebec, who act as co-chairs of the Commission.

Its mandate is to propose a comprehensive set of recommendations on the design, operation and implementation of a form of government in Nunavik, more specifically on the powers of such a government, the electoral process, the selection of leaders and executive members, relations with other governments, financing, measures to promote and enhance the Inuit culture, including the use of inuktitut in the Nunavik Government, and transitional measures.

In order to achieve its objectives, the Nunavik Commission conducted a vast consultation. All villages of Nunavik were visited, and the Commission held public hearings, meetings with municipal councils, with high school students and with local and regional organizations. It examined briefs submitted by organizations currently involved in public services in Nunavik, and consulted departments from the Quebec and Canada governments. Moreover, the Commission held consultations with neighbouring Aboriginal organizations that have some interest in Nunavik, such as the Cree, the Naskapis and the Innus.

The Nunavik Commission is not the first step in the implementation of self-government in Nunavik. In fact, over the last 30 years, the Inuit of Nunavik have reiterated their will to establish an appropriate form of self-government. The James Bay and Northern Quebec Agreement granted them a form of administrative autonomy and, in specific fields such as education, some extended powers. Nevertheless, discussions regarding this issue have never really halted; the Inuit have tried to build a consensus among themselves regarding the type of government they wish to establish. The Nunavik Commission marks, then, a decisive step in this historical process. Indeed, the recommendations that will come out of the Commission should be used as a basis on which to start the negotiations between the three parties.

NORTH AMERICA

CANADA - I

First Nations Relations in Canada at the End of the Second Millennium

A ny attempt to select and discuss two or three key issues for the year 2000 requires a caveat. 2000 was the final year of a millennium in which the second half began with a debate as to whether "Indians have souls". The millennium culminated, in Canada, with a Royal Commission on Aboriginal Peoples devoting an entire chapter to the need for an entirely new inquiry into the effects of Indian residential schools – including a 50% mortality rate achieved by some of those institutions. So we must begin with a reminder that most First Nations relations continued in the way they have since Confederation, despite new ground being broken here and there.

The "here and there" where new ground was broken can be identified by three signal events: (1) the ratification of the *Nisga'a Final Agreement*, by the British Columbia Legislative Assembly and the Canadian Parliament; (2) the first full year of the new territory of Nunavut in which an Inuit majority holds sway for the moment (see also the article on Nunavut); and, (3) the aftermath of the two Supreme Court *Marshall* decisions, the first allowing that under a Treaty of 1760-61 the Mi'kMaq nation has a continuing fishing right which, the Court said, allows the members of that nation to gain "a moderate livelihood" and the second backtracking on that decision by emphasizing the right of the federal government to make fisheries regulations.

The "same old, same old" recurred in situations too numerous to mention. I shall touch only on the most evident: (1) the findings published in the *Canadian Medical Association Journal* October 2000 issue, that one key predictor of urban child poverty was being the child of Aboriginal parents in a Canadian city; (2) the continuing high rates of incarceration of First Nations people, largely for crimes arising from material impoverishment compounded by four generations of residential school child rearing; (3) the characterization of the Nisga'a treaty by the Official Opposition in both the federal Parliament and the B.C. Legislature as "race based" in a right wing move to deny reality to the national and cultural identity of the First Nations in general or the Nisga'a in particular, and (4) the federal Minister of Indian Affairs and Northern Development, Robert Nault, continuing - in the rhetoric of his predecessors - to deny that his

department had responsibility for First Nations people living outside of reserved land (as more than half the First Nations population
do) despite section 92(24) of the *Constitution Act, 1867* stipulating
that the federal Parliament has jurisdiction over both "Indians and
lands reserved for the Indians."

The significance of parliamentary ratification of a modern-day
treaty should not be under-estimated. Nor should either a Supreme
Court decision attaching even modest weight to a treaty signed
long before Canadian Confederation or the coming into being of an
Inuit majority territory.

The Nisga'a Treaty

The Nisga'a began petitioning for recognition of their Aboriginal
title over the Nass River Valley in British Columbia over a century

ago. Its proponents say that the treaty allows for a significant measure of self-government despite serious constraints, e.g. dependence on federal funding and a requirement to follow provincial standards in respect to education and health issues.

The willingness of the Liberal Government in Ottawa and the New Democratic Government in Victoria to press on with ratification of the treaty despite considerable parliamentary opposition testifies to genuine efforts to extend some respect to the repeated admonitions of the Supreme Court regarding the continuing force of Aboriginal rights. The messages on several First Nations web sites and e-mail lists show as much opposition to the treaty within the First Nations for reasons quite opposite to those of the parliamentary opposition: the self-government provisions do not provide genuine autonomy and the land title of the Nisga'a under the treaty covers a small portion of their traditional lands under dubious terms. First Nations adjacent to the Nisga'a said that the Nisga'a treaty prejudiced their prospects of a comparable deal. Right wing senators seized this plea as a further excuse to oppose ratification.

The Mi'kMaq and Fishing Rights

Most complex is the decision in the *Donald Marshall Jr.* case. Marshall, who previously served 11 years on a wrongful conviction for murder, was prosecuted for catching eels out of season. On the basis of a 1761 treaty guarantee of "a truck house" at which the Mi'kMaq and Maliseet might sell their catch from hunting and fishing, the Supreme Court decided that the Mi'kMaq had a continuing right to fish for a moderate livelihood. Following the Supreme Court decisions in the fall of 1999, fishermen up and down the New Brunswick and Nova Scotia coasts attacked Mi'kMaq fishing boats and lobster traps while the RCMP provided little or no protection. In an almost unprecedented move, the Supreme Court responded to a request from the Attorney General of New Brunswick and the West Nova Fishermen's Coalition to provide clarification. Although the decision chided the government and the opponents of treaty rights and rejected their petition, asking the Court to reconsider its previous ruling, the Court nonetheless responded in a decision known as *Marshall* 2. It also emphasized the government's authority to regulate the exercise of these rights. During the last lobster season, in fall 2000, the Government attempted to impose harsh limits on the Mi'kMaq fishery while offering to subsidize the cost of equipment for those Mi'kMaq fishers who would submit to their authority. This seemed to have more to do with the historic divide-and-rule strategies of colonialism than with the treaty-affirming approach of the Supreme Court.

On the other side of the Mi'kMaq fishing rights issue, the National Chief of the Assembly of First Nations, Matthew Coon Come, asked whether any other people in Canada were restricted by court order to "a moderate livelihood". At year's end, several legal cases were pending: federal fisheries charges against Mi'kMaq fishers; Mi'kMaq suits against the RCMP and the Dept. of Fisheries; and, Mi'kMaq suits against the province (and vice versa) regarding the application of the same treaty to other natural resources such as game and timber.

Government's Policy Pretensions versus the Supreme Court's Attempts to Extend the Rule of Law to First Nations: two different approaches

More than half the Aboriginal population of Canada live in urban areas. Urban Aboriginal people are materially more impoverished than their on-reserve relatives: they lack the prospect of supplementing their livelihood with subsistence fishing and hunting. Many move back and forth between reserve and city on a frequent basis. Those who spend more than six months away from their reserve lose federal benefits, including not only supplementary health care but also post-secondary tuition.

Observers of First Nations relations in Canada have remarked for quite some time that the decisions of the Supreme Court are far ahead of the conduct of the Government and, further, that the Government is not particularly compliant with the instructions and orders of the Court. My own refinement of this view is that the Government continually tries to find a position mid-way between the decisions of the Supreme Court – which view the guarantes of Aboriginal and treaty rights in the Constitution as a sacred promise – and the position of the Official Opposition, the Canadian Conservative Reform Alliance Party – which would repeal the constitutional guarantees, abolish Aboriginal and treaty rights and dissolve any protection for Aboriginal peoples. The continuing Liberal effort to find a middle ground harks back to the era of Prime Minister Mackenzie King in the 1930s and 40s. It was famously said of Mackenzie King that he would never do by halves what could be done by quarters.

This is a strategy that worked far better in an era of repression than in an era with pretensions of reconciliation. It is not a strategy calculated to reach out to the remote areas of Canada where some people carry on traditional pursuits, some youth sniff gasoline and many children go to bed hungry.

CANADA - II

The First Nations Governance Act and First Nations Financial Institutions Act

In Canada, April 17, 2001, marks the 19th Anniversary of the adoption of the Constitution Act 1982. Section 35 of the Canadian constitution recognizes and affirms the "existing aboriginal and treaty rights of aboriginal peoples."

Yet the federal government has announced it plans to use its massive Parliamentary majority to change the legal status of Indian communities, by passing the "**First Nations Governance Act**", which will impose municipal type status and is intended to alter the current legal status and capacity of an Indian Band. As this is written, details of this legislation are found in two federally-released documents. The first one describes the key aspects of the proposed law: Legal Status of First Nations (Band); Roles and Responsibilities of Chiefs and Councils; Delegation Capacity of First Nations and/or Chief and Council; Capacities to create Band corporations/commissions; Standards respecting legal proceedings by and against Council. Document 2 describes the core elements of the proposed law: Governance Authorities; Financial Management, Accountability and Redress; Elections Consent and Referenda. The proposed legislation will be connected to another piece of draft legislation, the "**First Nations Financial Institutions Act**", which is intended to facilitate the removal of the tax exemption most Indians (First Nations) currently possess.

In 1996, the federal government tried to amend the *Indian Act* but this was soundly rejected by 85% of the Indian Bands across Canada. On December 12, 1996, faced with such opposition from First Nations, the then Minister of Indian Affairs, Ron Irwin, decided - literally at the last minute - to declare that the *Indian Act* amendment package would be "optional". Despite this last minute maneuver, First Nations knew the federal intent was to force them into the new legal arrangement, and so they kept up their opposition.

In 1997, Bill C-79, the *Indian Act Optional Modification Act*, died a death when the 1997 federal election was called. The federal government is now trying once again to re-package the 1996-97 *Indian Act* amendments package into two pieces of legislation, the "**First Nations Financial Institutions Act**" and the "**First Nations Governance Act**".

The *Indian Act* has not been significantly amended since 1951, although there have been piecemeal changes to the lands, membership and elections provisions. The federal Minister is attempting to use the fact that there are over 200 cases before the courts involving the *Indian Act*. However, at a meeting with the Assembly of First Nations on April 11, 2001, federal officials acknowledged that the vast majority of the court cases involve disputes over membership provisions, not the sections of the Indian Act the Minister of Indian Affairs intends to change.

From the 1996-97 *Indian Act* amendment experience, it was clear then, and it appears to be the same now, that the federal desire to change the *Indian Act* has more to do with attempting to restrict the legal status of First Nations self-governing powers while simultaneously dismantling the fiduciary, trust-like responsibilities and obligations for providing ongoing federal programs and services to meet the basic needs of First Nations peoples.

To put it plainly, all indications are that the federal government wants to "off-load" or devolve responsibility for providing programs and services to First Nations onto the provinces and to the Bands themselves. The "First Nations Governance Act", along with the "Financial Institutions Act" appears to be a new "statutory and regulatory regime" for furthering this quiet objective.

An internal Department of Indian Affairs document concedes that program sustainability is uncertain because "Demographic price + volume demand are outstripping fiscal supply." This is an acknowledgement that the First Nations population is young and rapidly growing at a rate higher than the Canadian average and, of course, this means increasing costs to the federal government in order to maintain its responsibilities.

To conclude, Canada's Throne Speech of January 2001 and the Prime Minister's response both highlighted the need to address the particular needs of Aboriginal children, the majority of whom live in poverty. The question remains: will Prime Minister Jean Chretien maintain his out-dated views on the rights of First Nations, which were reflected in his "1969 White Paper Policy on Indians", or will he recognize, as the Canadian courts have, that Aboriginal and Treaty rights are now constitutionally protected in section 35, and that a "generous, liberal interpretation of the words of the constitutional provision is demanded"? The unilateral actions of his Minister of Indian Affairs to force legislation on First Nations seems to indicate that Prime Minister Chretien is continuing with his assimilationist views from the past, rather than recognizing the First Nations right to self-determination.

Resource Development and Self-Government

For the Northwest Territories' Aboriginal peoples, the past year was dominated above all else by one pressing issue: non-renewable resource development. World commodity prices and market demand have brought a resurgence of interest in the Territories' resource potential, and throughout the Mackenzie Valley there is renewed activity in the oil and gas, mining and forestry sectors. In the Slave Geological Province, this process is well underway, with the Ek'ati diamond mine in commercial production, the Diavik mine receiving regulatory approval in 2000 and now under construction, and a number of other diamond and base metal mine projects being actively pursued. The Deh Cho region has experienced a substantial natural gas rush around Fort Liard, which is expanding to include other communities, as well as interest from developers in several mine projects. The Mackenzie Delta/ Beaufort region has also seen increased spending by the oil and gas industry on exploration at levels not seen for years. After nearly a twenty five-year hiatus, serious consideration is again being given to the construction of a pipeline down the Mackenzie Valley, as one of several possible routes for bringing natural gas to southern markets. In just a short time, a broad consensus seems to have emerged among the federal and territorial governments, industry, and some Aboriginal groups, that a viable economic future for the NWT and its residents lies with the exploitation of its non-renewable resources.

With all these development pressures, Aboriginal governments are scrambling to keep pace and their already limited human and financial resources are being severely strained. In the past, mining and oil and gas developments in the NWT have always gone forward without Aboriginal consent, provided only temporary benefits to community residents, and too often left behind lasting environmental and cultural damage. As viewed by government and industry, Treaties 8 and 11 (and the associated "scrip" settlements with the Métis) cleared the way for development and leave the Dene and the Métis with only a minimal say over what happens on their lands. The Aboriginal leadership and elders are keenly aware of this legacy of exclusion and disruption, and are determined that it will not be played out again. They wish to strengthen the socio-economic foundations of their communities, by securing training, jobs, business opportunities and economic income from development projects.

Equally important, they want to ensure that developments are environmentally sound, and that there are no negative impacts on their traditional lands, waters and resources.

Clearly, the NWT is witnessing a significant shift in Aboriginal attitudes toward resource development. This is a far cry from the heated debates that raged in the 1970s over the proposed Mackenzie Valley Pipeline. Instead of opposing pipelines and other non-renewable resource projects, Aboriginal communities now seem prepared to give their qualified support so long as they are involved as full "partners" in developments that take place on their traditional lands. A basic goal shared by Inuvialuit, Dene and Métis alike is to ensure that, in any decisions about resource projects and about the terms under which these proceed, both government and industry respect the historical rights of the NWT's Aboriginal communities and the authority of their governments.

It is instructive to revisit the 1977 *Report of the Mackenzie Valley Pipeline Inquiry* (the so-called "Berger Report"). In this *Report*, Justice Thomas Berger argued that: "a consideration of industrial development and social, cultural and political progress in the north cannot be separated from a discussion of native claims." One of its key conclusions was that, before development could go ahead in the Mackenzie Valley, Aboriginal communities must have time to strengthen their institutions and to secure clearer recognition of their rights under Canadian law. For this reason, Berger recommended that any pipeline development be delayed for ten years to allow for the "settlement of native claims." This analysis seems just as relevant today as it was in the 1970s: the question of resource development in the Northwest Territories remains inseparably bound up with the issue of its Aboriginal peoples' governance and control over their traditional "homelands."

In the intervening years since the Berger Report, the NWT's Aboriginal peoples have made undeniable progress in developing their political and economic institutions, and in starting to address the social and economic problems of their communities. Three regional land claims have been settled—the Inuvialuit, the Gwich'in and the Sahtu—and implementation of these settlements has been underway for several years. Co-management of lands, waters and the environment of the Territories has become a reality in the past ten years, both at the regional and the Territorial levels. Aboriginal communities are now routinely consulted and involved in "multi-stakeholder" processes relating to major government initiatives or development projects. Community and regional organizations have also gained some sophistication in dealing with developers through Joint Venture and Impacts and Benefits Agreements. But, despite these advances, the Aboriginal peoples of the Territories have so far had very limited success in achieving practical recognition of their inherent right of self-government.

Self-government negotiations between the federal Crown and the different Aboriginal regions began in earnest in the NWT back in 1994. Seven years later, there is general consensus on the Aboriginal side that this process has been costly, time-consuming and ultimately unproductive. Probably the closest to finalizing an agreement is the Dogrib Treaty 11 Council, which has been negotiating Dogrib government as part of its comprehensive claim settlement: an Agreement-in-Principle was reached in the spring of 1999, with a final Agreement anticipated by the end of this year. In the Beaufort-Delta region, the Inuvialuit and the Gwich'in have been jointly pursuing a self-government deal with Canada to supplement their already completed land claims, and an Agreement-in-Principle is expected at this table sometime in 2001. Self-government talks in the Sahtu are currently community-based, with the Deline negotiations serving as a test case for the use of this approach elsewhere in the region. Discussions on Aboriginal governance in the Deh Cho region and in the Treaty 8 communities are in more preliminary stages and form part of much broader negotiations aimed at clarifying and elaborating the intent of the original Treaties with the Crown.

From the Aboriginal perspective, the governments of Canada and of the Northwest Territories bear primary responsibility for the difficulties that have occurred in these various self-government talks. On paper, the federal *Inherent Right Policy* appears to hold considerable promise. But, in actual negotiations, Canada has insisted that federal laws must be paramount over Aboriginal laws except in a few jurisdictional areas, and that outside Aboriginal "owned" lands, the rights and powers of Aboriginal governments and citizens will be largely subject to laws of general application. The territorial government's own Self-government policy is very vaguely worded and, in practice, the GNWT negotiators' underlying concern often appears to be to retain as much government power at the territorial level (i.e. in the capital, Yellowknife) as possible.

Time and again, there have been delays in negotiations as territorial and federal negotiators have sought Cabinet mandates to enable them to effectively address issues that arise at specific tables. One major sticking point has been the government negotiators' reluctance to consider strictly "Aboriginal" models of governance. Typically, they have pushed for public or hybrid forms of government on the grounds that the rights of non-Aboriginal residents must be respected in any agreement. Another has been financing, as Canada and the GNWT have played political football on the question of who will pay for the "incremental" costs of implementing self-government. Related to this, the territorial government in particular has dragged its feet in recognizing taxation powers for Aboriginal governments, being key instruments in raising their "own-source" revenues. A third point of contention has been Canada's refusal to negotiate jurisdictional authority over sub-surface development for Aboriginal governments outside of Aboriginal "owned" lands in their traditional territories, beyond sharing a small percentage of annual Crown resource royalties.

Compounding these difficulties further have been recurrent efforts by the territorial government to secure jurisdictional authority from Canada over Crown sub-surface lands in the Territories. Until recently, the so-called "Northern Accord" has been viewed by these two governments as a strictly bi-lateral matter, to be undertaken apart from self-government and other Aboriginal rights negotiations. As such, it has been resisted by most Aboriginal groups who recognized that this devolutionary transfer would only strengthen the powers of the territorial government and undercut the integrity of their self-government talks.

However, in the past two years, the terms of the proposed Northern Accord have changed, as both Canada and the GNWT have shown some willingness to include the NWT's Aboriginal governments as partners in a comprehensive transfer package. As presently conceived, this Accord would vest both Aboriginal governments and the GNWT with a share of Crown non-renewable resource revenues and jurisdiction over sub-surface development. This proposal is unprecedented in Canada and has potentially major implications for the future financial viability of the Aboriginal governments, who are rightly approaching it with great caution. In the past twelve months, the Inter-governmental Forum—involving Canada, the GNWT, and the NWT's Aboriginal governments—has emerged as a key mechanism for working out the details of a Northern Accord transfer. At this point, whether the Forum will succeed in this difficult task remains an open question.

CANADA - IV
THE INNU NATION

The leadership of the Innu Nation and in the two Innu communities in Labrador continue their struggle to find ways of dealing with alcohol and substance abuse. A radical step was taken in mid November by the Innu leadership when they asked the provincial government of Newfoundland to remove a group of troubled children from their homes. It has come to the point now, said the President of the Innu Nation, Peter Penashue, where there are a substantial number of young people, as young as seven years old, sniffing gas in the community. One of the health hazards prompting this action was that the children were sitting by campfires in the forest sniffing gas from plastic bags.

An underlying issue here is that the Department of Social Services has the legal means to take such action, and has the resources necessary to provide the needed support, as opposed to the Innu Nation or the Band Councils who do not.

Education

As mentioned in last year's *Indigenous World*, in November 1999, the governments of Canada and Newfoundland entered into an agreement with the Innu Nation to transfer control of education and policing their own communities, for example using Innu constables, to the Band Council in each community, and to give the Band Councils the jurisdiction they need to handle the alcohol and solvent abuse. It has frustrated the Innu leadership that governments have not followed up on this agreement. "We realize that the problems afflicting our communities will not be resolved by outside governments or agencies, "says Peter Penashue in a press release from the Innu Nation in November 2000, "but we can't even pass a bylaw against littering, much less take action against alcohol and gas sniffing, deliver education to our children or effectively police our community. Until the agreements we have reached are given some effect by Canada and Newfoundland, we will never have the tools and resources that we need to be effective."

With respect to schooling, it is an enduring problem that while the children all speak Innu as their first language, the curriculum is all in English, except some material provided in the first grades. It is also a major problem that the curriculum in no way reflects the culture and life of the Innu.

Land Claim Settlement

In June of 2000, the Innu Nation tabled a proposal with Canada and Newfoundland for a fair and just settlement of their land rights. In a press release, the Innu Chief Negotiator Daniel Ashini said that the Innu Nation's proposal would provide recognition for Innu self-government powers over 10,000 square miles of territory in Labrador: "On this land, we would be able to govern ourselves in accordance with the treaty, and develop an economy while protecting the land and our traditional way of life. This size area is consistent with many of the other land claim settlements in the Northwest Territories, Nunavut and in the Yukon. We also want to participate in co-management arrangements with Canada and Newfoundland over a larger region of Labrador. In these areas, Innu could also benefit from royalty and resource development revenues, giving us a chance for economic self-sufficiency." On the basis of a positive response from the federal government of Canada and the government of Newfoundland, the Innu Nation believes that it could conclude an Agreement in Principle by the end of the year, and a Final Agreement within 2 years. In an article published in December in a major Canadian newspaper, *The Globe and Mail*, the President of the Innu Nation Peter Penashue writes: "We are currently in claims negotiations and we remain hopeful that Canada and Newfoundland will change their positions on the amount of land and resources they want the Innu to give up. If Canada's and Newfoundland's proposals prevail, we won't have sufficient land and resource revenues to build a self-sufficient economy; we will remain welfare dependent. Is that what Canadians want? Even as the Innu are negotiating claims with Canada and Newfoundland, Canada and Newfoundland continue to give our land and resources to third parties to develop. The Upper Churchill hydro-development, Voisey's Bay nickel mine and the massive hydro-development of the Lower Churchill River are but a few examples. The Innu have asked for a moratorium on these developments until their claims are settled. Canada and Newfoundland have refused.

In good faith, we have been negotiating with Voisey's Bay Nickel and Newfoundland and Labrador Hydro with respect to the current proposals for Lower Churchill and Voisey's Bay, but we take the position that these projects cannot go ahead without our consent. If these projects prove compatible with our way of life, and we can get the same rate of return that all Canadians would find fair, then perhaps the projects can proceed. But we refuse to give our land and resources away."

Military Training

Military flight training over 130,000 square kilometres of Labrador and northeastern Quebec has been conducted by European countries under a Multinational Memorandum of Understanding from CFB (Canadian Forces Base) Goose Bay since the early 1980s. The majority of the approximately 6,000 annual training flights are conducted by fighter jets flying at low level (less than 100 feet above ground level). Innu people have long opposed military activities over their homeland, primarily due to concerns about the impacts of jet noise and pollution on humans and wildlife.

An environmental assessment of low-level flying activities was conducted on the basis of an environmental impact statement (EIS) prepared by the Canadian Department of National Defence in 1994. The 1994 EIS stated: "The LLTA's (low level training areas) are not approved for supersonic flight, nor are there any plans to approve any such supersonic flight under the Multinational Memorandum of Understanding." In spite of this, in July 2000 the Canadian Department of National Defence gave the Innu Nation three days notice that Royal Netherlands Air Force would be conducting supersonic test flights over the Innu hunting grounds. When the Innu Nation launched a court challenge, the flights were postponed until June 2001.

The rationale given by the National Defence for breaching the 1994 prohibition is that it was based on a project description, which, at that time, did not include supersonic flights. With the introduction of the new fighter aircraft (the Eurofighter Typhoon), which will be operational approximately three or four years from now and which will have supersonic cruise capability, they now see a need to facilitate supersonic flight training at Goose Bay.

Of particular concern to the Innu Nation are the potential risks of supersonic activities on Innu hunters and wildlife. One expert explains that supersonic flyovers at 5,000 feet can generate shock waves that can produce irreversible damage in human lungs, viscera, ears and can also cause brain damage. A human being directly under the flight path of an aircraft flying supersonically at 15,000 feet would be likely to be exposed to sound in excess of 130 dB, which is the threshold for pain.

Sources

Innu Nation, Environmental advisors Larry Innes and Stephan Fuller
The Globe and Mail, December 7, 2000

THE UNITED STATES OF AMERICA

With the beginning of the new millennium, Native peoples in the United States continue to battle for greater self-determination. Consequently, indigenous peoples are addressing issues concerning the sustainable development of reservation lands, the protection of sacred sites on public and private lands, the ownership of intellectual property, the gambling industry, problems with the Native American Graves Protection and Repatriation Act, and the role of state and federal agencies in tribal affairs.

Demographic realities and health factors are major obstacles to more self-governance and self-sufficiency. According to the 1999 census, 2.4 million people identify themselves as Native Americans. Only 1.7 million of these individuals are actually enrolled in a federally recognized tribe, however. Of enrolled tribal members, approximately 900,000 live on reservations. The remaining population resides mostly in urban areas located in one of six states: Oklahoma, California, Arizona, Alaska, Washington, or New Mexico.

Because of high mortality rates, the average age amongst Native Americans is eight years younger than the population at large. Cardiovascular disease is the leading cause of mortality among Native peoples. Among teenagers and adults in their early twenties, homicide, suicide, accidents, and alcohol-related deaths are endemic problems. The Bureau of Indian Affairs [BIA], the agency that oversees Native affairs, estimates that alcohol-related deaths among Native peoples are four times greater than the United States average.

Unemployment continues to plague Native peoples. Approximately 50% of the adults living on the more than 300 reservations in the United States are unemployed. Of the adults employed, 30% live below the poverty guidelines established by the Department of Health and Human Services. If all enrolled Native Americans are included, unemployment stands at 14.4%, as compared to 6.3% for the rest of the United States' citizens.

In order to fulfill President Clinton's Native American Initiative discussed during his visit to Pine Ridge Reservation in 1999, the Bureau of Indian Affairs (BIA) has requested $9.4 billion dollars for 2001 from the federal budget. This is 14% more than was requested in 2000. With this money, the BIA wants to strengthen programs critical to the future of Native peoples. These programs include the education of 50,000 elementary and secondary students attending 185 schools; the continuation of 25 tribally-controlled community colleges; the training of law enforcement personnel; social services for the elderly and disabled; better management of trust land resources; the maintenance of over 25,000 miles of roads on rural and isolated reservations; and the implementation of land and water claim settlements.

Sustainable Development of Reservation Lands

Two conditions, chronic to reservations, limit the ability of tribal councils to create opportunities for sustainable development. First of all, reservation land is held in trust by the federal government. As a result, the BIA's responsibility to aid the efforts of Native communities to obtain greater self-determination are in conflict with the agency's role as protector of the reservation's resources. The case Cobell versus Babbitt clearly illustrates this problem. As Secretary of the Interior during Clinton's administration, Babbitt oversaw the Bureau of Indian Affairs. While acting as Secretary of the Interior, Babbitt was sued by Elouise Cobell over the Bureau's management of trust funds. As the lead plaintiff, Ms. Cobell was requesting that the BIA provide the records of over 500,000 individual trust accounts. These accounts include royalties for the leasing of allotted land to ranchers and farmers as well as corporations involved in resource extractions. Currently, the Department of the Interior cannot find records for 100 million trust funds or 2.4 billion dollars held in escrow for Native peoples. In 1999, Royce Lamberth, a Federal District Judge found Babbitt, as well as the Secretary of the Treasure and former Secretary for Indian Affairs, in contempt of court. The judge is demanding that the BIA determine all monies owed to Native peoples, beginning with the Allotment Act of 1887. Presumably, the problem will be resolved by Gale Norton, President Bush's appointment to the Secretary of the Interior.

A second factor that limits a tribe's ability to gain greater self-sufficiency and self-determination is the often abysmal educational facilities on reservations. According to the 2001 BIA budget report, many reservation schools are structurally unsound and/or of insufficient size to educate incoming students. Only 65.5% of Native peoples graduate from high school, compared with 75.2% for the U.S. population as a whole. Even worse is the fact that a mere 9.3% of Native students graduate from college versus 20.3% for the nation at large. Without decent educational opportunities, few businesses are interested in investing resources on reservation lands.

President Bush promised to provide 1 billion dollars to Native American schools during his campaign. Whether this will be reflected in his budget is not yet known. Without these funds, though, it will be impossible for the Federal Government to meet the goals

Photo: Michaelle Vignes

of the American Indian Initiative [AII]. Introduced during the end of President Clinton's term, the AII's purpose was to channel medical, economic, and educational resources into the reservations.

Native American Gaming

Native American gaming has become for some Native reservations a viable economic alternative to unemployment and high poverty rates. In 1987, the Supreme Court of the United States passed the Cabazon decision, which permitted gambling on Native reservations. Due to the phenomenal growth of the industry, Congress passed the Indian Gaming Regulatory Act (IGRA) in 1988. Basically, this act provided a regulatory framework and supervisory body for reservation gambling. Half of the over two billion dollars generated from this activity is received by ten of the 184 tribes involved in the industry. Although the Supreme Court permitted Native communities the power to determine whether or not they wanted to offer gambling, the IGRA has successfully ruled that a tribe must enter into a compact with the state in which the reservation is located. Some states have been hesitant or even hostile to the possibility of legalized gambling within their boundaries. This has proved to be of major controversy in the state of Nebraska, for example. In this area, the Santee tribe has opened a casino that provides slot machines. Twenty-three jobs have been created as a result. Unfortunately for the Santee, Nebraska legislators perceive the casino as illegal since the tribe never entered into a compact with the state. Each day that the casino remains open causes the tribe to be fined several thousand dollars. Even so, the tribe held a special election and voted to keep the casino operating. Ultimately, they hope that the people of Nebraska will also vote to permit them to continue running a casino. Unfortunately, the legislature has yet to allow the issue to be voted on by the citizens of the state. During the last two years, the state committee responsible for this issue has kept the other legislators, as well as the state's citizens, from voting on the Santees' right to offer gaming.

It is unclear if Gale Norton, in her role as the Secretary of the Interior and the ultimate overseer of Indian affairs, will aid the Santees' struggle against the state of Nebraska. Her views on state versus tribal rights are difficult to determine. At the time of her confirmation to Bush's cabinet, Norton stated, "decisions of government are best made by those who are affected. What is true for states is true for tribes. Self-governance is important and I support this as a concept."

Environmental Protection of Native Lands

Beginning in the 1980s and continuing through the 1990s, the Nuclear Regulatory Agency has attempted to entice reservation communities to accept nuclear waste. As an incentive, Native councils willing to listen to various proposals concerning the creation of nuclear dumps were offered financial incentives of several hundred thousand dollars. Because the state of Oklahoma has the most Native communities, with varying amounts of land, these tribes have become the main targets for the agency. In response, 31 tribes in Oklahoma formed the Inter Tribal Environmental Agency [ITEC] to keep these dumps off of their lands. At a national level, Native communities have formed the National Environmental Coalition of Native Americans [NECONA] to help maintain reservations free of nuclear waste dumps.

In May 2000, Native communities in the Mojave Desert of California successfully halted the storage of nuclear waste in Ward Valley. With the help of NECONA and a consortium of environmental groups, the project was stopped in order to protect the desert tortoise and running trails sacred to Native peoples in the region.

Hopefully, the Pyramid Lake Paiute tribe of Nevada will be equally successful in halting the development of a sewage treatment plant by the Truckee Company based in California. According to the Paiute, the 42 million dollar sewage expansion project will negatively impact on the Truckee River and Pyramid Lake. Both of these regions are important to the subsistence needs of the Pyramid Lake Paiute community.

Protection of Sacred Sites on Public and Private Lands

Native peoples have had little success in protecting sacred sites that are not located on tribally-owned land. Invariably, the Supreme Court has ruled against Native peoples on this issue. In 1996, President Clinton addressed the issue by requesting that federal agencies, (1) accommodate access to and ceremonial use of Indian sacred sites by Indian religious practitioners and (2) avoid adversely affecting the physical integrity of such sacred sites. A caveat to these laudable points, however, is the fact that they are mere suggestions. Currently, federal agencies are under no legal obligation to protect sites that affect the usage of lands under their control. As a result, land containing sacred sites can continue to be used according to the mandates of the federal agency regulating the region. If the site is on public lands, it cannot legally be set aside for the sole purpose of Native activities. According to the Supreme Court, no one ethnic group can be allowed greater access to the nation's public space than any other persons residing in the United States.

In response, some federal agencies, particularly some members of the National Park Service, are providing information to visitors requesting them to respect Native uses of the area. As a result, rock climbers are requested not to use pylons on sacred mountains in the Southwest, California, the Northwest Coast area, and the Black Hills in the Northern Plains. In addition, tourists are asked not to take pictures of Native peoples involved in religious activities at sacred sites on public lands. At this time, a person's adherence to these guidelines is totally voluntary.

Land Claims

Numerous Native communities have fought to regain land illegally taken from them in the past. Although, in 1983, the Timbisha Shoshone Tribe was promised a permanent land base in Death Valley, they have yet to be given any acreage. This battle is currently wending its way through the federal court system. Numerous other Native communities are striving to gain federal recognition and also to obtain ownership of land illegally taken from them. This has led to some infighting between federally and non-federally recognized communities. Since Congress tends to limit the amount of money they appropriate to Native peoples, federally-recognized tribes are concerned that an influx of newly-recognized communities will diminish the amount of monetary resources available. This fear is not unfounded. In general, Congress tends to split the pie into smaller pieces rather than adding money to the whole. Presently, over thirty Native communities are attempting to gain federal recognition. This is an arduous journey, as the community needs to meet numerous criteria to gain federal affiliation.

Intellectual Property

Native peoples are continuing to fight for the right to control the use of their symbols, names, and knowledge. Many names used by professional and amateur sports teams have been appropriated from Native peoples. At the professional level, the Atlanta Braves and the Redskins have yet to change their names even though Native leaders have continually asked them to do so. There is a similar situation with numerous high school sports teams as well. So far, the courts have ruled that tribal names and symbols are in the public domain and consequently are considered to be unprotected by copyright law.

Native American Graves Protection and Repatriation Act

Passed in 1990, the Native American Graves Protection and Repatriation Act [NAGPRA] protects skeletal remains, burial goods, and ceremonial objects associated with federally-recognized tribes. NAGPRA only covers items that are held by institutions receiving public funds, however. Items owned by private collectors, located on private lands, or taken during battles are not covered by the act. In addition, skeletal remains of unknown tribal affiliation are not covered by the act. In an unprecedented decision, the University of Nebraska agreed to return all unaffiliated remains to Native peoples in the Great Plains. Unfortunately, indigenous communities in the region have yet to come to an agreement on a place for the burial of these individuals. Hopefully, they will design a structure to deal with these individuals of unknown ancestry and return them to the earth.

MEXICO AND
CENTRAL AMERICA

MEXICO

The most noteworthy events in Mexico of significance to the indigenous world can be summarised in two: a) the electoral process, in which an opposition candidate was the victor and, b) the successful Zapatista march/motorcade, held during the months of February and March 2001, the main aim of which was to build a national consensus around recognition of the rights of indigenous peoples.

The combination of the transformative interval (which opened up the path to political alternation) and the Zapatista march has created, since December 2000 (date when Vicente Fox of the National Action Party – PAN – took over as President of the Republic) an extraordinary opportunity that has opened up real possibilities for the Congress of the Union – Chambers of Deputies and Senators – to spend time creating the necessary consensus around constitutional reform in the areas of indigenous rights and culture, responding to the commitments made by the federal government to the Zapatista National Liberation Army (EZLN) and which were reflected in the so-called San Andrés Larráinzar Accords of February 1996.

Nonetheless, by the end of the first half of April, two weeks following the Zapatista withdrawal from Mexico City, things were not clear with regard to the extent of the rights to be recognised. The main point at issue, repeatedly expressed by the main political actors, is their doubt as to the scope of indigenous rights, in particular in relation to recognition of the right to self-determination and its achievement through autonomy.

Once the commitment to reform the Constitution was made by the legislators, it still remained to be seen how deep such a reform would be able to go. And whilst, in fact, following the Zapatista march, conditions to legislate on indigenous rights have never been better, it is nonetheless not certain that the results - in terms of the scope of rights - will maintain a high profile. The Mexican political class – particularly the political parties – have shown a tendency to gradually reduce the extent of what was achieved at San Andrés. This concern is a valid one given that, between 1996 and 2000, each

Zapatistas gathered at a meeting, Mexico. Photo: Franziska K. Nyffenegger

time the negotiations were opened for re-negotiation, they were constantly reduced, both in profile and in scope.

Despite these challenges, it is clear that since Vicente Fox's triumph and the Zapatista march/motorcade, the stage may now truly be set for achieving recognition of the indigenous right to autonomy.

The Indigenous in the 2000 Elections

The results of the Mexican presidential elections on 2nd July 2000 were unexpected. For the first time in more than seventy years, the Institutional Revolutionary Party (PRI) was defeated. But the vote in the indigenous regions brought no surprises. As in the past, the PRI won once more in these regions. The PRI's corporatist system functioned yet again, oiled by a political system that operates via the clientilistic use of social policy resources, particularly those destined for the poor. But, on this occasion, these votes were insufficient to avoid the victory of the PAN candidate, Vicente Fox, who took over the presidency on the basis of the votes in the urban areas and the west and north of the country. The newness of indigenous participation in the electoral process was part of the strategy adopted by some of the indigenous organisations which, on this occasion, did not vote unconditionally for the opposition parties – particularly those of the Left – because these parties had refused to negotiate alliances.

In 1994, a block of the main indigenous organisations in the country organised the First Indigenous National Electoral Convention. At this event, they listened to the indigenous programme and proposals of all the contesting party candidates, with the exception of the PRI candidate, who did not attend the debate. It was also an opportunity for the organisations to put forward a political agenda specific to the indigenous movement. Within the context of the Zapatista uprising and a climate of strengthening within the indigenous movement, the political parties negotiated alliances with some of the indigenous organisations. The result was that the LVI Legislature (1994-1997) had the greatest number of indigenous legislators in the country's history.

However, in 2000, the opposition parties refused to establish agreements with the non-partisan indigenous movement. And so, in May 2000, a block of 6 national indigenous organisations – of all colours, from the Plural National Indigenous Assembly for Autonomy – ANIPA, to the Mexican Indigenous Council, affiliated to the PRI – decided to draw up an indigenous political agenda, which they presented to all the candidates contesting the presidency of the

Republic[1]. Some of the most noteworthy points proposed were: a demand for the fulfilment of the San Andrés Accords, approval of the draft Law formulated by COCOPA, the creation of a Centre for Indigenous Languages, the creation of a National Council for the Development of Indigenous Peoples, demilitarisation in indigenous regions and a call for the cancellation of indigenist policies, enabling indigenous peoples themselves to run the government institutions in charge of indigenous policy.

This list of demands obtained no response from either the PRD or the PRI candidates. To the surprise of the Indians and the rest of the Mexican population, it did obtain a response from Vicente Fox, an overwhelming one in fact: on 14th June 2000, in the daily *La Jornada* newspaper, he published a complete plan in which he took on board the list of these organisations' demands and committed himself to taking up COCOPA's proposed reforms as his own, transforming them into a government initiative, which he would issue on the first day of his government, if he were elected.

In fact, on the first day of taking over as President of the Republic, in his role as supreme chief of the armed forces, President Fox gave instructions to commence the withdrawal of some military posts, to reduce military numbers and to dismantle some of the military camps in Chiapas. At the same time, he sent an initiative for constitutional reform to the Congress of the Union that reflected CO-COPA's proposals in the area of indigenous rights and culture within its text. The resistance from the executive power that had been evident during the government of President Ernesto Zedillo was at last gone, although rejection of the proposal was from then on to be concentrated in the hands of the deputies and senators.

At the same time and on the same date, the EZLN announced that it would leave Chiapas for Mexico City in search of a meeting with the senators and deputies in order to gain approval of the mentioned reform. From the moment the march was announced, the Zapatistas made it quite clear that they were going to the capital to support COCOPA's proposal, and that they were not going to meet with the executive or any of its members, and that its motorcade did not have the aim of signing peace or handing over arms. This would not happen until the three conditions for reopening dialogue, the "three signs of goodwill", were fulfilled by the federal executive power.

On 28th March 2001, the climax of the successful motorcade, the EZLN *comandantes* (commanders) were in the Chamber of Deputies appearing before the nation. There they presented their reasons and arguments in favour of indigenous rights, thus fulfilling the goal of the motorcade. And although the results of these negotiations have yet to be made concrete given that, at the time of writing, the Senate of the Republic has still not issued its report on the COCOPA-Fox initiative, the process has now begun and it is hoped that it will be concluded by April. With this event, one stage will draw to a close, and a new era for indigenous rights in Mexico will commence.

The Colours of the Earth Motorcade for Indigenous Rights

The return of the 23 indigenous *comandantes* and *sub-comandante* Marcos to Chiapas, safe and sound, and with the goals achieved plus a good deal of legitimacy gained for their movement and the indigenous cause, was possible thanks to the involvement of many actors, both national and international. And although the balance is positive, it could have been the opposite. For the 36 days of the march/motorcade, a deeply divided Mexico could be observed in the capital, a political class polarised into two broad blocks. The issue of indigenous rights was the backdrop against which two projects for the country were discussed, one aspiring to the possibility of a Mexico accommodating the Indians with full rights, and the other continuing to maintain the idea of a *mestizo*[2] State, a mono-ethnic State, into which the Indians had to be forcibly incorporated.

The march/motorcade took place despite the fact that, in the early days, threats were received, along with a simultaneous and fierce confrontation with power. The first battle was with representatives of President Fox, who requested a discreet meeting with the EZLN in order to reach agreement over issues relating to the security of the march. The Zapatistas refused. The EZLN preferred the accompaniment of the International Red Cross. However, this organisation declined, a refusal that generated an irate response from the Zapatistas, accusing representatives of President Fox of having put pressure on the international body to prevent it from being involved.

The start of the march was preceded by declarations condemning the march from the country's different power groups. Various representatives of business groups demanded the arrest of the Zapatistas the moment they crossed the Chiapas border. Another businessman played down the importance of the indigenous demands, saying, *"the root of indigenous problems can be found in alcoholism, sexist customs and in rows stemming from stupid quarrels. They are just a bunch of idiots."* Yet another representative of this sector described the motorcade as a "Hollywood-esque spectacular".

Some members of the political class contributed to the lynching of the march. The governor of the state of Querétaro called for the death sentence for the Zapatistas, while a local deputy from the state of Morelos challenged sub-comandante Marcos to a duel. A member of the Church, the Bishop of Ecatepec, was of the opinion that sub-comandante Marcos was "nothing but a poor devil" and wrote off the motorcade. Yet others debated the legality of the march, the use of balaclavas and the presence of arms among the protestors. Others, the majority, asked for respect and tolerance.

President Fox himself called on his party members to act sensibly and requested their collaboration in ensuring the safety of the Zapatistas. Alongside this, the Zapatista leadership decided to implement its own security system (initially made up of an Italian solidarity group known as the "Monos Blancos" – an allusion to their white overalls) and decided to hire buses for the journey, leaving their arms in the community of La Realidad, the Zapatista leadership headquarters, under the protection of comandante Moisés.

The EZLN left La Realidad on 24th February, thus commencing a long journey that was to last 36 days. On leaving Chiapas, sub-comandante Marcos gave a speech in San Cristóbal de las Casas and proclaimed the motorcade for *"the rights of those the colour of the earth"*. It is important to note that the aim of the Zapatista march/motorcade was to contribute to peace. When the EZLN withdrew from the negotiating table, it stated that it would only return if the government fulfilled the commitments it had made at San Andrés Larráinzar. Given that the aim of this motorcade was to argue personally in the Congress in favour of constitutional reforms so that these commitments could be fulfilled, the Zapatistas were subscribing to fulfilment of the said Accords. If the deputies and senators kept these commitments, they would be clearing the path for a resumption of dialogue.

The other conditions made by the EZLN (the so-called "three signs" demanded of the executive power before any resumption in dialogue could take place), such as the release of Zapatista prisoners and the dismantling of certain military bases, are gradually being fulfilled and so it is possible that, during the second half of 2001, the dialogue process interrupted in 1996 may be able to be resumed[3]. Prior to coming out of the forest, the EZLN told President Vicente Fox, *"...the Zapatistas do have a voice. If the three signs demanded are fulfilled, there will be dialogue. If there is a serious and true desire for dialogue and peace, the EZLN will respond similarly."*

The Boundaries of Optimism

The Zapatista motorcade achieved what seemed to be the impossible: to unite thousands of Mexicans to the indigenous cause. After the deep polarisation the country experienced during the first two weeks of the march, passions finally died down and the threat of a divided or "Balkanised" Mexico gradually diminished.

On 29th March, the day after the Zapatistas appeared before the National Congress, the national daily newspaper *Reforma* published a survey regarding the legitimacy of the demand for indigenous rights and the need for their recognition. More than 90% of those questioned confirmed the need to legislate on indigenous rights. At the same time, those taking a more radical position, such as deputies from the government party itself, the National Action Party (PAN), opposing a President from their own party head-on and refusing to receive the Zapatistas, even having reservations about discussing the issue, in the end agreed to join the legislative commissions formed to debate COCOPA's proposal, transformed into an initiative by President Fox.

It has to be remembered that these events are completely new to Mexico. Dominated by strong presidentialism, with parliamentary life previously dominated by the PRI, no one dared contradict mandates from the President of the Republic. Now, political alternation has brought with it a new relationship between the executive, legislative and judicial powers, which are beginning to become true counterweights. A lack of democratic practices and institutionalised paths for parliamentary debate means that this episode is being characterised by fierce confrontation between parties and powers. Nonetheless, in the end, the debate on the "rights of those the colour of the earth" remains on the nation's agenda.

It is worth noting the importance of the national indigenous movement in these events, grouped around the National Indigenous Congress (CNI), which validated and accompanied the motorcade. Its presence minimised the strength of the arguments that attempted to discredit the Zapatistas as representatives of all Mexico's indigenous peoples. The most important, it concluded, more important than the "representativeness" of the Zapatistas in relation to "all Mexico's indigenous peoples" was that they were, before the Congress of the Union, the bearers of the indigenous agenda that had been expressed in the San Andrés Accords, particularly in terms of recognition of the right to self-determination and its achievement through autonomy. And it could hardly have been any other way. In the course of events, from 1994 to the present day, it has become clear that indigenous rights in Mexico would have gained no visibility, nor any relevance on the national agenda, if they had not had the backing of the guerrillas. Only the force of arms made it possible for the political class, and Mexican society in general, to understand the importance and legitimacy of Indian rights for the democratic life of

Indigenous peoples protesting in San Cristóbal de las Casas, Mexico. Photo: Heidi Moksnes

the country, an understanding which, despite events, still has difficulties in finding its concrete expression.

Given the great resistance and difficulties the San Andrés Accords have had to face up to, optimism regarding the results of the march and what is going to be included within the Constitution needs to be tempered with realism. In fact, everything points to the fact that the scope of indigenous rights to be recognised by Congress will not go as far as that which was agreed at San Andrés and it is even feared that the "spirit of the agreements" may be lost. This is not without reason. The EZLN agreed to sign the San Andrés Accords under protest. The EZLN signed them but called them "minimum agreements".

One of their main objections was that it was not expressly noted in the Accords that autonomy was to be achieved by means of an "Autonomous System", to name but one of the omissions[4]. There was reason for concern. Since the Accords, the so-called "autonomy" has been reduced to a catalogue of rights that are called "autonomous" but which do not fall within the framework of an autonomous system. Nor was the scope of their implementation specified. And so, even though there may have been an intention to maintain the integrity of the COCOPA-Fox initiative, this is limited to a catalogue of "autonomous rights", restricted by and subordinate to State action. And there is a danger that they may yet be even further reduced.

For these reasons, one of the main issues of debate in the said reform revolves around specifying the scope of its fulfilment. Apparently, the most that is likely to be achieved is that it will be established at the community and municipal levels. Thus the scope of autonomous rights will remain reduced to "community autonomy" and "municipal autonomy". Despite these limitations, for the deputies and senators that are now revising the COCOPA-Fox proposal, such rights are "unconstitutional", and so they insist on eliminating some of the commitments signed at San Andrés. Many of them have proposed omitting rights related to "self-determination", "autonomy", "peoples", "communities" and that it should remain limited to "municipal autonomy".

In other words, the indigenous deputies and senators propose recognising indigenous rights but without modifying the Mexican State, without modifying the homogenising principles that underlie the Mexican Constitution: in short, "plus ça change, plus c'est la même chose". And, unfortunately, these limitations have not been overcome, not even in the oft-quoted COCOPA proposal. The model for formulating the recognition of "autonomous rights" drawn up by this body and taken up by President Fox is constructed in such a way that it grants rights at the same time as it limits them. Let us take a look at some examples of rights that are recognised, and the limitations from which they suffer:

- Right to self-determination and, as an expression of this, to autonomy (Art. 4)
  Limitation: as part of the Mexican State (Art. 4)

- Right to decide: their internal forms of co-existence and social, economic, political and cultural organisation (Art. 4)
  Limitation: as part of the Mexican State (Art. 4)

- Right to apply: their system of law in the regulation and solution of internal conflicts (Art. 4)
  Limitation: Respecting individual guarantees, human rights and, in particular, the dignity and integrity of women; their procedures, judgements and decisions will be validated by the State jurisdictional authorities (Art. 4)

- Right to elect: their own authorities and to exercise their own forms of internal government in accordance with their regulations within the sphere of their autonomy (Art. 4)
  Limitation: guaranteeing the participation of women under conditions of equality (Art. 4) and guaranteeing the unity of the National State (Art. 115)

- Right of access: to the collective use and enjoyment of the natural resources on their lands and territories, these being understood as the whole of the environment used and occupied by indigenous peoples (Art. 4)
  Limitation: except those under the direct control of the Nation (Art. 4)

In spite of all the influences that the validity of "autonomous rights" suffers from, it is clear that progress is being made. However, there are still many challenges in the path that obscure the view. There is the fear that once constitutional reform has been achieved, it will remain dead letter. This is what has happened in the past. The Mexican Constitution was reformed in 1991 and included recognition of indigenous rights within Article 4. This reform was never applied because the deputies never got round to sorting out the regulations governing it. The same can be said of ILO Convention 169. Although Mexico was the second country to adhere to this international regulation, it was never taken on board in any serious way, neither by the executive nor (indeed far less) by the legislature. Some jurists have even insinuated that, indigenous rights being "unconstitutional", they could be taken to court and overturned.

This is the state of affairs following the Zapatista march: the climate remains very sensitive to the possibility of a scenario that will lead to dialogue and the signing of peace in the medium term. This is apparently a realistic expectation, the Zapatistas have repeated their desire and the need to achieve peace now. In this context, however, there remain doubts as to the future of indigenous rights once the Chiapas indigenous have returned to the "rule of law".

Notes

[1] Their position was publicly announced in an article published in *La Jornada* on 19th May 2000
[2] "Mestizo"- people of mixed (generally including a large proportion of Spanish) descent - trans. note
[3] The almost one hundred Zapatista prisoners throughout the country have been gradually freed; and by 2nd January 2001, 53 military posts had already been withdrawn from the state of Chiapas
[4] The Zapatista lack of agreement is expressed in the document *"Punto y seguido"* ("Full Stop")

GUATEMALA

The last century bore witness to many events in relation to the recognition of the world's, and particularly Guatemala's, indigenous peoples (*Campaña Continental de Resistencia Indígena, Negra y Popular* - the Continental Campaign for Indigenous, Black and Popular Resistance; Rigoberta Menchú's Nobel Peace Prize; the signing of the Agreement on Identity and Rights of Indigenous Peoples within the framework of the peace process; ratification of ILO Convention 169, etc.) These events helped to transform the Mayan movement into the true representatives of the Maya people. This transformation is currently going through a period of stagnation, or even reversal, which is due to a lack of coherence amongst the leaders, often because these leaders are not responding to the demands of the rural communities and are focussing their work in the city, through lack of a well-defined politico-ideological project.

Maya children, Guatemala.Photo: Anette Molbech

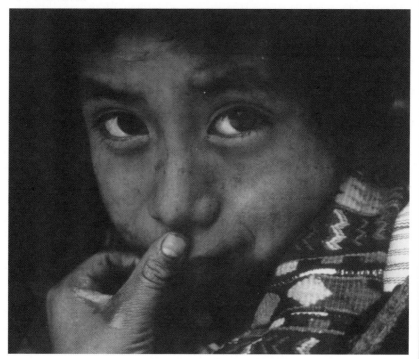

The situation merits a deep and critical analysis at a number of different levels, taking into account the fact that the demands of the Maya bear no relation to the recent armed conflict but find their origins in the time of the Spanish invasion and colonisation.

In Terms of Politics

It must be remembered that a new government came to power in 2000. The Guatemalan Republican Front (FRG)[1] took office, nominating Alfonso Portillo as President, a contradictory person in both his discourse and his political leaning.

For the first time, the URNG (Guatemalan National Revolutionary Unity) participated in the electoral contest and, in alliance with other left wing groups, participates in the Congress with eight deputies, of which few now remain because the previous left-wing candidate, Alvaro Colom, who always had leanings to the Right, has now set up a new party known as the National Union for Hope (UNE), to which deputies from the old PAN[2] and the ANN[3] have defected.

It is important to emphasise that many indigenous leaders who had been involved in the different organisations of the social movement participated in the electoral process. Whilst it is clear that this is the first time a considerable number of Maya have gained access to Congress, albeit through the different parties and, in particular, the FRG instead of strengthening the process of the Mayan movement, the participation of some leaders in the political parties has brought it to a standstill as they have lost sight of the rationale of the organisations and have become mixed up in party political propaganda.

Currently, some Mayan groups are making efforts to form political parties. This is born out of the experience of some civic committees, for example, the case of Xelju'[4] in Quetzaltenango. Another example is the *Asociación Política de Mujeres Mayas* (Political Association of Mayan Women), including amongst others, Nobel Peace Prize winner Rigoberta Menchú; ex-deputies Rosalina Tuyúc and Manuela Alvarado; the Minister for Culture, Otilia Lux de Cotí, and the peasant leader, María Toj. The Association's main aim is to support the initiatives of any indigenous woman who is looking to become involved in politics.

It is clear that these political projects can be good but, unfortunately, they are creating the basis for personal ambition. This was the same system that was used by the Left and the Right to organise indigenous communities by creating certain figures who, instead of strengthening the movement have, at the end of the day, divided it.

In Terms of Economics

The process of globalisation promoted by the United States, Europe and Japan has caused the greater impoverishment of indigenous communities and the over-exploitation of Mayan families in rural areas, along with increasing levels of unemployment and under-employment in the towns. These are important factors when considering the standard of living and poverty.

The government - and often the NGO - concept of rural development results in infrastructure developments (bridges, roads, health centres, markets, etc.) but does not envisage a concept of integrated human development, which would imply a change in structure and attitudes and a new relationship between rural and urban areas.

In the peace process, an Agreement on Socio-Economic Aspects and the Agrarian Situation was signed. For many years, the URNG maintained its struggle for access to land as this was the focal point of indigenous community development. But, unfortunately, in the Agreement, whilst it clearly recognises the indigenous communities' philosophical concept of land, it does not propose the urgent restructuring of land tenure, by not providing for a new land registry. In other words, it does not touch upon the issue of agrarian reform.

The Land Fund was created and peasant organisations joined the National Coordinating Body of Peasant Organisations, CNOC[5]. The struggle for land has always been an unjust one for the peasants and, in this case, instead of resolving the problems the Land Fund has made them more complicated. One of the problems is that the government buys the farms from those who have made themselves rich on the communities' resources for many years. Another problem is that to have access to this land, the peasants have to buy it and, given their economic status, they are becoming ever poorer. Whilst it is clear that nowadays nothing comes free, selling land to its legitimate owners is not the right approach to providing peasants with resources.

As a consequence of this economic and social situation in the communities, increasing migration of indigenous and peasant families to the United States and Mexico can be observed and, in addition, the appearance of prostitution amongst indigenous women.

In Social Terms

Guatemala is a signatory to the Declaration on Discrimination against Women, has ratified ILO Convention 169 and has an Agreement on the Identity and Rights of Indigenous Peoples, signed during the peace process. But this does not mean that discrimination against indigenous peoples has decreased; this is a structural evil entrenched in the very heart of the State itself.

Whilst it is clear that there are a great number of women amongst the Mayan movement's leadership, they continue to be advised by men or it is the men who continue to make the decisions. In the communities, too, women are greatly disadvantaged in relation to men. The militarisation suffered by the indigenous communities increased the levels of sexism and gender differences. The concept of complementarity in life which, according to the Mayan world vision, is one of the principles of marriage between Maya, is now a Utopia, given that in recent years a high degree of family disintegration has taken place, along with all the problems a dislocated community suffers from (youth gangs, drug addiction and begging).

In Educational Terms

The Agreement on the Identity and Rights of Indigenous Peoples clearly speaks of an education in keeping with the pluricultural and multilingual reality of the country and the urgent need for Educational Reform is stated.

And so a Consultative Committee for Educational Reform was established within the Coordinating Body of Mayan Organisations of Guatemala (COPMAGUA)[6]. All civil society organisations and, particularly, the Mayan organisations, made a contribution, both the organisations of displaced people, united in the Consultative Assembly of Displaced People (ACPD)[7] and the large number of Mayan organisations (popular, development, academic, women's). The result was the Plan for Educational Reform.

The Portillo government has given this plan very little consideration. With the appointment of the Vice-Minister for Education, Dr. Demetrio Cojti, and the Minister for Culture, Otilia Lux - the former a member of the Consultative Committee for Educational Reform, the latter a member of the Commission for Historical Clarification, and both indigenous - many believed that Maya-related issues would be rapidly dealt with. On the contrary, they have stagnated and there has been very little progress in the area of education. The government has planned only palliative measures, such as the last Literacy Campaign, which created controversy in all sectors, as civil society was not consulted at all. For the Mayan organisations, it continues to be a project of Hispanicisation, as are all the programmes that have been promoted by the Ministry of Education. Nevertheless, some progress has been made in that some Mayan organisations have formed Mayan Schools, even though they are isolated initiatives. The Maya University is a Utopia, a dream and may be a means by which the State can clear the conscience of the many.

In Terms of Religion

In this area, there is a great development and strengthening of Mayan spirituality. Whilst Christian groups (Catholic and Protestant) have problems amongst themselves and are dividing communities at the same time as they are losing ground, Mayan spirituality is increasingly widening its scope. This way of viewing divinity and everything associated with it has enabled the Maya to recover their identity.

One of the problems is that, in their enthusiasm, it seems as if they may be falling into the same methodological trap used by Christian groups to gain followers. In other words, it is highly possible that they could become caught up in a Mayan fundamentalism and this could cause the role of spirituality to become distorted. Another problem is that some organisations have been using Mayan ceremony and priests as a means of getting their hands on financial resources.

In Summary

Whilst it is clear that it had been making good progress, the indigenous movement is now experiencing a period of stagnation or even backslide. This requires an analysis of the realities of the Mayan movement and its relationship with the Maya people. The movement also urgently requires a Strategic Plan to prevent further co-optation and the loss of leaders who have a great deal more to offer. Given these factors, the formation and strengthening of a Mayan intelligentsia is urgently needed. All that exists at the moment is a purely academic class, which is neither particularly creative nor proactive.

Notes

[1]   The FRG was established by General Efrain Rios Mont, a general who has combined politics with Protestant fundamentalism. He is the current President of the Congress of the Republic, but was responsible for the large-scale massacres that took place during the armed conflict in Guatemala.

[2]   PAN, the Plan for National Progress, is the party of the previous government. From this political group have appeared 'Unionists' and 'PANists'.

3   The ANN, the New Nation Alliance, is the alliance of political parties headed by the URNG, DIA and UNID, which formed the Left in the previous elections.
4   This is the oldest civic committee in Quetzaltenango. Its history began at the end of 1972.
5   CNOC was formed of various peasant organisations fighting for land, including: the Committee for Peasant Unity (CUC), the Kabawil Peasant Council, the National Indigenous and Peasant Coordinating Body (CONIC), etc.
6   COPMAGUA was, at the start, made up of the Council of Mayan Organisations of Guatemala (COMG), the Academy of Mayan Languages of Guatemala (ALMG), the Body for Mayan Unity and Consensus (IUCM), the Union of Maya Peoples of Guatemala (UPMAG) and the Tukum Umam Movement. Following an internal struggle, and due to personal ambition and inter-institutional problems, the first two organisations withdrew, leaving only the latter three, albeit accompanied by others.
7   The ACPD, made up of the CERJ, CONAVIGUA, CPRs, GAM, CUC.

NICARAGUA

Conflicts over land ownership and the fight against exclusion were the topics that marked the geography and lives of the indigenous peoples and ethnic communities of Nicaragua's Caribbean Coast during the year 2000.

Although the right to land is widely recognised in the laws of the Republic of Nicaragua, there are no mechanisms for demarcating and titling land in favour of indigenous peoples or ethnic communities. The lesson learned in this region was that you can move forward in unity when the interests of the majority are combined.

Defence of Indigenous Territories

In October 1998, the Presidency of the Republic presented a draft Law of Demarcation, which was discussed with the different communities and territories in which the country's indigenous peoples and ethnic communities live.

The Autonomous Regional Councils – regional governments on the Caribbean coast – approved this draft legislative bill by means of a consultation process that was made possible through the combined efforts of men and women from the communities, their leaders, churches, universities, municipalities, Autonomous Regional Coun-

Miskito children, Alamikamba, RAAN. Photo: Diana Vinding

cils and national deputies, along with the financial and logistical support of governmental and non-governmental bodies.

After two years, on 6th September 2000, the Autonomous Regional Councils of the North and South Atlantic Autonomous Regions finally presented the new *Draft Law for a System of Communal Ownership on the part of the Indigenous Peoples and Ethnic Communities of the Atlantic Coast of the Rivers Bocay, Coco and Indio Maíz* to the National Assembly.

A Little Background

The demarcation and titling of lands has been one of the most fundamental and historic demands of the indigenous peoples and ethnic communities of Nicaragua's Caribbean Coast, and has remained an inescapable commitment throughout the different phases of State development. This was reflected in:

- The Treaty of Managua of 1860
- The Harrison-Altamirano Treaty of 1905
- The Titling Commission of the Mosquitia of 1905
- Agrarian Laws of 1963 and 1981
- The Political Constitution of 1986
- The Statute of Autonomy, approved in 1987
- The Constitutional Reform of 1995

Articles 5, 89, 107 and 180 establish clear recognition of the indigenous peoples' communal ownership of their territories. Article 89 clearly states, "The State particularly recognises the indigenous peoples' forms of communal ownership of lands in all that which concerns the right of ownership of their lands."

The submission of a *Draft Law for a System of Communal Ownership* responds to the need for a legal instrument that specifically governs the demarcation and titling of the lands of indigenous peoples and ethnic communities in order to ensure the effective application of their rights.

The Current Situation

Whilst some indigenous communities enjoy real and legally registered property titles, the majority of communities do not: they are recognised as the owners of their land but the boundaries have not been defined.

Various businessmen and companies voraciously exploit the fishing, mining and timber resources, along with the biodiversity, of these territories, most of them uninterested in resolving the issue of ownership of the indigenous territories.

Poor peasants from other regions of the country see new opportunities for survival in these "promising and underutilised" indigenous lands. The question people continually ask is why so few people claim so much territory?

We will now present some examples of how this conflict manifested itself in the year 2000. The examples are unresolved conflicts, such as the demand for a fair law to establish clear mechanisms by which to recognise the ancestral inheritance of the indigenous peoples over their lands and waters, vital elements for the preservation of their cultures, languages, religions and ways of life.

Prinzapolka: *Gringos* against Indigenous

The peaceful atmosphere of the plains lining the river Prinzapolka was lost because the inhabitants refused to allow four United States citizens linked to logging companies to strip them of the lands populated by the Miskito people.

Richard Clearence, Joseph Patten, Robert Burrinson and Paul Stauder Morales are four Americans who reopened a lawsuit against nine indigenous communities, accusing them of seizing property and falsifying legal documents in order to obtain more than 58,000 hectares of moist tropical lands in the areas along the river Prinzapolka in the North Atlantic Autonomous Region (RAAN).

This conflict, better known as the "Prinzapolka Case", has already been submitted twice to the courts in Puerto Cabezas and, on both occasions, the decision found in favour of the communities, who have lived on these lands for more than one hundred years.

However, the Americans' lawyer last year managed to get another judge to accept a new appeal, accompanied this time by criminal proceedings against the indigenous people, and the case has thus been reopened.

"I do not understand how someone who is not from this country has the right to say that the indigenous people are invading private land, when it is they who come here to buy the sacred communal lands of the indigenous, lands which the communities own through the Law of Autonomy. Nicaragua does not belong to the North Americans and this needs to be clearly stated," notes the Moravian priest Norman Bent, president of the Coastal Committee.

Bent says the Coastal Committee has spent several years working on the issue of communal property in the Atlantic Coast and that, in the Prinzapolka case, they have requested the government to cancel all tenancy agreements that may have been made between some communal organisations and the North Americans, as they were contracts signed by organisations that are no longer in existence.

According to experts, the properties in conflict were acquired by a North American citizen in 1909. With the passing of time, the lands were sold and inherited, which explains how the claimants now number four.

To lose 58,000 hectares of territory would mean the indigenous would be left without land on which to plant banana, cassava or *malanga*[1], without access to the river and its natural resources: in short, condemned to die from starvation.

The Prinzapolka Case was denounced in an international forum held in Geneva at the end of last year. A delegation of community leaders was able to participate, with funding from the Office of Humanitarian Promotion and Development of the Atlantic Coast (OPHDESCA).

Cayos Perlas: A Pending Dispute

Leaders from the communities of Laguna de Perlas, Corn Island, Bluefields and Rama Kay are still awaiting the decision of the Civil District Court of Bluefields with regard to a demand to nullify the sale of seven cays to a Greek, Peter Tsokos, who is now trying to resell – via the Internet – this area of communal territory.

The origin of the conflict dates back five years, when the Greek "bought" seven cays from the Hooker Jackson family for C$ 60,000. Several years previously, the Hooker Jackson family had acquired the cays in payment of a debt owed by the father of Amos Briton Archibold, the supposed owner of the cays.

However, in a document submitted at the end of October 2000, the communal and regional leaders stated, "Everything indicates that the Hooker Jackson family obtained the decision for forced sale without presenting the titles that proved Dr. Amos Briton Archibold's right of control over the islets or cays in question. As he was not the owner, he did not have the title deed. The forced sale was thus undertaken without proof of ownership and in serious violation of the law."

According to Tsokos, the transaction was perfectly legal. He "bought" seven of the 18 islets: Claw Cay, Baboon, While Kale, Waters, Vincent, Great Kay and Link Kay from the Kirkland, Taylor, Hooker and Jackson families, who had supposedly held the title deeds for more than a century.

But Tsokos' purchase contradicts article 10 of the Nicaraguan Political Constitution, which clearly states that territories such as the Cayos Perlas belong to the State.

Alejandro Mejía Gaitán, president of the Governing Board of the South Atlantic Autonomous Regional Council, says they are sure the Cayos Perlas belong to the community members from the Laguna de Perlas Basin, and so the regional authority fully supports them in their demand for return of the lands to those who historically owned them.

Members of the Autonomous Regional Council and leaders from the different indigenous communities requested that cancellation of the forced sale of the seven cays be declared because, "you can't sell someone else's property" and that the corresponding record of registration also be cancelled.

Monkey Point against the Giant CINN

The inhabitants of Monkey Point are standing firm in their struggle against the driving forces behind the Nicaraguan Interoceanic Canal

(CINN), who are attempting to build a port in their bay for freight handling.

On 3rd November 2000, the indigenous communities of Monkey Point and El Rama submitted an appeal on the grounds of unconstitutionality to the Supreme Court of Justice against construction of the dry canal and requested a hearing from the National Assembly in order to explain the reasons why construction of the port and the arrival of large ships would be damaging to the inhabitants and the environment.

The communities claim that the actions demanded and omissions noted in the appeal constitute violations of articles 5, 46, 89, 90, 91 and 180 of the Nicaraguan Political Constitution, which together guarantee the rights to ownership and use of their lands on the part of the indigenous and ethnic communities of the Atlantic Coast, as well as guaranteeing the right to the integrity and cultural survival of these peoples. The communities furthermore claim that the concessionary contract, as it is drawn up and negotiated with the Government of Nicaragua, also violates constitutional articles 60, 102, 128, 129, 177 and 181.

For the moment, approval of the draft bill known as the Contract of Concession for the Study of the Feasibility, Final Design, Construction and Operation of the Nicaraguan Interoceanic Canal Project (CINN) is still pending.

However, indigenous fears persist. They consider that the CINN infrastructure would divide and isolate the lands traditionally occupied by indigenous communities.

In May, the indigenous complaint reached the Inter-American Commission on Human Rights of the Organisation of American States (OAS). This organisation presented questions to the Government of Nicaragua, which has yet to reply.

The indigenous have the backing of a support group formed by the Coordinating Body of NGOs of the RAAS (South Atlantic Autonomous Region), the Alexander von Humboldt Centre and the International Legal Group for Human Rights.

Awas Tingni at the Inter-American Court of Human Rights

The Mayangna community of Awas Tingni, in the North Atlantic Autonomous Region, requested that the Inter-American Court of Human Rights oblige the Government of Nicaragua to demarcate and title their ancestral communal lands.

The Court and the Inter-American Commission are part of the Inter-American System for Human Rights Protection, created in order to watch over respect for human rights protected by the American Convention. The States, like Nicaragua, that are signatories to the Convention and members of the OAS, are bound by the jurisdiction of the Court, and so the decision in this case, expected during 2001, will be obligatory upon the Nicaraguan government.

The Mayangnas claim State protection and respect for their rights over the lands. With no consultation of the community, the Ministry for the Environment and Natural Resources (MARENA) handed over 62,000 hectares of forest for timber exploitation to the Korean company Sol del Caribe, S.A. (Solcarsa) in a thirty-year concession. In 1997, following the indigenous complaint, the Supreme Court of Justice declared the concession unconstitutional, for which reason it was cancelled in 1998. But the case was already in the hands of the Inter-American Commission's offices in Washington, D.C., which endeavoured, for more than two years, to get the Government of Nicaragua and the Awas Tingni community to reconcile their positions, with no success.

The Court continued with the case, holding a first hearing last November. During the in-depth hearing, the Mayangna community of Awas Tingni presented to the Inter-American Court more than a decade of statements from traditional communal authorities, witnesses and experts of the stature of Dr. Galio Gurdián, Dr. Lottie Cunningham, Dr. Charles Hale, Dr. Roque Roldán and Dr. Rodolfo Stavenhagen.

The decision regarding the case of the Mayangna community of Awas Tingni will create a very important precedent, not only at national level for all the indigenous peoples of the Atlantic Coast of Nicaragua (Mískitos, Ramas and Mayangnas or Sumus), but also for the international community, because Awas Tingni is demanding that the Government of Nicaragua recognises its rights over its communal lands in practice, that it ceases to grant concessions over natural resources on its communal lands and that it pays reparations for the economic and moral damage suffered by the Community because of the government actions and omission regarding their property rights.

Future Prospects

Even though the Draft Law was presented more than six months ago, it has still not been approved, in spite of the fact that the main conflicts facing indigenous peoples and ethnic communities are closely linked to the problem of ownership of their lands.

In the final stages of 2000, it was difficult to negotiate the discussion and approval of the Draft Law because the national political scene was focussed on municipal elections. This year the situation will change little: there are further national elections, this time for the presidency and the National Assembly. Discussions focus more on the "worthiness" of the candidates than government programmes, and when plans are discussed, there is no mention of indigenous peoples or ethnic communities.

In the area of the BOSAWAS Biosphere Reserve, the indigenous Mískitos and Mayangnas are undertaking their own process of self-demarcation and recently entered into an agreement for gradual implementation with the Nicaraguan Institute for Territorial Studies (INETER). These could form models for other territories. While we await the law, other voices demand recognition of historical agreements whose validity has not expired.

Note

[1]   "Malanga" - a tuber not dissimilar to sweet potato - trans. note.

COSTA RICA

In Costa Rica, 39,264 indigenous people live over 23 territories[1], the total area of which amounts to 324,829.29 hectares. We are eight clearly established indigenous peoples: the Bruncas, Bribris, Ca-bécares, Guaymies, Malekus, Huetares, Chorotegas and Teribes.

Despite the fact that we form only one per cent of the Costa Rican population (totalling 3.8 million), important achievements have been gained. Nonetheless, these have been due more to the individual efforts of peoples and communities through their own organisations than to State policies.

Relations between the State and Indigenous Peoples[2]

The indigenous populations lack a State coordinating body to direct and technically guide common lines of public sector action towards indigenous populations.

The National Commission for Indigenous Affairs (CONAI) - a government organisation - has not fulfilled the overriding objective behind its creation, which was to serve as a coordinator of programme strategies and to defend the interests of the indigenous communities. More serious still, this body has become a mechanism of political power that divides the indigenous populations, a situation which can clearly be seen in virtually all of the country's indigenous communities, often ignoring the direct demands of indigenous inhabitants.

This has meant that it has been necessary to turn directly to the different Associations, Neighbourhood Committees, Women's Committees and Civil Organisations in order to find out indigenous needs, opinions and resolutions within the national life of the country.

The absence of control and a hierarchical vacuum have meant that this institution's behaviour has been the subject of criticism and complaint from indigenous inhabitants, within an environment of civil denial on the part of the communities themselves.

National Plan for Indigenous Development

During the year 2000, indigenous community members came to an agreement as to their own National Plan for Indigenous Development, aimed at providing a general outline with regard to the who, how, where and when of development programme implementation in the native communities. However, alongside this initiative, the Costa Rican State undertook a similar exercise, through the Rural Development Programme, producing another "Governmental Plan" as a result, and allocating it resources of a little over US$ 100 million. The government exploited the date of 12th October 2000 to publicise its "plan" and to calm indigenous voices. As you can imagine, allocation of the financial budget has been a farce; the plan has received not one penny and, what is more, it has undermined the whole negotiation process that indigenous organisations were entering into with different donors.

Meanwhile, the indigenous communities suffer ever-increasing poverty.

Environment

In January 2000, indigenous communities and environmental groups submitted an appeal on the grounds of unconstitutionality against the oil exploration concessions granted by means of resolution R-702-

The indigenous territory of Rey Curré and the future location of the Boruca Dam. Photo: CEDIN

98 of the Ministry for the Environment and Energy (MINAE) to the MKJ XPLORATION INC company, given that "no popular consultation process aimed at the communities of the Caribbean coast of Costa Rica, who will clearly be affected by these activities, has taken place".

In the appeal, they demanded respect for the commitments made in international agreements and pacts, particularly in relation to respect for and consultation of indigenous communities. Although the explorations were initially halted, they were allowed to resume some time later, provided they were not within indigenous territories.

Since June 2000, in the southern region of the country, concretely in the Rey Curré indigenous territory, a group of indigenous women have taken the decision to openly confront progress of the Boruca Hydroelectric Project, a megaproject promoted by the Costa Rican Electricity Institute (ICE) at a cost of around US$3,000 million. This project would completely flood their territory, partially flood those of Boruca and Térraba and indirectly affect three more, as it would form a lake of around 250 square kilometres.

Whilst the preliminary construction works continue, the dialogue between the community and the Project's Executive Board has broken down since 18th January 2001. However, the awareness generated in different sectors of society and environmental organisations would seem to presage an intense struggle of opposition, in which fulfilment of existing indigenous legislation will prevail (Indigenous Law 7172, Convention 169 and Law 7316, amongst others).

Complementary to this issue, constant requests have been made to the Agricultural Development Institute (IDA) to transfer the territorial rights to Rey Curré, Boruca and Térraba to their legally representative organisations. Strategically, the IDA does not want to grant them this right, as it would give these peoples greater tools in their struggle against the Hydroelectric Project.

Indigenous Women

As in many of the world's countries, indigenous women suffer from double discrimination: firstly, because they are women and, secondly, because they are indigenous.

In the short-term, a more active and broad participation on the part of indigenous women can be detected neither in their self-development nor within the mechanisms of the national movement. The opening-up of the organisations towards involving women in their membership or governing bodies is due more to the demands of international donors than to a conviction or change in attitude amongst the men.

The isolated efforts made by some women's groups, primarily in the Caribbean and the southern part of the country, are very valid and must be recognised for what they are for they demonstrate, on a small-scale, the contribution that can be made to national indigenous development. They are sowing seeds which, in the longer term, when they germinate and their branches link with the seeds sown on the other side of the Andes, will be a force capable of giving the change of direction necessary to eliminate the dependence, paternalism and, above all, conformity in which a large part of our peoples are submerged and that we will advance towards the development with identity of our indigenous peoples.

Conclusion

It cannot be concluded that, in recent years, indigenous peoples have gained significant achievements of benefit to the majority.

In spite of this, if we analyse the initiatives at regional and local level within the country, we find that the statement at the beginning of this article is nevertheless true: the communities have gained achievements, which have objectively verifiable indicators, through the individual efforts of their grassroots organisations, building from small bridges to schools, from small subsistence projects to self-sufficient marketing centres, from traditional agricultural projects to banana crops capable of supplying 75% of the national market, all generating change in the development of their respective communities.

If we add together all of these "isolated advances", we can conclude that the Costa Rican indigenous movement has made really surprising achievements. These have been obtained through a far more direct relationship between the local organisations and international donors and, to a lesser extent, through the interinstitutional relations with regional and sub-regional governmental offices, some - not all - of which have made efforts to cooperate with indigenous development. Nonetheless, due to the fact that this is not in line with government policy, their secretive efforts are few.

In response to great threats such as the Hydroelectric Project, the Governmental Development Plan and other initiatives during the first months of 2001, indigenous people are entering a period of turmoil that predicts gratifying results for them.

Although the Costa Rican indigenous movement as a whole has not shown perseverance in its actions, it is clear that the maturity of its grassroots organisations is making people understand the urgent need for consolidation and strengthening of national structures that are capable of maintaining a line of negotiation, of vigilance, of pressure and of constant struggle that will prove to the State and society in general the unity of our movement.

Talking with an indigenous friend of mine recently, we were analysing the current state of the indigenous movement, where the majority of organisations are born, grow and self-destruct with surprising speed, endangering both external and internal cooperation. He told me, "In reality, I believe it is the indigenous leaders who have fallen and disappeared and that the true indigenous movement, which involves the participation of the vast majority, has only just begun."

After some reflection, I think he is completely right.

Notes

[1]   One of these, Altos de San Antonio - of Guaymí origin -, has not been legally established.
[2]   Transcript of the Ombudsman's Report for the Year 2000, in its chapter on indigenous peoples, where it coincides with the majority perceptions of the native communities.

PANAMA

General Considerations

The indigenous peoples of Panama commenced the new millennium burdened by problems, frequently frustrated by electoral troubles but, in general terms, also active in their demands. Not only are they negotiating with the government's Executive but also with the Legislative Assembly, where laws are made at a national level and where the Commission for Indigenous Affairs is playing a remarkable role.

So far, five (5) indigenous territories have been legally recognised (Kuna Yala, Emberá Waunan, Kuna de Madungandi, Ngobe-Buglé Comarcas[1] and, as of June 2000, Kuna de Wargandi Comarca). This has led to other peoples who still do not enjoy this legality also demanding their recognition. Amongst these communities are the Kuna who live on the borders with Colombia (Pucuro and Paya or the Takargunyala Comarca), and the Nasos and the Bri-Bris on the borders with Costa Rica.

The creation of the National Council for Indigenous Development in January 2000 (CNDI, see **Panama** in *The Indigenous World 1999-2000*), attached to the Presidency of the Republic, gave rise to considerable expectations but, at the moment of being sworn in, it came as a great shock to the indigenous leadership that political elements from the ruling party were appointed to head this council although they had very little or nothing to do with the communities in question. A year on from its formation, it has not yet managed to meet because it comprises ministers and senior staff from autonomous institutions and universities who have shown no interest in sending their representatives. Meanwhile, indigenous affairs continue to be dealt with traditionally by the Ministry of the Interior and Justice, although this time in closer collaboration with the traditional authorities.

Another of the discussions of greatest impact has been the implementation of environmental projects or policies in different indigenous regions of the country, projects that come largely from the Inter-American Development Bank (IDB) and the World Bank. Most of these projects are aimed at the Darién forest, which is a small extension of the Amazon ecosystem within Panama.

Colombia's Internal Problem Overflows

This area of Darién is currently also falling prey to the expansion of neighbouring Colombia's internal problems. Incursions on the part of all the armed forces from this neighbouring country - military,

Kuna man, Panama. Photo: Andrew Young

paramilitary, guerrillas - are becoming a regular occurrence and the Darién forests have become an area of terror for the Emberás and Kunas who live there, as well as for the black population.

Previously, Panamanian life was respected but, over the last year, the situation has taken a different turn, and so the Panamanian police force itself has had to patrol the zone. Because of this increased militarisation, there have been reprisals on the part of the Colombians, and this is causing the mass flight of indigenous communities to other parts of Panama, particularly the capital, hence creating further social problems.

This problem reached its climax when an incursion on the part of one of the unlawful forces led to the murder of a young Emberá girl at the beginning of October 2000.

In the case of Kuna Yala, since the worsening of the situation in Colombia, a new military centre has been established within the Armila community and more than 100 young Kuna have been re-cruited to police the border under the military orders of the National Panamanian Police.

The General Kuna Headman, Carlos Inakelikinya López, Dies

On the 7th of August 2000, at 87 years of age, one of the most remarkable spiritual guides, a leader, historian and interpreter of Bab Igala (God) from the Kuna Yala Comarca, Carlos Inakelikinya López, passed away. He was also General Headman of the General Kuna Congress. López was the only living pupil of the great leaders and spiritual guides of Kuna Yala. He was also the only surviving eye witness of the Kuna Revolution of 1925. In 1997, he published the book *"Así lo vi, así me lo contaron"*, (What I saw, what I was told) a systematic evaluation of the bloody events that took place at that time.

Tabasará 2 Hydroelectric Project Suspended

One of the most controversial discussions to take place at national level related to the construction of large-scale hydroelectric plants on indigenous territories, particularly in the Ngobe-Buglé Comarca, on the river Tabasará, in the provinces of Veraguas and Chiriquí. The project consisted of two hydroelectric plants at a cost of US$105 million. The work anticipated the flooding of at least 500 hectares of land and would, in addition, have affected more than 5,000 indig-enous people.

Mobilisations and road blockades took place throughout the year, demonstrating the great organisational power of the Ngobe-Buglé people in defence of their territory. Action was undertaken not only by the indigenous population but also by peasants from the area, and the country's social organisations also joined in. The support af-forded by the Panamanian Ombudsman was very important, as was that of the Commission for Indigenous Affairs of the Legislative Assembly.

Given the lack of State response regarding where the more than 5,000 indigenous people forced to abandon their lands because of Tabasará 1 and 2 were to be moved to, the ex-President of the Ngobe-Buglé General Congress and natural indigenous leader, Al-berto Montezuma, ensured they continued to oppose both initia-tives, against which they would fight "to the bitter end".

At the beginning of December 2000, the Vice-Minister of Interior and Justice, Rodolfo Aguilera Franceschi, made known that, by means of a decision of the Supreme Court of Justice, the Tabasará 2 hydroelectric project had been suspended. Aguilera explained that the peasants and indigenous people had submitted a complaint regarding the environmental impact study, and the appeal had gone as far as the Supreme Court of Justice, which decided to reject the study and, finally, suspend the work.

New Legislation

During the year 2000, various laws in favour of the indigenous peoples of Panama were approved:

Law No. 20 of 26th June 2000 is a **sui generis** law on national and regional intellectual property, which provides new stipulations such as the creation of a Department for Collective Rights and Folkloric Expression (Art.7); the creation of a post known as the Examiner on Collective Indigenous Rights (Art.9), who is to protect the intellectual property and other traditional rights of indigenous peoples. And, lastly, as a new innovation, Article 25 establishes that, "For the purposes of the protection, use and marketing of the collective intellectual property rights of indigenous peoples contained in this Law, indigenous artistic and traditional expressions from other countries will benefit from the same stipulations established within it, provided they are undertaken by means of reciprocal international agreements with those countries." This is best described as a right of reciprocity with the other indigenous peoples of Abya Yala.

Through *Law No. 34 of 25th June 2000*, the Kuna Comarca of Wargandi was created. After several years of struggle on the part of this Kuna community, which lives right in the heart of the inhospitable Darien forests, it has seen its dream of having a separate geographical area comprising the districts of Chepigana and Pinogana, in the Province of Darién, covering an area of 77,500 hectares, come true.

In articles 3 and 6, the Law recognises the General Congress - as the highest traditional authority - and the local congresses. The General Congress and the traditional authorities will have the primary role of strengthening, developing, conserving and protecting Kuna culture, along with the traditions, language, unity and integrity of the inhabitants and natural resources of the Comarca, with the aim of promoting their social and economic development. Article 16 recognises the *Ibeorgun* religion as the main religion of the Wargandi Kuna. The Organic Charter of the Comarca will govern its promotion and dissemination.

Law No. 35, of 25ᵗʰ July 2000 provides for the creation of a Governing Board for Fairs for the Indigenous Peoples of the Republic of Panama, a body with legal status, its own assets, and administrative autonomy. The purpose of the Board will be to organise and hold national and international agro-forestry, handicraft and cultural fairs and exhibitions with the aim of promoting the national and cultural wealth of the indigenous peoples of Panama (Art.2).

Participation of Indigenous Women

Participation on the part of indigenous women in Panama has been much more active than in previous years and has taken place at all levels: economic, social, political and cultural. Many leaders are young, indigenous women and even professionals who have graduated from university. This has meant that some indigenous women are leading indigenous congresses, as in the case of the Emberás, and some are involved as leaders at community level, such as has taken place amongst the Kuna. The economic deterioration over recent years has meant that indigenous women have taken the reins of the household economy, as in the case of Kuna women who, through the sale of *mola* or blouses as art and handicrafts, have made this one of the most stable economies for their households. The same is occurring amongst other indigenous peoples, such as the Emberás and Ngobes. Significant cooperatives of indigenous women, and other organisations, have been created with this aim.

Indigenous women took part in all the mobilisations that occurred at national level to defend the rights of their communities, and their presence is very encouraging because the strength of indigenous women has meant that some processes were speeded up, such as the halting of the Tabasará 2 Hydroelectric Project.

At international level, this year saw the greatest participation yet on the part of the indigenous women of Panama. They attended virtually every international forum organised by the United Nations, by other regional organisations or by the indigenous peoples themselves.

Note and sources

[1] "Comarca" roughly translates as an administrative region (Trln.)
La Prensa, Panama 9ᵗʰ August 2000.
La Prensa, Panama 8ᵗʰ December 2000.
López, Atencio: "María Mecha y el Plan Colombia"
Official Gazette No.24 083, 27ᵗʰ June 2000 and No. 24 106, 28ᵗʰ July 2000.
Interview with Florina López, Person in Charge of the Women's Workshop "*Kikadiryai*" and leader of the Asociación Napguana.

SOUTH AMERICA

VENEZUELA

Constitutional Advances and Political Participation

With the approval of the new Constitution of the Bolivarian Republic of Venezuela at the end of 1999, indigenous peoples achieved fairly broad recognition of their specific rights, making the Venezuelan Constitution one of the most advanced in Latin America in terms of indigenous rights (see **Venezuela** in *The Indigenous World 1999-2000).*

In this context, during the first half of the year 2000 and, in the face of an election ordered by the National Constituent Assembly, national and regional level indigenous peoples and organisations devoted themselves to designing a strategy that would enable them to access - as an indigenous movement - these important spaces for political participation and decision-making within the dynamic of the Venezuelan State.

The indigenous organisations from each of the 10 states that have indigenous populations (Zulia, Amazonas, Bolívar, Delta Amacuro, Anzoátegui, Sucre, Monagas, Mérida, Apure and Trujillo) held local and regional Community Assemblies in order to appoint, in a participatory and democratic manner and according to custom and tradition, the candidates for each level of popular representation. This process of selection of candidates to legislative, municipal and government bodies enabled an important political growth and maturity on the part of the indigenous movement in its struggle to capture space for political participation.

When the elections were held on 30th July 2000, the National Indian Council of Venezuela (CONIVE) won the three positions of deputy to the National Assembly established by the Constitution: Noelí Pocaterra (Wayuú) for the western region; Guillermo Guevara (Jivi) for the southern region and José Luis González (Pemón) for the eastern region. Similarly, the Regional Organisation of Indigenous Peoples of the Amazon (ORPIA), the Regional Organisation of Indigenous Peoples of Zulia (ORPIZ), the Pumé de Apure Organisation and the Kariña from Sucre and Anzoátegui won deputy posts to the Legislative Councils plus posts of councillors in their respective

states. At the level of executive power, the political indigenous movement *"Pueblo Unido Multiétnico de Amazonas"* (United Multi-Ethnic People of the Amazon - PUAMA) gained control of the Government of the State of Amazonas, with the first indigenous Governor in Venezuela, Liborio Guaruya (Baniba) and three Town Halls in the Municipalities of Manapiare, Autana and Río Negro within the same state.

The success was such that, during the period covered by this report and on the basis of the rights recognised by the new Constitution, organised indigenous peoples managed to capture important spaces within the Venezuelan State political structures and this will enable significant progress in the area of indigenous rights over the coming years.

Approval of Favourable Legislation

Once the elections of 30th July had been held, the National Assembly was established and the three indigenous representatives managed to get a Permanent Commission for Indigenous Peoples created. This commission formulated a legislative agenda for the year 2000, which prioritised a Draft Law for the Demarcation of Indigenous Lands, drawn up with the participation of regional and national indigenous organisations, and also discussions on Convention 169 of the International Labour Organisation (ILO).

On 21st December 2000, after extensive discussions, the Law of Demarcation and Guarantee of the Habitat and Lands of Indigenous Peoples was approved and ILO Convention 169 was ratified.

The Law of Demarcation "has the aim of regulating the formulation, coordination and implementation of policies and plans relating to the demarcation of the habitat and lands of the indigenous peoples and communities in order to guarantee the right of collective ownership of their lands..." (Art. 1) and defines the indigenous habitat as "all of the space occupied and used by indigenous peoples and communities, and in which they undertake their physical, cultural, spiritual, social, economic and political life; this comprises the areas of cultivation, hunting, river and sea fishing, gathering, pasturing, settlement, traditional paths, river channels and routes, sacred and historic sites and any other areas necessary to guarantee and develop their specific ways of life." (Art. 2)

The national process of demarcation will be planned, implemented and coordinated by the Ministry for the Environment together with the indigenous peoples, communities and organisations and the National Commission for Demarcation of the Habitat and Lands of the Indigenous Peoples, appointed by the President of the Republic.

In the face of approval of this law, the different national sectors opposed to recognising the rights of indigenous peoples reacted by indicating - through the media - that approval of the Law of Demarcation was a threat to the territorial integrity of the Venezuelan nation. In this regard, the following was stated in a prestigious daily national newspaper:

> *"... we have warned of the dangers to Venezuelan territorial unity when theories and practices are promoted which - although the claims may be fair - as far as Venezuela is concerned relate to less than one per cent of the population...it is becoming ever more visible on the American continent, where indigenous movements have been increasingly consolidating their power, to the point of having formed alliances with other groups - as occurred in Ecuador at the beginning of 2000 - in order to demand and obtain governmental changes that are not shared with other broader sectors of society."* [1]

The Situation of Indigenous Peoples in Venezuela

In spite of the Constitution's broad recognition of indigenous rights and the notable progress made in the legislative sphere, the situation of the country's indigenous peoples continues to be truly critical, particularly in relation to land rights and the progressive deterioration in the health status of the communities. In fact, the serious problems caused by invasions of indigenous lands and their occupation for State development projects have continued, without effective measures being taken to resolve those problems.

Continuation of the Electric Power Line towards Brazil through the Lands of the Pemón People

During the year 2000, many Pemón communities of the Gran Sabana continued to protest against and denounce the occupation of their lands, the environmental damage and the secondary effects caused by the Venezuelan government's construction of the electricity power line towards Brazil, particularly its use for mining activity. As noted in the public statement made by representatives of National Social and Ecological Unity, the link between the electrical interconnection system in the south east and the mining development scheme proposed for Bolívar State is difficult to conceal, in spite of the Ministry for the Environment's statements to the contrary when attempting to defend the project in question.

The National Executive made considerable effort to come to an overall agreement with the Pemón communities, including direct talks between the communities, the President of the Republic, Hugo Chávez Frías, and the Vice-President of the Republic, Isaías Rodríguez. Nevertheless, the communities were divided. Whilst a good number of the communities accepted the agreement, which included (amongst other things) an obligation on the part of the National Government to proceed with the demarcation of their habitat and lands in the Gran Sabana and the creation of a fund aimed at the economic development of the region's communities, some communities declared that accepting the proposal violated indigenous custom itself, as the decision should have been taken by consensus.

In May 2000, these latter communities submitted an appeal on the grounds of unconstitutionality to the Supreme Court of Justice, in which they declared the unconstitutionality of the electric power line and requested a definitive halt to the work on the line because it affected their traditional way of life and the lands they had ancestrally inhabited.

The appeal was declared unfounded by the Supreme Court of Justice on 16th November 2000. Nevertheless, the decision rules that the Ministry for the Environment and Natural Resources should, with support from the Ombudsman and representatives of the indigenous communities, immediately design and implement a Plan aimed at checking and guaranteeing due fulfilment of the mitigation measures and conditions provided for in the administrative authorisations granted to the company *Electrificación del Caroní* (EDELCA) for occupation of the territory and the allocation of renewable natural resources for the purposes of construction of the electrical power line.

Following the decision, the Pemón communities opposed to the power line have continued their protest actions and have paralysed the work on various occasions by bringing down a number of the pylons that cross their communities.

Scientific Research in Indigenous Areas
In April 2000, the Piaroa indigenous communities of Manapiare in the State of Amazonas complained that the National Parks Institute had granted authorisation to representatives of the Venezuelan Scientific Research Institute (IVIC) and other foundations to carry out research into genetic resources in the Cerro Yutajé, Yavi, Corocoro, Guanay, Camani and Morrocoy natural monuments, which form the sacred places of the Piaroa people and are located within their territory.

This authorisation was granted without consulting the indigenous peoples and communities living in the area, as required by the Constitution of the Republic, and was undertaken within the framework of an access contract to the genetic resources granted to the IVIC on the part of the Ministry for the Environment and Natural Resources. This contract also granted the IVIC rights over the use and exploitation of those genetic resources. The complaint made by the communities and the Regional Organisation of the Indigenous Peoples of Amazonas (ORPIA) was dealt with by the Ministry for the Environment and the National Parks Institute and, following heated debate at national level on the issue of scientific research on indigenous lands, the permit granted by the National Parks Institute was repealed.

Along the same lines, during the year 2000 a series of complaints were made regarding scientific research undertaken during the 1960s in the area of Alto Orinoco (Amazonas State) amongst the indigenous Yanomami. In fact, following publication of the book *Darkness in El Dorado* by the North American journalist, Patrick Tierney, a great deal of controversy was centered around the issue of research in the area, as this book set out to prove that some North American scientists, in association with the United States Atomic Energy Commission, had used the Yanomami as a control group for the atom bomb, by introducing radioactive isotopes and using a vaccine against measles that led to the death of a considerable number of people in this ethnic group. The complaints in this case were taken to the Vice-President of the Republic and the Permanent Commission for Indigenous Peoples of the National Assembly, where investigations were initiated. However, these investigations have not yet reached their conclusion.

Coal Exploitation in Yukpa and Barí Lands in the Perijá Mountains
The mining concessions granted to public and private companies by the Ministry for Energy and Mines in the Perijá Mountains (Zulia State), traditional lands of the Yukpa and Barí, continue to affect the lives of these indigenous peoples. Faced with the granting of new concessions, the indigenous peoples submitted an appeal on the grounds of unconstitutionality in which they demanded that the Ministry for Energy and Mines should halt the process of granting concessions in this area that is under special administration. Nevertheless, this appeal was declared unfounded by the Supreme Court of Justice, on the grounds that a demand of such importance could not be granted by means of a brief and summary process such as this.

The Health Status of Indigenous Peoples
Despite the fact that the Constitution establishes the right of indigenous peoples to integral health care that takes into consideration their practices, cultures and traditional medicine, the health status of

several indigenous peoples continues to be truly critical. During the year 2000, outbreaks of cholera and tuberculosis have drastically affected the Warao people (Delta Amacuro and Sucre States) and the Kariña (Sucre State), where many deaths, particularly amongst the infant population, were caused by these and other illnesses. In the State of Zulia, outbreaks of cholera and dengue fever have seriously affected the Wayuú people. In addition, an increase in malaria in the states of Bolívar and Amazonas seriously affected many indigenous communities. With regard to the Yanomami, at the end of the year 2000, in the State of Amazonas, serious complaints were made about the increase in infant mortality, brought about largely by complications in respiratory illnesses, malaria and hepatitis B, which have become endemic diseases. In all these cases, the care provided by the Venezuelan State is remarkable in its insufficiency, to the extent that in some areas services are not provided at all or only intermittently, preventing effective measures from being taken to control the serious public health situation that many indigenous peoples find themselves in.

Reference

[1] **Adolfo P. Salgueiro:**. *El Universal* daily newspaper: 27th January 2001.

COLOMBIA

The 1991 Constitution and Indigenous Peoples

For indigenous people, the 1991 Political Constitution was unprecedented in the history of Colombia, as it enshrined our fundamental rights at constitutional level. It offered us the prospect, 500 years after the Conquest, of transforming a violent and oppressive encounter into a new and fertile one. We looked optimistically to the future.

Ten years on, there is no reason left to maintain this optimism. In part because, in spite of all the constitutional articles referring to respect for ethnic and cultural differences, the Colombian State has not identified itself with a willingness to revise its project of exclusivity. And, in part because, whilst the State opened its doors to indigenous peoples, the government of the time closed them in the economic sphere, which is a determining factor in well-being and in overcoming the conditions of opprobrium and marginalisation that indigenous peoples have experienced. It was thus a constitutional opening but not an economic one. What the Gaviria government called "economic opening" was aimed at the outside world, largely to attract capital that could be linked to the exploitation of mineral and energy resources.

Today, the structural problems of the Colombian economy and society continue to be the same. What is more, they have worsened: the social inequalities have grown and violence against indigenous peoples, against peasants, workers and afro-Colombians takes more victims than ever. Over the last decade, approximately 300,000 people have died a violent death in Colombia and more than one and a half million peasants have been displaced from their lands. These figures are comparable only to countries at war. Ten years after the new constitution came into effect, the rights of Colombians, even the most fundamental ones, now have no more than programmatic value and form part of a Utopia, awaiting better times in which to be achieved.

Indigenous participation in the National Constituent Assembly with their spiritual and ideological proposals, however, brought about positive change in Colombian society, as the behaviour and spirituality of indigenous peoples are now viewed with respect and admiration. Their systems of organisation, production, distribution, reproduction, their ways of applying knowledge and their ways of understanding development, offer alternatives in economic, social and technological terms and represent a broadening of Humanity.

Indigenous concerns regarding the destruction of ecosystems and living spaces have also been determinant in the emergence of protectionist and preservationist ideas, and in the formation of movements and schools seeking new conditions for economic development that guarantee a coexistence with nature.

Breaking down Indigenous Economies and Organisations

But these ideas have not been echoed by the Colombian State. Despite the fact that the *ethnic and cultural diversity* of the Colombian nation is considered to be an asset (in addition to being constitutionally protected), the State tolerates (when it is not actually promoting) local, regional and national development plans that break down the economies and organisations of the indigenous peoples. The necessary autonomy required by the indigenous peoples for their economic and social development remains empty of content when the State implements a political vision that views the Colombian nation as one huge market, in which economic sectors compete freely.

In open contradiction to the National Constitution, which envisages a territorial reorganisation of the Colombian nation in which historical, geographical, environmental, ecological, cultural and ethnic criteria should prevail, the Colombian State is undertaking a different territorial reorganisation using current national, departmental and municipal investments, focussed on extractive, agro-industrial, hydro-electric and infrastructural macro-projects. These investments, many of which are linked to multinational companies, are changing local organisation, transforming the regional economic dynamic and altering the territoriality of the indigenous peoples.

In the political sphere, the State tolerates no dissent from the population in relation to these economic policies. Social protest and mobilisation on the part of the social sectors affected are highlighted as attempts to destabilise the country and erode the rule of law on the part of guerrilla forces. It is this attitude on the part of the State that has led to the emergence of paramilitary units which, in recent years, and precisely in those regions where economic macro-projects are underway or envisaged, have carried out military actions against the population, with the previously mentioned results.

The Problem of the Pacific in the Context of Colombian Society

Around 100,000 indigenous people belonging to the *Tule*, *Embera*, *Katío*, *Chamí*, *Eperara-Siapidaara*, *Wounaan* and *Awa*[1] peoples live in the Colombian Pacific. We have different languages, customs and beliefs but we are united by the forest and by the lush and generous natural environment, which provides us with food, shelter and clothing. We also share a history of denial and struggle to preserve our territories, cultures and the right to live according to our traditions, to choose forms of government in accordance with our needs and to decide our future autonomously.

We have lived side by side in these forests with Black populations, brought from Africa to work in the mines. We share with them the desire for freedom and independence and we mutually recognise our differences. This afro-Colombian population, today close to 80% of the population of this region, arrived on our lands fleeing slavery and adopted many traditional practices from us in terms of the use and management of nature.

114

Embera handicraft production. Photo: Alberto Achito

Embera village. Photo: Alberto Achito

This region, paradoxically called "the Pacific" is, in reality, the epicentre of much violence. In percentage terms, it is the region with the most displaced people and the most violent deaths. And it is also one of the most neglected regions of the country. For the State and its economic model, we indigenous do not exist, for our lands are not for sale and our production does not obey mercantilist demands but is aimed primarily at satisfying our needs. For this reason, we are a useless figure in the country's Gross Domestic Product and a blank box in the State's accounts. But the official accounts do not put a value on forest conservation or protection of nature, for the biogeographical Pacific is one of the areas of most biodiversity on the planet.

The problems Colombia is experiencing contribute to nurturing and reproducing the crisis that we indigenous of the Pacific are suffering. This is related to:

A crisis in State legitimacy and the deinstitutionalisation of the Nation

In Colombia, there is a long tradition of disobedience towards State laws. And there are good reasons for this for, in the past, they permitted the legitimate appropriation of collective goods and wealth for private use. But this disobedience towards a State, *to the service of privileged private interests,* has been overwhelming in recent decades: tax evasion, smuggling, illegal land possessions, the plundering of public funds, the private appropriation of the Nation's wealth, fraudulent elections, vote buying, kidnapping and, last but by no means least, drugs trafficking, with all the consequences of corruption, violence and destabilisation this brings with it, have all ended up deinstitutionalising the country.

Clientilism, the crisis in political representation and the establishment of force and intimidation to guarantee partisan loyalties

All these factors have undermined the legal code and the application of justice in law, the monopoly of which should fall under the sole responsibility of the State. As the State has been rolled back in the area of justice, the social spectre of those who assume the legal authority to impose and apply their own law, by means of action, has grown. This *Supplantation of law by the rule of violence and power of force* has contributed to a loss of civic harmony. At the moment, violence is the issue that attracts the most attention on the part of Colombians. And this is inevitable, as the armed conflict in Colombia has entered a process of humanitarian degradation the likes of which has never before been seen in this country. Over the last decade, the yearly average number of deaths by violent means has been 32,000 people, making it the number one cause of death in the country.

With the escalation of the war, women have been forced to take on new social roles, as displaced widows or mothers who have to safeguard the sustenance and survival of their families and, on many occasions, the unity and permanence of their communities. Due to the fact that they are women in a male-dominated environment that undervalues women's political capacities, they are not subject to the same pressure and intimidation from the armed actors in the conflict. Nevertheless, the emotional impact of the assassination or disappearance of their children, husbands or close relatives is immense. This is an issue of great concern in our communities and is one of the central themes of indigenous Assemblies and meetings, for when the war affects not only our organisations but also our families, and women in particular, there is growing family breakdown and this is the beginning of the social and cultural disintegration of our peoples. What we here call an "acculturation of illegality" has thus emerged, which is benefiting those *powerful sectors that resort almost exclusively to the use of force* to achieve their political and economic aims, primarily the control of profits associated with the exploitation of natural resources, possession of fertile lands, control of geopolitically strategic territories and the establishment of *an economy based on illegal crops (coca and poppy)* over wide areas of the national territory. These regions are currently the subject of dispute between armed sectors, for control over them and this economy is vital for the financing of their armies and actions.

For indigenous peoples, the fact that we hold territories endowed with natural resources has been disastrous, for their extraction, together with the production of illegal drugs, are the most profitable activities. The exploitation of gold, oil, emeralds, coal, fine woods etc. are the favourite lucrative activities of the economic powers (legal or illegal). The greatest inconvenience in these economic extractive activities is the misery and violence their exploitation causes to the surrounding environment. Paradoxically, the regions most endowed with natural resources are those where the most conflictive focuses of the country are to be found, with the highest number of displacements, murders and kidnappings. Relatively young regions have, in a matter of a few years, become dilapidated zones on entering the mechanism of this economic activity. Misery and violence come to these regions to stay: the emerald zones of Boyacá, the oil zones of Arauca and Casanare, the coca-producing areas of Guaviare, Caquetá and Putumayo all typify this situation. With gold, timber and, most recently, coca[2], with its great rivers, its seas, its strategic position[3], with its natural wealth[4], with its great biodiversity and its lands aspiring to extensive livestock farming, the Pacific entered this dynamic and we are already feeling the consequences.

The eyes of many greedy "businessmen" with their capital flows are on this region; they move from one place to another in search of profit. And so we indigenous are seen as an obstacle to their path and, along with the Black and peasant populations, we become the object of all kinds of outrages on the part of the loggers, drugs traffickers, landowners and their paramilitary armies.

Because of this, we can understand why the *U'wa* indigenous people in the east of Colombia, consistant with their cultural ethos, radically oppose the exploration of hydrocarbons on their territory to the point of being prepared to commit suicide before permitting the entry of the oil companies.

A Work Agenda to Make our Dreams Concrete

We have shown how the principal problems oppressing us in the Pacific have to be seen within the national context. The solution to these problems, of necessity, requires structural political and economic change at national level. Nevertheless, we know that defence of the Pacific begins "at home". For this reason, we are currently in the process of drawing up our own agenda for struggle and making new adjustments to our organisations in order to adapt them to the situation of social, cultural, economic and territorial crisis our peoples are suffering. This will strengthen us internally to continue this already long struggle in defence of our territories. We hope that the Afro-Colombian communities of the Pacific will do the same. The future of the Pacific and of our peoples will depend upon it.

Within the macro-region of the Pacific, we are currently organised at a local, zonal and regional level. Some indigenous organisations are broader and have greater organisational scope, others are only a few years old and are in the process of consolidating their programmes of work. These organisations include, amongst others, the *Organización Regional Embera-Wounaan del Chocó* (the Regional Embera-Wounaan Organisation of the Chocó - OREWA), representing 240 communities and the same number of local Indigenous Councils. The 40,000 indigenous people it represents belong to five peoples: the Embera, Tule, Katío, Chamí and Wounaan; the *Organización Indígena de Antioquia* (the Indigenous Organisation of Antioquia - OIA), representing 13,500 indigenous people in the Department of Antioquia, belonging to the Chamí, Katío, Tule and Zenú peoples; and the *Unidad del Pueblo Inkal Awa* (the Union of Inkal Awa People - UNIPA), which is a zonal organisation grouping together 22,000 indigenous Awa in the Department of Nariño[5].

Recently, these organisations and indigenous peoples have decided to join forces and efforts to confront the threats and violence they are suffering from and to be able to defend their territories and lives together. This is materialising in the form of the *Coordinadora Indígena del Pacífico* (the Indigenous Coordinating Body of the Pacific), which is receiving support from IWGIA.

This indigenous coordination has as its main tasks the processes of cultural consolidation and economic and organisational appropriation of the indigenous territories in the Pacific region, in order to seek the political strengthening of our peoples with a view to becoming true social actors with the capacity to intervene in the region and to avoid the ethnocide that is in the making amongst our peoples. This desire for joint work is, in our opinion, one of the most important achievements of our organisations over the last twelve months and a challenge for the leaders and traditional authorities of our peoples.

Notes

[1] The Colombian Pacific covers an area of approximately 80,000 square kilometres. With 1,300 kms of coastline, it stretches from the border with Panama as far as Ecuador and is cut off from the rest of the country by the western mountain range.

[2] Drugs trafficking is gradually taking control of the region. Previously, its excellent geographic location was used to ship the drugs. Now this has extended to coca growing. Drugs trafficking is affecting all the region's productive activities and plays a role in the funding of political campaigns and paramilitary activity.

[3] The creation of a road network linking the Atlantic with the Pacific is considered to be a substantial development activity and there are four road macroprojects.

[4] The development of the oil, mining and energy sectors, along with biological and genetic exploration, are considered priority economic activities.

[5] The others are: the organisations of the Eperara Siapidaara people, being 7,000 people in the coastal area of the Departments of Valle, Cauca and Nariño; the *Cabildo Mayor Awa de Ricaurte* (the Awa of Ricaurte Higher Council), representing 8,000 indigenous Awa from the Municipality of Ricaurte en Nariño; the *Asociación de Autoridades Wounaan del Pacífico* (the Association of Wounaan Authorities of the Pacific), grouping together 29 Wounaan and Eperara Siapidara communities from Bajo San Juan; and the *Cabildos Mayores Embera-Katío del Río Verde y Río Sinú* (the Higher Councils of the Embera-Katío of the River Verde and River Sinú), with 3,500 indigenous Embera-Katío from the Departament of Córdoba.

ECUADOR

The most recent uprising, which took place in Ecuador during the last week of January and the first week of February 2001 (in other words, one year after the uprising that led to the fall of President Mahuad), shaped the nature of the socio-political dynamic of this country: a mono-ethnic State in structural crisis, controlled by an oligarchic and corrupt political and business elite, a bankrupt economy in which the poor (largely indigenous) constitute 80% of the population and who are constantly the most affected by the ubiquitous and draconian policies dictated by the International Monetary Fund, alongside an organised indigenous population embracing more than 40% of the country's population, and which has become a true social power capable of overturning government decisions with uprisings that paralyse the country, as was demonstrated during the last protest. Within this context, the indigenous nationalities and peoples of Ecuador thus move forward in a constant "toing and froing" with the government of the moment.

Year 2000: A Carrot and Stick Policy

Once installed in government – by the armed forces – President Gustavo Noboa experimented in his strategy of relating to indigenous peoples, with the supposed aim of "dealing with indigenous demands". It was lack of fulfilment of these that had led to his predecessor's downfall. The indigenist policy adopted by Noboa spoke for itself. Via decree and with grandiose offers he created the G.A.N.E: the "Great Ecuadorian National Agreement", led by a young lawyer "friend of and expert on the indigenous" with the support of anthropologists and sociologists who were "experts on Indians".

Prior to implementation of the government strategy, CONAIE, together with other social organisations in the country, initiated a campaign aimed at collecting signatures in support of a Popular Consultation on aspects inherent to the reform of the State and Ecuador's foreign policy. The main questions proposed for the Consultation related to: suppression of the three State powers (Legislative, Executive and Judicial); extradition of the corrupt bankers still on the run from justice; withdrawal of US military presence from the Manta base. The official presentation of the petition regarding the Consultation (according to opinion polls it had the backing of more than 90% of the general public) took place in August 2000.

At the market, Otavalo, Ecuador. Photo: International Labour Office

Young indigenous girl, Embabura, Ecuador. Photo: Rolf Blomberg

While this was going on, however, the GANE had become a real joke long before August. Six months of prolonged meetings demonstrated its ineffectiveness. After some thirty meetings, known as "tables for dialogue", the frustrating proof emerged of a lack of will on the part of the government to reach any real agreement. The GANE paradox ended in failure and a breakdown in dialogue. CONAIE's resolution to instigate another uprising was swift. In the face of this, and in order to neutralise the mobilisation that was now threatening to topple another president, the government displayed a creativity that harked back to the tragic era of the 16th century, focussing on distributing tins of tuna and wheelbarrows (in the communities considered to be the "most aggressive").

The call for an uprising, planned for September 2000, fell on deaf ears and the government celebrated the triumph of its supposed good policy over the Indians. To this event was added the much-publicised verification of the petition's signatures in support of the Consultation proposed by CONAIE and the other social organisations. According to the Supreme Electoral Tribunal, this contained a series of irregularities such as falsification of the majority of signatures. With this, the possibility of an unprecedented event - that the whole country should pronounce itself in favour of political reform proposed by indigenous people - evaporated into thin air. There were accusations of all kinds and an imminent criminal lawsuit against the President of CONAIE, Antonio Vargas, seemed increasingly likely.

Internal Control?

The falsification of signatures and the failed uprising were the ingredients that put CONAIE in the eye of the storm. In the case of the petition, although the non-indigenous social organisations were also jointly responsible for the failure, they never suffered the consequences. Demands for an internal purge of CONAIE were not long in the making. An Assembly held in November 2000 adopted a resolution to bring forward the renewal of CONAIE's leadership in March 2001.

However, this resolution did not discuss the role of the regional indigenous organisations nor of the grassroots of the different peoples and nationalities, for all these bodies were involved in decision-making around the Consultation, as well as in the failed uprising. All these bodies should and must take their responsibility as actors involved in these events, instead of passing all responsibility on to a few members of the Governing Council of CONAIE.

For this reason, the internal handling of this issue seems more like a kind of witch-hunt, and yet this can still be rectified. For this is everyone's responsibility, both leaders and grassroots, in the same way that decision-making functions.

Indigenous Reassertion

In these circumstances, and in the face of an apparently weakened indigenous organisation with no powers to organise, at the beginning of January 2001 the government began to adopt the traumatic adjustment measures prescribed by the IMF. CONAIE, which has maintained a line of radical opposition to these neoliberal policies, immediately commenced consultations aimed at taking a position opposed to this action. The measures were primarily linked to an increase in fuel prices.

In the face of the government's scepticism, in mid-January 2001, CONAIE announced an imminent indigenous uprising at national level. It began gradually, from 21st January on, with the celebration of the anniversary of Mahuad's fall. On 28th January, Quito was stormed by approximately 10,000 indigenous people. As all public spaces had been occupied by the military with the aim of avoiding being taken over by the indigenous, it was decided to request space from the Salesiana Polytechnic University and to remain there until the government responded positively to the Indian movement's demands which, in short, were a repeal of the measures.

Between 29th January and 1st February, the government unleashed a violent and racist repression. All access points to the university premises were closed off by the police, who prevented the entry of food, medicines, provisions and water. Even the electricity, telephone and water supplies were cut off. The approximately 10,000 indigenous people, including hundreds of children accompanying their mothers, remained in a kind of huge concentration camp, whilst in the streets pitched battles were taking place between indigenous supporters and mounted police who, on several occasions, bombarded the interior of the University with tear gas.

Only on 1st February, when the government realised that the uprising had taken hold all over the country and the effects (shortages of food and fuel supplies) were being felt in the urban centres, did the government choose to propose a dialogue. However, the repression did not stop and on 5th February came to a head when the army instigated a massacre in the Amazonian town of Tena, in which four people died and dozens were wounded. Following suspension of the dialogue by the President of CONAIE, the government finally agreed in large part to the Indian proposals.

123

On 7th February 2001, a 23-point Agreement was signed between the government and the country's Indian organisations and, since 20th March 2001, ways of making these concrete have been under discussion by means of various negotiating tables. The Agreements are basically short-term, and economic. Paradoxically, they do not include basic issues inherent to collective rights, the autonomy of Indian peoples or reform of the State model. It is undoubtedly essential that, at the same time as negotiating the points of the Agreement, the Indian movement initiate a dialogue with other social sectors regarding an agenda that proposes meaningful changes to the Ecuadorian politico-administrative system. The Ecuadorian indigenous movement has all the necessary qualities to lead this.

The reassertion of the Indian movement as a real social power and the firm and intelligent way in which the uprising was conducted has strengthened the leadership, particularly that of the President of CONAIE, Antonio Vargas. Following this action, the renewal of the Governing Council of CONAIE was postponed until October. There is fierce dispute among a number of figures from Andean organisations for CONAIE's Presidency.

Indian Peoples and the Decline of the Liberal Monoethnic State

"Zapatismo is one of the most important anti-neoliberal popular movements in the world, and if it can manage to link with other social groups at international level, it could change the course of history." Thus spoke the American intellectual, Noam Chomsky, in the Mexican "La Jornada" newspaper.

A path that has been trodden step by step, in which the footprints of the men and women of the other Mexico remain more deeply in the land their ancestors walked upon, long before Cortés and throughout the whole time when a minority was organising and flourishing – as occurred in all of the continent's ex-colonies – a democracy – as Chomsky asserts – designed to protect a wealthy minority from the majority or the "economically backward".

"Violation of national sovereignty"; "fragmentation of the Country"; "creation of a State within a State". These are the reasons given by the traditional economic and political elites opposed to the San Andrés Accords. We hear the same reasons in Ecuador. They are reasons that are shared by the upper echelons of all the ex-colonies. They are the reasons of those who defend the validity *ad infinitum* of the mono-ethnic State, the unsustainability of which - and the consequent urgency of profound changes - is more evident than ever. This represents what Marcos holds up as a fundamental condition for eradicating the spiral of social conflict: "Get to the roots of the problem, otherwise making policy will continue to be no more than the art of pretence."

President Fox has insisted on the signing of a Peace Agreement. One has to wonder why the San Andrés Accords are such a battleground for the government? The only things we have for a fact, a fact that is still a painful memory, are the massacres perpetrated by the federal army in Aguas Blancas and El Charco. Peace will only be possible on the basis of new political, social, economic and cultural rules meaning, in essence, respect for Indian peoples' right to self-determination. Events in Mexico are being repeated in Ecuador and in all the ex-colonial states of the world where Indian peoples are forced to live within mono-ethnic structures, where the *sui generis* adaptation of liberal democracy has reduced the public to the mere role of voting and observing. Paradoxically, at the same time as the world is witnessing the arrival of a much-trumpeted globalisation, it is also witnessing the decline of these mono-ethnic structures.

The Zapatista march, the uprising by the Quechua and Aymara Aylluss in Bolivia, the solitary historic right of the Uwa in Colombia, the Indian uprisings in Ecuador, all form stones that one by one chip away at the gigantic dome protecting the mono-ethnic structure that is supported by the sacred beast of wealth and corruption. These stones are called resistance, the form in which hope appears when times are bad.

Democracy or Ethnophagous Indigenism?

"Ethnophagous indigenism" is the concept by which Díaz Polanco defines the State indigenist policies that are implemented in Latin America in response to ethnic emergence and which consist of recognising a package of rights accompanied by declarations on the pluriculturality and multiethnicity of the States, whilst at the same time, however, largely maintaining the *status quo* and draconian economic models.

History notes that recognition of Indian rights has never been through the exclusive good will of the elites, nor through the validity *per se* of a western model known as "democracy" but through perseverance, struggle and resistance in order to gain recognition of the right to exist as peoples. For, when building the nation - as a democracy or not - Indians have always been ignored. In other words, the States were designed without the Indian peoples, in the image and style of a European or North American State. Consequently, there has been no other understanding of democracy and its ideals, no other reference point, than that universally taken on board by the West since the times of Ancient Greece. Hence this model is referred to as the only possible scenario in which to achieve multiple freedoms and the only way to gain the convergence of the most diverse conflicts and agreements; these are only processed within the strict parameters of the Western vision.

The application of collective rights is thus exceptionally difficult if not impossible, since the freedoms that are universally considered within the western logic are fundamentally individual ones. For this reason, we can also understand why an indigenous councillor, mayor, prefect or deputy is not elected within the current form of democracy. It is for this reason that the administrators of Justice and the Law schools do not recognise the existence of Indian legal systems. It is for this reason, too, that the autonomy proposed by the Indians scares the defenders of the unitary State and the proposal for a Plurinational State is understood within the logic of a Proletarian State or an Indian State. It is for this reason, too, that deeply ethnocentric, homogenising and anti-environment models of development are applied, alien to the indigenous philosophy of "good living".

For this reason, there is a need to redefine our understanding of Democracy. To build a democracy based on the multiple ideals and paradigms of the West and of the different societies in Ecuador, a democracy whose dynamic focuses on interculturality as the ontological code of conduct in all tasks of daily social, political, economic, cultural and religious life. Merely stating that Ecuador is multiethnic and pluricultural does not make us intercultural. Interculturality must be understood as a process of communication whose point of departure is not the sender but the receiver of the message. We need to reconceptualise democracy, beginning by stripping it of its cosmogonic western essentialism. The challenge is to reinvent a "multiparadigmatic" democracy.

If not, in the belief that the Indians must participate in the democratic game, the same logic of indigenist policies in force until the 1970s may occur once more, policies that proposed integrating the indigenous peoples into "national society", making them renounce their own identity in order to assimilate them. A meeting and harmonisation of the different democratic cultures existing in Ecuador thus needs to be put forward in order to bring an end, via new structures and relationships, to ethnophagous indigenism.

PERU

General Outlook

The mood of profound instability and political turbulence that has characterised Peru in recent years was maintained, and taken to an extreme, during the second half of 2000. The expected electoral fraud was quite openly confirmed, due to an overconfidence in the possibilities offered by an absolute control of absolute power, the aim of which proved to be to remain in power. Nevertheless, the strong popular reaction of 28th July and a growing lack of confidence on the part of international human rights organisations began to deflate the arrogance of a military leadership headed by the leader of what is nowadays considered to have been a "band of gangsters" but which ruled the country for 8 years under the façade of being a legitimate government.

The usual methods of twisting information gradually became more ineffectual and a frustrated attempt at camouflaging a large network of drugs traffickers and arms dealers as a success of the Intelligence Service was the trigger for a series of processes that were to end up impacting severely on well-organised structures, ranging from the intelligence service to the military.

On 14th September, the first in a long series of documentary films appeared, proving the extent of generalised corruption. On 16th September, President Fujimori announced his retirement and, following the denunciation of enormous sums of money transferred to Montesinos via different Swiss banks, on 10th November the President fled the country.

The new government, which took power on 22nd November with a transitional programme aimed at creating fair conditions for new elections, created a space for hope and democratic credibility which, however, did not fully manage to rid the people of their profound disappointment in the political class, making the electoral outlook and the country's future uncertain.

The Situation and the Indigenous Agenda

The uncovering of a generalised immorality ended up being of assistance to a series of demands indigenous people had been making over recent years, particularly with regard to the political manipulation of State resources and of funds from large multilateral-funded projects, the enormous significance of State corruption within public bodies, the armed forces and the police, not to mention the judicial powers, as well as a generalised atmosphere of immorality at local level, by means of the apparatus organised by Absalón Vásquez[1], the "Montesinos of civil society", through the prefectures, town halls, Temporary Councils or special projects.

The authoritarianism and deep social crisis have offered an environment that is not particularly favourable to significant progress vis-à-vis long-term proposals such as those characterising this stage of the Peruvian indigenous movement's development, whose agenda includes issues such as:

- proposals for local government based on intercultural civil pacts;
- the Plans for Life[2];
- the proposal for an Indigenous Law or the regulation of institutions, such as consultations on key issues, for example, hydrocarbon or mining exploration or regarding the protection of knowledge (practices and innovations);
- implementation of Convention 169 and systems of administering indigenous justice and
- the design of guidelines for managing culturally protected areas (the Sira, the Amarakaere Reserve, Vilcabamba, Kubaim-Morona and others).

Nevertheless, and in spite of serious difficulties, the Peruvian indigenous movement has been surmounting the many obstacles in order to protect its rights at local, regional and national level, in a tense and hostile environment in which clientelism and blackmail were the only things on offer from the State and in which indigenous interests have habitually implied a hindrance to the discretion required when making public "deals" relating to natural resources and budgets.

In contrast, opportunities and settings open to indigenous proposals and initiatives and offered from the level of central government have not been lacking, although these proposals have never managed to form stable spaces for coordination.

In no case has it been possible to control the actual dissemination of these opportunities, and far less the fate of the results of consultations, and so the limited openings for dialogue never led to a sufficient basis of trust and did not culminate in practical results, with the exception of the relations established with the Ombudsman (*Defensoría del Pueblo*).

The Municipalities have not led to the democratic space that was expected of them the year previous. In general, their role has been reduced to that of a link in the distribution chain of privileges and co-optation, forcing their complicity in the receipt of partially or totally imaginary works and programmes. For their part, the ma-

This woman is a "Mashco Piro" who used to live in voluntary isolation. After an accident, she and her sister were forced to leave their group and they are now living in an indigenous community where they also have married.
Photo: FENAMAD

nipulation of votes and the scandalous electoral fraud committed against indigenous candidates (in the municipalities of Manseriche, Tahuania, Pastaza, Rio Tambo, etc.) remain unpunished.

With few exceptions, we can mention the other spaces for popular participation, whose development had been taken as guidelines for work over the period. Faced with a non-existent State, agreements - of necessity provisional and uncertain - have been of very little significance. Another issue prioritised in the original plan was that of Peru-Ecuador bilateral relations, which promised to open up a wide range of opportunities for the consolidation of cross-border indigenous peoples. For the moment, it is another of those issues that is raised temporarily but soon dropped, as it is given no expression in concrete proposals for actions and initiatives that could be implemented.

With regard to hydrocarbons, after a long period of negotiations, indigenous demands were flagging due to the dynamic of the process itself. There are very few exploratory initiatives that continue to be active and, in these cases, the indigenous population has managed to effectively control the situation. New drilling is rare and new finds nil. Nevertheless, the problems could re-emerge in the short term: the unconditional resistance of the Achual[3] people in the face of the ARCO Company's plans resulted in this company transferring its rights to OXY, a company with far less scruples, with strong political links and with precedents for placing communities in jeopardy and which has already begun to issue warnings concerning its firm intention to enter the concessionary territory, no matter what. Given these contextual difficulties, the indigenous movement has played a fundamental role in some regions. We will now go on to look at some of the most outstanding events of the period.

The Process in Madre de Dios

In the case of Madre de Dios, the mining and forestry problems and the aggression towards the indigenous population in isolation have again triggered a significant indigenous reaction.

Faced with the serious social problems of the Department of Madre de Dios and the aggressive depredation of the forests on the part of large logging companies, the popular organisations called upon all of the departmental associations to join forces and put forward a joint platform of needs to the government.

This call for unity was organised by those organisations considered as being the strongest in the region: the Departmental Agrarian Federation of Madre de Dios (FADEMAD) and the Native Federation of Madre de Dios (FENAMAD).

An initial awareness-raising activity was successful in uniting all the associations, women's and students' organisations and agreement was achieved on the aims of the initiative, agreeing a common platform that was discussed with the local authorities. This was not favourably received and so the regional assembly declared the First Regional Strike in August, supported by more than five thousand people, including farmers, indigenous people and the population at large.

The town was paralysed for three days and indigenous men and women, like the rest of the inhabitants, had to withstand harsh and indiscriminate repression. The presence of commissions of Congress members and Ministers enabled the Platform for Regional Struggle to be discussed and supported, a number of commitments being made.

With regard to the needs put forward by the indigenous population, the government agreed to respect the decision of the indigenous population in isolation, to thoroughly analyse the mining problem, to recognise ways of including indigenous territorial control within the communal territories and natural protected areas and to conclude the definitive categorisation of the Amarakaere Communal Reserve.

A maximum 10-day period was established in which to tackle the different lists of demands or, failing this, an indefinite stoppage would occur.

The Second Regional Strike was held once this period had expired and an indefinite stoppage began that continued from 18th to 26th September, at which date the Government agreed to some of the demands, resolving - amongst other things - administrative problems in timber extraction.

The strike gained massive support from the population. A large number of police contingents brought especially from Lima violently clashed with the demonstrators, resulting in two peasants wounded by gunfire and two indigenous people tortured, with 120 demonstrators arrested.

For their part, since August 2000, the communities most affected by gold mining on their lands have begun actions to evict the miners, thus intensifying the confrontations.

Despite the fact that they have made efforts to come to an agreement on four occasions, all the meetings have unfortunately ended in failure, with the miners maintaining an inflexible and arrogant attitude. They are led by the mining employers, who have held leadership positions in the professional organisations. Faced with these events and the indifference of the authorities, the communities have maintained their decision not to allow the miners to re-enter their lands.

In September 2000, FENAMAD had the opportunity to meet the Vice-Minister for Mining in Lima, in order to try to find an answer to the mining problems in the communities. At the meeting, the previous government's Vice-Minister and his technical team, as well as FENAMAD and its team, arrived at a joint agreement to resolve the problem in the following way:

- In order to avoid the granting of new concessions, a Supreme Decree would be issued ordering that new reports in the areas occupied by the communities would NOT BE ACCEPTED.
- For the cases of miners already operating: given that they have acquired rights granted by the Mining Registry, an inspection and environmental audit would be undertaken with the aim of checking fulfilment of environmental obligations and fulfilment of the obligations provided for in the mining law itself, such as the prior agreement of the landowner or the payment of rights. If lack of compliance was found, fines or cancellation of the concession would be applied.

The Ministry fulfilled the inspection and audit in three communities, where the reports proved a lack of compliance of legal obligations on the part of the miners. Further commitments remain incomplete due to the change in government.

FENAMAD has recommended negotiations with the new Transitional Government in order to continue with its aim of resolving this problem at the highest level of government authority, and has the support of tutelary offices such as the Ombudsman and SETAI (Department for Indigenous Affairs).

On the other hand, there is a great deal of interest on the part of the logging companies in extracting timber from the area of activity of the indigenous populations in isolation, for which reason they have asked the government to declare this a permanent forest extraction zone.

However, in recent months a series of events have occurred that prove the presence of indigenous populations in isolation, such as the attack on a group of fisherpeople in September 2000, which resulted in a young boy of 18 being wounded by an arrow in the back of the neck. Events such as these confirm the need to restrict access to the zone. With this aim, FENAMAD has undertaken a study on territorial demarcation with funding from IWGIA and which is now in its final stages.

Alongside this, pressure on the government to refrain from granting forestry concessions in the area continues. In addition, through the Territorial Reserve and Defence Campaign, which began in October 2000, the zone is under surveillance and the corresponding complaints against the loggers made who, in spite of being informed of the risks existing in this area, continue to work within it.

In spite of this, the authorities decreed a suspension of the closed season for mahogany and cedar in the area, increasing the entry of loggers and other illegal extractors onto the lands of the isolated indigenous peoples. This has led to this indigenous population defending itself, afraid of the threat of the foreigners, causing one case of an arrow wound suffered by one of the members of the brigades making incursions into their territories.

Finally, on 12th February 2001, there was a clash with a group of isolated indigenous people in the Santa Cruz community, leaving a considerable number of isolated indigenous wounded and possibly seven dead, according to as yet unconfirmed reports from FENAMAD.

Spaces for Coordination

Largely with funds from multilateral financial organisations, a good number of coordinating initiatives have been undertaken which, in the view of the indigenous organisations, were not generally aimed at resolving indigenous problems.

The following are worth mentioning:
• The AIDESEP-Ombudsman Agreement aimed at protecting the fundamental rights of indigenous peoples.
• The Consultation on an agenda of legal initiatives to be introduced to the Congress of the Republic (due to time limitations

restricted to the Law of Intercultural Bilingual Education and the Law of Indigenous Justice).
• The definitive launch of the Indigenous Affairs Committees within the legislative and executive powers.
• Specific legal consultations (such as the System for the Protection of the Collective Knowledge of Indigenous Peoples or the Regulations governing the Forestry Law).

This opening up is in contrast to the unexpected promulgation of the new Forestry Law. In this case and, being a law that profoundly affects indigenous interests, it was not the subject of consultation, apart from the superficial consultation that was undertaken with some NGOs on a text that differed substantially from the final official text.

Forestry and Wildlife Law No. 27308 is the product of a very long history of "one step forward and two steps back" relating to the modernisation of a sector which, at this precise moment, forms one of the areas most opposed to social control. The events in Madre de Dios, initially denounced by FENAMAD and other popular forces, brought to light the Mafia-like handling of concessions to the service of the mass depredation of the national forests by national and international companies, guaranteed impunity on the part of the regional authorities.

Nevertheless, the new Law, welcomed by some as the most modern on the continent, does not imply significant advances in terms of indigenous peoples' rights over their territorial heritage and, instead, consolidates State control over decisions in this regard. Whilst the indigenous organisations are trying to define operational rights in the Law's regulatory framework, the ambiguity with which the rights of indigenous peoples are depicted within it makes it clear that, in any case, this is not an attempt to legislate for them but with complete disregard for them.

In many people's opinion, the promulgation of this law, like the others that form the framework for the expropriation of indigenous peoples' natural resources (the so-called Law of Lands and the Law of Exploitation of Natural Resources), all (despite their importance) adopted without consultation, shows the other face of the "consultation game" which, in view of its results, could be understood as having been intentionally unsuccessful.

The Events in the Central Forest and Decree 15-2001-PCM

Yet again, the Asháninka population of the Central Forest has been the major player in the inventory of indigenous struggles. The mass invasion of San Ramón de Pangoa, considered strategic in definitively overcoming indigenous resistance and dividing their traditional territory in two, once more caused indigenous populations and settlers supported by the local authorities to clash. On 30th January 2001, an attempt to legally evict the invaders took place which, due to the reduced number of police, was unsuccessful and left an unknown number of people wounded. The withdrawal of the police left the indigenous population of the community at the mercy of a mob of furious settlers who tried to blow up the San Ramón bridge and stoned the judicial authorities and staff of the Ombudsman's Office who were in the area. On 31st, 1,500 settlers with eight guns entered the community and overpowered the indigenous patrols[4], setting fire to three houses and threatening to destroy the community.

In the face of these actions, on top of the two decades of suffering and genocide already suffered, the indigenous organisations of the Central Forest embarked upon a march to Lima and undertook an intense lobbying and awareness raising campaign that obtained significant results, succeeding in putting the issues directly to eight sectoral Ministers and to the new President of the Republic, Dr. Valentín Paniagua.

As a result, and recognising the country's moral obligation to the Indigenous Peoples, on 14th February by means of Supreme Decree 015-2001-PCM, the President established a Multi-Sectoral Commission at inter-ministerial level to agree - with the national indigenous organisations - a solution to the eight priority points within a period of 60 days and to formulate, within a further 120 days, integrated proposals to guarantee the full validity of the constitutional rights of indigenous peoples and communities and to promote their well-being.

What the Future Holds

Due to this important and historical organisational achievement, the period closed with very promising perspectives that create new possibilities for real and effective dialogue between the State and indigenous peoples, possibilities that were unthinkable throughout the whole of the past decade of authoritarianism.

For many, it may well be a period full of opportunity as it is certain that, in many cases, the involvement of some of the most outstanding elements of the political class within the transitional government has been secured, and that there is a general environment of judicial "cleaning up" that could encourage solutions to the problems of indigenous peoples that had been dragging on during all the years of the shady management of public affairs.

With their characteristic pragmatism, many organisations have decided to test out these opportunities and are preparing processes for agreements with the transitional State apparatus in search of long-term solutions to their problems. It is very possible that these agreements, which are understood as opportunities of the moment, will take up a good part of the indigenous movement's attention over coming months, along with the preparation of agendas to receive a new government.

At the end of the period, the Indigenous Movement was obliged to undertake urgent tactical changes in all negotiating processes being held with the State apparatus. This was not only due to a change in government but to a whole revolution in objectives, styles, expectations and procedures on the part of central government, along with the resistance of local powers to abandoning the comfortable positions obtained during the dictatorship.

Conversations and negotiations underway have been taken up by a transitional government full of good intent and with great popular sympathy, but limited by circumstances. The atypical nature of a period such as the present (and the one to follow is unlikely to be very different) has caused bursts of acceleration and sharp braking, changes of direction and the reconstruction of agendas at uncommon speed. The transitory nature of the current political moment (with a government that is not going to last but whose prestige could promote the consolidation of some important achievements) is forcing the organisations to be alert to the opportunities and to distinguish those that could last from those that are merely contrivances of the moment.

Routine, the culture upon which more solid processes are built, is not - at this precise moment in time - (as can be seen), the natural environment of the Peruvian indigenous movement.

Notes

1   A former member of the APRA party and the principal confidante of Fujimori. He was the great organiser of the "local bases" of Fujimorism and, through one of the party's of the pro-government alliance, "*Vamos Vecinos*" ("Come on, Neighbours"), he was responsible for the redistribution of social funds in the Provinces and Districts throughout Peru.

2   In AIDESEP's view, the Life Plans are mechanisms for collective reflection that attempt to evaluate the history of an indigenous people during the years of contact with national society and attempt to establish broad lines of action for that people from a long-term perspective.

3   The Achual belong to the Jibaroana linguistic family and live in the north Peruvian and south Ecuadorian forests, largely along the rivers on the Pastaza river basin plains.

4   Communal forces with the sole aim of self-defence.

BOLIVIA

During the year 2000, peasants and indigenous peoples realized that government policies with regard to land distribution and natural resources in practice denied them the territorial rights they had obtained over the previous decade through constitutional and legal reforms. In a context characterized by a diminution of their rights, the only alternative has been mobilization by the people in order to generate spaces for negotiation with government agents through such action.

The Water War

Inhabitants of the valley regions of the country were faced with the Potable Water and Sanitary Sewer System law, which was approved in October 1999. This law opened the door to the privatization of water resources. Following approval of this law, water was privatized in the Department of Cochabamba when, by means of a concession, the government surrendered the water sources that provided drinking water. Traditional users were excluded from the right to access this resource and small-scale infrastructure constructed by communities passed into the hands of a private company. From this point on, they had to pay this company for water extracted from their own lands and by their own methods. By the middle of January, various social sectors had united to form the *Coordinadora del Agua* (the Water Coordinating Committee)[1] and blockaded the city of Cochabamba. Through these actions, they managed to ensure that the company which had purchased the concession would not control community irrigation systems. During the first days of February they took over the city, an action that was called the "water war" because of violent confrontations between the Army, police, and demonstrators. This takeover forced the government to commit itself to changing the law. However, in April a third demonstration was necessary to ensure that the law was actually changed and the concession contract annulled, legal actions that were needed in order to safeguard the rights of the users.

The Rural Blockade

In September, the highland peasant movement and coca producers in Chapare blockaded the main national highways for a month, leaving

Indigenous peoples demonstrate, Bolivia. Photo: Alejandro Parellada

The Third Indigenous and Peasant March, June 2000. Photo: IWGIA archive

the country's central axis (La Paz-Cochabamba-Santa Cruz) immobilized. These actions were a reaction against government policies and a development model that gives them only marginal possibilities of surviving in conditions of dignity. These prolonged actions made the government subscribe to agreements in which, among other things, it committed itself to modifying the main laws relating to land and natural resources. It also agreed to definitively suspend construction of the military bases in Chapare that were part of the process of eradication of surplus coca crops.

The Third Indigenous and Peasant March for Land, Territory and Natural Resources

By the beginning of the year, several of the indigenous organizations that had presented claims for *Tierras Comunitarias de Origen* (indigenous territories) and some regional organizations had come to understand that the process of consolidation of the rights recognized in national legislation was going down a road that would hopelessly lead to the elimination of those very same rights. Their fears were based on the following facts:

- The inexplicable delays in promulgating new regulations that would ensure the correct implementation of the *Ley del Servicio Nacional de Reforma Agraria* (the National Agrarian Service Reform law) that had been agreed upon with the organizations.

- The National Institute of Agrarian Reform - INRA, which is responsible for land titling, issued and hoped to implement technical norms that would enable illegal third parties[2] inside indigenous lands to consolidate their rights. This would have been to the detriment of indigenous peoples, who are the legitimate owners of these lands.

- The *Viceministerio de Asuntos Indígenas y Pueblos Originarios* (VAIPO, the Viceministry of Indigenous Affairs and Native Peoples), through supposedly technical spatial needs studies, systematically reduced the areas to be titled as indigenous territories[3].

- At the end of 1999, a Supreme Decree was approved, which converted former rubber and brazil nut concessions into forestry concessions. Through implementation of this decree, large areas of the northern Amazon would be consolidated in favor of *ba-*

rraqueros[4], areas in which thousands of peasants and native peoples live and carry out traditional activities[5].

- An arbitrary rejection of three appeals concerning the unconstitutionality of INRA's resolution 098/99 presented before the Constitutional Tribunal. With this resolution, INRA, part of the executive branch of government, claimed legislative functions, established a summary and almost secret process to provide forest concessionaires with vast areas of forest lands, and avoided the legal *saneamiento*[6] procedure.

As a result of these measures, the process of titling indigenous lands initiated in 1997 did not produce satisfactory results. The process reached a point where, in practice, the territorial claims were not viable. Faced with this situation, indigenous peoples initiated a strategy of mobilization by creating links with other social organizations, such as peasant and settler organizations in eastern Bolivia, who were also faced with serious land tenure problems.

In April, these organizations presented their demands to the government and informed it that they would mobilize until they achieved effective solutions to their main problems. As a result, the government rushed to expedite the new regulations for the INRA law. However, as the organizations feared, some of the articles of these regulations were changed to facilitate and consolidate, through the administrative measures mentioned above, recognition of the property rights of private individuals and to grant large areas as forest concessions.

The government did not provide any answers. The march began on June 28 in the Department of Pando, where several hundred peasants and indigenous people traveled from their communities to the city of Riberalta. There they were joined by the *Central Indígena de la Región Amazónica de Bolivia* (CIRABO, the Indigenous Organization of the Amazon Region of Bolivia), the *Federación de Trabajadores Campesinos de la Provincia de Vaca Díez* (Federation of Peasant Workers of the Province of Vaca Díez), and the *Central Campesina de Guayaramerín* (Peasant Organization of Guayaramerín). Together they traveled to Trinidad. They arrived in Santa Cruz on July 6 where they were joined by delegations of indigenous peoples and peasants organized by the *Coordinadora de Pueblos Étnicos de Santa Cruz* (CPESC, the Coordinating Committee of Ethnic Peoples of Santa Cruz) and federations of peasant workers and settlers from the Department of Santa Cruz. Later, peasant federations from the Beni and the Gran Chaco province of Tarija, as well as organizations representing the populations of three indigenous territories being claimed in the Department of Beni (the Multiethnic territory - TIM, the Isiboro Sécure Indigenous Territory and National Park - TIPNIS, and the Mojeño and Ignaciano territory - TIMI), joined the third march.

Before the march left Santa Cruz, the National Director of INRA and the Vice-Minister of Indigenous Affairs (VAIPO) rushed to make small offers so that the natives would stop the mobilization. However, the march continued and demanded definitive solutions to their demands. In the city of Montero (45 km. to the north of the city of Santa Cruz), 6 government ministers arrived to negotiate with the leaders of the march. The dialogue took two days and lasted until dawn each day. The dialogue bore fruit and the organizations achieved concrete agreements to resolve their demands, which they had sent to the President of the Republic two months earlier.

The fact that the government initiated the dialogue and, without major changes, accepted the solutions proposed by the organizations proved once again that the rights of indigenous people and peasants only become reality through the use of pressure tactics.

Achievements of the Third March

The achievements of the march were significant. The decree that transformed the *barracas* into forestry concessions and the administrative resolution that authorized INRA to declare lands available for concessions were annulled. Prior to the march, nearly 3,800,000 hectares were ready to be granted in concession but, as a result of the march, these areas will now be titled as indigenous and peasant lands. In the decree that changed the new regulations of the law, INRA's ability to continue declaring lands as forestry concessions was limited, and it was established that such actions could not be taken without first carrying out the *saneamiento* of agrarian property, for which a specific regulation was instituted.

These changes to the new regulations of the INRA Law were aimed at guaranteeing the legal paperwork for the *saneamiento* process of indigenous lands and impeding the award of land rights to owners of unutilized lands or to those who had illegally acquired lands inside indigenous territories. With these changes, one of the main problems that led indigenous peoples to march was resolved because the implementation of technical rules issued by INRA had led to properties of up to 2,500 has. being consolidated in favor of third parties even though they did not fulfill legal and constitutional requirements. This had led to massive reductions in the size of indigenous territories throughout the country and, in some cases, the disappearance of these territories altogether. These clearly illegal technical rules had been contested by the organizations affected and, in response, INRA put a halt to their respective *saneamiento* processes. This is exactly what happened during the titling process of the Monte Verde territory claimed by the Chiquitano people. With these changes to the regulations, these technical regulations automatically disappeared and processes that had been suspended could now continue.

VAIPO's ability to recommend areas to be titled for indigenous peoples was eliminated and the timeframes within which the processes had to be completed were reduced.

Advances in the Titling Process of Indigenous Lands

In just 15 days, what had seemed impossible during four years of fruitless *saneamiento* of agrarian property, costing large sums of money contributed by international donor agencies, was achieved. Although it had been four years since the approval of the INRA law, which required that 16 territorial claims be titled in a maximum span of 10 months, up until then only 657,736 has. had been titled. This area included the claims of the Ayoreo people and a part of the claim of the Guarayo people[7]. The march obtained legal authorization for the issuing of titles for the following indigenous territories: the Multiethnic II in the northern Amazon, Lomerío in the Chiquitanía and Yuracaré in the tropics of Cochabamba. The total area of these territories is 832,735 has. Another 1,077,115 has. are close to being titled, including the Monte Verde territory.

The Multiethnic II Indigenous Territory

The northern Amazon was one of the main protagonists of the march. The mobilization in this region was characterized by a strong alliance between indigenous peoples and peasants, which was important in defeating the government's decision to convert nearly all of the Department of Pando and the northern sections of the departments of Beni and La Paz into forestry concessions.

As of December 1999, according to INRA's projections, of the 441,000 has. claimed by the Multiethnic II territory the *"barraqueros"* would receive approximately 156,000 has. and the peasants 45,000. Coincidentally, in its preliminary spatial needs report, VAIPO recommended the titling of 236,000 hectares. Once dialogue was initiated, the study was modified to recommend the titling of 407,000 hectares.

Following the march, third party rights were revised on the basis of new rules and INRA issued the titling resolution for the Multiethnic II territory, with a total area of 391,000 hectares. This meant that the area that was supposed to be awarded to the *barraqueros* was reduced to less than 6,000 hectares, since peasants still received the projected 45,000 has. However, two more mobilizations were necessary: 1) a blockade of roads for several days during December carried out in coordination with transport workers, so that the resolutions corresponding to third parties were emitted, a prerequisite for final titling; and 2) one more blockade in February, which lasted until they obtained the executive title. This title was emitted on the 23rd February and was for 289,000 hectares. The reduction is due to the fact that a group of 36 third parties contested the titling resolution for an area equal to 102,000 hectares.

With this title the Esse Ejja, Tacana and Cavineño indigenous people, with an approximate population of 4,000, will have their territorial property rights guaranteed. At the time of writing, they had already organized a management and administrative committee for their territory.

The Chiquitano Indian Territory of Monte Verde

The titling process for this territorial claim had been at a standstill for more than six months. This extended delay in the titling process was INRA's response to the objection that indigenous organizations presented against the technical rules it had issued, which valued the properties of third parties in order to establish the legality of their titles and to determine whether they were fulfilling a socio-economic function. These objections sought to prevent the territory being given to landowners in the region.

Once the legality of the *saneamiento* process was restored through changes in the regulations governing the law, the process recommenced. Since the many illegal interests that conspired against the titling of this territory no longer had the backing of the technical rules mentioned above, it appeared that the process would culminate satisfactorily in the terms agreed upon with the government. However, INRA delayed its completion and opened up an unexpected and inconvenient reconciliation process with third parties.

On September 29th, INRA issued the titling resolution but without the accompanying resolutions for each one of the properties of third parties and with incomplete and erroneous geographic information. The area the resolution gave to the natives did not include areas that legally belonged to third parties, as well as 120,000 hectares claimed as forestry concessions. As a result, it only provided the Chiquitanos of this region with 881,000 hectares of the 1,060,000 hectares they had originally claimed. Although it disregarded provisions in the law and a recent decision by the Supreme Court of Justice[8], the decision to consolidate the forest concessions was ratified by the Minister of the Presidency, reneging on commitments made during the third march.

The protest marches by the communities and organizations of this territory led to the suspension of implementation of this resolution by INRA. In order to convince the organizations to accept the consolidation of forest concessions, INRA offered to compensate them for all the areas given to third parties and already granted as concessions. In this way, the final area titled would be equal to the surface area originally claimed (1,059,964 has.). However, at the same time, INRA summoned all third parties to a "reconciliation hearing", an extraordinary process that led to third parties placing more pressure on indigenous people in order to increase the size of their properties. In fact, third parties were able to effectively increase the area they were to receive by nearly 30,000 hectares.

The agreement between INRA and organizations representing the indigenous people of Monte Verde was signed in November. However, by the end of the year, INRA had not issued the new titling resolution. This made it possible for large landowners to appeal to the National Agrarian Tribunal against the resolution issued in September, thus paralyzing the process once more. Third parties subsequently presented an appeal concerning the unconstitutionality of several articles of the new regulations, with the pretence that the final part of the *saneamiento* process should be redone.

The titling of Monte Verde currently depends on a decision to be made by the Constitutional Tribunal. A surface area of 851,000 has. within the area claimed and 208,964 has. more outside of it are still waiting to be titled.

The Chiquitano Territory of Lomerío

In spite of all the technical problems that came to light, the *saneamiento* of the Lomerío territory was concluded by the middle of June. Up to that point, VAIPO had not presented the corresponding identification of spatial needs study. This study was presented during negotiations with leaders of the march and recommended the titling of 384,000 has. or, in other words, 84,000 has. more than what had been originally claimed.

For its part, INRA committed itself to issuing the title resolution by the beginning of August. This did not happen until 20th October

2000, and the resolution was issued for an available surface area of 275,000 has. During this period, INRA attempted to establish a "reconciliation" process, as it had done in Monte Verde, but the leadership and the communities stood firm, avoiding the opening of this process.

Since the area to be titled is less extensive than the area recommended by VAIPO, the communities have already requested compensation for the difference. The indigenous organizations have identified areas that can form part of this compensation, and these are precisely those areas that were previously declared as concessions by INRA. Following the march in July, the government had also agreed to give these areas to indigenous peoples and peasants. Once the titling process has ended, the next step will be to initiate the compensation process, which should not present any major obstacles.

The Yuracare Territory

The titling process of the Yuracaré territory has generally been the least conflictive. *Saneamiento* was carried out with teams from the respective zones of the territory, and the indigenous technical expert worked efficiently. It is worth highlighting that, in this region, the natives never worked as peons on large estates and maintained extensive control over their territory. The few non-natives living in this area accepted the titling of land in favor of the Yuracaré people and were able to retain the areas they occupy as they are members of communities.

Nevertheless, VAIPO recommended the titling of nearly 22,000 has. less than what was originally claimed. Despite this recommendation, INRA decided to title the whole area claimed, which was 244,335 has. The executive title was formally issued in October last year.

The First Indigenous Territorial Claims (TIM-TIMI-TIPNIS)

The first territorial claims of the Bolivian indigenous movement were recognized by means of presidential decrees enacted between 1990 and 1992. However, 10 years on, the *saneamiento* process, which leads to the final titling of territories, had still not begun and it seemed unlikely that it would be carried out. The Isoboro Sécure Indigenous Territory and National Park (TIPNIS), the Multiethnic Indigenous Territory (TIM) and the new territorial claim of the Moxeño-Ignaciano indigenous people (TIMI) had been put on hold for some time amid conflicts over access to forest (timber) and oil resources.

The organizations that had claimed these territories decided to join the on-going march. The difficult weather conditions made it hard for community members to leave their territories, which is why they did not join the march until the night when the final text of the agreement was being discussed, a text that was eventually signed by the government and the leaders of the march.

In spite of their last minute arrival, organizations from the Department of Beni managed to incorporate part of their demands into the agreement. They managed to obtain resolutions that led to the initiation of the *saneamiento* process for the Multi-ethnic and Mojeño-Ignaciano (TIM and TIMI) territories. They also obtained a precautionary immobilization measure that prohibits new settlements and the titling or awarding of land to non-indigenous people.

In the Isiboro Sécure Indigenous Territory and National Park (TIP-NIS), the *saneamiento* of an area totaling 30,000 has. has been concluded. Third parties had sought to gain land rights to all of this area. In the end, the communities consolidated slightly more than 24,000 has., and they continue to believe that their entire territorial claim (1,236,296 has.) will be consolidated, given that it is categorized as both a national park and indigenous territory. However, a wealth of timber resources and biodiversity has made this area very tempting for landowners and land traffickers as well as exploiters of timber and natural resources. Although INRA has resources for the reorganization of two more areas, it has not included this territory in its schedule.

The Day after the March: Regressive Proposals

It has already been noted that many of the agreements obtained by the third indigenous and peasant march have been implemented. On the other hand, others have not.

The Vice-Ministry of Indigenous Affairs and Native Peoples, which became a Ministry after agreements were reached between the government and the peasant movement in October, has bypassed the changes to the regulations governing the law. These changes had eliminated its capacity to recommend the surface area to be titled for indigenous communities. It continues issuing such recommendations and substantially reducing the areas claimed. The territories now being affected are those in the southern Amazonian region.

In addition to this non-fulfillment of agreements, an entire process of counter reform has begun in order to revert legal changes obtained by the march and promote new rules directed towards recovering preferential treatment for certain sectors in the land titling process.

First, before the end of the year, a law was introduced in parliament that was to recover the benefits of the annulled *barraquero* decree.

Then, a proposal was presented to the *Comisión Agraria Nacional* (CAN, the National Agrarian Commission) to regulate the number of hectares per head of cattle. This proposal would be applied to cattle ranching properties throughout the land titling process. In accordance with this proposal, for each head of cattle[9], ranchers would be awarded from 6 has. in the humid tropics up to 47 has. in the Chaco region.

Finally, the CAN was presented with a decree that intends to revert all the changes to the regulations of the INRA law. Besides giving back to the Ministry of Indigenous Affairs the capacity to recommend surface areas to be titled for indigenous peoples, it re-authorizes INRA to be able to declare State lands as forestry concessions. It also restores legal provisions that favor the consolidation of properties by third parties who do not possess rights and proposes to change the minimum amount of land to be titled for families involved in extractive activities in the northern Amazon. If parliament approves the above-mentioned law, this last measure would pave the way for implementation of the *barraquero* law.

This counter reform process has taken place within a current Bolivian context in which businessmen have taken a prominent role in national public opinion by demanding that the government implement specific measures to attenuate the serious economic crisis, which has particularly affected the agricultural sector.

If the previous regulatory proposals are approved and implemented, cattle ranching activities would be legalized, northern Amazonia would be surrendered to *barraqueros* and forests to loggers, and there would be no land left for native peoples, peasants and poor settlers. Such a situation would extend and consolidate the excessive concentration of rural property and the age-old poverty of rural communities.

The organizations are attentive to what can happen. When the third march ended, the organizations made a commitment to continue a united struggle to defend their rights, and they have already announced new mobilizations for the first months of the year.

Notes

1   This organization brought together peasants, industrial and transportation workers, and urban and rural civic committees from the Department of Cochabamba.
2   Translator's note. In Bolivia, private individuals, businesses or non-indigenous peoples occupying or with a claim on lands inside indigenous territories are known as third parties (*Terceros*).
3   Based on official data, in global terms, of a total of 11,047,988 has. immobilized as part of the titling process of indigenous lands, VAIPO recommended titling 8,401,484, that is, 24% less.
4   Translator's note. *Barraqueros* is the name given to owners of *barracas* in Bolivia. At the beginning of the 20th century *barracas* were rubber extraction concessions. Later, when the rubber boom ended, they focused on extraction of brazil nut. *Barracas,* in effect, functioned like *haciendas* where workers toiled as peons. The size of these *barracas* ranges from 5 to 30,000 hectares.
5   These *barracas* functioned as places for the storage and processing of brazil nuts and rubber. According to INRA, at the beginning of 2000, after the enactment of Supreme Decree 25532, 240 *barraqueros* had requested a total of 3,400,000 has. as forestry concessions.
6   Translator's note. *Saneamiento* is a procedure through which INRA measures, demarcates, and investigates the legal standing of rural properties. *Saneamiento* is but one component of the titling process of indigenous peoples' territories. As the term has no equivalent in English, the Spanish term is used throughout the text.
7   Between October and December 1999, four Ayoreo territories were titled, with a total area of 244,736 ha. as well as an area of 413,000 has. of the Guarayo territory. The total area of the Guarayo territory is 2,205,369 has.
8   In May, the Supreme Court of Justice issued a decision that put an end to objections presented by indigenous organizations in 1998 against the granting of forestry concessions inside their territories. This decision indicated that concessions should be reduced by the necessary amount in order to title indigenous territories.
9   This is equivalent to 400 kg., which is the average weight of a mature head of cattle.

PARAGUAY

Socio-Political Context

Following the events known as the *Paraguayan March of 1999* (which included the assassination of Vice-President Argaña, 7 dead and hundreds wounded in public demonstrations, and the political trial and resignation of the then President Raúl Cubas) the Government of National Unity emerged, led by the Colorado Party and made up of the other most important political parties. Expectations for change following the acute political and social crisis have been increasingly frustrated by this government's performance.

For example, it has undergone several face changes and reformulations; the Liberal Party, for example, withdrew in the first half of 2000 only to join once more, winning the elections for the Vice-Presidency in August of that year.

This crisis of political actors has impacted on the social players, who gained few answers to their demands. The public fund deficit gradually increased to the point where the government, at the end of the year 2000, did not have enough funds to cover ongoing expenditure. From that point on, structural adjustment, so fashionable in other Latin American countries during the 1990s, was called for by various industrial and business sectors as the means by which to resolve the situation. The government and the political class have echoed this position, and various measures have been taken with which to embark upon the so-called "Reform of the State" which, in principal, envisages the privatisation of public companies, an increase in the price of basic services, the reduction and/or elimination of public expenditure, etc.

The Paraguayan Indigenous Institute (INDI) has been included amongst those organisations which - due to their excessive size, corruption and scarce social productivity - are to be reformed or eliminated. Put to the test, probably no State institution could pass the requirements for effectiveness and transparency but, undoubtedly, in the eyes of the government, some cutbacks have less political cost because of who they affect.

An Indigenist Policy of Denial

Whilst the President of INDI at the beginning of 2000, Mrs. Leni Pane de Pérez Maricevich, had indigenist experience, her administration was misguided and negative in relation to the interests of indigenous peoples. This management team commenced with a budgetary cut (see further on), which Mrs. Pane came to terms with as an important and determining but not absolute factor. Nonetheless, 2/3 of the scarce funds for land restitution were misappropriated through the purchase of overvalued land. To this had to be added the arbitrary management of the institution, which earned it the opposition of it's Council. INDI's internal conflicts went beyond this and the government sought to settle the discontent by dismissing Mrs. Pane and replacing her with Mrs. Olga Rojas de Báez, at that time a member of the opposing Council.

Mrs. Rojas, the eigth President of INDI since the start of the Paraguayan transition (1989), took up her post on 17th September 2000 with the promise to defend indigenous territories, fight for a fair budget and encourage the communities' self-sufficiency. However, her good initial intentions and even her open support of conflictive cases, has brought no advances to the indigenous situation.

In order to understand the government's current indigenist policy, we need to look beyond the changes in management within INDI, and take into consideration the following indicators: the budgetary cuts for land purchase during 2000 and 2001; the rejection of a request to reprogramme the land purchasing budget made to the Treasury Department in May 2000; the refusal to expropriate historical land claims in Parliament; funding for INDI's organisational running costs budgeted only until June 2001; and, finally, the presentation, by the Department for the Reform of the Executive Power, of a draft bill amending Law 904/81, considered unconstitutional and in contrary to indigenous rights, which should be considered by Parliament next March.

In the first place, the allocation of funds for the purchase of lands claimed by the indigenous peoples was reduced - initially - by more than 50% from 1998 to 1999, then by 84% from that year to 2000 and **by another 40% for 2001,** leaving it reduced to a sum of approximately US$400,000 at the current exchange rate (this amount could resolve hardly 1% of the current territorial claims). In other words, the latest cuts (2000-2001) more or less constitute the final blow in a series of cutbacks aimed at the effective disappearance of INDI.

The rejection and withdrawal of various projects for the expropriation of lands in favour of indigenous communities (see further on) by both chambers highlights the fact that Parliament has had no qualms in flagrantly violating the constitutional and legal mandate for restitution of lands to indigenous peoples. In opposition to these demands, the Paraguayan Rural Association (ARP) - the cattle farmers affected and politicians close to their interests - in alliance with the media, undertook a campaign to delegitimise the land claims and their justification, deeply insulting the organisations linked to the indigenous people and presenting the large estate owners as the victims.

In accordance with what was envisaged in the draft bill from the Reform Department, INDI will have to be substituted - in theory as of July 2001 - by a Department for Indigenous Affairs of lesser administrative status. This draft also stipulates the transfer of human and financial resources to the provincial governments and a reduction in the minimum land basis that can be demanded from the State on which to maintain indigenous families.

On top of these negative indicators, there are other equally serious situations: the indigenous migration to the towns - or rather to their rubbish dumps - through the dispossession of and/or insecurity on their lands; the exploitation of labour; the sale of private lands to the Moon Sect, which affects the territories of the indigenous peoples of Upper Paraguay (and even half of a national Municipality); the threat of megaprojects indifferent to or excluding indigenous rights and interests, such as the *"Corredores de Integración"* (Integration Corridors) project of the Inter-American Development Bank (IDB), the Project for the Sustainable Development of the Chaco (PRODE-CHACO), the Waterway and others. All these are phenomena and circumstances that point to a deterioration in the living conditions of indigenous peoples.

Finally, faced with the prospect of a generalised violation of their rights on the part of the State, indigenous people have increased their involvement in the public sphere, expressing their demands with increasing clarity and firmness through different organisational initiatives and before different authorities, beyond the sphere of the traditional leaders. Of these, the following can be mentioned: *Coordinadora de Líderes del Bajo Chaco* (the Coordinating Body of Leaders of the Bajo Chaco), the *Asamblea de Pueblos Indígenas* (the Indigenous Peoples' Assembly), the *Organización Nacional Aborigen* (the National Aboriginal Organisation), the *Unión de Comunidades Indígenas de la Nación Yshyr* (the Union of Indigenous Communities of the Yshyr Nation - UCINY) and, in particular, for their newness and distinctive nature, two political movements in the Chaco. The first to organise was the *Movimiento Indígena 19 de Abril* (Indigenous Movement of the 19th April), which launched its Religious Political Council on 12th October 2000 in the department Presidente Hayes; and the *Movimiento 11 de Octubre* (11th October Movement) whose headquarters are in the department of Boquerón but which has still not been officially launched. Both movements are made up of people from different indigenous peoples.

The Coordinating Body of Leaders of the Bajo Chaco has repeatedly denounced the Provincial Administration of the Department of President Hayes for embezzlement of funds and manipulation of indigenous peoples in its actions aimed at them. The UCINY managed to obtain agreements with the government for the exclusive stockpiling of caiman skins, thus avoiding exploitation at the hands of non-indigenous middlemen. The 19th April Indigenous Movement gained wide publicity at its launch and its members claim to be seeking an indigenous politics outside of traditional electoralism.

Indigenous Territorial Demands

In spite of a clear and favourable legal framework for the restitution of lands to indigenous peoples and the relative simplicity of their solution in financial and political terms, the State has made no progress in this regard over the last few years. On the contrary, it has tended to simply deny the problem. Today, for example, the indigenous peoples of the Chaco are claiming scarcely 3% of their territory (in round figures approx. 750,000 hectares) and those of the eastern region less than one quarter of this area, the purchase of which - from the private individuals holding them - would cost no more than US$50 million.

By way of example, it is worth noting recent and relevant events that serve to demonstrate the generalised violation of indigenous territorial rights:

The process of cutting back INDI's budget for land acquisition, INDI's disappearance and the possible creation of an unconstitutional State indigenist body
The draft bill from the Reform Department is the final nail in the political coffin of INDI, and clearly seeks to overturn the achievements gained in legal terms by indigenous peoples and their allies. This law, for example, reduces the minimum quantity of hectares the State must return to each indigenous family (from 100 to 50 hectares in the Chaco, from 20 to 10 hectares in the Eastern Region) which, on the one hand, contradicts the National Constitution itself where it mentions the return of land to the indigenous peoples *"in sufficient quality and quantity for the preservation of their particular ways of life"* (Article 64) and, on the other, seeks to legitimise the current situation of lack of compliance with the minimum requirements for territorial return.

The approval and/or acquisition of unclaimed lands and irregularities with regard to their processing
One example is the Paso Itá S.A. case, of around 1,350 hectares located in the Horqueta district, department of Concepción. Mrs. Pane ordered two payments for these lands to the Treasury Department for a total of Gs. 1,000 million (U$S 280,000). The cost per hectare approved by INDI was 7 times greater than that established by the Institute for Rural Welfare (IBR) for lands in the area.

The National Parliament's rejection of proposals to expropriate indigenous territorial claims
The most significant violations and acts of an arbitrary nature have been committed at parliamentary level, given the importance of this

authority and the consequences of the positions and decisions adopted by the senators and deputies.

Firstly, the example of the Xakmok Kásek (10,700 hectares) and Sawhoyamaxa (14,404 hectares) communities can be given. Both submitted their demands to Parliament in June 1999, after 9 and 8 years of wasted administrative procedures due to the intransigence of the owners in selling the claimed lands. From that point on, an innumerable number of humiliating events took place for both communities: only one group of commission members visited the communities in the first place; almost one year later and due to a demonstration on the part of the communities in Asunción, the Agrarian Reform Commission issued a favourable report on both cases and, then, because of the insulting campaign and lobbying against the decision, headed by the cattle farmers in question, the commission decided to postpone dealing with the cases and to undertake a second visit. During this visit, the indigenous people had no time to put forward their concerns and the parliamentarians decided in favour of the cattle farmers' arguments. The commission subsequently issued another report, this time with a majority against (several members radically changing their initial position) and, finally, the Senate rejected both requests on 16th November 2000.

Another two expropriation projects, that of the *Ayoreo Totobiegosode* (78,000 hectares) submitted to the Senate and that of the *Enxet* of *Yakye Axa* (18,186 hectares) submitted to the Chamber of Deputies, had to be withdrawn due to negative reports.

The government's lack of preventive and dissuasive measures
The government has taken no preventive or dissuasive measures to prevent the occupation of indigenous lands - guaranteed or being processed - on the part of poor peasants or to defend the indigenous environment from depredation at the hands of third parties.

The emigration is due to the fact that lands, mainly of the *Mbya Guaraní* people of the department of Caaguazú, were invaded by landless peasants or unscrupulous logging companies, encouraged by agents from the Colorado Party. The Police and Ministry of the Interior have been reluctant to ensure respect for the judicial measures that protect the indigenous lands in question and to apply orders for eviction of the illegal occupants.

BRAZIL

A Tumultuous Year for the Indigenous Peoples in Brazil

The year 2000 was a tumultuous one for the indigenous peoples in Brazil. The government of Fernando Henrique Cardoso proved unable and unwilling to render effective solutions in order to grant the indigenous people a dignified and safe existence within Brazilian society. The present delays in the demarcation process, due to ongoing Parliamentary Committee Inquiries (CPIs) into FUNAI and NGOs in Brazil as well as military repression against legal indigenous demonstrations also point in that direction. On the other hand, the social mobilisation generated in the wake of the indigenous march in April against the official commemoration of Brazil's 500 years has strengthened the grassroots of the indigenous movement. It should also be acknowledged that the indigenous population in Brazil is growing once again and that new international programs for the protection of indigenous lands, such as the Project for the Protection of the Indigenous Lands and Populations of the Legal Amazon (PPTAL), an initiative financed by the G7 countries, have inspired new faith among indigenous leaders that the demarcation process will go forward despite official resistance.

The Indigenist Policy and its Permanent Crisis

The designation of Carlos Frederico Marés as the new president of the National Indian Foundation (FUNAI) in November 1999 raised hopes of a more just and pro-indigenous policy. Marés declared that he would only assume the post on the condition that the Raposa/ Serra do Sol indigenous reserve (among others) was immediately ratified. During the first months of his presidency, he developed the proposal for a new Indian Statute, which was handed over to the indigenous organisations during their protests against the commemoration of Brazil's 500 years. Sympathising with the indigenous protests, he declared himself in opposition to the official commemoration of the 500 years anniversary of the "discovery" of Brazil, and eventually resigned as a reaction to the violent repression by the military police (MP) against the indigenous march towards Porto Seguro on the commemoration day. He was eventually replaced by Glênio Alvarez, who became the 27th president of FUNAI since its foundation in 1967. This disheartened the indigenous organisations as Alvarez showed less willing to speed up the demarcation process.

The Indigenous March and Protest against the Commemoration of Brazil's 500 Years

The indigenous march was initiated at the beginning of March 2000, with caravans forming all over the country and heading for Porto Seguro in Bahia, the site for the official commemoration of Brazil's 500 years. The march was organised by the "Comitê Outros 500", consisting of members from CAPOIB (The Coordinating Council of Indigenous Peoples and Organisations of Brazil) and CIMI (The Indigenist Missionary Council) as well as independent indigenous leaders. More than 3,000 participants representing 140 different peoples from 21 states in the country held demonstrations and speeches in 23 major Brazilian cities before uniting in Coroa Vermelho, where the "Conference for Indigenous Peoples and Organisations of Brazil" was held.

The Indigenous Peoples' Conference

This Conference was attended by approximately 3,000 Indians, the largest number ever to attend a conference. Besides condemning the continuing invasion of indigenous lands and the extermination of indigenous peoples, the final conference document also indicated new directions for indigenous resistance, emphasising the importance of building a broad alliance uniting indigenous, black and popular movements against the injustices of Brazilian society.

The principal demands of the indigenous peoples to the Brazilian State presented in the final document were:

- The fulfilment of indigenous peoples' rights as guaranteed in the federal constitution:
- The demarcation of all Indigenous Lands (TIs) before the end of the year 2000.
- The withdrawal of invaders from all demarcated lands, compensation for and recovery of degraded areas and rivers.
- Recognition of the resurgent[1] peoples and their territories.
- Protection of the isolated[2] peoples' territories against invasion.
- Respect for the indigenous peoples' exclusive right to the usufruct of all natural resources contained in the indigenous areas, with special attention to bio-piracy.
- A halt to the constructions in progress of hydroelectric projects, power lines, waterways, railways and highways, and compensation for the damage caused by projects undertaken so far.
- The end of all forms of discrimination, expulsion, massacres,

Clash between military police and Indian protesters. Photos: J.Rocha

Tariano group presenting a ritual during the "Week of the Indigenous Peoples, Manaus" Photo: Christian Groes-Green

Indian protest march. Photos: J. Rocha

threats, acts of violence and impunity. Immediate investigation into all the crimes committed against the indigenous peoples over the past 20 years and punishment of those responsible.
- That the true history of Brazil be acknowledged and taught in State schools, taking into consideration the thousands of years the indigenous population have occupied the diverse lands called Brazil.
- That the indigenous peoples elect the president of FUNAI after recommendations from the regional organisations.

Official Repression and Violence

On April 22nd - the final day of the indigenous conference - the indigenous caravan was prevented access to the celebration area in Porto Seguro where it was supposed to join black and popular caravans and make a speech to the nation and the Head of State, Fernando Henrique Cardoso. On the direct orders of Cardoso, the Military Police opened fire and injured seven Indians, also arresting 140 sympathisers from the black and popular movement. In response to the aggression, indigenous demonstrators ripped their "white man's" clothes off and threw stones at the MP officers.

The year 2000 was, in general, characterised by violence against indigenous peoples. In Mato Grosso do Sul, farm owners shot two *Guarani-Kaiowá*, and wood workers in the same region assassinated a *Nambikwara* boy. In Acre, at least three unidentified Indians were murdered, allegedly by a city councillor. Among the *Yanomami*, the indigenous leader, Davi Kopenawa, reported that army soldiers had raped young girls and caused gonorrhoea epidemics. In Pernambuco, the federal police invaded the indigenous Truká area with helicopters and buses, arresting and beating up several individuals, claiming that they were involved in drug trafficking.

The reactivation of the military "Calha Norte" project in the Amazon has also caused fear and insecurity among the indigenous peoples in the region. The widespread military presence, the aim of which is to gain geopolitical control over the region, exposes many isolated peoples to harmful contact. The federal government justifies the choice of the Amazon as strategic region by asserting the need for an effective defence of the natural resources against foreign military invasion and exploration. In indigenous areas in the State of Amazonas, there have been reports of military personnel sexually abusing the women, distributing alcohol and entering indigenous villages without permission.

The New Indian Statute

The proposal for a new Indian Statute, worked out by FUNAI President Marés, was approved by the influential Amazonian organisations in April but fierce critique from indigenous leaders from the central and eastern parts of Brazil, in agreement with CIMI, made FUNAI suspend the proposal. The Federal Executive is now processing an alternative proposal but the key question is whether or not the regional indigenous organisations can come to an agreement. The problem is that the Amazonian organisations, under the co-ordination of COIAB (CoordenaVão das OrganizaVões Indígenas da Amazônia Brasileira), believe that compromising with the government is the only way to influence its indigenist policy. Indigenous organisations from the central and eastern regions, however, emphasise the clear deterioration of the Indian Statute in comparison with the draft law from 1991 and the 1973 Statute in force. *Kayapó* and *Xavante* representatives, for example, refuse to accept the clause in the present draft that impedes unlimited prospecting by indigenous people and the clause dealing with the limitation of the FUNAI tutelage, upon which both of these groups are particularly dependent, as well as the clause that deprives so-called "acculturated" Indians of their right to impunity.

Indigenous Health

The Pro-Yanomami Commission (CCPY) reports that the Yanomami experienced severe health problems during the year 2000. Of particular concern was the immigration of ill Yanomami families from Venezuela. Uhiri, a non-governmental health organisation, found 453 of these immigrants with serious illnesses such as malaria, acute respiratory infections and dermatological diseases. This immigration process, caused by a lack of health services among the Yanomami in Venezuela, is disastrous, firstly, since the immigrants have to undertake exhausting walks and cross Yanomami areas where they are not welcome, which puts them in an extremely vulnerable situation. Secondly, because these desperate immigrants might be the transmitters of dangerous diseases, which could have catastrophic consequences for the Brazilian Yanomami areas.

Demarcation of Indigenous Lands

Only five indigenous lands comprising merely 149.276 hectares were demarcated in the year 2000, making it the second worst year in terms of demarcation for the last ten years. In March 2001, the general juridical-administrative situation regarding the *terras indígenas* (TIs) in Brazil was as shown below:

Legal situation	No (number of TIs)	HA (hectares)
To be identified	135	
Identified	16	2,275,007
Delimited	55	10,394,545
Demarcated	19	1,917,403
Ratified	34	10,376,906
Registered	321	76,297,577
Total	580	101,261,438

Out of a total of 580 TIs in Brazil, so far more than 60 per cent have been demarcated covering an area of 76,297,577 hectares, which corresponds to 12.3 per cent of the area of the national territory. More than two thirds of the total number of concluded demarcations have occurred within the last decade.

FUNAI anticipates the demarcation of 34 TIs during the year 2001, 17 of which will be demarcated with resources from the G7 countries' PPTAL program. In the State of Amazonas, 12 lands inhabited by the *Kokama, Mundurucu, Tucuna, Apuriña, Mura, Tenharim*, and *Torá* peoples will be demarcated. In the State of Roraima, the demarcation of *Macuxi* and *Wapixana* lands is expected, as is the demarcation of the *Mundurucu* territory in the State of Pará. This does not mean that the process of demarcation will proceed without severe obstacles in years to come. By way of example, the year-long impasse regarding the demarcation of the Raposa/ Serra do Sol area inhabited by approximately 12,000 Indians was not solved in the year 2000. Local farm owners and prospectors (*garimpeiros*) working in the indigenous areas, as well as the State Government of Roraima and rightwing politicians in the Senate are joining forces to suspend the demarcation process. Farmers and prospectors claim their right to stay on certain lands in the area, and agitate for the decree signed by the Minister of Justice in 1996 suggesting a 300,000 hectare reduction of the area originally identified by FUNAI as covering 1,6678,800 hectares.

A more general problem regarding the demarcation process in Brazil is that few resources are available to finance the demarcation of TIs outside of the Amazon. This is because, at the moment, the only solid source of funding at FUNAI's disposition is the resources available from the PPTAL program, all of which are aimed at the Amazon region. Political interests in the mineral resources are the

Sateré-Mawé selling their handicraft during the "Week of the Indigenous Peoples", Manaus.
Photo: Christian Groes-Green

primary reason for the general delay in the process of demarcation. In collaboration with the right wing deputies making up the "Amazonian Faction", the Federal Senate has set up a CPI of NGO activities in Brazil justified by an alleged fear of internationalisation of the Amazon. The objective of this absurd initiative is obviously to hinder the international support of indigenous and environmental interests in the country thus facilitating access to minerals and other resources in the indigenous and nature reserves. Notably, the "Amazon Faction" approved the report, which concludes the CPI of FUNAI suggesting that:

- The limits of the TI Raposa/Serra do Sol should be revised by segmenting the indigenous areas out of respect for the lands of local landowners and occupants.
- Inquiries should be made into the activities of the Centre for Indigenist Work (CTI).
- Future ratifications of demarcations should be scrutinised by the National Congress.
- Inquiries into the partnership between Indians from the TI Raposa/ Serra do Sol and NGOs should be initiated.

These anti-indigenous initiatives are linked to the approaching implementation of "Avança Brasil", a huge development program made up of dozens of major infrastructure projects intended to accelerate economic development in terms of industrial agriculture, timber and mining activities. According to an article by William F. Laurance et al. published in *Science*, the Brazilian Government's investment of more than $40 billion over the years 2000-07 will be used on highways, railroads, gas lines, hydroelectric projects, power lines, and river-canalisation programs. Should this program be completed it will have catastrophic consequences for the indigenous peoples in Brazil and their environment.

The Brazilians' Attitude towards Indigenous Peoples

A comprehensive national inquiry carried out in February 2000 by the Socio-Environmental Institute (ISA) reveals that the vast majority of the Brazilian population acknowledges indigenous rights and supports the demarcation of indigenous territories. For example, 82 percent of the population believes that the federal government ought to act to prevent the extinction of indigenous peoples and to promote their defence. In spite of the Brazilian State's lack of will to defend indigenous interests, and its continuing repression of its indigenous peoples, the population's attitude points towards the possibility of a future climate of respect and coexistence between the different societies.

Notes and Sources

[1] Resurgent is the expression used to designate indigenous groups that had been considered extinct, disappeared or non-existing but that somehow have resurfaced and have been rehabilitated.
[2] Indigenous peoples living in voluntary isolation or who are believed never to have been contacted.

Boletim Yanomami, No. 12, 25/04/01.
Brasil Indigena, No. 21, April 2001.
Coordenação das organizações indígenas da Amazônia Brasileira, COIAB (nd.): *Relatório da marcha indígena 2000.* COIAB, Manaus.
Conselho Indigenista Missionário, CIMI (2001): *Marcha e conferéncia indígena.* CIMI, Brasília.
Conselho Indigenista Missionário, CIMI (2001): *Agora são outros 500.* CIMI, Brasília.
Conselho Indigenista Missionário, CIMI (2001): *Situação jurídico-administrativa atual das terras indígenas no Brasil.* CIMI - Secretariado National, Brasília.
Conselho Indigenista Missionário, CIMI, homepage: www.cimi.org.br.
Fundação National do Indio, FUNAI (2001): *Terras indígenas tradicionais - procedimento demarcatório.* DAF - FUNAI, Brasília.
Instituto Socioambiental, ISA (2000): *Povos indígenas no Brasil: 1996-2000.* Instituto Socioambiental, São Paulo.
Instituto Socioambiental, ISA, homepage: www.socioambiental.org.
Porantim - Em defesa da causa indígena, No. 229, October 2000.
Porantim - Em defesa da causa indígena, No. 230, November 2000.
Porantim - Em defesa da causa indígena, No. 231, December 2000.
Science, Vol. 291, January 2001.

ARGENTINA

A new government in Argentina, new authorities in the National Institute for Indigenous Affairs, new directives, new ideologies. But what results have there been?

Back-Pedalling in State Indigenism

In spite of the fact that the country is witnessing a resurgence in the indigenous movement, Argentina's political leaders continue to ignore this. During the year 2000, the new authorities of the National Institute for Indigenous Affairs (INAI) thus submitted a programme of action that merely harks back to the old integrationist/developmentalist ideology of past decades. Consequently, a clear back-pedalling has taken place in State indigenism: programmes and activities that were being implemented have been brought to a standstill and the approval of others has been unacceptably postponed, highlighting the fact that this country has still not adopted a consistent policy for the indigenous peoples living within it and that everything is approached without prior planning and with no respect for indigenous rights. And so, when the civil servants change not only do the policies change but also the ideologies and principles on which they are based. It seems that Argentina's political leaders "don't know what to do with the indigenous". Consequently, cyclically, "indigenous affairs" remain subordinated to the swings of party politics, accentuating a clientilistic dependence and welfarist paternalism. And so, whilst other citizens have a number of organisations through which to make their demands, the indigenous have only INAI.

Convention 169:
Neither indigenous consultation nor indigenous participation
In fulfilment of indigenous hopes, although in terms of the above this could seem paradoxical, the Argentinian Foreign Office ratified ILO Convention 169 in July of last year, in response to a demand that had been extensively reiterated by indigenous organisations.

However, whilst the National Constitution and Convention 169 prescribe the necessary consultation and participation of indigenous peoples with regard to all areas that affect their lives, this was not respected during the year in question. A few examples serve to illustrate this: 1) Fifteen years after passing the law that created INAI, and as a result of a legal ruling regarding a request that was to initiate the Indigenous Association of the Argentinian Republic (AIRA), in August 2000 a presidential decree provided for the immediate regularisation of INAI as a decentralised body with indigenous participation and its own budget. Several months passed, and the Institute was still under the control of the Department of Social Development, with no indigenous participation and with the aggravating factor of a significant reduction in the budgets allocated to it. Of these, only 20% had been implemented by the end of the financial year. 2) The absence of indigenous consultation and participation can be demonstrated by a health programme that was implemented without the beneficiaries even having had the chance to give an opinion in its regard. On 24th July, the Ministry of Health submitted to the President the *"Programme of National Support to Humanitarian Actions for Indigenous Populations"* (ANAHI), which "will implement the article of national indigenous law 23302 that guarantees the indigenous populations' right to health". In summary, the programme consists of the establishment of a primary health care system based on the work of indigenous community health agents. A system which, albeit with shortcomings, had already been implemented for a number of years. For this reason, in practice this meant no more than a change in name and a replacement of the people in charge. Apart from this, the decree creating this programme provided for the functioning of a Consultative Council in which not one indigenous representative has participated. The members of this Council met four times during the year but have still not been able to establish a programme to take forward. Nonetheless, a number of employees collect a salary for their "work" within ANAHI.

A Review of INAI's Management during the Year 2000

Programme of regularisation of indigenous lands
There are three agreements signed between INAI and the provinces of Chubut, Río Negro and Jujuy, which provide for budgetary contributions to the parties in question. This programme forms part of the spectacular announcement - made in 1996 by President Menem - that 2,000,000 hectares of State lands would be returned to its legitimate owners. Four years on, the results have been poor. In 2000, some provinces made progress on their own, as INAI systematically failed to ensure the policy of land regularisation.

Meeting of the Lhaka Honhat General Council of Caciques, San Luis, Salta Province, Argentina
Photo: Morita Carrasco

Bulldozer destroying the burial grounds of the Wichis living in Hoktek T'oi village,
Salta province, Argentina. Photo: John Palmer

Management priority for 2000: student grant programme
In line with the integrationist/developmentalist ideology that characterised INAI's conduct over this period, the most important activity, and that which took up a major part of the resources - to the detriment of other programmes such as the land programme, so unjustly postponed - was the implementation of a system of grants for secondary school and university students. This system consists of granting a monthly stipend (US$60 for secondary school level and US$200 for university level) to young indigenous people so that they can achieve better integration into the formal State education system under the supervision of a tutor. Following a complex and extended selection process, 1,354 grants were awarded to secondary school students, many of which were still unpaid as of December 2000.

International development cooperation in indigenous communities
INAI is the local counterpart in three programmes that have international funding from different sources and which each have different methodologies.

The "Ramón Lista Integrated Development Programme" (DIRLI): Through an agreement with the European Union (US$8,000,000 over four years with national counterpart funding), this programme is being implemented in the Province of Formosa. Its goal is: "to improve the living conditions of Wichí communities, on the basis of the activation of an endogenous and self-sustained development process that targets the protection of their cultural identity." Following stagnation caused by a delay in the funds being made available, the programme was initiated, giving priority to improvements in housing and water provision with funds provided by the provincial state. The Wichí population benefiting from this programme is approximately 6,000 people..

The "Attention to Indigenous Peoples Component" (CAPI) of the Programme of Attention to Vulnerable Groups of the Inter-American Development Bank (IBD) (approximately US$4,000,000 over four years with national counterpart funding) is being undertaken in three provinces: Jujuy, Salta and Chaco. It covers communities and organisations from different indigenous peoples. Its main objective is: "to strengthen the operational management capacity of grassroots and intermediary indigenous organisations." So far, social appraisals have been carried out, training meetings have been held on legal status and project design and specific projects have been initiated in some communities.

The "Indigenous Community Development and Biodiversity Protection Project" receives funding from the World Bank (US$6,000,000 plus national counterpart funding) and its aim is to strengthen the indigenous communities in chosen pilot areas with an emphasis on "sustainable development with identity" and, secondly, to discuss alternative forms of legal support to protected areas. The project has been at a standstill since October 2000, waiting for the President of the Nation to pass the respective decree for final approval. As of the beginning of 2001, the programme's future is uncertain, for if the stated decree is not passed, the Bank may decide not to continue with the programme.

Recognition and Defence of Rights

The Catholic Church

On the 12th May 2000, an official document from the Catholic bishops, referring to the National Constitution recognising the right to community possession and ownership of lands on the part of aboriginal groups, championed an "acceleration of the devolution of lands to the indigenous peoples, whether State lands or private".

Ordinary law

The lack of application of constitutional rights has led indigenous people to resort to legal paths to submit complaints. And, surprisingly for a country with such little respect for cultural differences, during the year 2000 some judges issued encouraging decisions for the recognition of their rights. These included the following:

In the Province of Neuquén, a Mapuche community achieved the right to receive a bilingual education, a Mapuche language and culture teacher joining school No. 319 Paraje Aucapán Abajo. Through this case law, it was expressly recognised that Argentinian indigenous communities have a right that can be legally requested and which must be satisfied by the State.

In the Province of Santa Cruz, a family from the Tehuelche people came out on top in a century-long legal dispute for recovery of their territory. The judge in the town of Río Gallegos passed judgement that, following five years of forced absence, the Tehuelche could return to their ancestral home. This case marked, for the first time, the application in Santa Cruz of the 1994 constitutional reform guaranteeing property rights over indigenous territories.

Violations, Threats and Attacks on the Physical, Territorial and Cultural Integrity of the Indigenous Peoples

Occupation of indigenous lands

Land occupations continue in a number of different provinces, without the slightest respect for indigenous land rights. The communities of the Mapuche people in the provinces of Río Negro and Chubut, in particular, have had to repeatedly denounce violations of their rights to the courts and demand their respect. By way of example, we quote the following:

Within the context of aggressive proceedings, the members of the families forming part of the "Vuelta del Río" Mapuche community, the largest aboriginal reserve in Chubut, created in 1899 by presidential decree, are being pursued through the courts following a formal complaint of misappropriation presented in 1994 by the descendants of a landowner of the area, who claim ownership of the lands traditionally occupied by the Mapuche. The community, made up of 25 families, have no electricity and no school, they live in poor housing on 15 plots of 625 has each..

In the Province of Río Negro, the Kom Kiñe Mu - Arroyo Las Minas - community is faced with proceedings for their removal. In order to defend their right, they submitted an administrative appeal denouncing the illegitimate action of the Provincial Department for State Lands, pending resolution in the Supreme Courts.

In the Province of Salta, the Hoktek t'oi community of the Wichí people finds itself cornered onto 27 hectares, suffering the depredation of its environment by a forestry company. A request to expropriate these lands (approximately 3,000 hectares of their traditional territory of 75,000 has.) and put a ban on the company, Los Cordobeses S.A, is currently going through the National Congress. This company was trying to evict them from an extra 17 has. of native forest bordering onto the community.

In the Province of Chubut, the Argentinian army is arguing that it is the owner of the lands of the Prane community, and is endeavouring to evict the Mapuche families from this area.

In the Province of Salta, the Tinkunaku community of the Kolla people cannot use 80,000 has. of mountains where their animals pasture due to the fact that they are faced with a legal procedure for return of the donation, initiated by the Tabacal Seaport Corporation Refinery. In the meantime, the company is seeking to divide the indigenous organisation by buying its members off financially and attempting to confuse them and wear them down so that they denounce their right.

Attack on an indigenous leader

Jorge Santucho, from the Amaicha del Valle community in the Province of Tucumán, was set on fire by the Cruz family. In a dispute over control of the area of the Quilmes ruins, Jorge Santucho was sprinkled with petrol while using the community tractor to seize lands that had been fenced off by this family with no prior consultation. Several years ago, this family had obtained a dubious licence to carry out a hotel undertaking in the area where the important archaeological remains of the Sacred City of Diaguita de Quilmes are located. Following a long period in hospital, Jorge Santucho was able to return to his community.

Oil contamination
In the Province of Neuquén, two Mapuche communities continue to fight a long battle against the Repsol/YPF oil company. In June, members of the two communities decided of their own accord to prevent implementation of maintenance work on installations located in the Loma de la Lata oilfield as a protest at the extension of oil exploitation contracts. They took this opportunity to make an appeal to the provincial authorities to put a stop to the personal, material and cultural aggression they were suffering as a consequence of this company's activities.

Land conflicts in the international arena
The complaint made to the Inter-American Commission on Human Rights by the Lhaka Honhat Association of Indigenous Communities against the Argentinian State because of a lack of environmental impact studies and claiming ownership of their territory in the Salta Chaco continued to be processed. In November, a hearing took place in Buenos Aires between the interested parties, with the president of the Commission in attendance. At this meeting, it was agreed to commence a dialogue process with the aim of formulating a proposal for an amicable solution to be presented to the Commission at the next hearing to be held on 1st March 2001.

CHILE

The year 2000 has been no exception to previous years and, right from the beginning, the newly-elected socialist president Ricardo Lagos and his government were set a hard task in attempting to solve a number of conflicts between the indigenous peoples of Chile and Chilean society - conflicts which, to a large extent, have been inherited from former governments.

At the forefront has been the year long conflict between timber companies and private farm owners on the one hand, and the largest group of indigenous people, the Mapuche Indians in the south of

Chile on the other (see **Chile** in *The Indigenous World 1999-2000*). The organisations *"Consejo de Todas las Tierras"* and the *"Coordinadora Arauco-Malleco"* have been the moving spirits behind the mobilization all along. The Mapuche demands for the recovery of land and for recognition as a people poses a serious challenge to the forest industry, and to Chile's economy in general, as the industry is a major contributing factor to Chile's economic growth. For this reason, Chilean governments have, in many cases, neglected recognition of the land rights of indigenous people. A case in point was the approval of the Ralco Dam by the former Eduardo Frei government, even though it is being constructed on land defined as indigenous, and will entail the relocation of around 700 indigenous people (see *The Indigenous World 1999-2000*).

As a consequence, the demands of the Mapuche movement had been met with strong reservations from Eduardo Frei's government, even though the 1993 indigenous law in fact gives legal grounds for the claiming of vast areas of indigenous land. In an attempt to maintain political stability, the Frei government had used the State internal security law against the so-called Mapuche "terrorists" in a repressive political action which, in some ways, echoed the days of Pinochet. The government of Ricardo Lagos took over power in a very critical phase of the conflicts, as the negotiations had reached a deadlock and the line of action against the co-called "terrorists" had already been settled.

The Human Rights Situation

The year 2000 has been marked by many conflicts, all of which reflect a general distrust or even hostility towards the Chilean government, and accusations of racism and violations of human rights have been repeatedly propagated by the Mapuche movement. One example was the case of 10 Mapuche leaders and activists who, during February and March, were charged with a number of very serious crimes ranging from arson and timber theft to kidnapping, violation of the national internal security law and the attempted homicide of three security guards working for the timber company Mininco. Among those arrested was the leader of the organisation "Coordinadora Arauco Malleco", Víctor Ancalaf Llaupe, who was arrested for kidnapping and violation of the State internal security law after occupying the Court of Justice in the city of Collipulli on March 28, 2000. The courthouse was occupied in order to protest against the imprisonment of Pedro Maldonado Urra and Luis Ancalaf, who were charged with the attempted homicide of the three security guards.

Mapuche demonstrating on October 12 – the anniversary of Colombus' discovery of America. Photo: Dorthe Kristensen

The arrested Mapuche, along with their organisations, denied any responsibility for the homicide attempt. Instead, they accused the timber company, Mininco, of being responsible for the act. That accusation has been given further credence by a written confession from several timber company security guards and read out on the national radio station, Bio Bio, in February 2000 in which they admitted to carrying out acts of assault and vandalism with the intention of blaming the Mapuche movement for the incidents. So far, however, no security guards have been arrested or charged. On the other hand, the arrests of the Mapuche were enforced without hesitation. Afterwards, these arrests were reported as irregular, as one of the confessions was given after 15 days of solitary confinement and torture, while the law permits only 10 days of solitary confinement. This confession, however, became the principal evidence in the charge against the 10 Mapuche. In addition, the families of the arrested, particularly that of Víctor Ancalaf, suffered harassment as well as serious threats, allegedly from employees of the Mininco timber company. Gradually, the Mapuche were conditionally released from prison. The last to be released - in August 2000 - was Víctor Ancalaf, after five months of imprisonment. The serious charges are, however, still being investigated.

Many Mapuche saw this case as an example of the human rights violations repeatedly being committed by the Chilean government. The imposition of the State internal security law in this case was seen as an attempt to avoid confronting the serious historical problems that the Mapuche movement was addressing. The arrest of Mapuche leaders for crimes that had an almost total lack of evidence was regarded as a reflection of the government's wish to stifle the demand for autonomy. Those arrested were therefore regarded as political prisoners. The case was subsequently viewed as proof that the Chilean government primarily serves the interests of strong economic groups, and that the "democratic" laws do not protect the more marginal groups. The radical Mapuche organisations claimed that the repressive politics of the government left them no choice but to respond in a similar way. A new spiral of violence seemed inevitable.

Another case, which was followed closely by the Chilean press during 2000, was the indigenous students' protest against a presumed closing of various student residences for indigenous students followed by demands for improved grants and credit. The student residences, which had never been officially recognized by the Chilean government, were now denounced as a cradle for Mapuche terrorists. On these grounds, the residences were placed under close observation, the electricity was cut, and meals and grants were denied. In protest, the students occupied the buildings of the State Corporation for Indigenous Development (CONADI) in Temuco and Santiago.

Dialogue, Solutions and Limitations

All these conflicts, and many others, are just some of the issues that Ricardo Lagos has had to address during his first year in office. He has done so by trying to establish a dialogue with the Mapuche organisations in order to find some long-term and sustainable solutions.

Wishing to demonstrate his opposition to the Frei government, he announced the creation of a "Commission of Historical Truth" on March 31, 2000. In addition, he initiated a dialogue with the indigenous movement through the establishment of a negotiating table. Mapuche representatives, primarily from the state Corporation for Indigenous Development (CONADI), were invited to participate along with academics, representatives from the Church, businesspeople and others related to the Mapuche people. However, the leaders from the more radical organisations such as the *Coordinadora Arauco-Malleco* and the *Consejo de Todas las Tierras* were not invited, and this caused strong criticism from the outset of the negotiations. The results of the dialogue were published on June 1, 2000. Not surprisingly, the conflict was first and foremost viewed as an economic problem rather than a political one. As the conflict was defined as one resulting from poverty, the measures agreed upon were based accordingly on this premise. In a ceremony in the building of the parliament, "La Moneda", Ricardo Lagos published 16 measures, including:

- The foundation of regional work groups
- Co-operation with indigenous representatives in the establishment of projects
- Grants of 100,000 pesos to 10,000 small farmers (US$180)
- Distribution of 50,000 hectares of land before December 2001, and 150,000 hectares in total during the Lagos period in office.
- The national celebration of the day of indigenous peoples on the 24th June.
- The development of a project regarding constitutional recognition of indigenous peoples.

For the Mapuche organisations, these measures seemed promising but far from satisfactory. The measures concerning the "soul" as it was put, for instance, the national celebration of the day of indigenous peoples, were generally met with satisfaction. This was also the case for the last item on the agenda – constitutional recognition, which is the most crucial issue to the Mapuche Movement.

On the other hand, the fact that the ratification of ILO Convention 169 concerning indigenous peoples had been postponed resulted in strong criticism from the Mapuche organisations. Furthermore, it had not been defined to which of the indigenous peoples of Chile - the Mapuche in the south or the Aymara, Quechuas and Atacameños in the north - the 150,000 hectares of land were to be allocated (*La Tercera*, August 8, 2000). It also proved difficult for CONADI to find plots of land that could be bought with special reference to transferring them to the Mapuche. In addition, the funds for the purchase of land proved inadequate, as prices soon rocketed. CONADI's indigenous adviser, Hilario Huirilef, thus estimated that the US$11,000 that had been granted would be far from sufficient to purchase the targeted 50,000 hectares in 2000 (*El Mercurio*, August 7, 2000). The fact that private landowners were speculating in and profiting from the conflict was difficult to deny. Finally, the case of the Ralco dam had not been dealt with, as Ricardo Lagos had avoided considering the problem by leaving it to the law courts to decide whether the construction of the dam was illegal or not.

In summary, the reactions towards the government measures were quite negative, as they seemed to be improvised rather than in-depth solutions. The attempt to balance neo-liberal politics with international standards concerning indigenous peoples proved very difficult. Instead of solving the conflict, the dialogue seemed to escalate it, fundamentally because the principal demands from the representatives of the more radical organisations had not been dealt with.

The Struggle for an Account of the 'Real' History

During 2000, the extent to which a solution to the Mapuche "conflict" will implicate a rethinking of the historical relationship between the indigenous peoples of Chile and the Chilean nation-state has become more and more evident. In this context, it is interesting to note that the process called "the recovery of territory", which initially seemed to be primarily a protest against the marginalization and increasing impoverishment of the Mapuche Indians, has increasingly been accompanied by efforts to revitalize traditional structures and by a demand for recognition as a people along with the corresponding rights to territory and autonomy. The discussion of what the word autonomy implies, however, has only just recently begun.

However, the majority of politicians continued to deny the political and cultural roots of the problem, reducing it to a matter of economic hardship. In the same line of discussion was the polemic between the historian, Sergio Villalobos, winner of a national history prize, and a number of Mapuche and Chilean academics. On May 14, 2000, Sr. Sergio Villalobos published an article in the newspaper *El Mercurio* in which he depicted the "pacification" of the Mapuche as inevitable, since a meeting between a highly developed culture and a less developed one will always result in the former dominating the latter. Villalobos further proposed the view that, in the case of the Mapuche, this process was indeed a positive one, as it, among other things, brought civilization and "the practice of justice instead of revenge, the practice of monogamy as well as the punishment for homosexuality, which before was a current practice." It was hardly a coincidence that this article was published shortly after the publication of the first results of the dialogue. As such, it could be seen as an example of the Chilean nationalistic discourse, which profoundly conflicts with the demands of the Mapuche organisations. It is hardly surprising that the responses from the Mapuche and academics sympathetic to the Mapuche demands, were very critical. To mediate between these two positions will therefore be a hard challenge for the Commission.

By Way of Conclusion

The objective of the "Commission on Historical Truth" was to establish new forms of indigenous participation as well as to give an account of the true historical relationship between the Chilean government and the indigenous peoples. The measures of June 1, 2000 gave the first guidelines for the work of this commission. In autumn 2000, however, dissatisfaction with the results of the government became increasingly visible. The mobilizations started anew, land was symbolically occupied, and individuals wearing hoods, supposedly Mapuche, were reported to have committed crimes such as attempted homicide, arson and timber theft. Many Mapuche Indians were arrested, which they reported as having taken place with an exaggerated use of violence; people were left wounded and houses were ravaged. However, the Chilean press was primarily concerned with the supposedly "violent" action of the Mapuche, rather than the examples of torture and mutilation that the communities involved in the "conflict" experienced.

As a result, the suspicion that the radical organisations, rather than being in dialogue with the average Mapuche, had been infiltrated by "foreign terrorists" was propagated first and foremost by right-wing politicians, whose vision of Chile as a homogeneous society was threatened by the Mapuche demands. Investigations were initiated with the aim of "revealing" the degree to which foreigners had organised the mobilizations. According to right-wing politicians, the more radically and violently the Mapuche movement sought to propagate its demands, the more reasonably it seemed to deny the demand of "splitting" the country in two which, in their view, would be the consequence of a ratification of ILO Convention 169. Not surprisingly, the parliament, which still has a large percentage of right-wing politicians, definitively rejected ratification of Convention 169 in November 2000.

On January 18, 2001 the commission was renamed the "Commission for Historical Truth and New Treaty". The former president of Chile, Patricio Aylwin, was elected as president of the commission, and leaders from the more radical organizations, among these the leader of the "*Consejo de Todas las Tierras*", Aucán Huilcamán, were invited. However, at the first meeting of this commission on March 12, 2001, the more radical representatives of the movement were not present (*El Mercurio* March 13, 2001).

Sources

El Diario Austral
El Mercurio
El Metropolitano
La Tercera
El Siglo
El Sur
See also project **Nuke Mapu**, http://www.soc.uu.se

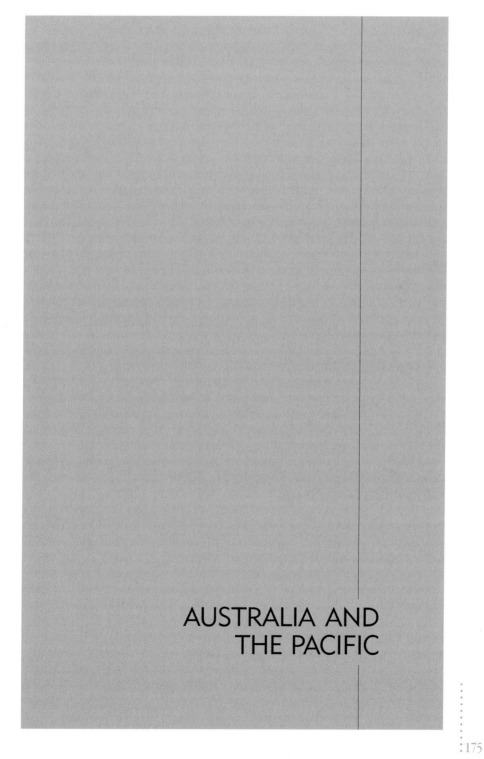

AUSTRALIA AND
THE PACIFIC

AUSTRALIA

In Australia, three processes have been entangled during the past year. One is the Howard government's repudiation of international human rights scrutiny in general and by the United Nations in particular. Another is the climax of the 10-year work of the Council for Aboriginal Reconciliation – and the evolution of black-white *reconciliation* on which it has focused. The third we might call *the celebration syndrome,* in which Australians reflect on their past and present. The celebrations themselves are one hundred years of Australia's Constitution uniting six former British colonies as one country, the new century, the new millennium, and the Sydney Olympics.

Rejecting the World

Federation, i.e., the constitutional union of six colonies on January 1, 1901, had racial anxiety at its heart. Not only were British and Irish newcomers wresting the lands, freshwater, and coasts away from their Aboriginal and Torres Strait Islander inhabitants, but the new Australians feared the moral (!) and social effects of, and possible conquest by, the dark-skinned peoples of the South Pacific and the many-hued populations of Asia to the north. *Vis-à-vis* Aborigines and Torres Strait Islanders, the new Australian government had no power and, indeed, was constitutionally forbidden to exercise any. The former colonies, renamed 'states' from 1901, had sole power and, given that farming, settlement, pastoralism, and mining were the key to state livelihoods and revenue, indigenous peoples were pushed out of the way more or less brutally[1]. Only in 1967 did the national government obtain power in principle through a referendum to act in these matters but it has since left matters largely to the states. The referendum was itself in part a response to international perceptions of Australia and its treatment of Aborigines as racist.

Since the 1992 High Court decision in *Mabo* recognising Torres Strait Islander and Aboriginal land rights in principle, many white politicians have tried to stir up white anxieties. Targeting blacks by encouraging white fears that they will seize your home and prop-

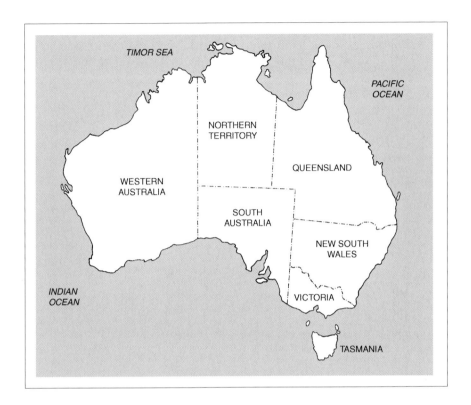

erty, or that tougher laws and policing are needed to put them in jail
because they are unemployed and thieving or violent, or that their
gobbling up of white tax dollars is improper because they are just
bad people who refuse to help themselves... these have been explicit
and implicit political themes at state, Northern Territory (NT), and
federal government levels. At the same time, however, Australians
have been learning through the media, speaking visits, and docu-
mentaries that other countries like Australia – notably New Zealand,
Canada, and USA – have been discussing indigenous political and
legal rights and have moved towards greater indigenous control of
their own lives, lands, and coasts.

In these contexts, the Howard government (elected March 1996)
has led a national reaction against the indigenous renaissance and
what it calls 'the Aboriginal industry'. Howard, who has been his
own minister in charge of Aboriginal and Islander[2] affairs, has
generally avoided policy debate on indigenous issues. He has been
content with one-liners and old-fashioned platitudes, and the abrupt-
ness of his language and responses to reform or recognition proposed by or for Aborigines betrays his disdain and lack of under-

standing. When Aboriginal leaders began to travel abroad to explain their situation and ask for foreign support, he called this 'stunts'. His own government, of course, collects information on indigenous issues abroad.

In 2000, Howard took his worldview a step further. As reported earlier (*The Indigenous World, 1999-2000*), he warned Kofi Annan on arrival in Australia not to speak of Northern Territory (NT) policies towards Aborigines. When Kofi Annan tactfully kept silent, his visit to Australia being to thank Australia for support of the UN in East Timor, Howard claimed in public that this silence proved that the UN found no fault with Australia's human rights practice. This was untrue, of course. A number of UN fora were finding fault with Australia's policies (and with its clumsy handling of international procedures and discussion of these). On August 29, 2000, Howard sent three ministers to tell the media that Australia would now refuse to cooperate with the UN on domestic indigenous and other rights matters[3]. Howard himself went to the UN in New York and announced this policy. The Howard doctrine is that decisions of Australian federal, state, and territory governments are beyond scrutiny by outsiders but that Australia, being a morally superior country, will continue to criticise others.

The intriguing question is whether this was a pre-emptive move before some new outrage attracts world criticism. Handing NT Aborigines and their lands and coasts over to the profoundly anti-Aboriginal NT government, i.e., by granting statehood as a gift to 'celebrate' Federation, would be one such possibility.

Reconciliation

The formal Reconciliation process climaxed on May 27, 2000, with the presentation of documents to the Prime Minister in the Sydney Opera House in the presence of the country's white political leaders. Many impressive speeches were made by both whites and blacks. Howard did not shout at the audience as he had done three years earlier at the previous Reconciliation convention but was quietly resistant all the same. Aboriginal leaders and the Council for Aboriginal Reconciliation had become so angry in preceding weeks and months with the Howard government's intransigence on issues of concern that they had strengthened their statement. The Council's Declaration reads:

Aboriginals regard their flag with pride. Photos: IWGIA archive

Aboriginal boy, Australia, painted for dance. Photo IWGIA archive

We, the peoples of Australia, of many origins as we are, make a commitment to go on together in a spirit of reconciliation.

We value the unique status of Aboriginal and Torres Strait Islander peoples as the original owners and custodians of lands and waters.

We recognise this land and its waters were settled as colonies without treaty or consent.

Reaffirming the human rights of all Australians, we respect and recognise continuing customary laws, beliefs and traditions.

Through understanding the spiritual relationship between the land and its first peoples, we share our future and live in harmony.

Our nation must have the courage to own the truth, to heal the wounds of its past so that we can move on together at peace with ourselves.

Reconciliation must live in the hearts and minds of all Australians. Many steps have been taken, many steps remain as we learn our shared histories.

As we walk the journey of healing, one part of the nation apologises and expresses its sorrow and sincere regret for the injustices of the past, so the other part accepts the apologies and forgives.

We desire a future where all Australians enjoy their rights, accept their responsibilities, and have the opportunity to achieve their full potential.

And so, we pledge ourselves to stop injustice, overcome disadvantage, and respect that Aboriginal and Torres Strait Islander peoples have the right to self-determination within the life of the nation.

Our hope is for a united Australia that respects this land of ours; values the Aboriginal and Torres Strait Islander heritage; and provides justice and equity for all.

The Howard government considered this statement too radical in several places to accept. The document was accompanied by four strategies for addressing social disadvantage, economic advantage, and Reconciliation work in future, and a National Strategy to Promote Recognition of Aboriginal and Torres Strait Islander Rights[4]. When the Reconciliation council handed its final report to the government in December 2000, the last two recommendations were the crucial ones:

5. That each government and parliament:

- *recognise that this land and its waters were settled as colonies without treaty or consent and that to advance reconciliation it would be most desirable if there were agreements or treaties; and*
- *negotiate a process through which this might be achieved that protects the political, legal, cultural and economic position of Aboriginal and Torres Strait Islander peoples.*

6. That the Commonwealth [national] Parliament enacts legislation (for which the Council has provided a draft in this report) to put in place a process which will unite all Australians by way of an agreement, or treaty, through which unresolved issues of reconciliation can be resolved.

A *Federation Forum* wound up the 10 years work of what one might call 'the white man's' reconciliation body, the Constitutional Centenary Foundation, created to build greater national cohesion, identity, and purpose through constitutional discussion and reform. Like the Reconciliation council, the CCF went out 'not with a bang but a whimper'. However, the Forum's summing up included a recommendation that:

There needs to be wide-ranging national debate within the framework of the reconciliation process about the representation of Australia's indigenous population. In this context, Australia should consider as one option the recognition within the structure of the Australian federation of the Aboriginal and Torres Strait Islander nations[5].

Celebrations

Sport is a matter of basic national pride and identity in Australia to a degree unknown in other countries. The desire of political leaders to be photographed with sports heroes reached its dazzling zenith at the Sydney Olympics in September 2000 when the Prime Minister tried to join every Australian medallist as foremost 'cheerleader', as he put it.

The Olympics, especially their opening and closing ceremonies showcasing Australian performance art and cultural references – some droll, some solemn – were important for how Australians saw themselves and how they showed themselves to the world. Everyone performing and watching understood this. So the prominence given to Aboriginal and Islander artists, motifs, and athletes, especially runner Cathy Freeman, was significant. Many Australians regard Aboriginal and Islander flags and assertiveness as un- or anti-Australian. However, for most people they are merely statements of pride and are quite non-threatening.

The various 2000-2001 celebrations, and the urge of so many authors, artists, academics, commentators, and public persons to think about the past and how we are doing in the present, have inevitably made the Aboriginal and Islander issue central. With the recent bicentenary of the first white settlement at Sydney in 1788 and the flood of books and re-appraisals issued then, Australia has had more than its fair share of excuses to ponder itself. Howard and many like him regard national self-appraisal as unnecessary or even treacherous. In his view, people who dwell on Australia's 'blemishes', as Howard calls past massacres of Aborigines, are self-hating. They are betraying their country, which is 'quite magnificent', in endless ways, which his speeches enumerate. His view of Australia was further startlingly revealed when, during the Olympics, he told us how foreign visitors had come up to him and said, 'Mr Howard, your Australian people are nice and friendly'. With such a leader many Australians complain that their country is demeaned, but his comments on Aboriginal issues have been the particular focus of public unease.

While the country had appeared to be building a consensus as a confident, outward looking, inclusive, sophisticated, internationalist but caring society, the Howard government brought that to a halt. Its brand of nationalism is phobic, not forward-looking. But for any national identity, Aborigines and Torres Strait Islanders are central. The Howard government goes to Geneva to tell the UN that indigenous communities are wallowing in squalor and that past 'self-determination' policies are to blame[6], while the more extreme Right populist rhetoric of One Nation is more obvious in grasping the moral legitimacy of being the first citizens, which is held by Aborigines and Islanders[7]. The Right now has a reliable little band of newspaper columnists, some of them academics, as well as the journal *Quadrant*, which has been ranting about Aborigines and trying to deny or downplay their pain and history since the former editor was fired some years ago for becoming too sympathetic to indigenous woes. In other words, the national assertiveness that had been growing wholesomely enough in Australia has now become entangled with 'the culture wars' of intellectuals and the wilder perspectives and revisionism of the populist Right.

What Next?

While the newcomers to Australia battle over their visions of who they are, who they were, and who they may become, the indigenous political agenda is evolving more surely. Howard's intransigence over recent years (see especially *The Indigenous World 1998-99*) has in a sense encouraged unity and a more serious focus among Aboriginal leaders on a 'treaty' or whatever such a document or documents might be called[8].

A negotiated process leading to a treaty or similar framework is agreed broadly across the indigenous spectrum, whether ideological or regional. There is now a website[9] and momentum is building. Meanwhile, in regions like Torres Strait, the Cape York Peninsula, and Central Australia, grassroots work in indigenous communities seeking official partners or allies is pushing self-government in a desperate attempt to address the human ills, which government programs have so spectacularly failed to do.

The Howard government has attempted to reject and roll back progress achieved in indigenous rights and policy over the preceding 30 years by governments including the Fraser Liberal government in which Howard was a leading member. Howard, like his hero Margaret Thatcher, believes that society and culture are part of one's childhood, not something understandable in a wider sense.

With the UN world racism summit in South Africa, and the British Commonwealth heads of government meeting (CHOGM) in Brisbane, and a national Australian election sometime during 2001, there will be many contexts in which Aboriginal and Torres Strait Islander grievances and needs will be played out against an intransigent national government.

Notes and References

1   For a general history of this anxiety, see Day D, 1997: *Claiming a Continent: a new history of Australia*, Angus & Robertson (HarperCollins), Sydney. For specific regional histories see Reynolds H, 1987: *The Law of the Land*, Penguin, Melbourne; and Reynolds H, 1995: *Fate of a Free People*, Penguin, Melbourne. Reynolds' other works such as the *Frontier* books are also highly recommended.

2   'Islander' in this report means Torres Strait Islanders specifically, not South Sea Islanders in general.

3   Their media release was euphemistically entitled, 'Improving the Effectiveness of United Nations Committees', and was so obscure in its wording that one would learn little from reading it. The ministers, according to journalists, were extremely embarrassed at their press conference because they knew, presumably, even if the Prime Minister did not, what outrageous nonsense the whole exercise was.

4   For further information see the Reconciliation Process' website: http://www.reconciliation.org.au/

5   Paragraph 2.4.3. of Communiqué, *Federalism Forum*, October 19-20, 2000.

[6]   Such comments show that the Howard government, apart from all else, has no idea what self-determination means. For UN speech see July 29, 1999, Australian government statement delivered by indigenous affairs minister John Herron, online: http://www.atsia.gov.au/fr_press.html

[7]   **Jull P, 2000:** 'Hansonism and Aborigines and Torres Strait Islanders', *The Rise and Fall of One Nation,* ed. M Leach, G Stokes & I Ward, University of Queensland Press, Brisbane, 206-219.

[8]   **Jull P, 2000:** 'Treaty, Yeah, Treaty Now!' *Arena Magazine,* No. 48 (August-September 2000), 20-21.

[9]   http://treatynow.org/

AOTEAROA (NEW ZEALAND)

A general election in late 1999 saw a change of government, with the defeat of the National Party-led coalition. New Zealand's electoral system, with mixed member proportional representation, means it is unlikely that any one political party would ever get enough votes to form a majority government. The centre left Labour Party won the most seats but not enough to form a government. It subsequently formed a coalition government with the left wing Alliance Party. Labour secured victory largely because of the overwhelming support from Maori voters. This support won Labour all 6 seats reserved for Maori in Parliament. In 1996, Labour had lost all Maori seats to the New Zealand First Party after continually taking the Maori vote for granted and selecting poorly performing candidates to contest the election. The mixed member proportional representation system has led to more Maori elected to parliament. There are currently 17 Maori members of parliament, of which 10 are government members.

"Closing the Gaps" Policy

One of the key government election policies was closing the social and economic gaps between Maori and other New Zealanders. In Labour's pre-election policy document, the leader of the opposition, Helen Clark, was unequivocal about the policy:

"My commitment to those policies is absolute. Closing the gaps between Maori and other New Zealanders is a fundamental goal of the new Labour government." [1]

The government even trumpeted its new policy at the meeting of the United Nations Working Group on Indigenous Populations at Geneva in July 2000, saying that:

"A major priority of the new government in New Zealand is to close the gaps between Maori and non-Maori."[2]

The term itself was not new and had in fact been used by the Ministry of Maori Development as part of its monitoring of programmes for Maori during the previous administration. After the election, the Prime Minister Helen Clark confirmed her commitment to the policy and formed a powerful cabinet committee to be headed by her to monitor it. Further, government departments were put on notice that their performance in implementing the policy was going to be monitored and chief executives were going to have performance clauses included in their contracts. The budget earmarked NZ$258 million a year for 4 years to close the gaps[3].

At first there was general support for the programme. However *pakeha* – the Maori term for a New Zealander of European descent - became increasingly alarmed as the government unveiled various affirmative action programmes. Firstly, and most controversially, a government bill to parliament included a provision in new health legislation, which required the law to be interpreted consistently with the Treaty of Waitangi[4]. Many in the public believed that such a clause would give Maori preferential health care. It was amended and clarified but the damage had been done. Other initiatives targeted at Maori included anti-smoking campaigns (a third of all Maori women die from smoking-related diseases), hepatitis B screening programmes, diabetes screening and free contraception advice. The opposition waded in to the debate looking for electoral gain on what it said was racist legislation. The Race Relations Conciliator, an independent statutory body, warned that positive discrimination would incite racial division and resentment. In his annual report to parliament he said:

"People consider that government policies are' pandering' to Maori with more public funds, following large Treaty of Waitangi settlements and affirmative action programme".[5]

He also added that:

"Gap reduction policies would probably have legitimacy in the public perception if they were targeted against poverty, rather than particular ethnic groups." [6]

This had come immediately after the publication of a report by a senior civil servant that said poverty and deprivation were based on class not ethnicity[7]. This seemed to undermine the government's programme of targeting Maori rather than those in poverty. In the face of these reports and public pressure the government retreated, formally abandoning the 'closing the gaps' title. The programme was broadened to include all disadvantaged New Zealanders, not just Maori. In October, the Prime Minister noted that closing the gaps was:

"Not about gaps between Maori and Pacific peoples and others but about poverty."[8]

Treaty of Waitangi Settlement Policy

Another of the government's key election promises to Maori was its Treaty of Waitangi settlement policy for breaches of the Treaty of Waitangi. Its election policy stated that:

"Labour is committed to the Treaty settlement process and is committed to reaching a fair and just settlement on a case by case basis."[9]

Despite 10 years in opposition, it took the incoming government 8 long months to develop and release its policy. This was done without any consultation with Maori. Six key principles were adopted to guide the government in negotiating settlements for breaches of the Treaty of Waitangi. They were:

- Good faith
- Restoration of relationship
- Just redress
- Fairness between claimants
- Transparency
- Direct negotiation with the Crown[10]

Other key principles enunciated were

- The scrapping of the fiscal envelope concept[11].
- Claims to oil and gas and other Crown minerals were ruled out.

- Conservation land (wilderness land) would not be readily available to be returned for Treaty settlements[12].
- A comprehensive review of the Treaty of Waitangi Act, which established the Waitangi Tribunal and was the source of its jurisdiction (to enquire into breaches of the Treaty of Waitangi), was to be undertaken.
- Existing Treaty of Waitangi settlements would be used as benchmarks for future settlements.

Maori were openly critical that the policy was little different from that of previous governments. Given Maori expectations, the policy was underwhelming. One Maori leader summed up the general feeling when he said:

"This is meaningless. It simply means that the status quo remains." [13]

It is understood that the Maori government members were particularly upset about the exclusion of natural resources from Treaty settlements. Tribes with natural resource claims before the Waitangi Tribunal were damning in their condemnation of the policy.

The Ministry of Justice was also directed to develop policy on claims to rivers, lakes and foreshore. This has postponed an inevitable showdown with tribes who have claims to rivers. In 1999, the Waitangi Tribunal released 2 reports on rivers[14]. It found that, under the terms of the Treaty of Waitangi, the tribes were guaranteed full exclusive and undisturbed possession of their traditional properties. The Tribunal found that the tribes had proprietary rights in the rivers akin to ownership rights based both on the Treaty of Waitangi and the common law doctrine of aboriginal title. In both cases, it recommended the Crown pay compensation for the appropriation and use of a resource it did not own. The government refused.

The government also stated that it wanted claimants to enter into direct negotiations with the Crown, bypassing the Waitangi Tribunal which, it said, was too slow. There are currently hundreds of claims waiting to be heard by the Waitangi Tribunal. It does not expect to complete these until 2014.

The government's approach and criticism and the policy to review the Tribunal itself were seen by many as a deliberate attempt to undermine the Tribunal. One of the main reasons for the delays has been the consistent refusal by successive governments to fund the Tribunal at a level necessary to carry out its statutory duties. The Tribunal requested an extra NZ$2 million but this was refused. As a consequence, the number of hearing days was reduced and claims mothballed. This refusal was completely at odds with the government's pre-election promise to:

" Ensure that the Waitangi Tribunal is adequately resourced."[15]

In a speech at a ceremony to celebrate the Tribunal's 25th anniversary (October 2000), Chief Judge Joseph Williams[16] responded to these concerns. He noted that the Tribunal process gave Treaty settlements legitimacy and:

"Enhanced the likelihood of settlement in my experience."

He also noted that the Tribunal needed to be funded to do its job[17].

The Oil and Gas Claim

A Treaty claim[18] was lodged with the Waitangi Tribunal by a tribe in 1999 for the oil and gas beneath its traditional lands. Under current legislation, the Crown owns all minerals. The claim was granted urgency and was set down for a hearing before Chief Judge Williams. However, before the hearing had commenced, the cabinet minister responsible for Crown minerals stated publicly that the claims were:

"A waste of time." [19]

He said that the government would retain ownership irrespective of what the Waitangi Tribunal said[20].

Again, this seemed to fly in the face of its own key principle of good faith.

Judge Williams was not impressed and issued a curt reminder to the government of the constitutional implications of predetermining a case[21].

The question over ownership of natural resources is not one the government is going to be able to put in the 'too hard' basket for much longer. It is sure to test the loyalty and effectiveness of Maori government members of Parliament.

Treaty of Waitangi Settlements

Recently, the crown and the claimants have signed Deeds of Settlement settling 2 land claims on agreed terms[22]. Both followed earlier settlements and an apology was given with cultural address and cash settlements of NZ$2.6 and NZ$15.25 million respectively. Six Heads of Agreements have been signed between the Crown and claimants but are still under negotiation before Deeds of Settlements can be signed. Some 13 claimants are in pre-negotiations and 6 claims are still before the Waitangi Tribunal[23].

Sea Fisheries

In 1992, the government concluded a controversial settlement with Maori negotiators on all Treaty of Waitangi and customary rights over sea fisheries. This was in response to litigation, which threatened the government's fisheries quota scheme as a device to conserve and manage fish stocks. Under the terms of the settlement, the government provided cash to purchase the Sealords Fishing Company, which held 23% of the fisheries quota. This would meet the Crown obligation under the Treaty of Waitangi. The fishing quota would then be allocated to tribes on a basis to be determined by an independent Maori fisheries commission.

However, a number of tribes opposed the settlement and the attendant extinguishment of Treaty and customary rights. They said that the negotiators had no mandate to sign away their rights. Subsequent court action failed to halt the settlement. In 1993 a communication was lodged with the United Nations Human Rights Committee under the Optional Protocol of the Covenant on Civil and Political Rights. In November 2000, the Committee expressed its views that, on the facts, there had been no breach of the Covenant[24].

When a Maori Fisheries Commission was appointed under the 1992 settlement to develop a scheme for distribution of the fish quota to tribes, it was initially thought that this would only take a short time. However, after 8 years of continued and cripplingly expensive litigation, no final allocation has been made. Inter-tribal litigation exists between tribes who want the allocation made on the basis of population and others who want it on the basis of their coastline. To complicate matters further, pan-tribal urban Maori groups have entered the litigation claiming they are a modern manifestation of a tribe and should be allocated a quota. The new Government has appointed new commissioners to reach an acceptable compromise. The millions of dollars spent on litigation demonstrate the dangers of quick-fix global settlements.

Notes and References

1   He Putahitanga Hou - Labour on Maori Development 16 October 2000.
2   New Zealand Statement to the United Nations Working Group on Indigenous Populations, Geneva, 24-28 July 2000.
3   *New Zealand Herald,* 30 December 2000.
4   The Treaty of Waitangi was signed in 1840 by a number of Maori tribes and the British Crown. For an excellent Maori analysis see Tino Rangatiratanga site at http://aotearoa.wellington.net.nz
5   NZPA 25 November 2000.
6   *Ibid.*
7   *Maori Socio-economic Disparity.* Simon Chapple, Department of Labour, 2000.
8   New Zealand Herald 30 December 2000.
9   He Putahitanga Hou *2000:9.*
10 For further details and for an explanation of the term Crown see: www.exective.govt.nz and www.ots.govt.nz
11 The fiscal envelope was introduced in 1994 by the then National Government. It proposed to limit all compensation to Maori for all breaches of the Treaty of Waitangi to NZ$1 billion NZ dollars. This led to unprecedented protests, land occupations and was unanimously rejected by all tribes.
12 This meant that even land confiscated by the government during the land wars in the 1860s in breach of the Treaty of Waitangi would not be returned. Tribes were left landless as a result.
13 Evening Post 21 July 2000.
14 WAI 16: *Whanganui River Report* and WAI 212:*Te Ika Whenua Report.*
15 He Putahitanga Hou 2000.
16 Speech delivered at the 25th anniversary of the Waitangi Tribunal on 11 October. Judge Williams was a very experienced and brilliant Treaty lawyer prior to his elevation to the bench.
17 *Ibid.*
18 WAI 793 Nga Ruahine Oil and Gas claim.
19 *Daily News,* 17 October 2000.
20 The Waitangi Tribunal powers are mostly recommendatory and are only binding in some very limited circumstances.
21 *Dominion,* 18 October 2000.
22 Te Uri o Hau and WAI 33: *Pouakani Report.*
23 See www.ots.govt.nz for further information.
24 Mahuika and others v. New Zealand CCPR/C/70/547/1993.

THE PACIFIC ISLANDS

The year 2000 brought new hope but also challenges for the 5 million indigenous peoples of the Pacific that live scattered over more than 6,000 islands.

Of the 50 island nations of the Pacific, 20 have gained their political independence in recent decades (1960-80s), while the remaining colonies are still struggling for their right to self-determination and independence. But, as can be seen from the following country reports, the plight of the indigenous peoples of the Pacific transcends colonial boundaries and reaffirms the many similarities shared among the numerous islands. Here, three cross-cutting issues should be highlighted:

Women

The issue of violence against indigenous women and sexual abuse of women and children continues to be of growing concern, particularly those in situations of armed conflict. In Bougainville, the Solomon Islands and West Papua women have reported that rape and sexual violence were used against them during the armed conflicts.

Nevertheless, women continue to play a major role in addressing struggles for peace within indigenous communities in the Pacific. Their strength has been visible in promoting peace-building initiatives in situations of political and social unrest, such as those experienced in Bougainville, the Solomon Islands and Fiji. Yet, despite their key role in facilitating the peace process, women continue to be marginalized as participants in the actual negotiations between conflicting parties.

Environment

The increasing strain on the environment in the Pacific today is clearly threatening the very existence of indigenous cultures and communities in the region. The indigenous concept of 'vanua' (land), which is equally shared by all indigenous Pacific communities, maintains that people are inseparable from the environment. As such, the demise of one means an equal fate for the other. In parts of the Pacific, the living spaces, land and waters of indigenous peoples are targeted by industrialised nations for nuclear testing and dumping of radioactive wastes from industrial or military operations. Furthermore, threats posed by natural resource extraction (mining, logging, fishing, coral extraction, etc) on the part of transnational corporations and the emerging effects of climate change and rises in sea level are also having devastating effects on the ecosystems, culture and livelihood of indigenous peoples in the Pacific.

Demilitarisation

Most strategic analysts in the region have noted that the main threat to national security in the Pacific islands is internal rather than external. Military doctrines have turned inwards to deal with threats to the security of the State from: failed politicians and political factions; resource and landowners; indigenous groups and movements for democratic rights. Of equal concern are the sources from which arms are obtained. Soldiers who took over the Fijian Parliament in May 2000 were armed and trained by the very same governments who preached good governance and a return to democracy – Australia, New Zealand, the United States, Britain and France. The 12,000 plus lives lost in Bougainville as well as in the Solomon Islands and Fiji were the result of ammunition ultimately sourced from Australia. The increased militarisation of the Pacific will continue to be a major threat to the social fabric, struggles and value systems of indigenous peoples in the region.

WEST PAPUA

During the year 2000, the indigenous peoples of West Papua consolidated their efforts and activities both nationally and internationally to reaffirm their ultimate goal of independence.

The first West Papuan Congress, held in February 2000, was a landmark in determining the process of uniting the various factions struggling for their self-determination. This Congress reaffirmed its rejection of the outcome of the 1969 Act of Free Choice and reiterated its desire for self-determination. The communiqué stressed the consensus of the Council as follows:

- That it is our desire to choose freedom and to separate from the Republic of Indonesia, as was conveyed to President Habibie and members of his reformation cabinet in January 2000.

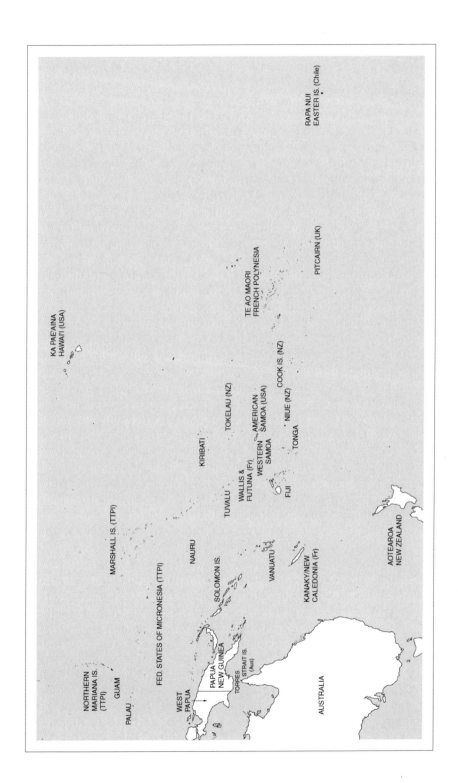

NORTHERN
MARIANA IS.
(TTPI)

GUAM

PALAU

FED. STATES OF MICRONESIA (TTPI)

MARSHALL IS. (TTPI)

NAURU

SOLOMON IS.

WEST
PAPUA

PAPUA
NEW GUINEA

TORRES
STRAIT IS.
(Aus)

VANUATU

KANAKY/NEW
CALEDONIA (Fr)

AUSTRALIA

KIRIBATI

TUVALU

WALLIS &
FUTUNA (Fr)

WESTERN
SAMOA

TOKELAU (NZ)

AMERICAN
SAMOA (USA)

FIJI

TONGA

NIUE (NZ)

COOK IS. (NZ)

KA PAEAINA
HAWAI'I (USA)

TE AO MAORI
FRENCH POLYNESIA

PITCAIRN (UK)

RAPA NUI
EASTER IS. (Chile)

AOTEAROA
NEW ZEALAND

- That we shall pursue dialogue in a peaceful and democratic way in order to secure the agreement of the Indonesian government.

The Congress elected Theys Eluay and Tom Beneal as chief executives of the Papuan Presidium Council. The 18-member Presidium included representatives of churches, women, customary landowners, former political prisoners, students, youth and the professions. A second and much larger Papuan People's Congress was held between 29 May and 4 June 2000 in the capital, Port Numbay (Jayapura). Over 3000 delegates attended, including representatives from central government and provincial administration, Papuan leaders living in exile, supporters of the *Organisasi Papua Merdeka* (OPM) as well as observers from Aceh and Riau. On 4 June 2000, the National Congress issued a Declaration of Independence. Congress leader, Theys Eluay, again reiterated the West Papuan Movement's wish to proceed peacefully towards independence.

Foreign countries, including those who were allowed to attend the Congress as observers, immediately issued statements condemning the declaration of independence and renewing their support to Indonesia. Australia, China, the USA, Japan, the Netherlands and the European Union all said they would not recognize Papuan independence and would not interfere in Indonesia's internal affairs.

However, the Nuclear Free and Independent Pacific (NFIP) Movement, recognizing the genuine aspiration for self-determination of the indigenous peoples of West Papua (April 2000), placed West Papua as its priority campaign on the issue of decolonisation and, in September 2000, the World Council of Churches and the Pacific Conference of Churches Meeting, held in Suva, Fiji, called on the governments of the Pacific to support the re-listing of West Papua on the United Nations list for decolonisation.

Support to West Papua was also stated on several occasions by the President of the Republic of Nauru, Bernard Dowiyogo, and at the United Nations Millennium Summit held in New York in September 2000, both he and Vanuatu's Prime Minister Barak Sope raised the West Papuan issue – the first countries ever to declare support for West Papuan independence at the United Nations.

Nauru's support became visible with the presence of key West Papuan leaders in the official Nauru delegation to the 31st South Pacific Forum in Kiribati in October 2000. It was an historical moment when the Forum passed a resolution on West Papua expressing its "deep concerns about past and recent violence and loss of life in the Indonesian province of Irian Jaya (West Papua)".

By the end of 2000 and the beginning of 2001, new West Papua solidarity groups and networks had been set up everywhere, notably in Australia, New Zealand, the United States and throughout Europe.

In October, the Indonesian government and the military increased their violent and bloody crackdown on West Papuan assertion towards self-determination. Thirty people were killed in riots after police forced down the Morning Star Flag, the Papuan symbol of Independence. A month later, about ten leaders of the West Papua Presidium Council, including the Chairperson, Theys Eluay, were arrested and continue to be detained by the Indonesian authorities without trial.

On December 1, as West Papuans prepared to celebrate the anniversary of the West Papuan Declaration of Independence in 1961, police enforced a ban on raising the Morning Star Flag, in what has been described as a calculated move to heighten tensions. Two policemen and a public servant were killed when independence supporters attacked a police station in response to Indonesian brutality while arresting independence activists. Nearly one hundred people were detained for several days following the attack, with three students killed in custody. At least ten independence supporters were killed in Merauke.

In search of safety, hundreds of West Papuans have crossed over to Papua New Guinea and are being held in church care centres in addition to existing refugee camps. The recent border crossers have not been recognized as refugees and have been brutally treated by the Papua New Guinea security forces. Leaders have been arrested and are awaiting trial in Papua New Guinea.

BOUGAINVILLE

After more than ten rounds of negotiations held throughout the year 2000, a major step forward took place when a referendum on Bougainville's independence was agreed to and finalized in January 2001 between Bougainville leaders and the PNG government.

The war of independence in Bougainville between 1989 and 1998 led to more than 12,000 deaths, in a clash between the Papua New Guinea Government and rebel forces under the Bougainville Revolutionary Army (BRA) and Bougainville interim Government (BIG).

Hundreds of children have been born as a result of the repeated raping of Bougainville women and girls as a weapon of war used by the PNG military forces.

The 1998 Lincoln Agreement initiated a peace process, calling for the gradual withdrawal of Papua New Guinea Defence Force (PNGDF) troops from the island, and the disarming of the BRA and the pro-Papua New Guinea resistance forces. People on Bougainville welcomed the end of the conflict under a Peace Monitoring Group involving Australia, New Zealand, Vanuatu and Fiji. Reconstruction efforts are in progress under the supervision of the South Pacific peacekeeping forces and the United Nations.

However, the total withdrawal of PNG military forces from Bougainville, as scheduled in the Lincoln Agreement, has not happened. As a result, the BRA and resistance forces have not put down their arms, although the BRA has submitted its proposals for a disarmament process to the Peace Process Consultative Committee, which oversees the peace initiatives on the island. Above all, the fundamental issue of self-determination has not been resolved.

In March 2000, what seemed to be a breakthrough in the peace talks later turned into another deadlock. PNG Foreign Affairs Minister, Sir Michael Somare, and Bougainvillean representatives (Leitana Council of Elders Joel Banam, Bougainville Governor John Momis and the BPC President Kabui) signed the Loloata Understanding. This included a commitment from the PNG Government to change PNG's constitution to allow a high degree of autonomy for Bougainville. But the PNG cabinet later reiterated its opposition to an independence option, which has since remained the major sticking point.

Speaking on the March 2000 talks, BPC international spokesperson, Moses Havini, expressed concern saying, "There is nothing in the understanding that pins PNG down to a fixed timetable or commitment to a level of autonomy or even when autonomy might be achieved. Acknowledging an 'aspiration' is a far cry from responding to those 'aspirations' . . . ."

In September 2000, Bougainville leaders and PNG officials praised another breakthrough in peace negotiations that saw an agreement towards a constitutional framework for a referendum on independence. This referendum, which must include the option of independence for the island – will be held no sooner than 10 years and no later than 15 years after the election of an autonomous government, expected in January 2002. Also under the agreement was the requirement that the Bougainville fighters hand over the weapons they have held since the late 1980s. But the BRA continues to question why the PNG government will not commit to do the same. However, joint leaders of the negotiating team emphasized that a breakthrough was only possible because both sides had been willing to compromise.

On 9 March 2001, peace talks re-convened in Port Moresby to revisit autonomy issues. With more than 20 representatives from Bougainville, as well as government officials and United Nations Executives, the meeting discussed areas of agreement as well as those that needed further negotiations. The issues relate to the kind of powers the State will have as opposed to what will be given to Bougainville. This will form the basis of a constitution to enable Bougainville to operate an autonomous government. However, critical issues that still need to be thrashed out include courts and judicial review, revenue-raising powers, human rights, foreign aid, intergovernmental relations, public administration and fiscal accountability. Furthermore, Bougainville women who were raped and used as weapons of war in the 10-year conflict continue to voice their frustration at the lack of justice in addressing the violations committed against them.

The question now is exactly which critical areas the Bougainville people will have full autonomy over.

THE SOLOMON ISLANDS

S ince 1998, the Solomon Islands has experienced a crisis that has threatened its very existence as a nation. The root cause of the crisis has been described in some quarters as ethnic differences between the peoples of Guadalcanal and Malaita.

The root causes of this crisis go far beyond this and can be found in the poor policies of successive governments, weak and ineffective structures and systems of government, poorly planned large-scale resource development, the inequitable distribution of development benefits and the need for institutional and constitutional change. The ethnic explanation alone is too simplistic and is unable to explain the causes of the conflict or contribute to its resolution.

Socio-economic and Political Issues

At independence on 7 July 1978, Solomon Islanders were faced with the daunting task of forging a national sentiment out of diverse societies: the Solomon population spoke over eighty-seven languages. Apart from issues of nationalism, the economy was dependent on the exploitation of natural resources by foreign companies and infrastructure development concentrated around Honiara, the national capital.

Honiara was also where most of the formal employment opportunities were concentrated, while Isabel, Makira/Ulawa, Temotu and Malaita Provinces accounted for 49% of the country's population, and only 15% of formal sector employment.

The distribution of benefits accrued from natural resource development became an issue in the decades following independence; natural resources were rapidly being depleted but not for the welfare of those who own them but to finance a government system.

Related to these developments was the issue of land. In the past decades, many Guadalcanal people (predominantly men) sold customary land around Honiara to people from other provinces. This was in spite of Guadalcanal's matrilineal society where females are the custodians of land. Furthermore, many individuals were selling land without consulting other members of their *laen* (tribe). This often caused conflicts within land-owning groups and between them and the new "owners". The sale of land has, over the years, been resented by women and a younger generation of Guadalcanal people who view the act as a sale of their "birth right".

In the 1980s and 1990s, the country's deteriorating economy saw the government accumulating debts well over its ability to repay. This was due partly to poor management practices such as uncontrolled spending and non-collection of revenue. The period also witnessed substantial fraud by public servants and huge amounts of money were given to members of parliament through the Constituency Development Fund (CDF). Consequently, a majority of the country's population suffered; a few became very rich at the expense of nation-wide development.

Since independence, there have been concerns that the provincial system of government was expensive and ineffective. In the report of the 1987 Constitutional Review Committee (CRC), one of the major recommendations was the establishment of a federal system of government. This, however, was ignored by successive governments.

Another issue raised by the 1987 CRC report was that relating to the freedom of movement and settlement. Although the Solomon Islands Constitution guarantees to every person the "freedom of movement . . . [which] . . . means the right to move freely throughout Solomon Islands, the right to reside in any part of Solomon Islands . . ." the CRC report highlighted the need to control the movement

Northern part of Papua New Guinea. Photo: Palle Kjærulff Schmidt

Man decorated for a sing-sing *tribal ritual. Highland, Papua New Guinea. Photo: Palle Kjærulff Schmidt*

and settlement of people. On Guadalcanal, the issues of migration and settlement were compounded because of the rapid growth of Honiara and the expansion of squatter settlements in areas around Honiara.

Another 1990s phenomenon, which goes a long way towards explaining the Guadalcanal crisis, was the Bougainville migration. Upwards of 9,000 Bougainvilleans fled to the Solomon Islands with the vast majority of them settling in Guadalcanal for long periods of time. They have definitely influenced Solomon Islanders.

But, the highlight of the 1990s was the 1997 national election. For the first time in the country's electoral history, voters dismissed more than half of the sitting parliamentarians. The election results sent a strong message to politicians that people would no longer accept "business as usual." They were demanding change, and quickly.

The Current Crisis

From early 1998 to late 1999, tensions between Guadalcanal people and Malaita settlers escalated to a stage where at least 50 people were killed and more than 20,000 people (mostly Malaitans) forced out of settlements on Guadalcanal, especially in areas around Honiara.

Throughout 1999, there were also continuous confrontations between the Royal Solomon Islands Police and the Guadalcanal militants, the Isatabu Freedom Movement (IFM). By April 2000, about thirteen IFM members had been killed by the police. The movement quickly attracted supporters from all over the island.

By the beginning of 2000, a group claiming to represent displaced Malaitans was formed and called itself the Malaita Eagle Force (MEF). This group's concerns centred around demands for compensation of properties damaged and destroyed by the IFM, the killing of Malaitans and the protection of Malaitan interests in Honiara.

The Search for Peace

Since early 1999, a number of attempts have been made to bring an end to the crisis. These processes involve attempts to address the underlying issues of the crisis and to deal with the demands of the various parties.

These attempts at resolution have included a *kastom* (custom) feast ceremony and five "peace talks" that have resulted in the signing of various documents: the Honiara Peace Accord (28 June 1999), the

Panatina Agreement (12 August 1999), the Buala Peace Conference (4 - 5 May 2000), the Auki Peace talks (9-10 May 2000), the Solomon Islands National Peace Conference (25-27 August 2000), and the Townsville Peace Agreement (9-15 October 2000).

If anything positive is to come out of the talks, all the parties involved in the crisis must be represented and the underlying socio-economic and political issues must be addressed. Furthermore, there is a need to look beyond ethnicity. We must explore the socio-economic and political issues that underlie the issues raised by the various actors in the crisis. In a way, there is legitimacy in many of the issues raised by Malaitans, Guadalcanal and others who are involved. Ethnicity is merely the avenue through which people's frustration becomes manifested.

KANAKY (NEW CALEDONIA)

The Government of New Caledonia has been working towards implementing the content of the Noumea Accord signed in May 1998 between the pro-independence coalition FLNKS (Front de Libération Nationale Kanak et Socialiste), the anti-independence majority RPCR (Rassemblement Pour la Calédonie dans la République) and the French government.

Although all parties to the Accord agreed on the principle of rebalancing the economy of the country and promoting greater participation of the indigenous Kanak people in the local economy, the Accord has already come under criticism from both member and non-member parties to the Accord. The French Government has been criticised by both major parties to the Accord for not playing its role as arbitrator in the implementation of the Agreement.

In a statement to the United Nations Special Committee on Decolonisation at the Pacific Regional Seminar 2000 in Majuro (Marshall Islands), the FLNKS representative raised concerns about power sharing within the New Caledonian Government, highlighting the failure on the part of the RPCR majority to release vital information to the opposition. The FLNKS questioned further the genuine commitment of the French Government to ensure the implementation of a genuine process of decolonisation for the indigenous Kanak.

The Social Pact

In addition to the difficulties of operating these newly established political institutions, Kanaky/New Caledonia has also been destabilised by significant events reflecting social disparity between the different communities.

In the lead up to the signing of the "Social Pact" by the local government and employers' organisations on October 20, numerous workers' strikes and factory seizures disrupted the fragile economy of the country. The pact was signed after extensive public debate started with its release in August. But some unions refused to sign the 20-page agreement; Union Syndicale des Travailleurs Kanak et Exploités (USTKE) described it as deceitful.

However, other parties saw it as a stabilising factor after many months of strikes and industrial unrest. It sets out conflict resolution procedures and compulsory "preventive" dialogue where strike actions threaten and requires five days' notice of a strike.

A key provision was that the country's minimum wage would rise to CFP Fr 100,000 per month within two years. However, in November a renewed attack on the pact was launched by a group of unions headed by Soenc-mines. They closed down the nickel mine in Kouaoua, disrupted others and organised a largely successful general strike on November 16. Next morning, the unionists positioned roadblocks on main roads in Noumea, disrupted the busiest highway intersection on the main island and pelted security forces with paving stones.

By afternoon, however, the troubles were over and the militants had won a new wage deal. On December 28, the government approved the new wages legislation.

On the Political Front

As a result of an unexpected coalition between anti-independence forces and pro-independence moderate parties within the new government, the political panorama has changed. In addition to such an unexpected coalition, Union Calédonienne (UC), the major party within the FLNKS faced serious divisions within its ranks.

In April, seven members of the New Caledonia Congress who were identified as FLNKS reverted to their UC identity, saying the decision did not affect UC's position within the FLNKS but would give the party an identifiable voice and role within the Congress. The breakaway group say they reaffirm the goal of UC and FLNKS to take the country to independence.

TE AO MAOHI (FRENCH POLYNESIA)

In French Polynesia, the debate over expected amendments to the French Constitution to allow the country greater autonomy and self-government is still high on the agenda of political parties. Like Kanaky/New Caledonia, the commitment of the French Government towards emancipation of the indigenous Maohi peoples in Te Ao Maohi remains questionable.

Although France has ended nuclear testing on Moruroa and Fangataufa atolls since 1995, the legacy of French nuclear colonialism in Polynesia is still very much alive in the minds of the Maohi people. A growing campaign for the opening of military archives related to the nuclear era in French Polynesia is drawing increasing support within the region and beyond.

Initiated by local Non-Government Organisations (NGOs) and Church groups, the call for transparency over the testing of nuclear devices in French Polynesia is also echoed by parliamentarians in France and international organisations in Europe and around the world. The petition for opening the archives is based on eyewitness testimony of former test-site workers published in "Moruroa & Us" (1997) as the result of a sociological survey carried out by local NGOs and the Evangelical Church of French Polynesia with support from other organisations in Europe. But, to discredit the testimony of the victims of nuclear tests, the Ministry of Defence manipulated the findings of an uncompleted epidemiological study conducted in 1998 by INSERM, and thus discharged the Board of the Centre d'Expérimentation Nucléaire (Centre for Nuclear Testing) of any responsibility in current serious health problems in French Polynesia.

In January 2000, replying to Emile Vernaudon - a Member of Parliament from French Polynesia who advocates the opening of the archives - Minister for Defence Alain Richard stated that France would not lift the "Defence Code" seal over the 193 nuclear tests carried out on the atolls of Moruroa and Fangataufa between July 1966 and January 1996. But documents unsealed by the "Defence Code" reveal that the tests had not been conducted under safe conditions for the people of French Polynesia or their environment.

The Jospin government recently approved a request from the Parliamentary Commission of Investigation into the massacres in Rwanda. In the light of such a precedent, the opening of military archives can no doubt be extended to the question of nuclear testing in French Polynesia.

In 2000, *the Comité de Suivi Moruroa e Tatou* ("Moruroa and Us" Follow up Committee) was established as an independent organisation operating with the formal support of the Evangelical Church of French Polynesia. Members of the Committee are rooted in civil organisations in Polynesia. The Committee is now playing an important role with the former test site workers, who want to establish a recognised committee to raise their concerns. During the year, the Committee attended meetings in Europe and lobbied French parliamentarians to support their call for opening the archives on nuclear testing.

The campaign has won support abroad and is networking with former nuclear test veterans, for example in Fiji and New Zealand. The Committee also initiated dialogue with the Ministry of Defence on the call to open the archives and has launched a postcard campaign to support their lobbying. A major activity of the Committee is to translate into *Reo' Maohi* the testimony of former test site workers published in "Moruroa and Us".

TOKELAU

The small island group of Tokelau has a population of approximately 4000 persons, 1400 located in Tokelau with a total land area of 12 square kilometres split into three atolls and the remaining 2,600 based mainly in New Zealand, Samoa and Hawaii.

Tokelau is one of the seventeen countries on the list of non-self-governing territories with the UN Special Committee on Decolonisation and is working towards self-governance and independence. In recent years, there has been a process to devolve powers from New Zealand to the people of Tokelau.

In forging Tokelauan nationhood, the village is the foundation of authority. The Village Council of Elders is the central authority in government, not some distant colonial administration located in Apia or Wellington (NZ). The Modern House of Tokelau is the initiative that will bring Tokelau that much closer to exercising its right to an act of self-determination.

The strong wish of the leadership of Tokelau (both traditional and modern) is for the UN Special Committee on Decolonisation to continue to have a presence beyond the year 2000.

Tokelau seeks to discuss further with its administering power a Comprehensive Plan outlining the major development components to be achieved and settled before a specific timetable for self-determination is considered. Of major concern to Tokelau at the present moment is its need for future economic survival. Accessing major funding resources to develop fisheries as the main natural resource and meet other priorities such as sea walls has proven difficult and the same applies to accessing funds from the international community for infrastructure development. Being a territory with extremely limited natural resources, the question of self-determination is difficult when one has to rely on meagre resources. If Tokelau gains self-determination tomorrow, it will not have the economic means to survive.

Tokelau, however, is seeking to reclaim land that will extend its Exclusive Economic Zone and preserve its culture and economy. A crucial concern is the return of Swains Island (Tokehega), which was granted to American Samoa in an agreement between New Zealand and the United States. Tokelau has cited external documents that support this claim. This is an issue of great pain to Tokelau. It is also an issue that could relieve the pressures on and the need for fertile land to grow food, the production of copra as well as untold marine resources.

Tokelauans see themselves as a unique people trying to survive. They are weak and need the support of the international community - both material and moral.

FIJI

Lead-Up to Coup of May 19th 2000

The revival of the Taukei Movement (TM) in Fiji in April 2000 heralded the political upheavals that Fiji continues to face to date. The TM is an indigenous nationalist movement that was instrumental in the political processes and actions that led towards the 1987 coups. It was revived with a public vow by one of its leaders, veteran politician Apisai Tora, that the Labour party-led People's Coalition government of Mahendra Chaudry would be overthrown. Tora said that Chaudry's actions and statements since taking office in May 1999 had been offensive to indigenous Fijian institutions and that Chaudry was literally inviting a coup. He said that the aim of the TM was also to change the 1997 Constitution to ensure Fijian political paramountcy. The Fiji Military Forces immediately issued a statement saying they would not be party to any attempt to overthrow the government.

The first TM's march against Chaudry's government was held on 20 April 2000 at Lautoka (Fiji's second largest city) with a turnout of 300 people. A week later, there was a bigger turnout with a protest march through Suva of about 5,000 supporters.

The main opposition party, Soqosoqo Vakavulewa ni Taukei (SVT), formerly led by coup leader and former Prime Minister Sitiveni Rabuka but now headed by one of the founders of the TM in 1987, Ratu Inoke Kubuabola, strongly supported the revival of the TM and planned activities. Chaudry's government maintained that the SVT was endorsing an extremist nationalist policy with the TM in order to regain its former political status. It said such extreme racial politics had no place in Fiji's multi-racial and multi-cultural society.

On 28-29 April 2000, the Bose Levu Vakaturaga or Great Council of Chiefs (BLV/GCC) met on the future of the Agricultural Landlord and Tenants Act (ALTA), which regulates leases to largely Indian tenants on indigenous-owned land. An amicable settlement to ALTA is seen as crucial to economic and political stability in Fiji as it directly affects the vital sugarcane industry. Most Fijian provincial councils have called for the scrapping of ALTA, to be replaced by the Native Land Trust Act (NLTA). In response, Chaudry's government stated that they would like to retain ALTA, which angered many chiefs and Fijian landowners.

The Opposition SVT Party and NLTA's Board (NLTB) also attacked the $28,000 cash payment made by Chaudry's government to cane farmers whose land leases had not been renewed, while landowners were provided $10,000 in assistance for land rehabilitation. Chaudry's government explained that $28,000 is the cost of resettling a tenant farmer, and is a one-off payment for the rest of their lives. The $10,000 for landowners is a form of affirmative action and designed to help them farm their own land.

Then there was the issue of the deal being negotiated by the government over the harvest and marketing of Fiji's rich mahogany plantations. While no deal was signed, the government was under attack for the way it conducted the negotiations. The US government accused the Fiji government of deceiving them, an American consortium said it would take the government to court for defamation, and the NLTB and landowners jointly accused the Government of lack of consultation.

Armed Takeover

Against this backdrop, on 19 May 2000, seven armed gunmen led by failed businessman George Speight stormed Parliament House whilst it was in session, and took Prime Minister Mahendra Chaudry, his Cabinet and members into hostage. The attempted coup happened exactly one year after the Labour party-led People's Coalition Government came to power.

The armed take-over coincided with a march by around 5,000 supporters of the Nationalist Party and the TM through the streets of Suva. Members of the take-over gang were later identified as soldiers of the elite First Meridian Squadron, the military's Counter-Revolutionary Warfare Unit established after the 1987 coups.

Participants at the march were largely unaware of the armed take-over. When informed of the take-over, the marchers immediately set off for Parliament. As news of the armed take-over spread through Suva, businesses began closing shops and left for home. It is believed that groups of criminals began smashing shop windows and looting. As this continued without police intervention, many bystanders joined in the rampage and took items at will. Suva quickly turned into a scene of all-out looting. People returning from work and school children were soon involved as whole supermarkets and shops were emptied, windows broken and the burning of buildings started. The helpless police could only watch. Fire services tried to stop the blaze from spreading. The looting continued for almost three hours before the Police organised, regrouped and began to stop the carnage, and arrest the looters. Police reported that 16 shops were burnt and over 160 looted within the vicinity of Suva, with damage estimated at between F$30-60 million.

Wrangle between Speight's Taukei Civilian Government and Ratu Sir Kamisese Mara

At his first media conference, Speight stated that he had abrogated the 1997 Constitution, and made himself head of state "by the will of the people of Fiji". He said he was acting on behalf of all indigenous people in Fiji and that they were one hundred per cent behind him.

On Saturday 20 May 2000, the partially military-backed civilian coup instigators announced Ratu Jope Seniloli as President of the self-proclaimed "Taukei civilian Government". Speight was sworn in as interim Prime Minister and his Cabinet was comprised of 13 others from the SVT Party, the Fiji Alliance Party and the Nationalist Party.

A state of emergency was imposed by the then President, Ratu Sir Kamisese Mara. Immediately the army, police and civil service rallied behind him. The BLV/GCC was convened a few days later and, together with the military, negotiations immediately began with Speight for the release of parliamentarians.

Speight insisted that the 1997 Constitution, the President and Prime Minister should all be removed. The BLV/GCC meeting from 23-25 May 2000 gave its full support to Ratu Sir Kamisese as President, and its blessing to his appointment of an interim administration. Speight rejected the BLV's/GCC's ten point resolution to resolve the political impasse.

Ratu Sir Kamisese Mara, quoting from Section 106 (1) of the Constitution (Amendment) Act of 1997 prorogued Parliament and then appointed Ratu Tevita Moemoedonu, a member of Mr. Chaudry's Cabinet, as the interim Prime Minister. Rt. Tevita Momoedonu was amongst the few parliamentarians who were not present in the House of Representatives on the day of the coup. Both Speight and the Labour Party denounced this move.

Military Rule and Negotiations with Speight

In a move to find a quick solution to the political impasse, Ratu Sir Kamisese Mara, after being approached by a group of senior military officers and after a short Fijian traditional ceremony, was "set aside" from the office of President to allow the military to take full control of matters in the country. The Fiji Military Forces claimed they did this in a bid to maintain security in the country. On 29 May 2000, Commodore Ratu Voreqe Bainimarama declared martial law and the military later issued a decree abrogating the Constitution (Amendment) Act of 1997 and a second decree allowing all laws to continue unless modified (Decrees No.1 and 2).

In spite of the above moves from the military, Speight continued to make more demands. The Commodore reaffirmed that amnesty was granted to Speight and the seven men who stormed the Parliament but the amnesty did not include immunity from criminal activities or the murder of a police officer.

Amidst all this, the economic crisis began to escalate, with a thousand garment industry workers being laid off, more professional people migrating from the country, the tourist industry suffering a 60% drop in bookings and trade bans being imposed by the Australian Council of Trade Unions and the Solomon Islands Council of Trade Unions. Schools on the main islands of Vanua Levu and Viti Levu and the University of the South Pacific were closed early, a rugby tour to New Zealand by a Fiji Under 21 rugby group was called off following the refusal of the New Zealand government to grant them visas, the public service commission announced that they had taken a 20% pay cut across the board and a couple of overseas governments recalled their students through security fears. On 7 June 2000, Fiji was suspended from the Commonwealth.

Governance with the Support of the Fiji Military Forces

With negotiations on the release of parliamentarians still continuing, the military announced a 17 member interim civilian administration led by Laisenia Qarase, with Ratu Epeli Nailatikau as Deputy Prime Minister and Minister for Foreign Affairs.

On 18 July 2000 (five days after the release of all remaining parliamentarians by Speight), Ratu Josefa Iloilo, following the endorsement of the BLV/GCC, was sworn in as the new interim Head of State and President by the military. A few days later, a second interim civilian government led by Laisenia Qarase was appointed. The second interim administration was made up of 24 Fijians, one Rotuman, one Indian and two part Europeans. There were five women in the new line-up, with one holding a substantive Ministerial position and the remaining four holding Assistant Ministers' positions.

One of the first items of business dealt with by the second Interim Administration was to seek the approval of the BLV/GCC for a ten-year development plan for Fijians and Rotumans and the revision of the Constitution (Amendment) Act of 1997. The BLV/GCC approved the formulation of a blueprint of actions.

The blueprint of action is aimed at enhancing Fijian and Rotuman interests and touches on issues such as agriculture, education, business, land ownership and leases. In a submission made by the Interim Administration its aim was stated as being to promulgate a revised constitution by 2001 and to hold general elections no less than a year after that. In his submission, Qarase announced that the new constitution would have three main objectives:

a) To address the concerns and aspirations of Fijians and secure paramountcy of their interests, which was derived from the Deed of Cession of 1874;
b) To provide a framework of good governance in Fiji including equal rights and freedoms for all citizens and groups, the rule of law and an independent judiciary, and a Parliament representative of all communities in Fiji; and
c) To put in place a constitution that will provide the framework for the communities in Fiji to work together and to promote national unity.

The blueprint had been described by certain groups within the community as racist but Qarase called on his critics to understand indigenous concerns and assured other races that they would be catered for. Critics of the planned constitutional review had also argued that this undertaking could only be decided by a group of elected representatives.

The continuing lawless actions following the release of hostages, especially the taking over of Korovou town (where Speight comes from), incidents of violence and the looting of property experienced by Indian rural communities, the detention of 400 Indians in Labasa and several roadblocks all culminated in the detention of George Speight and three of his closest confidantes by the military on 26 July 2000. The following day, during an early morning military ambush, 369 civilian supporters of Speight were taken in and detained at the Nasinu Police Station. Speight and twelve others were refused bail by the court and jointly charged with: consorting with people carrying firearms and ammunition, unlawful burial at the Parliamentary complex, unlawful assembly at Parliament and unlawful assembly at Kalabu Fijian Primary School to purposefully cause instability in the country. They remain imprisoned on Nukulau Island (off the coast of Suva).

Path towards Constitutional Law

In September 2000, Interim Prime Minister Qarase told the UN General Assembly that he would restore democratic rule within two years. He set up a Constitutional Review Commission with the task of reviewing the 1997 Constitution.

On 2 November 2000, armed counter revolutionaries began an onslaught on the Fiji Military Headquarters in Nabua, with random shooting. A heated exchange of gunfire ensued, killing eight soldiers (three loyal to Commodore Bainimarama and five from the mutineers) and wounding twenty-eight. Details of the mutiny stunned the nation, especially the indigenous Fijians, who hold the army in high regard and who have had a long-standing belief that the army (predominantly comprised of indigenous Fijians) is there to protect indigenous interests and would never turn on their own people.

On November 15 2000, a High Court Justice, Anthony Gates, ruled that the Constitution (Amendment) Act of 1997 remains the supreme law of the country after a farmer, Mr. Chandrika Prasad, sought justice from the Courts. Prasad and his family had been attacked by indigenous Fijians on their farm, their animals slaughtered and their property burned. Justice Gates also ruled that the former President (Ratu Sir Kamisese Mara) was still President and that Parliament should be reconvened for the appointment of a new Prime Minster. The Interim administration immediately sought an appeal on this decision from the Appeal Court.

Justice Sir Maurice Casey, who headed the Appeal Court, ruled that Gates' judgement "does not have any legally coercive effect" and agreed that the interim government should be allowed to present evidence it was unable to present before Justice Anthony Gates. On 1st March 2001 and in a landmark ruling, Justice Sir Maurice Casey, declared in the Court's judgement that:

a) The 1997 Constitution was still the supreme law of the country and had not been abrogated;
b) Parliament had not been dissolved but prorogued on May 27, 2000;
c) The office of the President became vacant on December 15, 2000 when Ratu Sir Kamisese Mara resigned. In accordance with Section 88 of the Constitution (Amendment) Act of 1997, the Vice-President may perform the functions of the President until March 15, 2001;
d) The State was to pay $50,000 to cover costs incurred by Mr. Prasad's legal team.

Immediately after the judgement, Ratu Iloilo called himself "Acting President" to show his compliance with the decision. He was supported by the BLV/GCC to continue as President with Ratu Jope Seniloli as Vice-President. Qarase at first resigned but was eventually reappointed for the third time to the position of interim Prime Minister. Mr. Qarase has not made any major changes to his Cabinet line-up from the second interim administration (28 members) but has been reported in an interview as saying that he will be proposing additional Indo-Fijians.

Future Challenge

The political crisis is not a simple clash between Indo-Fijians and Fijians. There is conflict within the communities as well as between them. Evidence has shown that the views of indigenous Fijians are polarised. There are those that see the situation as one of indigenous Fijians standing up with force and violence to assert their rights. There are those who see the situation as one of certain politicians and political parties using racist and nationalist sentiments to get back into power after being toppled in the May 1999 general elections by

Chaudry and his multi-racial Coalition government. There is also the subtle but prominent presence of provincialism, between the East, West and North of Fiji and between the three confederacies of Burebasaga, Kubuna and Tovata. And there are disagreements and crisis within Fijian political leadership and also amongst the chiefs, who have different views. There is the view of Fijian political dominance as a necessity and there is the view that that Fiji cannot move forward with racism or any semblance of first and second-class citizens.

Indo-Fijians are as much divided, as witnessed by the hostility with which many particularly viewed Chaudry's largely Labour-backed government.

There is also the element of militarisation in Fijian society. Events of 1987 and May 2000 could set off a dangerous precedent where guns and violence become the fashionable way of resolving differences. "No Other Way", the phrase Rabuka used to describe the motive of the two 1987 coups, is becoming popular.

The challenge for Fiji, which many had hoped was addressed in the internationally acclaimed 1997 Constitution, is how to balance indigenous rights and aspirations with democratic principles of equal rights and justice. Many of the problems Fiji is facing now are a result of colonialism, mismanagement of native land leases and also of indigenous rights, governance and justice in modern times. Finding a solution will not be easy but one will have to be found. The question Fiji must ask is what type of society it aspires to have and how to achieve it.

TONGA

In Tonga, the movement for democracy and change is gathering increasing support from within and outside the kingdom. As Tonga's Human Rights and Democracy Movement (THRDM) activist, Akilisi Pohiva confirmed, the movement will continue to pressure the government and the monarchy to push for a referendum for changes to the Constitution. THDRM will continue to push for dialogue and discussion with the Tongan government and the monarchy to effect the two major changes recommended.

Recommended Changes to the Constitution

The first recommendation calls for greater power sharing in the kingdom's administration. Furthermore, it is recommended that all thirty members of the Parliament be elected and that the monarch chooses his 12 Cabinet Ministers from the 30 elected people. This is contrary to the current Constitution, which provides for 9 members elected by the people, 9 nobles elected by other nobles, and 12 Cabinet Ministers appointed for life by the monarchy.

There has been no official response from the government since 1998 when the draft constitution was submitted to the cabinet. The Tongan Government turned down a further request from the movement for a national referendum to coincide with the last general election. The pro-democracy movement in Tonga also called on the nobles to share some of the benefits of the land with the people. To date, a major part of the land is still administered by nobles, who get the full benefit of land rentals and leases.

Overseas missions' representatives based in Tonga, e.g. New Zealand, Australia and Britain, have indicated changes in their stance and pledged support to the Tonga Human Rights Democracy Movement by not funding all of the government's activities put before them.

Environment and Resources Protection

In addition to campaigning and lobbying for constitutional change, the Tonga Human Rights and Democracy Movement is also active on issues of environment and resource protection. Following the groundbreaking discovery of hundreds of unknown marine organisms in the Tonga Trench by scientists from Australia and France, the THRDM called on the government of Tonga to claim ownership over marine organisms. As stated by Mr. Senituli from the THRDM, "It is absolutely essential that the government stakes its claim to ownership over these marine organisms now. In fact, the Government and the people of Tonga should have the naming rights over these new organisms since they are found inside Tonga's legal boundaries."

Under the World Trade Organization, the United Nations Convention on Biological Diversity (CBD) and the United Nations Law of the Sea Convention, the government of Tonga has rights of ownership over natural resources, including flora and fauna, found inside its geographical and legal jurisdiction.

Blood Sampling as Bio-piracy

The Tonga Human Rights and Democracy Movement condemned an agreement signed between the Tongan government and an Australian biotechnology corporation Autogene, to collect blood samples from Tongan nationals. The agreement, concluded without extensive public debate, opens the way for the commercialisation and patenting of DNA and genetic material.

Bio-piracy is not new in the Pacific. In 1992, the US Department of Commerce filed a patent claim over the human T-cell lines of a 40-year-old woman from a Western Province and a 58-year-old man from Guadalcanal in the Solomon Islands. Again in 1993, the US Department of Health and Human Services and the National Institute of Health laid claims over T-cell lines of 24 peoples from the Hagahai Tribe in Papua New Guinea.

More recently, an agreement was reached between the administration of the Norfolk Islands and Griffith University in Australia for DNA research on the island.

Asian Migrants

The only kingdom in the Pacific is faced with problem of Asian migrants displacing the Tongans from their economic and commercial activities. According to the Ministry of Labour and Commerce, there are 849 retail outlets on Tongatapu, the capital island, 67 of which are owned by Chinese migrants, and another 31 by Tongans but now operated by Chinese migrants.

According to Mr. Senituli, "The small retail shop is the final link between the manufacturer, the importer wholesaler and the consumer. Their owners are the human face of the retail industry, for they meet the consumers everyday and they know and understand all their family, social and financial problems. The Tongan small retail shops are not simply for buying and selling of goods. They are also waiting rooms for those who are in need of social, communal and financial assistance. On top of that the families of the owners of the small retail shops are usually the highest contributors to the 'fonua', the church and family activities. As such the small retail shops are an integral part of our social, economic and cultural system. The question is whether the Asian small retail shop owners can fulfil that role?"

Children ready for dance, Te Ao Maori, French Polynesia. Photo: Palle Kjærulff Schmidt

Women with tuna fish, Tonga. Photo: Palle Kjærulff Schmidt

MARSHALL ISLANDS

M arch 1ˢᵗ marks the annual celebration of Nuclear Victims' Memorial Day in the Marshall Islands. This year, emphasis was placed on declassified materials documenting the effects of radiation beyond the four atolls (Bikini, Enewetak, Rongelap, and Utrik) recognized in the Compact of Free Association. According to US Center for Disease Control (CDC) documents, Ailuk atoll contains the single largest source of atmospherically-released iodine 131 in the world (MI, 8 Aug 1998, 1, 5). Additionally the Center for Disease Control recommends that Ailuk, Jemo, Likiep, Wotho, and Wotje receive compensation for exposure to fallout from the Bravo test of 1954. Studies such as these will be used to argue a "changed circumstances" case in the upcoming compact negotiations. The changed circumstances clause of the compact allows for a reassessment of compensation if new evidence shows the current agreement is inadequate.

Kwajalein Missile Tests

The Pacific Concerns Resource Centre (PCRC) has criticised the continuation of US missile tests at Kwajalein Atoll in the Marshall Islands, saying the latest failed test highlights the folly of the new arms race in space.

Each anti-ballistic missile test at Kwajalein Atoll costs US$100 million dollars. The overall cost of the National Missile Defense system will be US$60 billion - money that could be put to better purposes, stated the Pacific Concerns Resource Centre (PCRC) in Suva, Fiji Islands.

On 8 July, the US military tested its National Missile Defence (NMD) system in the central Pacific. A missile fired from Vandenberg Air Force Base in California released a mock nuclear warhead over the Pacific Ocean. Another missile launched from Meck Island in Kwajalein Atoll attempted - and failed - to shoot the warhead from the sky. This Exoatmospheric Kill Vehicle failed to separate from the booster rocket, and the whole device completely missed the incoming target. A similar test in January 2000 had also failed. The NMD tests are part of a US effort to develop a new Star Wars system and the US government will soon make a decision on whether to deploy the weapons system.

The Marshall Islands government is currently asking the United States to pay extra compensation to Marshall Islanders who were irradiated by 67 US nuclear tests at Bikini and Enewetak atolls between 1946-1958. How can the US government justify this expensive missile-testing program when it refuses to face its responsibility for past nuclear tests? The Nuclear Claims Tribunal in the Marshall Islands has promised compensation to hundreds of Marshallese affected by the US nuclear tests at Bikini and Enewetak. But over one third of those due to receive compensation from the US government died before full payment could be made.

Economic Renegotiations

If the Federated States of Micronesia and the Marshall Islands leaders were anticipating tough economic renegotiations with the US, they received confirmation late last year that it was going to be an uphill battle to secure anything close to the level of funding the Americans have provided for the first 15 years of the Compact of Free Association. The Compact's economic provisions expire in October – with a two-year period of grace during which funding is guaranteed in case, as is likely, negotiations can not be wrapped up by the end of 2001.

The approximately $2.5 billion ($1 billion to Marshall Islands, $1.5 billion to Federated States of Micronesia) provided by Washington, "led to little improvement in economic development," according to a detailed General Accounting Office (GAO) report in September. It is a contention that most island leaders dispute, but the GAO report is giving ammunition to American Congressmen who want to slash funding to the two central Pacific nations. Thus representatives Doug Bereuter (R-Nebraska) and Don Young (R-Alaska) in an "op ed" column in the *Marshall Islands Journal* in mid-December stated that, while some of the responsibility lay with the US, the underlying problem with the current Compact of Free Association was not the level of funding provided. "We cannot ignore the failure of the Marshall Islands government to live up to its part of the contract. Despite massive aid, hospitals and schools are in disrepair and lack basic supplies." They implied that the one-year-old government of President Kessai Note was paying lip service to the reform process and called on the government to take action. But officials in the FSM and Marshalls say that many governmental reforms about which US officials are raising questions are already in place. Marshall Islands Ambassador to Washington, D.C. Banny deBrum said that, contrary to GAO claims, the Marshall Islands modernization of the "woefully inadequate social and physical system of infrastructure left behind by the (US) Trust

Territory has not only enhanced the quality of life in the Marshall Islands but also provided the necessary foundation for private sector growth."

Federated States of Micronesia Ambassador to Washington, Jesse B. Marehalau, disputed the GAO findings and called it a "disservice" for the GAO to suggest that the US Congress should approach the new Compact package "with the notion that the Compact assistance has been wasted." But that appears to be exactly how Bereuter and Young – two key leaders in the House whose committees control money for the islands – are approaching the talks. One of the major recommendations of the GAO report is that the "full faith and credit" provisions of the current Compact funding – which have guaranteed US payments each year since 1986 – be removed from any future agreement, to give the US more leverage to insure accountability. One criticism that irks island leaders is the contention that nothing has been done with Compact money. The American-administered trust territory was jokingly referred to as the "rust territory" due to its lack of development progress in the 1970s. "If we compare development now with the trust territory period, it's much different," said Jacklick. "I hope that the US government appreciates this."

The Gambling Issue

With a vote of 17 to 7, gambling has now been banned in the islands. While the two bills presented by Senator Ataji Balos (Kwajalein) had the support of the churches and the Council of Iroij (Chiefs), the pro-gambling group consisted of three government officials and their supporters. Public hearings were devoid of debate - not a single individual spoke to defend the right to gamble - as person after person spoke against the unregulated gambling that left children hungry. The pro-gambling coalition in the Nitijela centred its concern on replacement revenue for Kwajalein, which relied on slot-machine income as part of the atoll's budget. Yet, on the Nitijela floor, as the bills were presented, an inquiry revealed that the national government had received no revenue from the taxation of casinos. In the break before the final vote, Speaker Kessai Note announced that President Kabua, Senator Tony deBrum, and Minister Phillip Muller would not be permitted to vote due to their conflict of interest as owners of casinos. Others with similar conflicts were told to withhold their votes or be fined if evidence emerged later. An additional two members withheld their votes.

Passport Scam

The illegal sale of the Republic of the Marshall Islands passports is a considerable problem to the indigenous Marshallese, as migrants are taking over their jobs. However, for rich Asian migrants, becoming a citizen of the Marshall Islands provides security for investments in the tourism industry and in competing for resources on the very limited land area that makes up the atolls of the Marshall Islands. The illegal sale of passports is also an easy way for the Asian migrants to gain American citizenship.

GUAHAN (GUAM)

G uam's economy is still in trouble due to the Asian economic slowdown. Unemployment is running at 14 percent; the health of the government's General Fund is dismal, despite an employment freeze proclaimed by both the executive and the legislature, and calls for a 10 percent budget cut; the government deficit is currently at $114 million and not being contained with any sustained effort; and the island's main economic engine, tourism, is currently running some 16 – 18 percent below the previous year.

Another current issue is that of illegal immigration into the Territory. In late June 1999, in his first ever appearance before the UN General Assembly, the Governor of Guam had already expressed his concerns. Referring to Guam's non-self-governing status as a "threat to Guam's vision for social and economic progress" he stated that, "both legal and illegal immigration under the Administering power's regime threatens the balance needed to keep our fragile economy and environment from breaking under the strain" (Gutierrez 1999a, 2). In early March 2000, Congressman Underwood introduced House Resolution 945 calling for the amendment of the Immigration and Naturalization Act to prohibit claims of political asylum from being made on Guam by undocumented foreign individuals. After touring the tent "city" of illegal immigrants on Tinian and talking with UN officials there, Underwood amended his resolution. He concluded that asylum could be allowed but that the United Nations standards, which are stricter and more effective than those provided in US immigration law, should be used with respect to Guam. He urged his colleagues in Congress to reprogram some supplemental funds from continued efforts in Kosovo and Central America to the Immigration and Naturalization Service for its work in Guam and the Northern Marianas.

Chamorro Protest Imprisonment over Land Rights Struggle

The Colonized Chamorro Coalition in Guam held two demonstrations in early January. The first demonstration was on 7 January 2000, against the sentencing of Angel Santos to six months imprisonment for continuing his protest over the US government's taking of his grandfather's land. He had defied a restraining order imposed by the US District Court and was arrested for his defiance. The Court sentenced Mr Santos to six months imprisonment. While awaiting the Court's ruling, Mr Santos went on hunger strike to demonstrate his resolve and personal commitment to continue fighting for the rights of the Chamorro Nation until justice is served.

The second demonstration was on 14 January 2000 on the occasion of a visit by a delegation of US Congressmen to inspect military bases on the island. The Coalition listed four issues for the protest as follows: 1) War Reparations; 2) Return of Excess Lands Under Federal Control; 3) Political Status; and, 4) Environmental Clean Up of Lands used by the US military and other federal agencies.

Chamorro Oppose US Missiles in Guam

The Colonised Chamorro Coalition in Guam has hit out at recent moves by the US military to deploy conventional air-launched cruise missiles in Guam, saying they will strongly oppose any further militarisation of the island.

Almost 20% of the island has been given to the US Department of the Interior as "wildlife reserves" but Chamorro activists fear that these lands could be reclaimed by the US military for further militarisation. The fear is well-founded given the recent action by the US Navy to cancel the transfer of the former US Navy ship Repair Facility to the government of Guam. The Navy now claims it may have been "hasty" in its action to downsize the bases on Guam.

The recent move by the US military is alarming and, together with the testing of the Theater Missile Defence System in Kwajalein atoll in the Marshall Islands, signals a growing militarisation of the Pacific that must be opposed and condemned.

KA PAE'AINA (HAWAI'I)

Debates on the 'Reconciliation' Hearings and the Akaka 'Recognition Bill' were the major focus of the Kanaka Maoli struggle for
recognition and sovereignty in the year 2000.

The 'Reconciliation' hearings came after six years of inaction and
mounting Kanaka Maoli ferment following the 1993 US Congress
Apology Resolution (Public Law 103-150). Introduced by Kanaka
Maoli US Senator, Daniel Akaka, the joint resolution acknowledged
that the 1893 US conspiracy, armed invasion and recognition of the
white settlers' provincial government were in violation of treaties
between the two countries and international law, and a suppression
of Kanaka Maoli self-determination.

However, on 23 February 2000, the US Supreme Court ruled in
the Rice vs. Cayetano case, overturning a 1978 State of Hawai'i law
by a majority of 5 to 4 Justices. This court ruling means that the law,
which allows only Kanaka Maoli to vote for trustees of the State
Office of Hawaiian Affairs, is unconstitutional because it was based
on race. Thus, landless Kanaka Maoli who now comprise only 20%
of the 1.2 million population in their homeland of Ka Pae'aina are
considered racist under US law for exercising limited self-governance as wards under control of the State. According to Kekuni
Blaisdell, this meant that the Kanaka Maoli were in danger of having
their permanent political status determined for them by the US
government, and this was occurring without their initiation, input or
informed consent.

To counter fears that US federal health, education, housing and
other social programmes for Kanaka Maoli would be challenged in
the US courts, Senator Daniel Akaka announced the formation of a
'Native Hawaiian Task Force'. The Task Force was to represent the
people of Hawai'i and the US government, and prepare legislation
to protect US federal-funded programs for Kanaka Maoli by declaring Kanaka Maoli indigenous to the US. Thus, it was reasoned,
Kanaka Maoli have a legal, political and trust relationship with the
US similar to that of 'other Native Americans', the American Indians
and Alaska Natives.

At a 29 March forum at the University of Hawai'i, pro-independence Kanaka Maoli denounced both the Rice and Cayetano positions.
The Pro-Rice decision, according to Blaisdell, confirms that US colonialism with anti-Kanaka Maoli racism lives on. Anti-Kanaka Maoli
racism is evident in the position, supported by the State of Hawai'i,
Office of Hawaiian Affairs (OHA), the US Solicitor General and the
Hawai'i Congressional delegation, which states that the Kanaka

Maoli are 'Native Americans' and that this subordinate status should be affirmed by US Congressional 'federal recognition'. In May, pro-independence Kanaka Maoli met with Senator Akaka and urged him to adhere to acknowledgements in his 1993 Apology Resolution, such as US suppression of Kanaka Maoli inherent sovereignty and right to self-determination. The delegation also stressed the importance, under Article VI of the US Constitution, for the US to abide by treaties and international law, such as restitution, as 'the supreme law of the land'.

Undaunted by criticism, Akaka's second draft legislation was faxed to the press on 3 July, but not distributed to the Kanaka Maoli people.

From the onset, pro-independence Kanaka Maoli have opposed three main aspects of Akaka's legislation:

1. The intent is to reduce Kanaka Maoli to American Indian status, purportedly to save meagrely-funded federal Kanaka Maoli programs that promote colonial dependency. This intent is linked with the US's long-range policy to maintain US nuclearism, military occupation and economic exploitation of Kanaka Maoli Ka Pae'aina, in order to ensure US control over the Pacific Basin and Rim as essential to US globalisation policy.
2. The process is to pre-determine a permanent subservient Kanaka Maoli political relationship to the US, in violation of Kanaka Maoli inherent sovereignty and right to a true and full self-determination process, based on Kanaka Maoli cultural traditions and under impartial international oversight.
3. The bill's content destroys Kanaka Maoli as a distinct people and nation with their own territory, cosmology, history, culture, language and future.

Pro-independence Kanaka Maoli argue that the majority of Kanaka Maoli remain unaware of the damaging impact of this legislation should it become law.

In spite of stormy Kanaka Maoli protests during Honolulu hearings in September, the Akaka Bill was passed by the US Senate Indian Affairs Committee. The US House of Representatives also passed it on 26 September. However, it has yet to be brought to the US Senate floor for a vote because of Republican senators' new objections to Kanaka Maoli acquiring a political status analogous to that of American Indians.

Follow-up lawsuits by pro-Rice 'equal-protectionists' against Kanaka Maoli benefits and recent community forums on culture and race, dominated by non-Kanaka Maoli, have heightened non-Kanaka

Maoli expressions of the Kanaka Maoli sovereignty issue. This has created a curious and, for traditionally sharing and caring Kanaka Maoli, a painful paradox. Colonised Kanaka Maoli are being accused of racism because of their attempts to survive as a distinct people and nation. Laws made by colonising US settlers, such as those pertaiting to 'no race-based voting' and 'equal protection', are now being imposed on the dispossessed Kanaka Maoli to deprive them of any special rights as the host people.

RAPA NUI (EASTER ISLAND)

The indigenous people of Rapa Nui, who now number around 3,000, have survived 136 years of continuous oppression by the Chilean government, which deprives them of basic human rights in their homeland. In September 1888, King Atamu Tekena, Chief of the Ancient Council, signed an agreement with the government of Chile for protection of the remaining 350 Rapa Nui islanders in exchange for sovereignty. This treaty was violated in 1891 when Chile rented the island to a British company.

In 1914, Mr. Daniel Maria Chavez, Chief of the Ancient Council, organised a struggle for land claims, fair treatment, justice and human rights. Chilean officials arrested him and tried him in a court on a ship. He died mysteriously on the ship en route to Valparaiso, Chile. Similarly, two years later, Rapa Nui King Riro died in Chile where he had gone to sign an agreement with the Chilean government.

In 1933, the government of Chile registered Rapa Nui land under Article 590 of the Civil Code, stipulating that any land without a registered owner within the territorial borders of Chile belonged to the State. In 1979, after the Pinochet coup, the Chile government decreed a new law # 2885, which empowered the Chilean president to provide titles and deeds legitimating the State inscription of 1933. In 1989, the Rapa Nui Ancient Council filed a lawsuit against the State of Chile, charging land usurpation. As a result, the government of Chile created the indigenous law, which recognises and favours the rights and cultural values of the Rapa Nui people abiding under the principles and recommendations of the United Nations for natives and ethnic minorities across the world. However, the Chilean law is detrimental to the people since it legitimises the usurpation of land within the scope of Decree 2885 and the inscription of 1933.

During the year 2000, the indigenous people of Rapa Nui continued their struggle against the Chilean law. Isolated from the main routes in the Pacific, they do not have access to legal resources with which to support their land struggle. Support for the people of Rapa Nui is an important component of the broader decolonisation struggle in the Pacific.

NORTH AFRICA

NORTH AFRICA

THE AMAZIGH PEOPLES

The Amazigh peoples constitute a considerable part of the North African population. Yet the governments of the North African states do not disclose the correct statistics, and a number of the indigenous peoples are Arabized. All history books confirm that the Amazigh (a word which means 'the Free' in the Amazigh language), known in some history books as 'Berbers' (as foreigners call the indigenous peoples in North Africa), are the original population in North Africa. The Tuareg living in the desert form part and parcel of the Amazigh peoples.

The Amazigh Movement

The Amazigh Movement was started by Amazigh university students in the 1960s. The objectives of the movement were, from the very beginning, as follows:
- Recognition in the Constitution of their cultural, linguistic and civilizational identity;
- Integration of the Amazigh language into the education system;
- Integration of the Amazigh language into the media;
- Recognition of human rights and of cultural and linguistic rights on an equal footing.

In the 1960s, a number of cultural Amazigh movements came to the fore in Algeria, Morocco and in the European countries to which many citizens of these countries had migrated. These associations coordinated their activities and gathered at the International Amazigh Congress at which many associations from North African countries, Europe, America and Canada took part. Later on, the Amazigh movement joined the international indigenous movement.

Since its participation in the international human rights congress for the first time in 1993, the Amazigh movement has attended the meetings of the indigenous international movement held in Geneva, taken part in the political, social, economic and cultural daily activi-

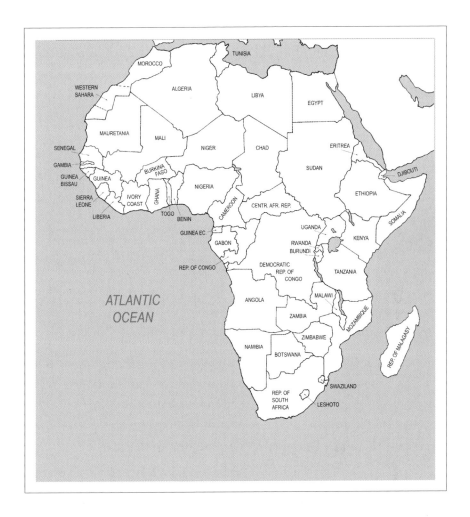

ties as well as in task forces of the United Nations on the rights of indigenous peoples.

The Amazigh movement's demands to amend the Constitution and take into consideration the multiple dimensions of Moroccan identity in its preamble was for many years ignored. The Arabization policy that was applied by the Nation-State following independence led to the severe discrimination, by all means possible, of the Amazigh people. The Amazigh languages were excluded from education, media and Administration. Artists were banned from taking part in national competitions because their products were in the Amazigh language. Amazigh activists from Morocco, Algeria and Libya were arrested for writing in their mother tongue. Children were deprived the use of their Amazigh names. The

Arabization policy prevented the majority of these peoples from acquiring an education and having access to the most fundamental aspects of a respectable life such as water, electricity, means of communication or health premises.

After many years of ignorance, arrests and outright attempts by the governments to harass the movement to silence, things seemed to develop in a different direction.

In 1998, the government recognized the Amazigh dimension of Moroccan identity for the first time in an official declaration. In a recent amendment to the Constitution in Algeria, the government officially recognized the Amazigh dimension of Algerian identity. An official institution was established for the first time in North Africa. The High Commission for the Amazighity was set up in Algeria to propose programs and regulations that could contribute to the relative integration of the Amazigh language within Algerian schools. Many other Amazigh organizations and associations saw the light of day in the Canary Islands, which in 1997 played host to the first Amazigh International Congress following its constitutive congress in 1995.

Despite some progress in the position of the official institutions, the circumstances of the indigenous peoples in North Africa have changed little. The formation of Amazigh associations in Libya is still forbidden. The situation of the indigenous peoples in Tunisia is deteriorating. Many setbacks have been noted in Morocco and Algeria in 2000.

Significant Events in the Life of the Indigenous Peoples in North Africa, Morocco in Particular

The greatest gathering of Amazigh associations in the regional seminar organized in association with the International Labor Organization in 2000
The regional seminar on Convention 169 concerning the rights of the indigenous peoples, organized on 21-22-23 January 2000 by the Tamaynut Association in association with the International Labor Organization, was an outstanding event in the history of the Amazigh movement in North Africa. Approximately fifty-five Amazigh associations and cultural and developmental Amazigh sections as well as representatives from many North and West African countries met for the first time to exchange ideas and opinions on the current situation of the indigenous peoples, examine future perspectives and propose recommendations and plans. The seminar's recommendations were dominated by the immediate adoption of Convention 169 on the rights of indigenous and tribal peoples. They then stressed

that the other rights that had already been declared relating to the fact that Constitutional recognition of the cultural, civilizational and linguistic identity of the indigenous peoples should be confirmed, and that the mother tongue should be incorporated into education and media. The importance of this seminar lies in the direct meeting of cultural associations defending human rights with economic and developmental organizations.

Announcement by the Amazigh Declaration and the Constitution of the 15-member committee on May 13, 2000

One thousand intellectuals and Amazigh cadres signed a political statement prepared by the academician Mohamed CHAFIK, in which they demanded official recognition of the Amazigh character of Morocco, in other words political recognition of the cultural, linguistic and civilizational identity of the Moroccan indigenous peoples. King Mohammed VI appointed a committee made up of the head of his cabinet, the head of the Royal Committee for Education, and the official speaker of the Palace. This committee has met with representatives of the signatories to the Declaration and conveyed to them that the King is prepared to consider their demands. Yet no reply has been given so far. In May 2000, an important gathering was held to discuss the strategy of the Amazigh movement with a view to democratizing the country and the regime in Morocco. The gathering also exchanged views on how to influence cultural and political decisions. At the end of the gathering, a 15-member committee was elected, ensuring fair geographical representation of the major regions of Morocco. This committee was entrusted with the task of preparing for the Amazigh Congress to be held at the end of the year 2001. It has also held many meetings to examine the possibility of collaborating with other Amazigh associations so that the Amazigh movement could proceed along two fronts, cultural and political, as suggested by an activist from the Amazigh movement in North Africa.

Expropriations in the province of Agadir and a sit-in by the Amazigh developmental associations on July 4, 2000

The nation-state superseded the colonizer in applying the French regulations regarding the transfer of lands, forests, oceans, minerals to the French State, (subsequently the nation state), ignoring the rules of the indigenous peoples that prevailed prior to colonization. During the year 2000, the government undertook expropriations of lands and forests in the region of Tafraout, in the south of Morocco. The local population fought this encroachment on their lands with protests and complaints. Yet this was not enough to put an end to this process. They thus organized a sit-in before the parliament in Rabat on July 4 2000, leading to the opening of dialogue and to a temporary freezing of the expropriation process.

Adoption of a Charter of Education and the protest of the Amazigh Associations – April 2000

At the beginning of 2000, the Royal Committee of Education (a committee set up with no participation on the part of the Amazigh associations), announced the Charter of Education. In the view of the Amazigh associations, this Charter does not respect the cultural and linguistic identity of the Amazigh population nor does it consider the Amazigh language as an official language. The Amazigh associations denounced this Charter, for it enshrines a policy of discrimination on the basis of language and it aims at Arabizing the Amazigh through a policy of Arabization presented in a Charter abusively called 'national'.

During the meeting of the parliamentary session in April 2000, the Amazigh associations staged a sit-in before Parliament to demand that a law preserving their cultural and linguistic identity be elaborated and that the Tamazigh language be incorporated into education and the media. Yet the government banned the sit-in despite the fact that it was organized in line with all the legal formalities. Police forces descended on the main avenue where the sit-in was expected to take place in a bid to prevent the protestors from protesting or from gathering in front of Parliament.

Amazigh children prevented from registering their names in the Family record books

The authorities continued to deprive the Amazigh of registering their children with Amazigh names. A great number of the children were not allowed to register their names in the Family record books on the excuse that these names are neither Moroccan nor Arab, which simply means that everything which is not Arab is not Moroccan ! **Tunarug**, **Titrite**, **Massine** are all names of children born in 2000 and they are still deprived of their right to take that name.

The march in support of women's rights (12 March 2000) – abandonment of the government's plan for women's involvement following a counter march

The majority of North African women suffer from discrimination in various ways. Illiteracy amongst women is sometimes as high as 90%

(in Morocco). This situation forces them to do only minor jobs for little return. Although the Constitutions of the North African countries recognize equality of political rights in theory, women are still deprived of these rights. This is because elections are still being rigged and the will of the people is not respected in North Africa. As to equality with regard to civil rights, this does not figure either into the Constitutions nor into current legislation.

The Amazigh woman suffers from a double discrimination. In addition to the said sufferings of women in general, the Amazigh woman is also deprived of constitutional recognition of her linguistic, civilizational and cultural identity. She has also been denied some other positive rights, which the ancient Amazigh regulations bestowed on her, such as *Tamazzalte*, a custom stipulating that the spouse has the right to own half the properties her husband acquires following marriage. Moreover, she has been denied the right to assume an effective role in cultural and political life because she is culturally marginalized, a direct result of not using the Tamazigh language in the media, the administration or in official life.

Some of the feminist associations organized themselves into a feminist movement, a framework that allows them to struggle for establishing equality, abolishing discrimination, and attempting to make the Moroccan government withdraw its reservations relating to the Convention on the abolition of all forms of discrimination against women, on the basis that some of its articles do not abide by Islamic legislation.

Because of all these things, and in order to apply the Beijing plan of struggle for women's rights, the feminist movement organized a huge march on March 12, 2000, to support a proposal put forward by one Minister to apply a plan for involving women in development. Yet the government did not proceed with this plan and the Minister who proposed the Plan was discharged from office in the government reshuffle in September 2000.

The discovery of oil and gold and the expropriation of Amazigh lands without consulting their owners in September 2000
In September 2000, it was officially announced that oil and gold had been discovered in marginalized lands that had been excluded from any developmental plan. This was the first time such news had reached the media.

It was announced that a big quantity of oil had been discovered in the Amazigh region of Talsint, in the south-east of Morocco. The lands of the local population were used without even consulting their owners, according to colonial rules promulgated by the French and used by the nation-state, taking into consideration neither its citizens, the nation nor the new international standards stipulated in Convention 169 on indigenous peoples in 1989.

The discovery of gold in the Amazigh region of Ta Ta came at almost the same time. Once again, the same colonial rules were applied that devastate the relationship between the people and the land on the basis of cultural and civilizational identity.

Despite all these riches, the State still refuses to recognize the minimum rights recognized internationally for indigenous peoples by Convention 169 on the rights of indigenous peoples and the International Declaration on the Rights of Indigenous Peoples.

Stifling of journalists, suspension of three newspapers, deterioration of public liberties, arrest and trial of protestors on the occasion of the International Day of Human Rights, December 2000

After the young King Mohammed the Sixth acceded to the throne following the death of his father in 1999, positive signs of change began to loom on the horizon. Yet some negative events still took place, such as the trial of a number of journalists, the concomitant suspension of three newspapers for publishing news relating to the purchase by the Minister of Foreign Affairs of a villa in Washington and for publishing a letter from an opponent of the Monarchy dating back to 1974, pointing out that the current Moroccan Prime Minister took part, along with the generals, in the failed 1972 coup d'état against King Hassan II.

The three newspapers were banned for 40 days. They were subsequently allowed to continue publishing. The year 2000 witnessed the greatest deterioration in the freedom of expression and in democratic liberties.

Activists from the Islamic Right and the Marxist Left chose to commemorate the day of Declaration of International Rights (10 December 2000) by organizing a peaceful march. But this march was banned and many activists were arrested, some of them are in jail and others are awaiting trial.

According to the international report on human development, Morocco moved from position 125 to 126 at the end of the year 2000.

Organization of the biggest gathering on land rights in Agadir 17-18 February 2001

The Amazigh movement is changing from a cultural into a social movement. The year 2000 opened with the first meeting on the rights of indigenous peoples attended by cultural and developmental associations. The latter organized the largest ever gathering on rights relating to land in Agadir on 17-18 February 2001. This gathering examined the current situation and protested against the fact that colonial laws still govern the relationship between the local population and the land. A representative of the Human Rights Center in Geneva took part in this meeting. The meeting recommended ratification of Convention 169.

People's hopes in the two governments of alternation shattered

All governments since independence have been the product of rigged elections, as attested to by the parties participating in these elections themselves. When the late King Hassan II appointed a government presided over by a socialist leader, hopes that the situation of the masses would improve began to appear. These hopes were reinforced when the young King came to the throne announcing 'a new concept of authority', constituting a committee entrusted with compensating the victims of arrest and torture during the rule of his father and addressing a letter on the occasion of the International Day of Human Rights.

Although the government of alternation came to power as a result of rigged elections, hopes for change were still strongly felt. Yet on February 4 2001, this government ended its third year with the situation of the population deteriorating on all the sides, political, social and economic. Regardless of the promises of change, corruption issues broke out and some negative events still persist, such as the trial of the young officer Adib in February 2000. He was jailed for three years for disclosing the corruption of his superiors. Children are still forbidden from using their Amazigh names, a sit-in of the Amazigh associations was banned, journalists were tried and newspapers were suspended in September 2000.

Summary

Despite all these events, the government still refuses to enter into open dialogue with the developmental and cultural Amazigh associations. It talks of democracy but exercises tyranny, and it talks of dialogue and yet still denies the rights of its citizens.

Nevertheless, the Amazigh movement pursues its peaceful means to achieve a true democratization of the State and to guarantee the right of participation in the cultural and political life under a democratic system that respects pluralism and the cultural and civilizational identity of the Amazigh peoples.

EAST AFRICA

EAST AFRICA

ETHIOPIA

Human Rights in the Gambela National State

The Ethiopian government claims to respect all fundamental human rights, to be dedicated and committed to the basic democratic principles of good governance, to justice, equality, and the rule of law. In practice, in almost all these basic areas of humanity, it demonstrates the contrary. Opposition political parties are not allowed to participate freely in public activities, their members and supporters are intimidated and affected by numerous breaches of the law and unconstitutional practices.

These have been extensively reported on in the past, during the elections of 1995 and again last year.

Numerous reports, notably by Amnesty International and the US Department of State, have been issued regarding the Ethiopian government's performance on human rights. The government has been criticised extensively. The latest report of the US Department of State, issued in February 2001, has this to say:

"...The Government's human rights record remained poor; although there were some improvements in a few areas, serious problems remained. Security forces committed a number of extra judicial killings and at times beat and mistreated detainees. Prison conditions are poor. Arbitrary arrest and detention and prolonged pre-trial detention remained problems. The Government continued to detain persons suspected of sympathizing with or being involved with the [Oromo Liberation Front]. The Government continued to detain and deport without due process Eritreans and Ethiopians of Eritrean origin. Since the outbreak of the border conflict in May 1998, as many as 75,000 such persons have left Ethiopia for Eritrea; the vast majority were deported, although a small number left voluntarily.... Although prompted by national security considerations, the expulsions and detentions raised fundamental concerns regarding arbitrary arrest and detention, forced exile, the forcible separation of families, and nationality issues, as well as the hardships and financial losses suffered by those who were detained or expelled. Despite some efforts, the judiciary continued to

lack sufficient trained staff and funds, which limited its ability to provide citizens the full protection provided for in the Constitution..... The judiciary also showed some signs of growing independence. The Government infringed on citizens' privacy rights, and the law regarding search warrants was ignored widely.

The Government restricts freedom of the press and continued to detain or imprison members of the press; however, fewer journalists were detained than in previous years. Most were accused or convicted of inciting ethnic hatred, committing libel, or publishing false information in violation of the 1992 Press Law. Journalists continued to practice self-censorship.... In July, legislation to create a constitutionally mandated Human Rights Commission and office of the ombudsman, which was passed in October 1999, entered into force; however, neither entity was operational at year's end. The Government generally respected freedom of religion; however, on occasion, local authorities infringed on this right. The Government restricted freedom of movement.... Violence and societal discrimination against women, and abuse of children remained problems....The exploitation of children for economic and sexual purposes remained a problem. Societal discrimination against disabled persons was a problem. Discrimination against religious and ethnic minorities continued. Child labor, particularly in the informal sector, continued to be a problem. Forced labor, including forced child labor, was also a problem, and there were reports of trafficking in persons...."

This certainly covers and reflects the general suffering common to all Ethiopians, irrespective of their ethnic origin, religious beliefs, geographical location, or social and economic background. However, the focus of all these reports remains largely limited to the centre, and to the "more developed" Tigrai, Amhara, Oromo and Southern Peoples states.

Details of human rights abuses against the indigenous peoples in the "less developed" peripheral states, Gambela, Afar, Somali, and Benshingul-Gumuze, which have common agro-pastoral economic and social backgrounds, have received far less attention.

In fact, human rights conditions in these lowland states provide exact details of the Ethiopian government's lack of commitment and respect for the internationally accepted human rights standards it claims to accept and implement. In these areas, opposition political parties, dedicated to improving the livelihoods of their people, find their members regularly mistreated, imprisoned, tortured, dismissed from civil servant posts, detained without trial, even killed. The local state governments, largely controlled by the ruling Ethiopian Peoples Revolutionary Democratic Front authorities in Addis Ababa, demonstrate a complete lack of interest in involving the general public, in promoting a culture of democratic rule and good governance, of freedom of expression and speech. The result is widespread practice of human rights abuses that are largely ignored.

Development issues, vital and particular to the indigenous peoples of these regional states, are routinely ignored by both the federal government and the local administrations, or kept secret. The people remain marginalized and neglected, unaware of social, political and economic activities in their own homelands. The general public in these national states is unable to participate actively in issues that directly affect their lives. Policies and programmes, though frequently claimed to incorporate local interests, are regularly imposed without consent or consultation.

Arrests and Detentions in Gambela National State
The Gambela State government recently launched a new crackdown, with the arrest of at least seven leading members of the oppositional Gambela Peoples Democratic Congress (GPDC) and community elders. They are:

- Ambassador Ophato Wa-Aliwo;
- H. Ogud Wu-Nyigwo (Capt.), a Gambela elder arrested in Abwobo district and now in Gambela prison;
- Omot Wu-Ojulu (Mr.), a member of the Gambela State Council, also arrested in Abwobo, and taken to Gambela prison;
- Ajau wu-Odol (Mr.), arrested in Gambela town and held in Itang prison;
- Okony Nyu-Omot (Mrs.), arrested at Itang and then transferred to Gambela prison;
- Beay Nyu-Ochar (Mrs.), also arrested at Itang and transferred to Gambela prison;
- Kuwot Wu-Teferri (Capt.), a member of the Gambela State Council, arrested in Abwobo district and now held in Gambela prison.

Ambassador Ophato Wa-Aliwo was released on bail after five days; the others are still (as of April 2001) held. No charges have been made against any of them. The arrest of Omot wu-Ojulu and Kuwot wu-Teferri, both members of the Gambela State Council, is in breach of the constitutional rights of the elected members of the state council.

These are only the latest detentions in a long list going back several years.

In May, 2000, the ruling Gambela Peoples Democratic Front (GPDF), the EPRDF's surrogate party in Gambela State, claimed an overwhelming victory in the general election. Claims by the opposition GPDC of widespread human rights abuses against its members and supporters were ignored by the government, as was the widely reported intimidation carried out by EPRDF soldiers against local people during the election campaign. It is common for youngsters to be picked up and detained in military garrisons, in the town centre or out of town. There they are severely beaten by the soldiers, sometimes leaving them with lasting injuries. Some have been issued with death threats should they remain in the region. The result has been to introduce a climate of fear. Many who have undergone such brutal treatment do not dare to talk about their experiences for fear of retaliation, concerned for their own safety if their names should appear in public. Many Anuak are fleeing the region, in some cases even across the border into Sudan; other ethnic groups in Gambela State are suffering equally.

In fact, members and supporters of the GPDC, the only opposition political party in Gambela, have been targeted since 1998. Many remain in detention without trial, others have disappeared or been killed. Today, more than 300 individuals accused of membership of the GPDC, or of supporting the party, are held in the appalling and over-crowded prisons of Gambela State. A few months ago, it was reported that Omot wu-Obang Onugi, one of the founder members of the GPDC and a former head of the Planning and Economic department of the Gambela State Council, had died in Gambela prison. He had apparently been denied access to medical facilities and suffered from serious mistreatment while in detention.

Many others are reported to be in critical condition for the same reasons:

- Last year, two Anuak, Gog wu-Omot and Abulla wu-Okello, were killed in military garrison posts outside Gambela town.
- Five members of the Gambela Peoples Democratic Congress, including the prominent political activist, Abulla wu-Obang, disappeared in Gambela town. Abulla wu-Obang was released from Gambela prison recently after being detained for 2 years without trial; Omot wu-Obang, Gurnyang wu-Obang, Ochaan wu-Okello, and Omot wa-Akway are still missing.
- Among the few educated Anuak are Opumo wu-Oboya and Ojulu wu-Bach. They were arrested in 1998 as a result of their active participation in forming the GPDC. Neither have been tried or even charged.

Local Elections

Local elections have recently been held in several areas of Ethiopia. There has been no information as to when they will be held in Gambela State. It is now believed that they will not take place until the next countrywide general election, five years from now. This is because of the difficulties the ruling GPDF had in winning a majority in the general election despite the corruption of the electoral system. The municipal positions for Gambela should be filled though a democratic election. Instead, it appears the GPDF is appointing people it sees as loyal, its own members, to fill posts without taking the risk of allowing even controlled elections.

Ethnic Conflict

Another danger is the growing threat of ethnic conflict. Already, conflict between the Anuak and the Nuer, who are the third largest ethnic group in Southern Sudan, is spreading to other areas of Gambela. There has been no sign of interest by either the federal government or the regional government regarding what has become almost chronic ethnic violence. Many Anuak have lost their lands and now live as refugees following clashes. Hundreds from Jokau and Akobo districts are displaced every year without any government interference. There is widespread suspicion that the government is actually encouraging tensions between the Anuak and the Nuer in order to keep control of a region that was virtually autonomous prior to the 1974 Ethiopian revolution. It was the revolution that largely destroyed traditional Anuak political institutions and culture, and lost the Anuak control over their territories.

There have been recent reports that over 20,000 armed Nuer have crossed into Anuak territories never previously threatened by their traditional foes, and settled along the banks of the Gilo River. Despite this move, which will destabilise the whole region, the government has remained silent. Escalating conflicts are also reported among different Nuer clans in Jokau and Akobo districts, and again there has been no government response. Tension between the Majanger (Ojang) and settlers from different parts of the country in Godare district is also rising and actual conflict is now likely. The Majanger are being displaced from their homelands by huge trading companies involved in the destruction of what is now the only remaining forest in Gambela State. The very future of the Majanger is under threat from highly profitable business activities that ignore their suffering as their environment and their way of life is destroyed.

Oil Exploration

The recent oil exploration deal signed between the Ethiopian government and the Gambela Petroleum Corporation (Pinewood Oil Company of Canada) has raised great concern among the Gambela community in the region as well as outside the country. The deal remains a secret between the Ethiopian government and the Canadian Oil Company, Pinewood. The indigenous peoples of Gambela State, the claimed beneficiaries, will certainly be affected by the investment of this foreign company. However, they have not been consulted at any stage of this alleged "development" plan, nor have they been informed of any of the details of the agreement. Even most senior local government officials, council members and community elders have not been informed about the government plan for their own lands. At every level, the Ethiopian government action is in clear contradiction to all basic constitutional principles as well as the international instruments, treaties, and protocols it has ratified and signed.

Not surprisingly, the indigenous Anuak are seriously worried by the potentially devastating effects of such a development project being implemented without either consent or much apparent planning. In the past, several such development projects have been instituted, claiming that they would lead to significant improvements. They have included such projects as the Abwobo (Abobo) State Farm and Alwero (Alworo) irrigation dam, still not in use to this day. These both deprived local people of large areas of fertile land, displacing them without any compensation and denying them access to ancestral burial sites, forcing people to become refugees in their own territories. Over 60, 000 people from the highlands were settled in Anuak lands, forcibly displacing the previous owners. The results have included a significant intensification of the levels of poverty, alcoholism and suicide among the Anuak, as well as other psychological, and emotional effects.

Nor is the oil deal the first government initiative affecting local peoples' ways of life and the environment. As early as the 1970s, there were attempts to clear Anuak lands along the Openo (Baro) River. This was blocked by the efforts of the international community, with the active participation of the European Commission (EC) and Anti-Slavery Society campaigns, ending the threat to Anuak society. Now, the current Ethiopian government, which has neglected, ignored and marginalized indigenous peoples, is attempting to undertake exactly the same developments again.

Given negative past experiences of development projects, the Anuak will resist the implementation of so-called "development" projects that are implemented without consultation or discussion.

They are already highly suspicious of the strategy of pilfering resources, a strategy that contributes nothing to social welfare and to the economic performance of Gambela State. Such projects, ignoring the importance of indigenous participation and representation, are all too liable to failure, bringing disaster to human resources, wildlife, and the environment in general.

Gambela is one of the under-utilised potential tourist areas in Ethiopia, with numerous varieties of wild animals and large numbers of different fish in the rivers, particularly in the areas targeted for petroleum exploration!

The current problems of Gambela cannot justify implementation of such an ambitious and destructive project. The indigenous people live from subsistence agriculture, hunting, gathering, and fishing. There has been little attempt by the government to involve them in any of the major economic activities of the modern world. It is no surprise to see that the benefits of such environmentally and socially destructive projects are not intended to benefit the indigenous peoples of the area. Moreover, additionally, social and economic institutions remain inadequate and will be unable to sustain or cope with the major health threats that will result from the implementation of this project.

The specific areas targeted by the government for exploration are: Adhura and Jor, both very short of health facilities. Both contain major fishing rivers, the Gilo and Adhura (Adura), much used by local indigenous people as a main source of food. The environmental effects of this project will be devastating on the Anuak community there, and will seriously reduce alternative food sources for the population of Gambela as a whole.

In fact, the deal threatens the destruction of the Anuak way of life, their culture and tradition, as well as the loss of control over their territory.

The previous regime had little regard for the survival of Anuak political institutions and culture, nor indeed for their very survival as a people, and the very existence of the ethnic group came under threat. Little has changed. It is widely believed that the present high level of human rights abuses against the Anuak is a calculated move to realise the long-term Ethiopian government plans, which have yet to be revealed.

Indeed, the oil deal, from which the Anuak are excluded, could easily lead to the complete disappearance of the Anuak. It is a concern that is widely shared by other indigenous people in the state, who see themselves isolated from the government in Addis Ababa.

KENYA

The Announcement of the Results of the Population Census

The results of the 1998 Population Census were announced in late 1999 and, for the first time in the country's history, the figures were broken down by district rather than by ethnic group. While the new style of presentation of figures is said to help reduce the significance of the ethnic or "tribal" factor (since it makes it difficult to deduce population figures of any ethnic group), it also tends to conceal the negative effects of high rates of migration into indigenous peoples' territories. Such migration has reduced the resource base of marginalized indigenous peoples and many of them have been made quite vulnerable as a result. This is in addition to becoming minorities in their own areas and the problems of being dominated in the political, social and cultural spheres.

The Constitutional Review Process

Over the past several years, Kenya has been trying to carry out a constitutional review process in order to change the constitution before the next elections in 2002. The process began with pressure being exerted for constitutional review prior to the last general elections at the end of 1997. Unrest and violence ensued. As a consequence, the parties represented in parliament formed the Inter-Parties Parliamentary Group (IPPG) for the purposes of directing the process. This group was later replaced by the Inter-Parties Parliamentary Committee (IPPC), which then organized a series of meetings with all stakeholders to discuss the modalities of constitutional review.

Negotiation among members of the IPPC then took place and was concluded with changes being made to the Constitution of Kenya Review Act, which was to form the basis for the review of the constitution. The review of the Act was finalized by the end of January 1999. However, application of this new law soon reached a deadlock when members could not agree on the formula for sharing out the 25 seats between the various political parties. Besides this, there was also disagreement on whether or not the review process should be undertaken by ordinary citizens or by their parliamentary representatives. The President contended that ordinary citizens, represented by the synonym of "Wanjiku" did not have the capacity to review the constitution, and that parliament should carry out the task on their behalf. After one full year, the deadlock eventually led to two parallel processes: the Ufungamano Initiative and the Parliamentary Group.

The Ufungamano Initiative and the Parliamentary Group

The Ufungamano Initiative started the process with a meeting organized by religious leaders to which all the 54 stakeholders named in the Review Act as amended were invited. The meeting was held at Ufungamano House, hence the name. Following this meeting, a Steering Council was formed to spearhead what was later to be called "a people-driven constitutional review process" to distinguish it from the "parliamentary review process". The Ufunamano process swore in commissioners and started collecting people's views on the proposed new constitution. However, since most members of the initiative were unelected by the people, their process was said to lack the legal mandate to make a new constitution. Doubts were also expressed as to how a constitution drafted by this team - which is outside parliament - would be implemented within the existing law.

Parliament for its part also set up a Parliamentary Select Committee to review the Constitution of Kenya Review Act and proposed some amendments to jump start the stalled process. It also allowed parliament to guide the process. The report of the Parliamentary Select Committee was adopted, a bill drafted, debated and enacted. A commission of 15 persons was appointed, chaired by Prof. Pal Yash Ghai, a member of the Minority Rights Group. After some disagreement, the two groups finally came together in the early part of 2001 and agreed on the basic principles of the Constitutional Review Act. The constitutional review process is now said to be on course and might be completed before the next general elections in two years.

Significant Areas in the Constitution

Under the Constitutional Review Act, the main areas to be examined by the review commission are as follows:

The composition and functions of the State organs; federal and unitary forms of government; existing constitutional organs, good governance and human rights; the electoral system; the judiciary; local government; property and land rights; public finances; citizenship; socio-cultural obstacles; the rights of the child; succession to office; treaty-making and implementation; principles directing State policies; and any other matters connected to the above. Some of these areas have a bearing on the lives of everyone including marginalized indigenous peoples as elaborated below.

The *composition and functions of the State organs* is essentially the separation of powers of the three branches of government - the executive, legislature and judiciary – to allow for a balance of power and check excesses of each one. The present constitution has granted the executive more power than is necessary at the expense of the other branches. No doubt a process that streamlines the State organs will be deemed beneficial to all citizens.

The choice between a *federal versus a unitary form of government* is one topic that dichotomises opinion, where the majority and more dominant communities find themselves on one side and the minority and more marginalized communities on the other. The present constitution of Kenya provides for a unitary form of government where power is centralized and the government exercises its power directly in all parts of the country, at the provincial, the district, the location and sub-location levels. Since Kenya has always operated under a unitary form of government, the communities - who do not feel that they are adequately represented in all administrative levels - have reached the conclusion that the problem is the centralization of power. They therefore propose change that allows for the devolution of power to the regional and district levels. In this way, they hope to exercise some autonomy in the management and control of their own affairs and resources, particularly land.

But discussion of a federal system of government in Kenya evokes feelings of fear and discomfort among the majority and more dominant communities for very specific reasons. While federalism exists in many parts of the world – the USA, Germany and Ethiopia are frequently quoted examples - it is not always clear what form it would take in Kenya, although the system known as *Majimbo* (from *jimbo* or region) had been the hallmark of the first main opposition party, the Kenya African Democratic Union (KADU) in the 1960s but it was defeated by the ruling party, Kenya African National Union (KANU).

A type of *majimbo* system was contained in the constitution that existed at independence. In that constitution, the country was divided into seven self-governing regions or jimbos along the lines of the present provincial boundaries. Each *jimbo* would have its own parliament, judiciary and executive, while the federal government would deal with matters relating to defence, foreign policy, foreign trade and any external contact.

The main fear of the *Majimbo* system arises from interpretations of the type of federalism that might be considered. According to one interpretation, the regions might wish to be ethnically pure, meaning that other ethnic groups who were not indigenous to that particular region would be expelled. This expulsion would bring about ethnic violence. For this reason, any possibility of introducing a *majimbo* form of governance is bound to be rejected by the dominant communities and welcomed by the marginalized indigenous communities, who feel overwhelmed by myriads of migrants flocking into their areas and taking away resources that rightly belong to them.

Given Kenya's history of ethnic tensions and individuals in power using their position to benefit their own communities at the expense of the rest, these reactions do not come as a surprise. Indeed, given the enormous power of the executive, the government has unilaterally settled people on land belonging to the weaker communities without any form of consultation or compensation, but never vice versa. At times, this has resulted in the attack on or eviction of migrants and a culmination in ethnic clashes. Enoosupukia, Mt. Elgon and Likoni are areas where ethnic conflicts were reported in the early and mid 1990s and they still pose a serious threat in other parts of the country.

Another reason why the form of governance creates differences of opinion is that a unitary form of governance is also perceived to tend towards uniformity in ways of doing things: one language, one culture, one set of structures for all, etc. This is perceived to be diametrically opposed to a system that allows for some diversity, an element to which most marginalized indigenous communities relate well, on account of the prime value they attach to their rich and largely still functional socio-political and economic systems. Following European colonialism and subsequent re-colonization by the more dominant communities, indigenous systems are threatened with extinction, and if a federal system is likely to be more sensitive to such sentiments, then it promises to be the choice for such communities. Because of these reasons, this particular point in the constitution will remain a contentious issue and one which indigenous peoples will always follow closely since the outcome is bound to have an impact on their lives in one way or another.

Existing constitutional organs, good governance and human rights is another area that is bound to be universally beneficial since it focuses on the essentials of a democratic society: transparency, accountability, commitment to the rule of law and the observance of human rights. The proposed constitutional review is expected to come up with a strong Bill of Rights and provisions confirming the country's commitment to the basic principles of democracy, fundamental freedoms and protection of human rights.

Besides the constitutional review process, which has tended to dominate a good part of these past two years, other events of a national nature include the creation of a number of commissions to deal with major public concerns. One is the Akiwumi Commission to look into ethnic clashes and the other is the Njonjo Commission to look into matters relating to land.

The Akiwumi Commission

There is very little to write about the Akiwumi Commission because, although it was mandated to examine the causes of ethnic clashes and come up with recommendations on what action to be taken, it is now two years since the commission completed its task and yet the results have still to be released. The findings of the commission would be very important in understanding the causes of ethnic clashes so that sustainable means of mitigating and controlling them can be sought.

The Njonjo Land Commission

Unconfirmed but plausible reports have it that the Njonjo Land Commission was formed in order to give the impression that something is being done about the numerous irregular land transactions in the country. One case that hit the headlines is the famous Loodo-ariak/ Mosiro Case, in which land was demarcated on paper and titles fraudulently issued to officials of the Ministry of Lands and others without the knowledge of the indigenous Maasai community who are ordinarily resident there. Since the land was a "first registration," according to the Laws of Kenya, it could not, apparently, be challenged in court. A new bill needed to be passed in order to correct the injustice.

With the help of the organisation "Survival International", a new Bill was drafted and lobbying was done to have it passed. It was published in the official Kenya Gazette and discussed in Cabinet. But, that was as far as it went. It was said that highly placed government officials, along with their relatives and friends, would stand to lose illegally acquired land. The next thing was the setting up of the Njonjo Land Commission with a mandate to investigate and come up with solutions to land laws that need to be amended, to report on land that was illegally alienated and suggest solutions for the return of such lands.

The commission was supposed to have given a progress report early this year but it is still collecting views from the public. It will

247

be a long time before the report is finalized and made public, if at all, although the chairman is on record as having promised that it will be done. There has been criticism that the commission may not be fully independent and that, since there are many highly placed people whose interests would be affected, it is possible the Commission's report may never see the light of day. And this would be to the detriment of peace in the affected areas of the country. Already, the people of Loodoariak and Mosiro have attacked and chased away persons trying to build structures on the land, and claiming to have title to it. And despite the existence of very clear regulations governing conditions for issuing loans, banks have allowed the mortgaging of those titles before it could be verified as to whether or not the land truly exists and whether it is viable for the purposes for which it is being mortgaged. This too is illegal. It is mainly marginalized indigenous peoples who are most affected by the outcome of the Njonjo report.

The Drought and its Effects

Over the past two years, Kenya has experienced a very serious drought that has resulted in the death of livestock and people. Officially, 3 million people - mainly pastoralists - were reported to have been left totally destitute. Since wildlife has also died in large numbers, hunter-gatherers are also affected. Some farming communities, who are usually food secure, were also not spared. The drought was first reported in northern Kenya and it spread to the south. The Samburu, Borana, Turkana, Laikipia Maasai, Rendille, Pokot, Somali and others all travelled south in search of pasture. The southern pastoralists moved to Nairobi and parts of northern Tanzania, having negotiated access with the communities there. The move was so great that, after the drought, the Kenyan government thanked the Tanzanian government for allowing the Maasai of Kenya to graze their stock during one of the worse droughts. Although an alert was sent relatively early, nothing was done about it until long after people had started dying of hunger. Then the World Food Programme and other relief agencies started moving in maize rations to the affected communities.

In the meantime, in order to ensure the survival of some herds, livestock had to be moved almost everywhere in search of pasture - private farms, national parks, forest reserves, recreation spots in the city and even to the compound of the State House in Nairobi. The movement of livestock created conflict, some of it real and some imagined. The real conflict was when the livestock was reported to have destroyed some crops on which farming communities depend.

But the imagined conflict was when the herds were moved into expansive private ranches with hardly any stock and into forest reserves and National Parks for the duration of the drought. Environmentalists complained bitterly about destruction of the forests by livestock and farmers called on the government to evict livestock from urban centres.

The drought brought to the fore the intensity of bias against pastoralists and their herds, both at the local level where legs of cattle were cut, and at the national level. In the face of so much desperation, the government, which is usually not very sympathetic about the use of reserved forests and National Parks, seemed to be rather understanding of the desperate situation. It even announced the imminent opening of the Kenya Meat Commission as a rescue measure to assist pastoralists in marketing their starving stock, an impossible feat given the fact that the factory had been closed for so long and the machinery was rusted. However, it gave some false hope to the herders.

The livestock that was moved to the forests perished in large numbers from disease and poor weather conditions. At the end of it all, high percentages of herders have either very few or no livelihood at all and are totally dependent upon relief food. Following the rains, while some farming communities have received seeds to re-start sustainable livelihoods, few herders have. And at any rate, their areas are too arid for crop cultivation. What they need are seeds in the form of young stock to facilitate restocking and to enable them to cease being dependent upon relief food.

Local Processes

The last two years have witnessed the demise of the Kenya Pastoralist Forum but also the birth of many small indigenous initiatives as well as wider individual community consortia and networks. The Borana have initiated the Movement for the Empowerment of Local Initiatives (MELI) and the Samburu have started Poverty Alleviation Awareness and Nutrition (PARAN) incorporating many small Community-Based Organizations (CBOs). And, besides numerous small organizations, the Maasai have also started the Maa Pastoralist Council that will bring together all Maa-speakers including the Samburu, Ichamus, Ilaikipiak and Ilparakuyo and others across the political divide. The Pokot for their part have also developed TOMWO into a regional cross-border network and have managed to involve quite a substantial number of Pokot. While these initiatives may be hampered by communication problems given the vastness of the areas and other factors, their existence reflects awareness and interest in self-determining their future in the context of serious neglect and exploitation. The initiatives will also reduce duplication of effort and facilitate the sharing of information and experiences, hence an easier search for possible solutions to common problems.

The campaign for the protection of the rights of the Ogiek people has been gaining force during 2000 and 2001. The Ogiek indigenous people are hunter-gathers living in and depending on the forests of the Mau escarpment. The area has been declared a protected area for watershed management by the Kenyan authorities, without regard for the customary territorial and foraging rights of the Ogiek. At the same time, the Kenyan government authorities have done little to stop encroachment and logging in the forest, they have allocated lands within the Mau forest to outsiders and tried to evict the Ogiek. The Ogiek took the matter to court and in 1997 the High Court declared an injunction on any further land allocations until the dispute had been resolved. Despite this injunction, the Ogiek have suffered continued harassment and threat of eviction, the latest being the government's announcement that 47,000 acres of Mau Forest would be degazetted and thus available for settlement by outsiders. The Ogiek have two court cases pending.

Women's Issues

There have been a number of interesting events in recent years that may have an impact on the situation of women. The Beijing Plus Five conference, which took place in New York, created pressure for a bill to be passed in Kenyan legislation establishing Affirmative Action. The discussion reached the floor of parliament but it has still to be finalized.

Meanwhile, the election of the first woman chair of the Law Society of Kenya has been an historic event. There is much excitement among women, who hope that women's issues will now be better articulated. The new chair, Raychelle Omamo, indicates that one of her priorities will be legal education.

Towards the end of the year 2000, a Maasai women's organization known as Reto organized a Maasai Cultural night, which brought together all Maa-speaking peoples from Kenya and Tanzania. The purpose was to raise funds to establish a gallery and resource centre for Maasai art; to establish a language school to teach urban children the Maa language, which is in danger of extinction; and to establish a facility for holding discussions and deliberations on issues of common concern for the purposes of seeking solutions.

The event was marked by song and dance, poetry, games, drama on topical issues of concern and cultural foods. Those who attended acknowledged the fact that the event was an historical one since nothing of the kind had ever been held before and that it should be held annually. Although the event took half the night, some people suggested that more time be allocated next time and that each event should address a particular theme. One or two competitive men expressed shock that women were becoming better than men!

TANZANIA

Overview of Indigenous Peoples of Tanzania

The indigenous peoples of Tanzania, as discussed here, are the hunter gatherer communities of the Hadzabe and Ndorobo, along with the pastoralist Barbaig and Maasai[1]. This summary discusses issues of primary concern to indigenous peoples in Tanzania over the last two years, i.e. 1999 and 2000.

Hadzabe and Dodorobo Hunter-Gatherers

The Hadzabe are descendants of the bush-manoid race and, until recently, were known in Tanzania as *Kangeju, Kindiga or Tindiga*. It is believed that the name Tindiga[2] was coined by the Nyisanzu, an ethnic community neighbouring the Hadzabe. In recent years, they have rejected these other names in favour of Hadza (pl. Hadzabe) which, in their language, means a person.

The Hadzabe are often thought to be related to the Sandawe of Dodoma since they both speak a click language. The Hadzabe have a distinct tribal identity and little else in common with their neighbours. They live in the semi-arid land surrounding Lake Eyasi in Northern Tanzania, where they occupy an area of about 25,000 square kilometers traversing Mbulu, Iramba and Meatu Districts in Arusha, Singida and Shinyanga regions. Around fifty years ago, the Hadzabe occupied twice their present territory, which has since been encroached upon by the Iraqw, Nyisanzu, Sukuma, Barbaig and others.

The Ndorobo[3] neighbour the Maasai in Kiteto, Simanjiro and Ngorongoro Districts of Arusha Region. They constitute a small minority
in the region and in Kiteto District they live in the following villages:
Amei, Loolera, Kilimoto, Palango, Iltirkishi, Enkusero,
Namelok, Napilukunya, Isinya, Kitwai and Nkapapa.

Although both groups are basically hunters they also gather wild
berries, tubers, roots and honey, which used to constitute about 80%
of their food supply, particularly during the dry season. In recent
years, however, food insecurity has become a recurrent problem
affecting the hunter-gatherers and, on occasions, the government
has provided food aid. However, it has often been supplied at the
wrong times.

In recent years, some government development programmes have
attempted to turn hunter-gatherers into farmers and livestock keepers. The Hadzabe have commenced cultivation of millet, maize, cow-
pea and, to a lesser extent, cotton in Munguli, Mongo-wa-Mono and
Yaeda Chini. Other crops include maize, millet and groundnut. The
government provided the villages with ploughs and some cattle but
the latter were stolen, and the ploughs had to be transferred to a
neighbouring Sukuma village, Paji, where they are not being used.
In addition, the crops introduced to them are considered strange by
the hunter-gatherers, who would prefer such crops as cassava, po-
tatoes, etc. which demand less attention, and withstand drought
better.

Livestock keeping is slowly gaining acceptance among the hunters. As a coping strategy, some of the hunters have also started
keeping chickens but it is only the younger generation that consumes
chicken and eggs. All in all, the hunter-gatherers find agriculture a
waste of time and often resort to their traditional ways of getting
food.

Conservation policies have also constrained the hunters' access to
their sources of livelihood. Hunting and gathering of wild berries,
which mediated their livelihood, became restrictive hence creating
uncertainty and perpetual food insecurity.

Pastoralists: The Barbaig and Maasai Peoples

The Barbaig are part of the Datoga cluster that comprise Buradiga,
Bisiyeda, Gisamjanga, Bajuta, Gidang'odiga, Biyeanjida, Darorajega
and Barbaig. Whereas the Gisamjanga section of the Datoga have been
assimilated by the Iraqwi, the Biyeanjida integrated into the Nyaturu.

The Barbaig are found mainly in Arusha and Singida Regions
along the Eastern Great Rift Valley, in the Districts of Babati, Mbulu,

Maasai Women. Ngorongoro, Tanzania. Photo: Frans Welman/WIA

Mongowamono Wahadzabe Settlement, Lake Eyasi, Tanzania. Photo: Frans Welman/WIA

Hanang, Singida, Manyoni and Iramba. Most of the Barbaig are currently concentrated in Hanang District at the foot of Hanang Mountain. They often migrate with their livestock across the borders of Arusha and Singida regions and, in recent years, following alienation of their traditional territory in Hanang, they have also started migrating into Dodoma, Morogoro and Shinyanga.

The Maasai[4] of Tanzania are divided into segments, the main group are the ones regularly referred to as the Maasai who live in four districts of Arusha region: Monduli, Simanjiro, Kiteto and Ngorongoro. The other segment are the Ilparakuyo (sometimes called Kwavi) who live in Tanga and Morogoro and a few have moved to Iringa and Mbeya.

Pastoralists and Resource Alienation

All pastoralists are under pressure from different land uses. The Barbaig have lost their prime lands to wheat production under the major wheat project implemented by the National Food Corporation (NAFCO), which was funded by the Canadian International Development Agency (CIDA). This has created serious land scarcity, subsequently causing perpetual conflict.

Similarly, the Maasai have also lost critical resources to wildlife conservation[5], large and small-scale farming, to mining companies and to infrastructural development. And in the same way, serious conflicts have arisen over these lost resources.

Development in the National Context

Indigenous Peoples live in an environment that is influenced by national and regional developments. The following are some of the highlights of important developments in the country, which have either a direct or an indirect bearing on the livelihoods of Indigenous Peoples.

Structural Adjustment Programmes (SAPS) and their Impact on Indigenous Peoples

Over the last two years, Tanzania has continued to feel the impact of the implementation of Structural Adjustment Programmes (SAPs). The specific objectives of the adjustment programmes that Tanzania signed with the International Monetary Fund (IMF) included arresting the economic decline, correcting imbalances in the external accounts, reducing government budget deficit, increasing the output of food and export crops, attracting investment and external resources and establishing instruments for efficient use of resources.

While virtually all Tanzanians have felt the impact of SAPs, the most affected segments of the population have been indigenous peoples, who are marginalized. Following the privatization of animal health services, prices for livestock drugs have risen beyond the reach of most pastoralists. Lack of infrastructure and marketing facilities have made it difficult for the livestock keepers to access livestock drugs. This combination has resulted in increased livestock diseases and losses.

Economic liberalisation has had its effect on pastoralism. Increased trends in the utilisation of forest products, mining extraction, charcoal burning and expansion of areas under crop production have all had a negative impact on pastoral production. They have all resulted in loss of grazing areas and alienation of permanent water sources. Many hunting blocks and wildlife management areas have increased competition for natural resources that are critical for pastoralism.

The banning of subsistence hunting has also negatively affected hunter-gatherer communities, since their livelihoods are dependent upon hunting game and gathering berries. Although hunters have been given a Presidential License allowing them to hunt without "paying fees", the difficulties in obtaining the licence lead to restrictions in accessing hunting.

The New Land Policy and Land Act of 1999

In 1995, Tanzania formulated a National Land Policy, which reaffirms the colonial legacy that declared all land in Tanzania to be public and vested in the presidency. In February 1999, the National Assembly passed a new land law, the Land Act and Village LandAct, 1999.

Also, because of the economic liberalisation, land is given a market value and priority is given to investors over the local people. Contrary to recommendations made by the Presidential Commission's Inquiry into Land Matters, which was chaired by Professor Issa Shivji, the Ministry of Lands officials are still in charge of land administration.

The new land law emphasises optimal use of land at the expense of security of tenure for subsistence farmers, herders and hunter-gatherers. A combination of factors, such as increased human, livestock and wildlife populations, expansion of agriculture, mushrooming of peri-urban centres, new forms of natural resource uses, have all increased the pressures on natural resources and a new class of landless Indigenous Peoples is emerging in Tanzania.

Displacement of indigenous resource tenure regimes and the imposition of alien models of property rights, with land vested in the presidency and administered by the executive, i.e. Ministry officials, is seen as the root cause of land alienation and insecurity of resource tenure in Tanzania.

Emerging Issues and their Impact on the Livelihoods of Indigenous Peoples

Shrinking territories

The indigenous pastoral and hunter-gatherer communities in Tanzania have traditionally occupied areas well endowed with natural resources. Such territories were adequate in size, and ecological parameters mediated and supported the sources of livelihood that formed the heritage of such communities. Indigenous knowledge systems evolved over time, and natural resources were utilised and managed in sustainable ways.

Over the years, the systematic alienation of key resources began to result in a shrinkage of their resource bases. Reduction of the resource base has reduced livestock holdings for the pastoral Datoga and Maasai. For the hunter-gatherer Ndorobo and Hadzabe, policies and regulations governing hunting have outlawed subsistence hunting. In addition, immigrants have depleted game resources and environmental degradation has significantly reduced the availability of wild berries, roots and honey.

Land alienation:

The alienation of land belonging to Indigenous Peoples in Tanzania for the creation of wildlife protected areas (Tarangire, Manyara, Ngordoto and Serengeti National Parks as well as the creation of Ngorongoro Conservation Area) and the alienation of Barbaig land for large-scale commercial farming, such as the NAFCO wheat farms in Hanang', small-scale farming in Kiteto district and gem stone mining at Mererani in Simanjiro, have all reduced the resource base for indigenous peoples, resulting in increased levels of land use conflicts.

Resource-based conflicts

Conflicts between wildlife and human activities originate in the historical approaches to conservation movements in the region. Official policies and attitudes relating to wildlife management in the region have tended to over-emphasise a law-enforcement approach. This method of conservation was inherited from the colonial era, during which time the rights of people occupying the same territories as wild animals were regarded as secondary to those of the wildlife. Accordingly, Park management training followed the same trend, whereby the development concerns of local people were disregarded in favour of wildlife.

Kilosa Killings

In early December 2000 (the night of 8th), violence broke out between the pastoralist Maasai and crop farmers in Rudewa village, Buyuni ward in Kilosa district. Nearly 31 people, mostly farmers, were killed and about 20 injured.

The nature of the conflict was resource-based, due to incompatible forms of land use between herding and crop agriculture. Reports in the media were clearly biased against the pastoralists, who were portrayed as "loose-foot herders who had no respect for other people's property".

The incident led to the suspension of senior government officials, the Kilosa District Commissioner, Edith Tumbo, and the O.C.D., Honoratha Chuwa. The Prime Minister and Inspector General of Police respectively suspended the two officials pending the setting up of an inquiry. A commission of inquiry was subsequently set up to investigate the cause of the conflict and advise government accordingly.

Multiple Marginalization, Increasing Levels of Vulnerability and Poverty

Levels of vulnerability and poverty are increasing. The ability of Indigenous Peoples to manage ecological uncertainty and spread risks has been reduced significantly. Some of the consequences of the shrinkage of their resource base are a decrease in the mobility of herds and changes in patterns of resource use. This has, in turn, led to livestock losses and increased levels of poverty and food insecurity. There are many levels of marginalization.

Economic marginalization is caused by a combination of factors. The reduction of the resource base significantly reduces livestock numbers. Livestock herders require large and ecologically variable grazing areas that facilitate seasonal mobility for optimal productivity. Mobility is necessary in order to allow range resources to regenerate and for optimal use. Restricting daily and seasonal livestock movements creates a form of economic marginalisation.

Reduction of the resource base also reduces game resources and wild berries, on which hunter-gatherers depend. A lack of infrastructure also makes areas occupied by indigenous people less accessible. The physical infrastructure is either lacking or is inadequate and this has had a negative impact on the coverage and quality of social services. Health facilities and health staff are few and far between, as are educational facilities.

The few available schools are poorly staffed and equipped. Because of poor facilities, pupils from the indigenous communities rarely make it to secondary schools. Serious shortages of teachers, equipment and books limit access to formal education. As a result, levels of illiteracy are increasing and there are inadequate professionals from these communities. This lack of own professionals in the fields of education, human and animal health, the judicial system and administration deprives indigenous peoples of representation on decision-making bodies. Overall, the denial of development constitutes a gross violation of fundamental human rights.

Extraction of natural resources from indigenous areas is largely benefiting outsiders, and nothing is ploughed back into such areas for the development of indigenous peoples and their areas. And this constitutes a denial of the right to their own resources. Since development priorities are defined elsewhere and not where indigenous peoples live, these peoples find themselves increasingly victimised and marginalized because of the abundance of valuable natural resources available in their areas.

In the case of the pastoralists, inadequate marketing facilities constrain livestock sales, resulting in perpetually low prices for livestock and livestock products. This has increasingly reduced the purchasing power of pastoralist Barbaig and Maasai, placing them in very vulnerable situations.

Cultural marginalisation comes about as a result of many factors. the loss of key resources that constituted the basic cultural rights of indigenous peoples has impacted on indigenous peoples' cultures negatively. *Endoinyio oolmoruak* is a special sacred site whose value to the Maasai community has been constrained by the loss of key resources.

There are also ritual occasions that are no longer observed because indigenous peoples are unable to afford the required stock to perform the ritual. It is also because of economic constraints that indigenous peoples have been systematically selling their valued art objects for a pittance, resulting in the removal of indigenous artefacts from the communities to trade centres (curio shops, museums and other tourist centres). Some of this art is used to decorate tourist hotels to which indigenous peoples are denied access.

The promotion of national languages and dominant cultures has been accompanied by the systematic suppression of indigenous languages and cultures, such that in urban settings it is becoming common for indigenous children whose parents work in towns not to speak their own languages.

An important segment of the community is also being drawn to urban centres in search of wage employment and this not only denies indigenous communities much needed labour but also removes the fabric that used to hold indigenous communities together. An example of this is the case of the *Ilmurran* who have been pushed - through loss of livestock - to work as security guards in urban centres because, being non-literate, these are the only available jobs.

In the political arena, all four indigenous communities in Tanzania have experienced the loss of their indigenous territories and they have been pushed into other areas. They now live in more than 15 administrative districts, where they constitute small percentages of the population of these districts. Consequently, they have ended up becoming a minority without adequate political representation in ten districts.

Regional Initiatives, Processes and Future Prospects

In June (5th to 8th) 2000, a total of 98 participants from 48 NGOs, CBOs, service providers and concerned individuals attended a workshop that deliberated on how to develop an umbrella organization that would act as the voice of all pastoralists and hunter gatherers, a body that would coordinate their activities and enhance lobbying and advocacy on issues of primary concern.

The establishment of a forum (TPHGC*) was designed to enable member organizations to share information and experiences; facilitate coordination of initiatives enhancing the development of indigenous communities; forge effective representation of indigenous communities at various levels - local, regional, national and international; promote service delivery to indigenous communities; facilitate processes to mobilize resources for indigenous communities; ensure advocacy and lobbying mechanisms for enhancing security of resource tenure for indigenous communities; build capacity for member organizations and networking.

In order to put this into practise, a task force was set up to carry out the above activities. The composition of the task force reflected the diversity of indigenous communities participating in the meeting. Two task force members were from the Maasai community, one from the Parakuyo community, two from the Barbaig community, one from the Hadzabe community and four were selected on the basis of their professional experience.

Community Research and Development Services (CORDS) was chosen to serve as an interim Secretariat. So far, the task force has prepared a constitution, has drawn up a newsletter to inform stakeholders about progress so far and has been fundraising for the purposes of operationalizing the Council's objectives, one of which is to call the same stakeholders together for an update and to undertake strategic planning for the Council.

Regional Developments

In January 1999, a workshop organised by PINGOS and IWGIA was held in Arusha, Tanzania. The workshop brought together indigenous participants from Eastern, Southern and Central Africa. One of the achievements of the workshop is that it helped indigenous peoples from the region to build their own networks. It also provided an avenue for African indigenous peoples organizations to link up with the African Commission for Human and People's Rights.

Later the same year, the Saami Council organized a course on Human rights and UN processes in which a number of indigenous peoples and organizations participated. The course lasted for three weeks and resulted in increased knowledge of the UN processes. It was during that time that the Organization of Indigenous Peoples of Africa (OIPA) was formed.

In June 2000, the UN High Commission for Human Rights organized a workshop, again in Arusha, to bring together indigenous peoples and minorities to discuss multiculturalism.

Notes

[1]   Discussion about other groups in Tanzania that may claim the identity of being indigenous peoples is beyond the scope of this paper.
[2]   Tindiga is used by the Nyisanzu to refer to people who live in the bush and live on hunting and gathering.
[3]   Ndorobo is a Maasai word that means someone without livestock and hence dependent on hunting and gathering
[4]   Although the Maasai are found in both Kenya and Tanzania, this section deals only with the Tanzanian side of the border.
[5]   Some of the protected areas carved out of Maasailand include Serengeti (Siringet), Manyara, Tarangire, and Nkordoto National Parks. Although Ngorongoro is supposed to be shared between people and wildlife, people have clearly lost out at the expense of conservation.

*   TPHGC: Tanzania Pastoralist and Hunter-Gatherers Council

CENTRAL AFRICA

RWANDA

A s a result of sustained advocacy efforts over the past years by the national Rwandese Twa NGO "CAURWA" (*Communauté des Autochtones Rwandais*), the dire situation of the Twa, and the fact that they have been hitherto almost invisible to policy makers, is at last beginning to be recognised by the Rwandese authorities. In April 2000, the newly established National Unity and Reconciliation Commission acknowledged: "The marginalisation of the Twa people is a dark side of our society...they have been systematically forgotten as if they do not exist... they have genuine concerns." The Commission recommended affirmative action for the Twa in terms of free education and health services. Four Twa community representatives subsequently participated in the Commission's National Conference in October, and spoke powerfully to the assembled participants of their sense of injustice and exclusion from Rwandese society. The Conference recommended in Resolution 11 that special attention should be paid to women, children, youth and Twa people and efforts should be made to help their organs acquire the capacity to participate in decision-making structures. Two youth and two women's representatives have been co-opted to Parliament but, so far, there is no similar representation for Twa.

In July, CAURWA sent an open letter to President Paul Kagame, urging the government to involve them more in the country's development efforts. The letter received national and international coverage and highlighted the fact that, in the five years since the Government of National Unity came to power, the situation of the Twa has not improved. Alienated from their traditional lands without compensation, they continue to suffer poverty, lack of education, lack of basic healthcare, social isolation and exclusion from decision-making.

A meeting of Central African indigenous organisations was held in Kigali in November, to strengthen the regional development of the International Alliance of Indigenous and Tribal Peoples of the Tropical Forests. This stimulated discussion within Rwandese ministries, NGOs and the press about "indigenousness" in Africa, a concept that is widely resisted by African governments and is particularly sensitive in Rwanda, given the post-genocide government's policy to discourage identification in terms of ethnic groups. The meeting elected national focal points for the International Alliance in each country in order to strengthen communications between indigenous groups within the region.

CAURWA and its member organisations have been active at local level, including dialoguing with local authorities to release communal land for the use of Twa families, organising house-building projects, providing tools, materials and aid to Twa communities, supporting Twa secondary school pupils, and setting up a network of prefectoral focal points to liaise between the communities and CAURWA. National coordination between Twa NGOs is increasing as five NGOs are now collaborating under CAURWA's auspices to carry out community projects. A comprehensive survey of Twa prisoners in all the detention centres in Rwanda carried out by the *Association pour le Développement Global des Batwa de Rwanda* (ADBR) revealed that the majority of the 700 Twa prisoners lacked dossiers, clothing, food and contact with their families. Without financial means or influence, they are unable to advance their cases. Only a handful of Twa have so far been tried. ADBR proposes working with local lawyers to bring the cases of those Twa with dossiers to court. An estimated 3000 Twa were imprisoned after the genocide, raising the question of what has happened to the remaining 2300 individuals.

THE DEMOCRATIC REPUBLIC OF CONGO (DRC)

The Twa in eastern Democratic Republic of Congo continued to be affected by the ongoing conflict between Uganda and Rwanda-backed rebel movements, ex-Rwandese Army (FAR) and Rwandese Interahamwe militias (perpetrators of the Rwandese genocide), Congolese Mai-Mai militias and DRC government forces. Severe human rights violations have been perpetrated by all the factions involved. It remains to be seen whether, following the assassination of President Laurent Kabila on January 17th 2001 and accession of his son Joseph Kabila to power, the Lusaka peace agreement negotiated in August 1999 between all the belligerent parties can be implemented.

Detailed information about the impact of the conflict on the Twa, Mbuti and other indigenous peoples of eastern Congo is not readily available. Intense conflicts between Hema and Lendu tribes in the Ituri region of north-eastern DRC, exacerbated by power struggles within the Ugandan-backed rebel forces, have caused thousands of civilian deaths and hundreds of thousands of displaced people. The effects of this fighting on the Mbuti is not known. In October 2000, UNHCR reported that, for the first time, over 100 Pygmies had sought refuge in Betou in the Republic of Congo, fleeing fighting between the Mouvement de liberation du Congo and government forces in north-western DRC. UNCHR considered that the Pygmies' presence was worrying, 'as these small communities are usually very self-sufficient and reluctant to move from their home areas unless faced with extreme hardship.' Attacks by Interahamwe militia, Mai-Mai and other armed groups around the Kahuzi-Biega National Park in south Kivu caused increased terror for the local population, including Twa communities, who have suffered arbitrary arrests, rape and pillage of property and animals. Each of the warring factions regards the Twa as being allies of the other side, and they thus fall victim to each successive wave of militias passing through the forest. Many Twa have left the forest for villages closer to Bukavu, putting a strain on the limited resources of already poor Twa communities. Completely destitute displaced Twa have reached Bukavu, Goma and other urban centres in search of food, shelter and basic necessities. Aid agencies cannot reach Twa communities still in the forest but the Twa say that even in accessible areas they frequently do not get a share of humanitarian aid because the distribution is manipulated and diverted by other more powerful groups.

Despite the ongoing difficulties, NGOs working for the Twa are continuing their work with Twa communities around Bukavu and developing their agriculture, education and health activities with Pygmy communities further afield. A number of new NGOs have emerged in the DRC, aimed at supporting Pygmy communities in education, agriculture and health care. This indicates a growing interest in Pygmy issues, albeit donor-driven in some cases. Most of these NGOs include some Twa individuals within their staff or associates. The *Programme pour l'Intégration et le Développement des Pygmées du Kivu* (PIDP) has begun a programme to respond to the needs of Twa women, and has made contacts with agencies working with Pygmies in North Kivu. PIDP is supporting a Twa student studying rural development in Bukavu. Legal action is being taken to contest the expropriation of a field cultivated by Twa at Bishulishuli. The Twa's lack of secure land for agriculture and housing is the main problem hampering efforts to improve their situation. A quarterly information bulletin *"L'Echo des Pygmées"* reporting on local and regional events has been started by the Bukavu-based

NGO CAMV (*Centre d'Accompagnement des Menages vulnérables et Autochtones minoritaires*).

Twa communities around the Kahuzi-Biega National Park continue to express their dissatisfaction with the restrictions imposed by the park, and their landless situation. The park authorities, the Congolese Institute for Nature Conservation and *Deutche Gesellschaft für Technishe Zuzammenarbeit GmbH* (GTZ), obtained food aid from humanitarian agencies for the Twa park guards. A plan to assist the Twa more effectively is apparently being developed by the park managers.

To celebrate the International Day of Indigenous Peoples, PIDP organised a conference of Twa women representing local communities from North and South Kivu and Maniema in August. A second conference was held in Bukavu in November 2000 to discuss Twa women's rights, the effects of the war on them and their contribution to the restoration of peace in the region. It brought together indigenous women from Rwanda, Burundi, the DRC and Kenya, as well as Twa community representatives, local DRC authorities and NGOs. The conference is likely to result in the establishment of a regional Twa women's network.

BURUNDI

B urundi's latest round of violence began in October 1993, following the assassination of the democratically elected Hutu president, Melchior Ndadaye, by the Tutsi-dominated military. Since then, violent conflict between different Hutu and Tutsi elite factions struggling for political power has ravaged the country. The Arusha peace process facilitated first by the late Tanzanian President, Julius Nyerere, and then by former South African president, Nelson Mandela, brought more groups to the negotiating table during 2000, and increased prospects for a political agreement. An accord was signed on 28th August 2000 by all parties except the two main armed pro-Hutu rebel factions CNDD-FDD and PALIPEHUTU-FNL, with the result that no cease-fire agreement was negotiated and fighting between opposing factions still continues. The possibility remains that the Arusha accord will be violently rejected.

The 30,000-40,000 Twa people of Burundi were not represented in the Arusha negotiations. The Accord provides for a National Assembly with 100 deputies and a Senate with one Hutu and one Tutsi representative for each of the 17 provinces. However, Twa representation is limited to three Twa co-opted to the Senate.

As a result of the civil war, an estimated 370,000 Burundians have fled to neighbouring countries, mainly Tanzania, and some 300,000 are internally displaced or re-grouped in sub-standard camps. The remaining 5.7 million Burundian citizens continue to suffer from violence and the erosion of State infrastructure, resulting in widespread failure of basic social services including health care, education, drinking water and sanitation. Two consecutive droughts and the displacement of farmers from their lands have caused serious food insecurity and environmental concerns. As occurred during the conflict in Rwanda, the Twa of Burundi were victimised by both Hutu and Tutsi belligerents and, being the most impoverished sector of society, have least resources to enable them to survive the harsh consequences of the conflict. They feel this as a particular injustice, since the war is not of their making.

In October, a meeting was held to coordinate the activities of the two Twa NGOs UNIPROBA (*Unissons pour la Promotion des Batwa*) and UCEDD (*Union Chrétienne pour l'Education et le Développement des Déshérités*), and an NGO working with Twa people, APDH (*Association pour la Paix et les Droits de l'Homme*). The three NGOs agreed to prioritise different areas of the country and to work on issues of education, land acquisition, agriculture, income generation, housing, prisoners and promotion of Twa culture. UNIPROBA has distributed materials to Twa farmers and is supporting Twa fisherfolk on Lake Tanganyika. Through their President, Mme Libérate Nicayenze, an MP, UNIPROBA is working to get land allocated to Twa communities. UCEDD is carrying out education and literacy work with Twa communities at Gitega and, in 2000, organised a meeting of Twa women to analyse their problems and identify strategies to empower them.

UGANDA

The establishment of the Bwindi and Mgahinga Forests as national parks in 1991 resulted in the enforced exclusion of the two thousand or so Twa of south west Uganda and the total destruction of their forest-based role in the local economy. They became landless labourers for local farmers. Some Twa received compensation, most received nothing. Meanwhile farmers, who had been destroying the forest and were therefore recognised as having land rights, received most of the available compensation. Much funding for the parks comes from the World Bank through the Global Environment Facility. Belated efforts by those responsible for the parks to help evicted Twa have been resisted by local farmers who, not recognising the Twa's unique dependence on their forest resource base, see land allocation and other support to Twa as favouritism. The Twa lack alternative livelihoods - access to the forest for subsistence and religious reasons is now illegal and risky for them and only two Twa are employed by the parks. Community development projects, funded by a Trust fund established by the World Bank and supported by the Dutch Government, have been very slow to deliver benefits to the Twa, despite pressure from the Dutch.

Over the last year, however, the situation of the two thousand or so Twa in south west Uganda has to a certain extent improved, although they continue to experience discrimination and impoverishment, and to be forcibly excluded from their forests. The Twa established their own NGO in February 2000 (OUBDU – United Organisation for Batwa Development in Uganda), and have begun to receive land as part compensation for their exclusion from the forests.

In December 1999, partly due to pressure from the Dutch, 70 acres of land was bought and distributed to 38 Twa households (less than 10% of landless households). In May 2000, UOBDU's representatives participated in a workshop on the World Bank's Indigenous Peoples Policy (see below under Advocacy at the World Bank). Later in 2000, partly due to pressure from the Twa themselves who had gained confidence and knowledge as a result of contacts made during the World Bank workshop, there were further purchases of about 100 acres of land. Potentially 25% of Twa will have received a small but vital amount of agricultural land giving them some sort of subsistence base, but 75% are still destitute and, in practice, almost all of them have still not been given any rights to enter their forests for subsistence or religious reasons.

Whether these actions are too little too late and will soon slow down, or whether the process of distributing land manages to gather momentum, it is too early to say. The process may begin to meet Twa needs if it is matched by genuine participative efforts from the conservation organisations and Twa can gain real benefits from the forests. This depends on Twa access to the forests for sustainable use and cultural purposes: a promise made since their eviction and exclusion in 1991 but which has not yet materialised. Instead, Twa are either too frightened to enter the forests (and the young are losing any chance of developing forest knowledge) or, for those that do enter their forests to worship or for subsistence purposes, a three-month prison sentence is often the consequence. Thus it is a matter of urgent concern that the relevant conservation bodies have not been able to move ahead speedily on questions of Twa access or rights to their forests. If dialogue with conservation bodies does not resolve the issue of forest access, compensation and restitution, the Twa are currently considering a possible legal challenge to the 1991 eviction and their subsequent exclusion from the Mgahinga, Bwindi and Echuya forests.

CAMEROON

B agyéli indigenous communities in south-west Cameroon will soon be faced with the environmental and social consequences of an oil pipeline passing through their territories carrying oil from the Doba fields in Chad. The controversial Chad-Cameroon oil pipeline project costing US$3.5 billion was approved on June 6th 2000 by the World Bank, which is supporting the project with loans of US$240 million[1].

A survey of Bagyéli villages carried out in April 2000 by the Bagyéli organisation CODEBABIK (see below under Advocacy at the World Bank) highlighted the marginalised and vulnerable situation of this indigenous group. The 4000 or so Bagyéli (Bakola) people lack Cameroonian identity papers, never participate in local elections and have no land rights under either national law or Bantu customary law. They mainly live by hunting and gathering, some farming and as occasional labourers in Bantu villages. They have not been well informed about the implications of the oil pipeline project for their future. The project presents real risks of increased impoverishment and marginalisation of the Bagyéli people.

Lobbying efforts at the World Bank by the Bagyéli and their supporters to highlight the concerns of indigenous peoples affected by the pipeline means that the project is now the subject of international public attention. The Bank Board views the project as a case that will test the World Bank Group's ability to deliver poverty reduction and safeguard the rights of indigenous peoples. Various measures such as an Independent Advisory Group (IAG) including social and development experts to report regularly to the Board on the progress of implementing this project, and an Indigenous Peoples

Three cases from Central Africa conc. World Bank projects affecting Indigenous peoples (see p.270)

Author	World Bank-funded project	Main Conclusions
CAURWA, Rwanda	Industrial forestry and cattle-rearing projects in Rwanda's Gishwati forest in the 1980s	The projects caused the involuntary resettlement of the Impunyu Twa of the Gishwati forest, and the loss of their previous forest-based livelihoods and culture, leaving the Impunyu landless and impoverished.
CODEBABIK and Planet Survey, Cameroon	Pre-project implementation consultations with the Bagyéli on the Chad-Cameroon Oil Pipeline Project	The consultations failed to properly inform the Bagyéli of the implications of the project for their future, mechanisms for the effective participation of the Bagyéli in decision-making were lacking and State agencies actively supporting indigenous interests do not exist. OD 4.20 was not implemented correctly.
UOBDU, Uganda and FPP, UK	Impacts of the Mgahinga and Bwindi Impenetrable Forest Trust on the Batwa of SW Uganda	The Trust's implementation of provisions for the Twa, particularly the appointment of a Twa officer, compensatory land purchase and community development projects has been sluggish and half-hearted.

Plan, are proposed but it remains to be seen whether the project will address the fundamental problems of discrimination and powerlessness facing the Bagyéli and bring them sustainable livelihoods, rights and equality.

Regional events

Conference on Moist Tropical Ecosystems of Central Africa (CEFDHAC)

Twa representatives from Rwanda, Burundi and the DRC, and a Bagyeli representative from Cameroon attended the 3rd Conference on Moist Tropical Ecosystems of Central Africa (CEFDHAC) in Bujumbura, Burundi in June. CEFDHAC is an interministerial process aimed at coordinating actions on forests across the central African countries. The objective of the conference was to examine issues of good governance in the forest areas of the Congo Basin. Despite the fact that the area covered by the countries in CEFDHAC is the area inhabited by Africa's indigenous "Pygmy" peoples, the CEFDHAC process makes little effort to engage indigenous or forest-dependent communities. Recommendations by the indigenous participants for greater involvement of indigenous peoples in environmental management, though approved by delegates to the Conference, did not make it to the final communiqué.

Advocacy at the World Bank

Central African indigenous peoples contributed inputs to an evaluation and revision of the World Bank's Operational Directive 4.20 for Bank projects affecting indigenous peoples, at a workshop in Washington, in May 2000[2]. The workshop comprised eight case studies, including three from central Africa(see p.269).

The workshop enabled indigenous representatives to make useful contacts with Bank staff and with indigenous people from other regions of the world. The case studies highlighted the need for stronger participation of indigenous peoples in Bank-funded projects, early action to safeguard indigenous lands and resource use, better monitoring of projects including inputs from affected indigenous peoples and NGOs, and measures to ensure correct implementation of World Bank projects, including stronger enforcement measures with borrower governments. The Bank's draft revised indigenous peoples' policy (OP 4.10) is expected to be published in February 2001.

New Publications

Video: *People of Clay: The Twa of Rwanda*. The history and present situation of the Twa of Rwanda, in the context of the international debate on indigenous peoples in Africa. Produced by CAURWA and Forest Peoples Programme.

Albert Kwokwo Barume. *Heading Towards Extinction? Indigenous Rights in Africa: The Case of the Twa of the Kahuzi-Biega National Park, Democratic Republic of Congo.* IWGIA and Forest Peoples Programme, 2001.

Jerome Lewis. *The Batwa Pygmies of the Great Lakes Region.* Minority Rights Group, UK, 2000.

J. van den Berg & K. Biesbrouck. *The Social Dimension of Rainforest Management in Cameroon: issues for co-management.* Tropenbos-Cameroon Series 4, 2000.

Notes

1   For further details see "What is in the Pipeline for the Bagyéli of Cameroon?" by the Forest Peoples Programme, UK (*Indigenous Affairs* No 3, July-Sept 2000).
2   The report of the workshop *"Indigenous Peoples, Forests and the World Bank: Policies and Practice"*, (organised by the Forest Peoples Programme and the Bank Information Centre) is available from FPP.

SOUTHERN AFRICA

SOUTHERN AFRICA

NAMIBIA

Drastic and Slow Measures

Certain decisions and plans of the Namibian Government in 2000 and 2001 have already had, or will have, critical consequences for certain San groups in the country.

The decision to allow the Angolan Armed Forces (FAA) to fight Unita rebels from Namibian soil has had extremely destructive consequences for the San in the Kavango and Caprivi Regions. Since this decision was taken in 1999, the San in these regions have lived in fear of stepping on landmines, being attacked by Angolan soldiers and being harassed by members of Namibia's Special Field Force. Arbitrary arrests of Khwe men have been frequent occurrences. In 2000, as happened for the first time in late 1998 following a secessionist uprising in the Caprivi, hundreds of Khwe fled to refuge in neighbouring Botswana, where the majority joined the 1,600 San at the Dukwe refugee camp where they took shelter in early 1999. Five of the eight well-established villages in West Caprivi are now deserted. Tourism in northern Namibia has declined dramatically due to the unrest in the area, and this decline has drastically affected the Khwe's community-owned N//goabaca campsite in West Caprivi: no tourists visited the camp in 2000, thus it generated no income. Some schools in West Caprivi have remained closed since late 1999, and many of the learners affected have no prospects for attending school elsewhere. Fearing for their safety, most Khwe women and children no longer gather food in the bush. Since the danger of landmines became a feature of daily life, Khwe farmers have cultivated only tiny pieces of their fields, if any. In early 2001, the Working Group of Indigenous Minorities in Southern Africa (WIMSA) received reports that the vast majority of the 6,000 Khwe of West Caprivi will not be able to harvest crops in the forthcoming season, thus if no solution is found they will go hungry until the next rainy season 10 months hence. Eventually, after many requests, the Namibian Ombudswoman has promised to visit the area in February 2001 to assess the situation.

The Namibian Government's plan to relocate the Osire refugee camp to the tiny settlement of M'Katta in Tsumkwe District West (formerly West Bushmanland) is regarded as counterproductive to the San's aim of obtaining a conservancy that will grant them control over natural resources in that area. The imminent placement of nearly 20,000 refugees on land that currently sustains approximately 4,500 !Kung will result in environmental devastation and a range of associated problems. The international organisation, Survival International, took action to prevent this from happening by launching a campaign in early 2001 to raise international awareness on the issue. The response to date has been a barrage of letters – *hundreds* in fact – addressed to the Namibian Ministry of Home Affairs. A 10-member task force formed recently to tackle this issue is comprised primarily of San representing the !Kung and Ju/'hoan Traditional Authorities of Tsumkwe District West and East respectively, as well as the Nyae Nyae Conservancy and WIMSA.

In 2000, Namibia's National Assembly finally approved the long-awaited Communal Land Reform Bill but the National Council (the second House of Parliament) rejected it. Namibian NGOs have also criticised the bill on the grounds that it lacks both an integrated natural resource management plan and clarification on the status of communal land that has already been fenced off – this being a widespread and illegal practice in Namibia. The Communal Land Reform Bill is of interest to the San traditional authorities particularly, as it provides for their involvement in land allocation procedures, and also recognises customary or traditional rights regarding access to land and natural resources. Each of the six broader San communities in Namibia has its own traditional authority and though all have applied for official recognition, to date the Government has recognised only two. The remaining four authorities will not be recognised until outstanding disputes within their respective communities, and between these and the Government, have been resolved.

Education

As in previous years, the Ministry of Basic Education, Sport and Culture (MBESC), UNICEF and NGOs have continued laying the foundation for the implementation of education programmes for San.

In September 2000, the draft strategy for the "Government of Namibia and UNICEF Programme of Co-operation, 2002-2005" was approved and endorsed. San representatives were invited to participate in the thematic working groups that prepared the draft strategy, and to sit on the steering committee that approved it. This invitation was a milestone for San: it was the first offer of direct representation on bodies tasked to strategise for such a programme. The strategy paper refers to vulnerability and marginalisation, and particularly to educationally marginalised children, the majority of whom hail from San or Ovahimba communities. It also imparts lessons on special protection from marginalisation, one such protection being that "financing for affirmative actions [should] include children of marginalised groups in education, health care and other services".

The document entitled "National Policy Options for Educationally Marginalised Children", published by the MBESC in 2000 concludes that, "San children are the most educationally marginalised in the country" and further that, "The challenge for the MBESC, and for the country at large, is to facilitate the education and training of San children and at the same time allow them to keep and be proud of their origin and culture." The document pleads for applying flexibility and creativity with a view to developing appropriate measures to ensure the participation of San children in the formal education system.

Training, early childhood education and formal and traditional education have continued to play a vital role in San communities during the period under review. However, Namibian schools are still registering a high dropout rate among San learners, and a high number of those who completed Grade 10 (the compulsory minimum level that a Namibian learner should attain) did not pass the end-of-year examinations. The few San who passed the Grade 12 examinations with results high enough to earn them admission to southern African universities must compete with thousands of other applicants for a place. By way of example, eight San applicants (one of them a woman) who applied to study at the Windhoek College of Education in 2001 competed with 1,800 other applicants for the 500 available places. Three of the eight (including the woman) were invited to take further tests and attend interviews, and eventually all three were enrolled for a Basic Education Teacher Diploma.

To increase school attendance and considerably decrease dropout rates among San learners in the Omaheke Region (in east-central Namibia), UNICEF has provided financial support and expertise to the Omaheke San Trust (OST), a small umbrella organisation serving the approximately 6,000 San in the region. The OST is currently identifying the problems faced by San learners in individual schools, developing a database on schools and San learners in the region, following up on learners who have dropped out, and facilitating dialogue between San communities and schools. The OST Board of Trustees welcomes this initiative, and some of its members are engaged in the programme.

The regional San education programme being run under the auspices of WIMSA with assistance from other stakeholders has entered its second phase after a one-year period of research into the educational situation of San children in southern Africa came to completion with the publishing of a report titled Torn Apart: San Children as Change Agents in a Process of Acculturation, authored by development worker Willemien le Roux. The second phase involves returning to all stakeholders in southern Africa to identify the efforts already in progress that seek to address the report's recommendations, the gaps that still need to be filled and the people best placed to fill them, and to open communication channels among the stakeholders. A workshop on education was held in November 2000 to address the specific problems experienced by San in Botswana. The workshop was well attended and one outcome was the appointment of a lobbying group on Education for Remote Area Dwellers (San) in Botswana, comprised of representatives from the Botswana Ministry of Education, San organisations and local councils. A regional San education conference hosted by the MBESC's Intersectoral Task Force Committee on Educationally Marginalised Children in Windhoek in May 2001 will mark the end of the second phase of the regional San education programme.

During the last WIMSA general assembly held in Gaborone, Botswana, in October 2000, the 47 San delegates from Botswana, Namibia and South Africa decided to form a nine-member Regional Education and San Language Committee and a six-member Regional San Heritage and Culture Committee. The latter will be an advisory body to the San Cultural and Training Centre situated near Yzerfontein in the Cape, South Africa, and for the San Oral Testimony Collection Project operating under WIMSA and the Panos Institute, an international information-dissemination organisation based in London.

San Women

A report entitled "A Gender Perspective on the Status of the San in Southern Africa" was completed in November 2000 and is due to be published as part of a series of five reports conveying the findings of a regional study entitled *A Regional Assessment of the Status of the San in Southern Africa*, funded by the European Union and co-ordinated by the Legal Assistance Centre (LAC) in Windhoek. (One report is a general introduction to the study and the other three are country specific. All five are likely to be ready for distribution in April 2001.) Authored by Silke Felton and Heike Becker of the Centre for Applied Social Sciences (CASS) at the University of Namibia, the gender report "firstly investigates the gendered aspects of the marginalisation of the San of Southern Africa, i.e. how it affects San men and women differently ... [and] secondly [focuses] on the changing gender relations within southern African San communities". The report discusses gender-related matters under themes such as division of labour, education, health, violence and abuse, policy frameworks and leadership, and makes recommendations in respect of each theme.

Capacity Building

For many San representatives, participation in the WIMSA General Assembly was one of the highlights of 2000. It became clearly apparent at the last assembly that the San delegates had developed a sense of unity, ownership of and responsibility for WIMSA. On that occasion, detailed and highly informative reports on each community were presented, critical questions were posed and practical solutions were found to some of the problems discussed. The discussion on indigenous intellectual property rights evoked particularly intense interest. The election of a new WIMSA Board of Trustees saw a shift from the middle-aged and elderly men and women to the younger and formally-educated generation. The members of the new and old boards pledged to co-operate closely with each other.

In the absence of San representation in practically all local and national government structures – only one San having been elected to date to the 72-member National Assembly, the highest legislative organ of government – San traditional leaders who have been formally recognised and are therefore members of the Council of Traditional Leaders are believed to be the most significant San representatives in Namibia at present. WIMSA, CASS and the USA-based First Nations Development Institute have continued to enhance the capacity of the recognised and designated San traditional authorities through tailor-made training workshops. During 2000, a series of workshops was conducted in the communities to provide an opportunity for interested community members to reflect on the tasks, responsibilities and rights of the traditional authorities. Where requested, communities were supported through the process of establishing community organisations.

The above-mentioned OST is already bearing fruit. This community organisation and its San trustees have gained recognition at government level within the region, national and international NGOs have expressed interest in working with it and funds provided by several donors have made possible the establishment of a few community projects. Gaining full recognition and respect among all ethnic groups residing in the Omaheke Region remains the OST's primary challenge.

Conclusions

It is hoped that the San – with the assistance of the international public and the United Nations Working Group on Indigenous Populations – will be able to influence the Namibian Government to revoke its plan to relocate almost 20,000 refugees to the home of 4,500 San who need their natural resources to realise their plans for the envisaged N=a Jaqna Conservancy. It is also hoped that the devastating consequences of the extension of the Angolan war onto Namibian soil will lead the Namibian Government to reconsider its "invitation" to the Angolan Armed Forces (FAA). If San were to be allowed to focus on their aspirations, plans and projects without interference from more powerful and dominating State structures and groups, they could gradually achieve their goals at local, national and regional levels.

BOTSWANA

A major concern of the approximately 53,500 San in Botswana during 2000 was whether or not San communities would be able to maintain their land and resource rights given changes that have occurred in Botswana government policies and the kinds of conservation and development initiatives that are being implemented there. According to San spokespersons and advocacy groups, such as First People of the Kalahari (FPK), Kuru Development Trust (KDT), and the Working Group of Indigenous Minorities in Southern Africa, there were four major areas of concern in 2000: (1) subsistence hunting rights, (2) land rights, (3) rights to benefits from tourism and from wildlife-related conservation and development projects, and (4) cultural and language rights.

Subsistence Hunting Rights

Subsistence rights are those rights related to the fulfillment of basic human needs (e.g. water, food, shelter and access to health assistance and medicines). The denial of the right to hunt and gather, according to some people, is an example of restrictions placed on subsistence rights. The San of Botswana understand full well the need for conservation of wildlife, plants and other resources. At the same time, they feel that they should be able to exploit resources as long as they do so in a sustainable manner.

From 1979 to 2000, Botswana was the only country in Africa that allowed its citizens who carried out subsistence hunting - hunting for the purposes of obtaining meat and other wildlife products for household consumption - to engage in legal hunting, which was made possible through the provision of Special Game Licenses under Botswana wildlife conservation legislation. In the rest of Africa, those people defined as subsistence foragers generally risked arrest and imprisonment if they engaged in subsistence hunting. In March 2000, the government of Botswana issued new 'National Parks and Game Reserves Regulations' (27 March 2000, *Botswana Government Gazette*). In Section 45.1 of these regulations, the following point was made:

> *Persons resident in the Central Kalahari Game Reserve at the time of the establishment of the reserve or persons who can rightly lay claim to hunting rights in the Central Kalahari Game Reserve, may be permitted in writing by The Director (of Wildlife) to hunt specified animal species and collect veldt products in the game reserve, subject to any terms and conditions and in such areas as the Director may determine (Republic of Botswana 2000).*

What this means, in effect, is that Special Game Licenses would no longer be issued to people. Instead, people in the Central Kalahari Game Reserve will have to apply to the Department of Wildlife and National Parks in the Ministry of Commerce and Industry in order to obtain hunting rights in the form of a Director's License. As of 2000, therefore, Special Game Licenses were no longer being provided to subsistence hunters in Botswana.

In the meantime, people continue to be arrested, jailed, fined, and deprived of their assets (e.g. horses, donkeys, weapons, bridles, saddles). Such an event occurred in July 1999, when 13 men from New! Xade, one of the resettlement locations, were arrested for allegedly engaging in illegal hunting. In this case, 7 of the men were arrested inside the CKGR, in contravention - allegedly - of section 2(3) of the 'Wildlife Conservation and National Parks Act, 1992'

A contemporary San settlement, Botswana. Photo: Arthur Krasilnikoff

Young San woman dressed for dance, Botswana. Photo: Arthur Krasilnikoff

(Republic of Botswana 1992). In addition, 6 men were charged with having killed a gemsbok in GH 10, one of the controlled hunting areas (CHAs) in Ghanzi District, sometimes called the Okwa Wildlife Management Area, and were charged with having contravened 19(3) of the 'Wildlife Conservation and National Parks Act'. The men who were arrested had Special Game Licenses, so the charge of hunting without a license was thrown out of court in October 2000.

Security Rights

A major concern of San and other rural people in Botswana relates to security rights. *Security rights* include the rights to be free from torture, execution and imprisonment, or rights relating to the integrity of the person. This set of rights is especially important in light of the frequency of allegations of torture and mistreatment of suspected "poachers" by game scouts and other government officials in Botswana. Such an incident allegedly occurred in late August 2000 in the Molapo area of the Central Kalahari Game Reserve (CKGR). The claims relating to this case are still uncertain, and investigations into the matter are ongoing. But some general information has been obtained.

According to field reports on the incident, 20 men and 4 women from Molapo in the CKGR were allegedly detained by the Botswana Police from Rakops and game scouts from the Department of Wildlife and National Parks for supposedly being involved in a poaching operation. Some of the people detained were taken into the bush away from Molapo and allegedly tortured for a period of 6 days. Subsequent to that incident, a prominent member of the Molapo community, Mathambo Sesana, died of a heart attack which, according to some reports, was a result of the treatment that he had received at the hands of the police and game scouts.

There were other incidents in 2000 in which individuals were arrested and detained for allegedly hunting without a license. In some cases, the charges were dismissed. In other cases, the individuals were kept in jail for inordinately long periods without being allowed to hear the charges against them or have access to legal representation.

The Central Kalahari Game Reserve
and Land and Resource Rights

Botswana has devoted a substantial proportion of its total land area to conservation purposes, including parks, game reserves and national monuments, all of which fall under the category of State land (17% of the country) and Wildlife Management Areas (WMAs), which are blocks of land in the so-called tribal land areas or communal lands of the country (71% of the country, about half of which is now zoned as Wildlife Management Areas).

One of the few game reserves in Africa that until recently allowed residents to continue to reside and earn a livelihood was the Central Kalahari Game Reserve (CKGR) in Botswana. As reported in *The Indigenous World 1997-98* (pp. 300-303) in May 1997, the government of Botswana relocated a sizable proportion of the CKGR's population, over 1,100 people, to two sites outside of the reserve, one in the Ghanzi District to the west of the reserve (New !Xade), and the other in the northern Kweneng District south of the reserve, Kaudwane, not far from Khutse Game Reserve. The populations of the new communities are so large, and the resources in the vicinity of the settlements so few, that the residents have been unable to sustain themselves through foraging, small-scale agro-pastoralism and rural industries, and have thus had to depend heavily on the government of Botswana's relief programs for economic support.

A Negotiating Team regarding the CKGR has been meeting with government officials for a number of years and it met with officials from the Department of Wildlife and National Parks several times during 2000. The Negotiating Team consists of representatives from First People of the Kalahari, Ditshwanelo (the Botswana Center for Human Rights), the Botswana Christian Council and WIMSA, along with a legal advisor, Glyn Williams, of Chennells Albertyn, a legal firm based in Cape Town. The Negotiating Team has pushed for recognition by the government of Botswana of the rights of the G/wi, G//ana, Bakgalagadi and other groups in the CKGR, including (1) residential rights, (2) hunting rights, (3) gathering rights, and (4) rights to a share in the economic returns from tourism in the reserve.

The Negotiating Team wants to ensure that the people who have rights in the reserve get some of the benefits from the tourism and other conservation and development-related activities in the CKGR. The Team has called for the inclusion of the needs of CKGR residents in the *Central Kalahari Game Reserve Management Plan,* which is currently in the process of being revised and updated by the government of Botswana. It is hoped that the new management plan will include "communal use zones" where people from local communities in the CKGR will be able to continue to obtain the resources necessary for subsistence and income generation.

The San in various parts of Botswana, with assistance from personnel employed by non-governmental organizations, notably First People of the Kalahari and Kuru Development Trust, were engaged during 2000 in the mapping of San territories (ancestral lands) and land use patterns as part of a strategy to gain government and district council recognition of San land and resource access rights. This process has been done using Geographic Positioning System (GPS) instruments and applying Geographic Information Systems (GIS) techniques. Such mapping work was carried out in the Dobe and !Goshe areas of western Ngamiland, in the Okavango Panhandle area, and in the Central Kalahari Game Reserve.

The Ju/'hoansi San of the Dobe area sought to further institutionalize their land and resource rights in western Ngamiland. One way that they have gone about this is through establishing new water sources, one successful one being at !Ubi (Qubi), a Ju/'hoan community that is the most important n!ore in the Dobe complex of n!oresi, (Ju/'hoan traditional territories). The !Ubi n!ore is some 230 sq km in size and is the only n!ore besides Dobe itself in which there are Ju/'hoansi residents living year round.

In the process of applying for water rights in western Ngamiland, individuals have on occasion attempted to outmaneuver their communities and obtain individualized rights over water points, something that has not gone down well with other Ju/'hoansi, who have pushed for rights to be given to communities rather than individuals, something much in keeping with Ju/'hoan traditions and sensibilities. Fortunately, these efforts have not been successful, and there is still a possibility that the various family groups at Dobe who have traditional territorial rights in the region around Dobe will be able to obtain title over their n!oresi, which they can then manage through a representative community body such as a trust.

Another way the San attempted to obtain land and resource rights was through engaging in community-based natural resource management (CBNRM). The Botswana government had passed legislation in the 1980s and 1990s that made it possible for local people in communal (tribal land) areas to gain rights to wildlife resources if they formed a community-based institution, usually a community trust, and then applied to the Department of Wildlife and National Parks for a wildlife quota for the area where they resided.

In October 1997, the people of /Xai/Xai, a community of some 350 people in western Ngamiland, formed the /Xai/Xai (Cgae Cgae) Tlhabololo Trust. In exchange for the sub-leasing of some of the wildlife of the controlled hunting areas to which the people of /Xai/Xai had access (NG 4 and NG 5, which together make up an area of some 16,966 sq km), the trust was in a position to make as much as P1,000,000 per year. In August 2000, there were 24 people employed by the safari operator, and food, medicines and other goods were being supplied to the population of /Xai/Xai as part of the joint venture agreement. There were at least half a dozen community trusts that had majority San populations in Botswana in 2000, some of them in and around the Okavango Delta region and others in the western part of the country in North West, Ghanzi, and Kgalagadi Districts.

In January 2001, however, the Ministry of Local Government stipulated that the community trusts that had been formed in the 1990s and early part of the new millennium in Botswana no longer had the right to retain the cash that was generated from their operations; the resources instead were supposed to go to the district councils. The Botswana government decision was challenged by non-governmental organizations, international donors, and San themselves. At the time of writing, no final decision had been reached on the status of the community trusts in Botswana.

Cultural and Language Rights

The language rights issue in Botswana has been an ongoing concern of the San for years. Botswana government policy is such that the languages taught in schools in the country are Setswana and English. There is no mother tongue education in the so-called minority languages, such as Ju/'hoan, Nharo or !Xoo. San children who go to school must learn Setswana when they start their education, and they are sometimes discouraged from speaking their own languages. The rights of minorities to speak their own languages and promote their own cultural traditions was the subject of a symposium held at the University of Botswana ("Challenging Minorities, Difference, and Tribal Citizenship") from May 23-26, 2000. At that meeting, several San spoke out on the importance of being able to use and teach San languages.

Efforts continued to be made in 2000 to engage in minority language education activities as part of the Nharo Educational Program at D'Kar in Ghanzi District, and the work of the Village Schools Program (VSP) in Namibia, in which the Ju/'hoan language is being taught, has important potential implications for Botswana San (see LeRoux 1999; Batibo and Smieja 2000). Thus far, however, the government of Botswana has not made a formal decision to allow mother tongue education in minority languages in the Botswana school system. The future of the San of Botswana depends very much on their ability to convince the Botswana government, international agencies, and non-governmental organizations of the importance of paying attention to social, economic and cultural rights, which they see as a matter of cultural as well as physical survival.

References

Batibo, Herman M. and Birgit Smieja, eds. (2000) *Botswana: The Future of the Minority Languages*. Frankfurt am Main and Bern: Peter Lang.

LeRoux, Willemien (1999) *Torn Apart: San Children as Change Agents in a Process of Acculturation*. Ghanzi, Botswana and Windhoek, Namibia: Kuru Development Trust and the Working Group of Indigenous Minorities in Southern Africa.

Republic of Botswana (1992) *Wildlife Conservation and National Parks Act, 1992*. Gaborone, Botswana: Republic of Botswana.

Republic of Botswana (2000) "National Parks and Game Reserves Regulations" (27 March 2000), Botswana *Government Gazette*. Gaborone, Botswana: Republic of Botswana.

SOUTH AFRICA

The policy situation for indigenous peoples in South Africa shifted repeatedly during 2000, with different government departments being more or less helpful but with no coherent policy guidance or political commitment emerging from the Cabinet or the President.

In 1999, President Thabo Mbeki demonstrated his government's commitment to redress for indigenous peoples by accelerating land restitution to the ‡Khomani, !Xû and Khwe peoples. However, this momentum did not continue into 2000. Mbeki's desire to stake out South Africa's leadership position on human rights in Africa and at the UN was eclipsed by other events at home, including a weakening currency and a debacle over the President's views on AIDS and other public relations problems.

South Africa Recognises Indigenous Peoples

The year started auspiciously with South Africa openly supporting the UN Declaration and the Permanent Forum during a Commission for Human Rights debate in Geneva in March 2000. South Africa stated unequivocally that it recognises the presence of indigenous peoples in South Africa and challenged other African countries to be honest about the issue. UN watchers noted that South Africa might be able to encourage Canada and other sympathetic countries to accelerate the speed of processing of the Draft Declaration on the Rights of Indigenous Peoples (UNDDRIP). The Department of Foreign Affairs was keen to develop a coherent policy on the UN Permanent Forum and UNDDRIP. However, South African foreign policy can only be articulated following clarification on related domestic policy, which has yet to be achieved (see below).

South Africa and Canada participated in a special joint briefing by the Indigenous Peoples of Africa Co-ordinating Committee (IPACC) and grassroots activists from Burundi and Algeria, where there have been cases of extreme human rights violations against Batwa Pygmies and Amazigh (Berbers) respectively.

At home, the chairperson of the South African Human Rights Commission (SA-HRC), Dr Barney Pityana, took the bold step of challenging the African Commission on Human and Peoples Rights to investigate the plight of indigenous peoples around the continent. The proposal was hotly contested by some Commissioners but was eventually accepted as a topic for research. South Africa then commissioned its own report on the status of indigenous peoples' rights in South Africa and related international issues.

The Concept of 'Indigenous Populations' Causes Delay in the Release of SA-HRC Report

A year on, the SA-HRC report on indigenous rights has yet to go on public release as it has become ensnarled in the bureaucratic system of the DCD / DPLG, which was being reorganised and reprioritised from above (see below). The SA-HRC report apparently deals with some of the conceptual difficulties of recognising an 'indigenous' population within a broader African society, as well as making a series of recommendations to help sustain indigenous identity and rights based on international experience. The most dramatic of these is likely to be the recommendation to facilitate cross border movements by indigenous peoples into Namibia and Botswana. The SA-HRC report allegedly argues that the right to cultural survival and equality requires such mobility. As borders are a very sensitive issue in Africa, this recommendation, which pits domestic constitutional principles against regional bureaucratic practices, is likely to cause some difficulties for Pretoria. As recently as 1999, ‡Khomani San were arrested for walking a few metres past the barbed wire fence that separates families living in South Africa and Botswana.

Concurrently, the Department of Foreign Affairs was stymied from any further policy initiatives until the Department of Provincial and Local Affairs (DPLA) had settled the domestic policy.

The Mandate of the Department of Constitutional Development (DCD) Causes Problems

The crux of the problem revolves around the mandate of the Department, which is meant to handle both Constitutional issues and the specific brief to investigate the claims of those identifying themselves as indigenous peoples in South Africa. This Department is also meant to guide the Cabinet in policy development, first at domestic level, then as foreign policy.

Originally, the Department of Constitutional Development (DCD) had a mandate to investigate the traditional chieftaincy system of the Khoe and San peoples. Historically the San did not have 'chiefs' but rather a complex system of family 'owners' of water sources, and other leadership roles, such as healers, trance-dance shamans, hunters, etc. Similarly, whatever chieftaincy system existed amongst Nama people in South Africa disappeared in colonial times. In contrast, Griqua groups still hotly dispute their respective claims to traditional leadership. The situations of Griquas and the other indigenous peoples in the country vary significantly. Griqua groups were more thoroughly assimilated into Afrikaans-speaking Protestant culture and the associated 'Coloured' identity of the colonial and *apartheid* periods. Nama groups along the Orange River and the ‡Khomani (or more accurately the N||n‡e) of the Kalahari have maintained their threatened language and many still have access to important traditional knowledge systems, including advanced knowledge of plants, animals and the environment. The !Xû and Khwe populations immigrated from Angola and Namibia bringing robust language and cultural traditions that were not so greatly eroded by the extensive aggression of the colonial and *apartheid* administration.

This diversity of historical experience and traditional identities became more complex when a new element claiming indigenous identity and insisting on participation in the DCD's investigation appeared. A group of people previously identified as being 'Coloured' (i.e. of mixed European, Asian or African descent), emerged to claim that they were the inheritors of historical Khoe cultural entities throughout the country. Relying on written historical documents, the Khoe-revivalists laid claim to chieftaincy status and reclaimed (Dutch) names of Khoe ethnic and cultural groups that had ceased to exist up to two centuries earlier.

The DCD was faced with a myriad of complicated claims to chieftaincy, on the one hand, and an evident situation of rural indigenous peoples without any chieftaincy systems but with serious economic and social problems typical of indigenous people around the planet on the other.

The DCD launched a research programme to clarify the claims and needs of the communities, including a report on traditional chieftaincy systems. Halfway through the year, the national government restructured the DCD, turning it into the Department of Provincial and Local Affairs (DPLA). The indigenous portfolio should have been shifted to the Department of Justice but, due to capacity problems and logistics, it remained with the DPLA, albeit with decreased importance and little hope that major policy advice would be forthcoming.

In 2001, the DPLA was again restructured and renamed the Department of Provincial and Local Government (DPLG). The DPLG has been stripped of all constitutional monitoring responsibilities. As a result, the report on Khoe and San peoples' needs and claims has been jammed in a bureaucratic process with no evident way out. The long awaited SA HRC report on indigenous rights has become one of the victims of this policy deceleration. The SA HRC report, which is itself tied to the African Commission on Human and Peoples Rights research project, is being held back by the DPLG Minister until other matters are resolved relating to broader policy on leadership amongst majority ethnic groups.

The Khoe and San research project is being incorporated into a larger DPLG process of reviewing the traditional chieftaincy system of the majority population (Bantu language-speaking peoples, recognised by both the colonial and apartheid regimes). There is little likelihood that the Black chiefs will accept that the term 'indigenous' should have a usage restricted to Khoe and San peoples, particularly when it is being associated with 'Coloured' nationalist revivalist groups. 'Coloured' South Africans are perceived to have enjoyed certain special concessions and rights during the apartheid period, a fact not forgotten by Black politicians and leaders today.

Implementation of Basic Language Rights Leads to Renegotiation of San and Nama Leaders' Status

On an optimistic note, the Khoe and San Language Body (KSLB), a constitutionally and legally created structure, has increased its capacity and started to have a policy impact. After a year-long organisational development process sponsored by the South African San Institute (SASI), the KSLB is starting to make its presence felt. KSLB has called for the restoration of Khoe and !Ui place names in the Northern Cape Province, including the restoration of the name of the Orange River, originally known as the *Kai !Garib*. The KSLB will mount increasing pressure on the government to implement Nama language education along the Kai !Garib, as well as insisting on the creation of effective alphabets for !Xû and Khwedam. San and Nama leaders see implementation of their basic language rights as the foundation for renegotiating their status within the country and winning back the respect of their own youth.

In Gordonia district, SASI helped the ‡Khomani community locate more of its elders who speak the almost extinct N|u language, the very last variety of the !Ui language family once spoken across South Africa. 25 N|u speakers have been found, although four died in 1999-2000. In October and November 2000, twelve elders journeyed back to the Kalahari, to their newly restored land, to teach their language to enthusiastic youth who have grown up in urban township areas. The language learning project is part of an overall co-operation between SASI and the community to help manage and restore cultural knowledge systems and traditional skills. Mapping of the history of the district's San is at an advanced stage and is being used in negotiating joint management and usage rights inside the Kgalagadi Transfrontier Park.

San Activists Press for Recognition of Rights within National Park

The topic of joint management of the National Park remains a controversial issue, and a high priority for San activists. Currently, the San have legal ownership of an unspecified 25,000 hectares inside the Park as part of the 1999 land settlement. However, San leaders are asking for broader recognition of other rights within the Park, including the right to visit grave sites, conduct research and training, conduct sacred rituals and, ideally, to sustainably harvest natural resources. The South African National Parks (SANP) remains ambiguous about whether it sees the land settlement as part of a joint management arrangement that would see greater use of traditional knowledge systems in conservation, tourism and management, or whether the land settlement is an attempt to contain the perceived threat to the Park.

!Xû and Khwe activists continued to advance the process of moving their 4500 people out of an impoverished tent city on military land to the new and fertile land at Platfontein, after their successful land claim. !Xû and Khwe leadership structures continue to strengthen, with a new generation of youthful leadership playing an important role in interaction with the State. The arts and crafts projects advanced very successfully, with a new shop opening in Cape Town to help market the variety of traditional and contemporary products. With the support of the South African Broadcasting Corporation (SABC), the !Xû and Khwe communities launched the first radio station to broadcast in San languages. Radio XK-FM broadcasts locally in both !Xû and Khwedam, neither of which yet have a written alphabet.

The International Labour Office (ILO) project on Indigenous and Tribal Peoples commissioned and published a report on South African Indigenous Peoples, looking at both needs and policy trends. The report is available from the ILO office in Geneva.

SOUTH ASIA

BANGLADESH

Chittagong Hill Tracts

D espite an agreement between the Government of Bangladesh and the Parbattya Chattagram Jana Samhati Saamiti (JSS) in December 1997, aimed at bringing peace to the volatile region of the Chittagong Hill Tracts, the situation remains fraught and uncertain. There is widespread concern that the Peace Accord has not provided the indigenous peoples of the CHT with their promised regional autonomy as the Government has not honoured its obligations under the Accord.

Three years on, the Accord remains unimplemented in key areas such as empowerment of the Regional Council, establishment of a land commission, rehabilitation of the internally displaced Jummas, resettlement of the state-sponsored settlers outside the CHT, and withdrawal of the armed forces from the region. But what has emerged as another complex issue in restoring peace to the CHT is the internecine tension between the JSS and the United Peoples Democratic Front (UPDF). The UPDF was formed by factions of the Hill People's Council (Pahari Gano Parishad), the Hill Student's Council (Pahari Chattra Parishad), and the Hill Women's Federation (HWF) who were opposed to the Accord which, in their opinion, does not meet the Jummas' demands for full regional autonomy.

Attempts have been made to resolve the differences between the two parties – which are more in terms of approach rather than in aims and objectives – such as the initiative of a group of respected Jumma elders including Upendra Lal Chakma of the Jumma Refugee Welfare Association. So far, the two groups have not yet come to an understanding although they have met on various occasions. In addition, members of both groups have been arrested and/or detained in police custody and in jail (especially from the UPDF group). On 12 January 2001, Sanchay Chakma, a leading member of the UPDF, was arrested during a public meeting in Chittagong, together with eight other UPDF members and supporters; they have not yet been released. Within this environment, recent reports indicate that there has been a rise in petty crimes and armed robberies. However, the most disturbing aspect is that this internal tension provides the Government with an excuse to justify the continued presence of the armed forces in the area.

Efforts are ongoing for the JSS and the UPDF to agree on cooperation towards strengthening indigenous self-rule in the CHT, including within the parameters of the Accord, and to terminate their confrontational relationship. It is hoped that the two parties will resolve their differences soon for the sake of the Jummas' collective interest.

Peace Accord

The implementation of the Peace Accord remains a contentious issue. Despite Government claims that 98% of its provisions have been implemented, the implementation process has been criticized both at home and abroad.

In September 2000, a parliamentary delegation of the European Union described the implementation as proceeding "very slowly" and emphasized the urgency for full devolution of powers to the Regional Council and the Hill District Councils, the withdrawal of the armed forces from the CHT and the resettlement of the Bengali settlers outside the CHT. The delegation clarified that the EU has decided to make future financial assistance contingent upon tangible progress in implementation of the Accord. Jyotirindra Bodhipriyo Larma, leader of the JSS and the chairperson of the interim Regional Council, has also been persistently demanding full implementation of the Peace Accord as per its terms and conditions. He has identified non-implementation of the Accord as the main reason for the increasing instability in the CHT.

Although some legislative steps have been taken vis-à-vis the councils, the practical implementation of a transfer of power to the Regional Council (RC) and the Hill District Councils (HDCs in Bandarban, Khagrachari and Rangamati) has not been achieved. The civil and military bureaucracy of the Government still retains the most important powers, such as law and order and land administration.

The active role played by the armed forces in the CHT also continues. The 1973 order imposing military rule in the CHT remains in force and only a few of the camps have been dismantled so far (a JSS report claims only 31 out of 500). There are reports of human rights abuses, arrests, intimidation and harassment committed by the armed forces, often in collaboration with settlers. Amnesty International reports that incidents have occurred that are reminiscent of past army practices, which resulted in the killing of indigenous people and setting their homes on fire (*Bangladesh: Hu-*

man rights in the CHT, 2000). There are also reports of rape, sometimes of young girls.

Land Rights
The erosion of the land rights of indigenous Jummas continues unabated by means of different measures, including non-implementation of the Accord and related agreements.

In April 2000, Justice Abdul Karim was appointed to lead the Land Commission, which is to be responsible for the adjudication of land disputes in the CHT. However, the commission is not yet fully operational and its other members, including the traditional chiefs of the CHT, have not yet been formally appointed. The Commission is to decide all land-related disputes in the CHT, and its decision is to be final. It is essential that the Land Commission is operational soon and that it adopts an objective and unbiased approach to conflictive land disputes.

This is of grave importance when analyzed within the context of the influx of some 400,000 non-Jummas, brought into the CHT between 1979 and 1984 by a state-sponsored population transfer programme. These settlers were allocated land that rightfully belongs to the Jummas, and the Jummas were either forcibly evicted from their traditional lands to make way for the settlers or, within the turbulent climate of settlement, militarization and oppression, sought refuge in neighbouring countries or in remoter forest areas. It is clear that most, if not all, potential land conflicts will be related to the population transfer programme, a practice that has been condemned in international law as unlawful and amounting to a gross abuse of human rights.

It is thus even more disturbing to note that the chairperson of the Task Force, set up for the rehabilitation of the returning Jumma refugees and the internally displaced, has decided to include 38,156 settler families as "internally displaced", much to the outrage of the indigenous peoples, including the JSS. They fear that this will enable the settlers to claim the lands they were illegally allocated by the Government.

Many of the Jumma refugees have not had their ancestral lands returned to them as was agreed by the Government as a precondition to their return to the CHT (some of these are under occupation by the settlers). In its recent report on Land and Human Rights in the CHT, the CHT Commission estimates that, with the 90,208 Jumma and 38,156 settler refugee families identified by the Task Force, more than half of the CHT population has been displaced by the 25-year long conflict (*Update 4*, 2000).

The acquisition and leasing of lands in the CHT also continues unabated despite the Accord and existing legislation. The forest department has been acquiring lands in order to create Reserved Forests for afforestation purposes. This will effectively debar the indigenous peoples from using the forest and its resources, and make any contravention a crime. Executive orders passed in 1992, 1996 and 1998 to demarcate nearly 220,000 acres as Reserved Forest remain in force despite repeated demands for their revocation.

There are also allegations that Deputy Commissioners in the three hill districts are leasing out lands to non-indigenous persons, and the military has taken out a lease over 30,000 acres of land in the Bandarban district for an artillery training centre, which will displace an estimated 25,000 indigenous people. These acquisitions and transfers are contrary to the provisions of the Accord as well as existing CHT legislation requiring that no lands may be leased, sold or otherwise transferred without the prior approval of the hill district councils. A protest rally against these land acquisitions was organized in Bandarban in October 2000, which was supported by all sections of the indigenous people, including the different political groups and their student and youth wings, and the traditional leaders.

Another threat to the land rights of the indigenous Jummas is that caused by mining. United Meridien Company of the USA found large reserves of gas in the CHT and there are plans to start drilling in the Baghaichari, Jurochari and Dighinala areas. This will not only result in displacing the indigenous peoples living in these areas; it is also a major threat to their health and well-being, in addition to causing environmental degradation. Since gas (and oil) are highly combustible, it is highly likely that swidden or shifting cultivation - which involves burning of vegetation - will not be allowed in the vicinity of the gas (or oil) drilling sites. This will almost certainly lead to further marginalization of the already impoverished indigenous farmers in the CHT.

What is even more alarming is a Government plan to raise the level of the Kaptai reservoir by 14 feet in order to produce two 50 mega-watt hydro-power units. The project is co-financed by the Japan Bank of Investment Corporation (JBIC). The Kaptai dam was constructed in 1960 flooding 40,000 acres of fertile rice-fields and uprooting over 100,000 indigenous Jummas (many of whom remain internally displaced). To raise the water level of the lake will have devastating socio-economic and environmental consequences for the indigenous peoples.

The Government's Power Development Board is eager to go ahead with the programme despite its adverse impact on the local people. The Board has publicly criticized community-based NGOs that have facilitated dialogue on the human rights dimensions of the proposed programme in an effort to highlight its effects. There are indications that the programme will be implemented despite the protests of the indigenous people.

Health and Education
A rural assessment report on Livelihood Security in the CHT published in April 2000 by CARE, an international NGO, finds that the Jummas face major health and education problems. It reports that "malaria and diarrhoea are endemic in the CHT and constitute the most common causes of child mortality", which is already high in the CHT. It reports that only 26% have access to safe drinking water, especially in remote areas, where tube wells often run dry for part of the year. The report also examines the education level in the CHT and finds that it is low, with a high drop out rate, especially among girls. It attributes this to the fact that instruction is in Bengali, which is not the mother tongue of the indigenous children, and discrimination against indigenous students.

However, the major issue was the finding that most indigenous communities face moderate to severe food shortages caused mainly by the scarcity of land, which is exacerbated by the influx of plains settlers onto the ancestral lands of the Jummas, as well as by the practice of turning traditional lands into reserve forests and leasing of lands to non-indigenous persons (about 5,000 acres in Rangamati district alone). There have been reports of starvation in remote areas of the Hill Tracts and, although some international agencies have provided emergency relief, the problem continues.

Religious Intolerance and Discrimination
The indigenous Jummas face discrimination in all areas of their daily lives. This problem is highlighted by the interim report of the UN Special Rapporteur on the Elimination of all forms of Religious Intolerance (9 August 2000). The Special Rapporteur, Mr. Abdel-fattah Amor visited Bangladesh, and the CHT, in May 2000 and points out in his report that although the Constitution of Bangladesh does not formally recognize the indigenous peoples as such, the Prime Minister - in her 1999 speech to the Hague Appeal for Peace Conference - referred specifically to the question of the CHT and to the right of an indigenous people to preserve its own identity, culture, tradition and values.

The report refers to the Babu Chara Bazar incident of October 1999 when the army, assisted by 150 settlers, attacked Jummas at the bazaar and ransacked a Buddhist temple, attacked the monks and desecrated statues of the Buddha (many Jummas are Buddhists). The Special Rapporteur also reports that the indigenous peoples are often subjected to "covert pressure from Islamic NGOs, and even Muslim extremist groups seeking to convert them to Islam, notably in return for services or money. Certain representatives interpreted the financial assistance provided by the State for the construction of new mosques and madrasahs (religious schools) as a discriminatory policy favouring Islam since, in contrast, indigenous religious institutions received meagre public subsidies."

In his report, the UN Special Rapporteur finds that the State appears to be "more sensitive to the interests of Muslims", and that this is reflected in the obstacles faced by non-Muslims in terms of access to public-sector jobs, especially to positions of responsibility. He goes even further and identifies this approach as the reason for the delays in full implementation of the Peace Accord in favour of the ethnic communities/indigenous peoples in the Chittagong Hill Tracts. In conclusion, the Rapporteur encourages the authorities to apply the Accord fully, and as rapidly as possible, as this Accord is fundamental for the survival of the indigenous peoples of the CHT and the preservation of their ethnic, religious and cultural identity.

Development

Since the Peace Accord, a large number of national and foreign NGOs and international agencies (UNICEF, UNESCO, World Bank, Asian Development Bank) have commenced operations in the CHT. However, with the implementation process of the CHT Accord lagging behind, and the Regional Council and the Hill District Councils not yet fully empowered, the indigenous peoples do not feel that any development undertaken in this interim period will be fully sustainable, unless and until it is undertaken with their consent and participation at all levels. However, many initiatives are simply implemented without any meaningful involvement on the part of the indigenous peoples and without taking into consideration their special characteristics, and for this reason many of the major national NGOs have also been criticized.

The European Union adopted a Resolution on 17 January 2001 calling on the Government of Bangladesh to accelerate implementation of the Accord, including empowerment of the Regional Council and establishment of the Land Commission. It also reiterated its support for the full resettlement and rehabilitation of the Jumma refugees and internally displaced as well as for the possible resettlement of the 400,000 Bengali settlers outside the CHT. However, it reaffirmed that any financial assistance would be conditional upon substantial progress in implementation of the Peace Accord and the need for culturally appropriate projects (B5-0048/2001/rev.1).

However, Denmark, a member country of the European Union and a leading protector of indigenous rights in international fora, has entered into a co-financing project with the ADB for an infrastructure project in the CHT, primarily for roads and bridges, at an estimated cost of $60.3 million. Given the continuing militarization of the area, the Jummas fear that this will only serve state interests to the detriment of their rights.

The Garos: Update on the Chailtachara Incident

On 18th December 1999, a group of Bengali Muslims attacked the Chailtachara Garo village in the district of Moulvibazar, with the intention of occupying the village and its surrounding forest lands. The village Headman, Gregory Nokrek, was stabbed and houses were looted. At that time, Gregory Nokrek appealed to the police for justice, but this was not forthcoming (see *The Indigenous World 1999-2000*, p. 293f). National newspapers, intellectuals and writers reported on the incident and expressed their concern and support. In the meantime, however, the Garo village of 20 families with 168 acres of hill forest has been occupied by Bengalis in the name of Kormodha Bohumukhi Saamity, an organisation led by the chairman of the Bengali Union Council. The trees have been cut down and sold. Headman Gregory Nokrek has fled to India. It is reported that he is now working in a coal mine in Meghalaya, India. There is no information as to the whereabouts of his wife, son's wife, brother's daughter or the one-year old grandson who were all abducted.

Garo and Khasi Communities Threatened by Eco-Park

Recently, a plan for the establishment of an eco-park on Khasi and Garos land in the *Moulvibazar* forest area was revealed. More than 1,000 Garo and Khasi families will be evicted if this plan goes ahead. The Environment and Forest Ministry did not consult with local indigenous people before planning this eco-park.
The National Adivasi Coordination Committee opposes the creation of the eco-park. In February 2001, a large public gathering and hunger strike to stop the eco-park on Khasi and Garo ancestral land was organized.

NEPAL

Indigenous Peoples Demand Constitutional Amendments

The Nepalese Indigenous peoples are campaigning for the amendment of the present Constitution of the Kingdom of Nepal. A National Consultation on Integrated Strategies in Promoting the Rights of Indigenous Nationalities in Nepal, held at Dhulikhel in Kavre District (Central Nepal) from January 16 to 20, 2000 and organized by the Nepal Federation of Nationalities (NEFEN) and Minority Rights Group International (MRG), had proposed constitutional changes to abolish all the discriminatory clauses of the constitution, statutes and common laws in the country. This national consultation was preceded by two regional meetings: Eastern regional consultations were held from January 4 to 5, 2000 at Dharan, Sunsari District, and Middle and Western regional consultations from January 7 to 8, 2000 at Narayanghat, Chitwan District. The central meeting was attended by representatives of NEFEN, legal professionals, intellectuals, representatives of indigenous peoples' organizations and different political parties, human rights activists, former members of Parliament, a former member of the Constitution Drafting Commission of 1990 and members of the Indigenous Women's Organization. In total, 59 delegates participated in the national consultation, 17 of them women. The national consultation reviewed:

1. developments pertaining to the protection and promotion of the rights of Indigenous nationalities in Nepal,
2. constitutional common law provisions and statutes affecting indigenous nationalities in Nepal,
3. consideration of the use of international bills of rights, declarations, covenants, agreements, other constructive arrangements and emerging rights and declarations regarding the rights of indigenous peoples in the context of Nepal,
4. legal and other provisions affecting the rights of indigenous women in Nepal, and
5. policy recommended for the promotion and protection of the rights of indigenous nationalities and the strategies to achieve this.

As a result, a number of recommendations for constitutional and legal amendments were passed. 27 proposals for constitutional amendments were listed and seven concrete strategies were decided on. Another seven amendment proposals concerned the Muluki Ain (civil code), also accompanied by different concrete strategies. 37 amendment proposals concerned 30 other laws, and nine proposals were made on indigenous women's issues. Finally, the consultation demanded the formation of a Constituent Assembly for drafting the constitutional amendments.

The consultation also proposed demanding self-government by indigenous peoples of their social, cultural and political development. Under the present Local Self-Government Act, the local administrative units are the 75 District (DDC) and 4,000 Village Development Committees (VDCs), which have not been created in accordance with the interests of indigenous peoples. Indigenous groups are also not properly represented in these units. The consultation demands for the re-division and re-organization of these units on the basis of region, language, and numerical strength of the ethnic groups. The election system should also be arranged in such a way that the majority people of the concerned area were properly represented. A customary rights act should be framed in order to safeguard the intellectual property right of the indigenous peoples and, in order to guarantee access to, and control and management of, traditional lands and other resources by indigenous groups, the respective laws should be amended.

Not only the indigenous peoples but also the mainstream people and major political parties have now taken up the discussion on amending the present constitution.

Communities Demand Equal Language Rights

Despite the constitutional and legal recognition of the many languages spoken by the different ethnic groups in Nepal, in June 1999 the Supreme Court issued an order against the decisions to use local languages as additional official languages on the part of the Kathmandu Metropolitan City, Dhanusha District Development Committee and Rajbiraj Municipality (see *The Indigenous World 1999-2000*).

The different language communities believe that the decision of the Supreme Court is highly prejudiced and against their aspirations. The Nepal Federation of Nationalities (NEFEN) therefore organized the First National Conference on Linguistic Rights, which took place in Kathmandu from March 3 to 4, 2000. 78 indigenous and human rights organisations, including representatives from 44 language communities, gathered in support of the cause for equal language rights. The Conference formulated a doctrine of equality in the language sphere and passed the National Declaration on Linguistic Rights, containing 31 articles. The conference rejected the decision of

Photo: Sv. Å. Lorenz Christensen

Photo: Sv. Å. Lorenz Christensen

the Supreme Court and demanded amendments to the articles of the 1991 Constitution of the Kingdom of Nepal related to language discrimination.

The Nepal Bhasa Sangharsa Saamiti organised a one-day national symposium on how to implement the National Declaration on Linguistic Rights in Kathmandu on March17[th], 2001. Nepal Tamang Ghedung has formed a drafting Committee of Lawyers under the Chairmanship of Ex-Attorney General Sarbagya Ratna Tuladhar to prepare a draft "Bill of Language Act" with the aim of presenting it at the forthcoming session of parliament.

Language Communities all over Nepal observed a "Black Day" on June 1, 2000 in commemoration of the day the Supreme Court of Nepal issued an order to stop the use of indigenous and local languages in local self-governing bodies. Nationwide mass demonstrations, poster and pamphlet campaigns, processions and mass meetings were organised. It was decided to continue the "Black Day" until the Government changes the laws and by-laws of the country to ensure equal language rights.

Bill on Nationalities Still Not Tabled in Parliament

The government had promised to table the bill on the "National Academy for the Upliftment of the Nationalities" at the 1999 parliamentary session. By 2000, however, it had still not been taken up. The bill was simply thrown into the pigeonholes of the members of the parliament. It is also important to note that in the bill, which was prepared by the Ministry of Local Development, the name of the Newar people has been dropped from the approved list of 61 indigenous nationalities. This signifies a continuation of the same divide-and-rule tactic the government has used to control the indigenous peoples over the last 233 years. The ninth development plan of Nepal also states that the government will form an "Indigenous Peoples' Council" at district and central level for the development of indigenous nationalities all over the country. And yet nothing has materialised.

Campaign to Include Ethnic Identity in Population Census

For many years, the national population census has been used by the ruling cast Hindu to confirm their majority in the country. The government has in the past refused to publish population data broken down by ethnicity. Owing to mounting pressure from the indigenous nationalities, the State for the first time published preliminary data on ethnic/caste population in 1991. However, many indigenous communities were not identified in the 1991 census, and the population figures for many of those who are on the list are too low. Furthermore, while the government of Nepal has recognised 61 groups as indigenous nationalities, 35 of these are not enumerated in the officially published list of the 1991 Population Census. Since the government of Nepal is again conducting a population census in June 2001, indigenous nationalities are now campaigning to be included in the forthcoming census. A delegation of indigenous organisations under the leadership of Mr. Parshuram Tamang, General Secretary of NEFEN, met the Vice Chairman of the National Planning Commission and presented a memorandum demanding the inclusion of all ethnic groups in the population census. Nepal Tamang Ghedung (NTG), an indigenous peoples' national organization, has also demanded the establishment of a "National Population Census Commission" to guarantee an impartial census.

Move to Combat Trafficking of Women

Trafficking of women is a growing problem in Nepal. To date, approximately 200,000 girls and women have been trafficked from Nepal, one third of them under the age of sixteen. Estimates of the number of women trafficked from Nepal to India every year vary widely, from 5,000 to 20,000. 90% of these women and girls come from indigenous communities. Nepal Tamang Ghedung organised a round table to bring NGOs and governmental bodies together to review the existing State policy and activities with regard to this problem and to draw up an action plan for the future in 2000. On the basis of the recommendations of the round table, Nepal Tamang Ghedung has asked the government to institute a new law to combat the trafficking of women and girls in Nepal, to discuss with the Government of India possible cooperation to repatriate trafficked women, and to push the proposed convention of the South Asian Association for Regional Cooperation (SAARC) against trafficking of women and girls in South Asia.

Human Rights Violations Continue

The Nepal Communist Party (Maoist) has been involved in an armed struggle known as the "People's War" to establish a socialist republic for five years now. More than 1,500 people have been killed during the fighting between the government forces and the Peoples' War Group. Most affected by the armed conflicts are the indigenous peoples and their territories. In these territories, it seems, two governments are present: the representatives of the Kathmandu government in the District Headquarter, and the People's War government in the rural areas. The indigenous peoples' lives and property have increasingly come under threat. Human rights violations such as rape, indiscriminate killing, kidnapping, torture and disappearances are common. It was expected that there would be dialogue between the government and the Peoples' War Group to minimize human rights abuses. But the long awaited dialogue did not happen, allegedly largely because the government failed to create an environment conducive to dialogue.

Fourth National Congress of NEFEN

The Nepal Federation of Nationalities held its Fourth National Congress from August 7 to 8, 2000 in Kathmandu, demonstrating the variety of culture of the various ethnic groups of the country. The ornaments, dress, languages and faces of five dozen indigenous nationalities at the opening ceremony on 7 August 2000 reflected how diverse Nepal is in terms of religion, culture and language. When the federation was set up ten years ago, only eight groups were attached to it. NEFEN's fourth national congress was attended by representatives from 33 member organisations. Although just a decade ago, ethnicity and indigenous issues were limited to academic exercise, today they are the subject of a lively national debate.

Kamaiyas Struggle for Survival

For many Kamaiyas, the Tharu indigenous people who became bonded laborers, the 17th July, 2000 was a day of victory. On that day, the Government of Nepal decided to outlaw the practice of keeping Kamaiyas, which has been prevalent in Banke, Bardiya, Dang, Kailali and Kanchanpur districts of Nepal (see *The Indigenous World 1999-2000*). But the Kamaiyas could not know that the victory would soon be followed by anguish. A month after the government decided to liberate the bonded laborers, thousands were kicked out of their shelters by the landlords, and 2,525 families were reported to be roaming about homeless during the monsoon. They were asked to pay back their debt to their former "owners", and cases were reported of Kamaiyas being thrashed, attacked with weapons, and their shelters being set on fire. Ultimately, all this is the result of the lack of a rehabilitation program. The Kamaiyas have appealed for help to Village Development Committees, District Development Committees and non-governmental organisations in their thousands, due to their lack of food, medicine and shelter. Some of the political organisations have turned a blind eye to the plight of the Kamaiyas since they see them as supporting rival political parties. While the government has talked of a relief package for the Kamaiyas, no such aid has so far reached the remote districts. Furthermore, on December 6, the government promised between one *kattha* (3,645 square feet) and five *kattha* of land for each displaced family. None of them has yet has received any land. Apart from the fact that this amount of land would be insufficient to support a family, no system is in place to facilitate the redistribution of land. The former bonded laborers are deeply frustrated by the authorities' inaction. Many of them are now occupying the main highway linking west and east Nepal, exhibiting their plight and demanding their rehabilitation. NGOs blame the government for their inaction and the government blames the NGOs for mishandling the cause to their benefit.

Indigenous Peoples of the Terai Organise

For the first time, indigenous peoples of the lowland Terai region organised themselves with the aim of coordinating the implementation of the recommendations of the workshop held in Damak, Jhapa, eastern Terai, Nepal from December 29 to 30, 2000. The workshop was jointly organised by Nepal Tamang Ghedung and the International Alliance of Indigenous and Tribal Peoples of the Tropical Forests, South Asia Desk, Kathmandu, Nepal. The theme of the workshop was "The Terai (Lowlanders) indigenous peoples and their problems". The workshop was attended by 37 indigenous persons from the nine Terai communities and, as a result, a regional committee of the Terai indigenous peoples was formed. These indigenous peoples number less than 10,000. They are the original inhabitants of the Terai who have been dispossessed by the government's so-called "land reform". Because they could not produce documents to the Government officials, their land rights were not recognized and they became landless and homeless. Today, they are sandwiched by immigrants from neighboring India and the hill region of Nepal. Many of the Tharu people, for example, have ended up as bonded labourers (see paragraph above).

INDIA

Biodiversity Bill Introduced in Parliament

In May 2000, the Biological Diversity Bill 2000 was introduced in Parliament in fulfilment of the Convention on Biological Diversity 1992 to which India is a signatory. The objectives of the Bill are the conservation, sustainable use and equitable benefit sharing of biological diversity. The Bill seeks to regulate access in order to ensure the equitable sharing of resources and knowledge use, to protect intellectual property, local/community knowledge, to protect and rehabilitate threatened species and to involve traditional self-governance institutions. The Bill is applicable to foreigners, foreign corporate bodies and non-resident Indians (Clauses 3,4 and 6), who will have to obtain "permission" to research on and use biodiversity resources and local knowledge. The Bill provides for a centralised regulatory structure with a National Biodiversity Authority (NBA), followed by the State Biodiversity Board and the local level Biodiversity Management Committee. The NBA acts as a civil court in matters arising from the Bill's prescribed punishments for violations of its provisions, as well as for violating NBA directions.

Although this Bill has been hailed as "revolutionary" by even progressive environmentalists, this piece of paper is condemned by Adivasi and indigenous peoples' organisations as just another piece of colonial legislation. To date, the lack of regulatory legislation has paved the way for the widespread plunder of both germ plasm and knowledge - especially of Adivasis - through devious means, under the guise of research, tribal development and nature conservation by both foreigners as well as their Indian partners. The government has always shrugged it off under the specious plea of a lack of appropriate legislation. With globalisation and WTO regimes being put in place, it becomes imperative that rules be set for the efficient entry of transnational capital in order to profitably exploit the biodiversity and knowledge of people and, in fact, for its own very rapid development. Indeed, the Bill is almost explicit in its approach of neatly arranging a link-up between foreign capital and Indian capital in their plunder while parading a nationalist cloak. Indians and Indian companies need only "inform" (not get permission from) the State Biodiversity Board! In other words Indian capitalists are handled softly and given a liberal leash as if they were any better than foreign capitalists. In fact, since Indian and foreign capitalists often work in collaboration, the bill paves the way for the entry of foreign capitalists through the backdoor.

The place where the bodies of the victims of the police firing in Tapkara have been buried. Photo: IWGIA archive

Jharkhand. Photo: Roger Begrich

There is also the added threat that some bio-rich areas would be declared as "heritage sites" from which people would be displaced. Already, of the more than 600,000 displaced from around 421 Wildlife Sanctuaries and 75 National Parks, 500,000 are Adivasis. Contrary to the UN Convention on Biological Diversity, the community - the Gram Sabha - does not feature, despite the Panchayat Raj (Extension to Scheduled Areas) Act 1996, which provides primacy and supremacy of the Gram Sabha, including command over resources and ownership over minor forest products. The citizen is expressly prohibited from going to court regarding those provisions that fall within the scope of the Bill. Quite naturally, the structure implementing the Act makes no provisions for community representation. The All India Coordinating Forum of Adivasis/Indigenous Peoples in its National Workshop on Biodiversity and Adivasis/Indigenous Peoples held in New Delhi from 29-31 January 2001 had pointed out these and other weaknesses, demanding a major revision of the Bill.

Supreme Court for Big Dams

In an illogical, dangerous and anti-people verdict, the Supreme Court of India allowed the unconditional and unfettered construction of the controversial Sardar Sarovan Project (SSP). The Apex Court, in its majority judgement in Narmada Bachao Andolan's Public Interest Litigation against the SSP on 18th October 2000, refused to take any cognisance of serious issues such as cost-benefit, the claims of benefits and environmental aspects of the project along with the large displacement and rehabilitation problems. The Narmada Bachao Andolan condemned the court for apparently playing into the hands of the dam builders, dominant economic and political powers. It accused the court of neglecting its own orders and logic of previous orders, which had resulted in the suspension of the work on the dam for about five years. It was understood that the government would definitely make use of the judgement to displace people without resettlement. The court unfortunately agreed to further construction without any plan or land on which to rehabilitate the 35,000 affected families already recognised, and the almost same number of unrecognised families. In its press release, the NBA wondered how, in view of the Madhya Pradesh state government's officially acknowledged inability to provide land for resettlement of the displaced people due to the 90 meter high dam, the court envisaged the rehabilitation of more people in the event of a higher construction, when many who had been displaced 10 to 15 years ago would again have to be rehabilitated.

World Commission on Dams Report

Although the Government of India did not allow the World Commission on Dams to hold a public hearing in the country its report, which came out immediately after the Supreme Court judgement, exposed the pro-large dam bias in the judgement with unbalanced praise for the dams and the beneficial and unsubstantiated premise that rehabilitation has brought a higher standard of living for the people affected by the project. The WCD Report clearly vindicated the issues that peoples' movements had raised and struggled for during the past half century. Large dams were planned, pushed through and justified with no respect for peoples' rights to resources and development planning, and no or little place for social and environmental impact assessment in their decision-making.

The Report showed that:
- Large dams have forced 40-80 million people from their homes and lands, with impacts including extreme economic hardship, community disintegration and an increase in mental and physical health problems. Indigenous, tribal, and peasant communities have been particularly hard hit. People living downstream of dams have also suffered from increased disease and the depletion of the natural resources upon which their livelihoods depend.
- As against benefits in terms of water and power services, the price too often paid by people especially in social and environmental terms, is unacceptable and unnecessary.
- The benefits of large dams largely went to the already well-off while poorer sectors of society have unjustifiably borne the costs.

Government Secretly Preparing to Amend the 5th Schedule

The world's rapidly increasing demand for mineral resources is putting at stake the very existence of many indigenous communities and cultures. The first year of the millennium saw the battle lines of globalisation at the doorsteps of their homelands in India.

The founders of the Indian Constitution put in a few safeguards in the form of Schedules for the protection of the indigenous minorities. The 5th and 6th Schedules were the two most important protective legislation preventing transfer of indigenous land to non-indigenous persons. Violations of these schedules, however, have continued ever since. Samata, an NGO in Andhra Pradesh, took up the matter and got an historical judgement from the Supreme Court in September 1997, preventing the transfer of indigenous lands for commercial purposes. A judgement that sent ripples through the corporate world at a time of liberalization. The Indian Government was quick to react and, in an article in Mining Journal, London, assured the prospecting MNCs that they need not fear.

Subsequent appeals by the Andhra Pradesh Government and Union Government were dismissed by the Supreme Court. Unbridled commercial interests and plunder by private and global capital has thus legally been kept out of the Scheduled Areas.

However, with globalisation and liberalisation having gained ground in India, private corporations and multinational companies have put pressure on the government. The National Democratic Alliance (NDA) government at the Centre, snubbed by the Supreme Court, is now secretly preparing grounds to amend the Fifth Schedule of the Constitution, the proof of which was a secret note from the Ministry of Mines of 10 July 2000 (No.16/48/97-M.VI). The note clearly puts the interests of "foreign corporate bodies" superior to the interests of people and scheduled tribes, and suggests that the Supreme Court's judgement can effectively be subverted by effecting "the necessary amendments so as to overcome the said SC judgement by removing the legal basis of the said judgement". This is now sought to be accomplished by making an amendment to Article 244, clause 5(2) removing the prohibition and restrictions on the transfer of and sale by Adivasis to non-Adivasis for undertaking any non-agricultural operations including prospecting and mining. The secret document goes on to say that "The impasse created by the Samatha judgement can perhaps be resolved only through an amendment of the Fifth Schedule to the Constitution as opined by Attorney General. One way could be to add the following explanation after paragraph 5(2) in the Fifth Schedule:

"Explanation: The regulations framed under paragraph 5(2) shall not prohibit or restrict the transfer of land by members of the schedule tribe to the Government or allotment by Government of its land to a non-tribal for undertaking any non-agricultural operations including reconnaissance or prospecting or mining operations under the provisions of MMDR Act 1957."

The attempted way out within the realm of the politico-administrative system is to simply drop (de-notify) the respective areas from the Scheduled Area list itself so as to make the SC judgement and the 5th Schedule inoperable. With the coming into force of the Panchayat Raj (Extension to the Scheduled Area) Act 1996, the struggle for self-rule at the village level has certainly received a boost (see *The Indigenous World 1996-97* p. 217-9). The Adivasis as a whole and all democratic sections of the country in general upheld the SC judgement in the Samata case as a progressive step towards understanding the right spirit of the Fifth Schedule of the Constitution. However, the attempt now to change the Constitution itself or to modify its area of application is a constant reminder that the struggle has primarily to be waged in the political arena and the space for legal action is collapsing. These plans, now exposed, are condemned by Adivasi organisations.

It was in July 2000 when the National Alliance of Mining Affected People (mm&P) got hold of the confidential letter sent by one of the State Government officials to the Union Ministry requesting them to alter the powers of the 5th Schedule. When indigenous groups got knowledge of it, a strong campaign was launched all over the country to counter the nefarious designs of the present Government. If these Schedules are amended, it will open the floodgates to alienation of tribal land.

National Alliance of Mining Affected Communities Founded

A big event in the history of communities fighting mining companies is the formation of a National Alliance of Mining Affected Communities called "mines minerals & People" (mm&P). At their National Convention in Hyderabad in May 2000, 87 different mining-related groups met under the theme *Our Land, Our Minerals, OUR RIGHTS*. Breaking the isolation of resistance groups, mm&P has been playing a supportive role in campaigns and advocacy.

Formation of New States

After a prolonged struggle for political autonomy, the indigenous peoples of the eastern region of the central tribal belt of India eventually succeeded in achieving statehood in the form of Jharkhand and Chhattisgarh, bordering each other. However, the indigenous peoples of the cultural region of Jharkhand living in the present non-indigenous dominated West Bengal and Orissa felt defeated and frustrated because of the failure to include their areas in the newly-formed Jharkhand state. The indigenous peoples of the Jharkhand region in general felt that the Central Government did injustice to them by forming a state named Jharkhand in which, contrary to what they demanded, they form only 27% of the total population. Chhattisgarh, with 44% of its population indigenous, was also denied the status of a state dominated by indigenous peoples by not including the border areas of neighbouring Orissa. Thus, the formation of these two states took place not on the basis of the indigenous peoples' demand for cultural autonomy but on that of administrative convenience and, as the activists of the separate state movements pointed out, of the evil design of the state, forever promoting the interests of the industrialists and transnational companies, to frustrate the cause of the people.

Jharkhand

The Tapkara Massacre

In a horrific act of State repression, the police of the newly-formed Jharkhand state opened fire on an unarmed assembly of the Mundas and killed 8 persons, seriously injuring 16 others on the 2nd February 2001 in Tapkara, the center of the Koel-Karo anti dam movement. One of the deceased, however, belonged to the minority Muslim community. The police apparently committed this heinous crime to break the unity and the struggling spirit of the indigenous peoples of the region, who had been able to stall the construction of large dams on the rivers Koel and Karo for the last 25 years or more.

This barbarous act, however, failed to dampen the struggling spirit of the people. According to the Munda Chief of the Guria lineage, the incident exposed the class-biased nature of the present government under the Right Wing Bharatiya Janat Party. In the ensuing public meetings, the people demonstrated their unity and reiterated their determination to stop the construction of the proposed dam at any cost.

The killing of the unarmed Adivasis roused strong condemnation all over the country. In Jharkhand, all the opposition political parties, peoples' organizations and civil society organizations accused the Government of being anti-Tribal and demanded its immediate resignation as well as the scrapping of the Koel-Karo Hydroelectric Project. They took up campaigns in support of the demands.

Successful Non-violent Protests in Chandil

Unlike in the case of the Koel-Karo Hydroelectric Project where the government tries to lure the project-affected people into agreeing to be relocated by offering attractive rehabilitation packages, it is doing little to rehabilitate the people affected by the Chandil dam on the Subarnarekha River in West Singhbhum district of Jharkhand. The government had completed construction of the dam's spillway by 1990/91 and had consequently fully or partially submerged 52 villages. In all, 5,000 families were displaced. Of these, only 12 % have been resettled, and these inadequately. The situation of the rest remains shocking.

The government started installation of the radial gates in December 2000. Work has, however, been stopped by the *satyagraha*, a non-violent protest in front of the office of the Superintendent Engineer near the Chandil dam site starting on 23 February this year. The protest has been initiated by the Visthapit Mukti Vahini, a people's movement functioning in the area since 1987. The VMV activists point out that if installation of the radial gates is completed (the government target is to complete it by June 2001), the dam's height will be increased by another 15 metres. This will cause large-scale submergence and displacement of another 10,000 families. To them, the government has no moral right to initiate any further dam-related work that will cause further displacement, until those already displaced by the dam are properly rehabilitated.

Jharkhand Save the Forest Movement
In response to the depleting forest cover and its extremely adverse impact on the indigenous peoples' livelihoods in several villages, the people formed 'Village Forest Protection Committees'. A forum was formed under the banner of the Jharkhand Save the Forest Movement on 19 November 2000 in Murhu, Ranchi District, with a view to uniting all these scattered initiatives. The major demands raised in the meeting were:

1. Restoration of the people's rights over forest to as they were before the advent of British colonial rule in the region in the 19th century.
2. Immediate scrapping of the Bihar Private Protected Forest Act (1952), which empowers the government to take over the legally recognized ancestral forests of the Mundas in the name of 'scientific management'.
3. Conversion of the villages within the reserved forest areas into revenue villages.
4. Arrest and punishment of the forest mafias and corrupt forest officials

To mark the occasion a website, http://jharkhandforest.com, was launched.

Orissa: Firing on Indigenous Protestors

Rayagada in Orissa is now a battlefield between indigenous people's organizations and Utkal Aluminium Industries Ltd. (UAIL), a consortium of aluminium companies including Canada's ALCAN and Norway's Norsk Hydro. Backed by the State government, UAIL has waged war against those people resisting land acquisition. For the past five years, people's resistance has been effective in not allowing UAIL to start construction. On December 16th 2000, at Maikanch Village, four Adivasis were killed and over fifty injured when the police fired on them. The incident took place as a consequence of the villagers protest against the extraction of bauxite from the nearby Bapilimali hills. In the early morning of the fateful day, 130 policemen together with the local Block Development Officer came to the village to enquire about the confrontation that had occurred the previous day between the villagers and the local political party leaders who were trying force people to give up their struggle against mining. The police were looking for the male members of the village. They beat up a woman and fired in the air to trace the absconding men. At this point, some men who were hiding in their houses came out and ran towards the hill. The police chased and fired at them from behind, indiscriminately leaving four men dead on the spot and over fifty injured. They also killed four cows. Later, the local bullies manhandled the members of the fact-finding team of the Eka Parishad when they paid a visit to the village.

The firing was no doubt part of the police strategy to demoralize and threaten the people and weaken the organizations fighting against displacement. Orissa has the dubious distinction of the largest number of multinational companies and the largest number of displaced Adivasis.

Source
Eka Parishad, Orissa

Madhya Pradesh

Indigenous Forest People Killed
On April 2, after a weeklong operation during which the houses of the predominantly Bhil, Bhilala and Korku tribes were demolished, the district administration of Dewas, Madhya Pradesh, delivered the final blow, shooting dead at least four of them in a demonstration of repressive State power.

The Dewas killings are another incident in the confrontation between the state and the Adivasis, dating from the time when the British colonial rulers made forests State property, a policy enthusiastically followed since independence. Contrary to the view of the Adivasis that holds the forest officials-contractors-politicians nexus responsible for the depletion of forests, the state's view is that the illegal use of the forest resources by the Adivasis is the main reason for the destruction of the forests, which must be stopped with a heavy hand. Thus, in Dewas, the administration targeted the Adivasi Manch Sangathan, a forum of many tribal organizations, established to assert their rights on forests. The Dewas collector, Ashok Burnwal, in at least two speeches at Pipri and Udainagar in the past two months, thundered that the Adivasis and their organizations would be crushed in six months. Beginning from March 28, he and the Superintendent of Police supervised the destruction of houses, village after village in Kadudiya, Potla, Patpadi, Jamasindh, Katukiya, Mehendikheda etc. In order to justify the crackdown, the police spread a rumour that the Naxalites (underground armed Marxist forces) had penetrated the area and were misleading the Adivasis. However, finally the people mustered the nerve to assemble at Mehendikheda in order to register a protest. The police fired at them, killing four. Evidence suggests the absence of any returned fire and thus the cold-bloodedness of the killings.

Source
Vinod Raina, SACW News

Targeting Peoples' Organisations - Yet Another Black Law

"Madhya Pradesh Special Areas Security Bill 2000" was passed by the M.P Legislative Assembly on 27 November 2000 without any significant debate and discussion. It is now awaiting the President's assent. It is publicised as a law to curb the illegal activities of certain peoples' organisations and the Naxalites.

Any organisation or group of people can be banned if their activities are declared illegal. Organisations and group ranging from an informal group of people to trade unions can be banned and they need not be registered in order to fall within the scope of this proposed law, which applies to those termed as their supporters. The lists of activities defined as illegal are very general, for example, activities that disturb the law and order or peace or have the tendency to create obstacles to the maintenance of public order etc.

The government is not bound to divulge the reasons for the ban. It does not give any opportunity to the organisations/groups to present their case before declaration of the ban. There is a provision for forfeiture of all the movable and immovable properties and assets of the banned organisations/groups. Unlimited powers have been granted to the District Collectors and the Superintendent of Police.

This law, if enacted, would have wide reaching powers and is intended to suppress all kinds of peoples' dissent, resistance and movements in Madhya Pradesh. This is made clear in the objects and reasons for the Bill, which states that danger from illegal activities of some peoples' and Naxalite organisations necessitates this. But it would be used against those who are working to protect the basic human rights of the common people.

Out of the six activities that have been defined as illegal, only one can be said to relate specifically to Naxalite activities. That is: using violent and terrorist means to create fear in the minds of the public or using arms and explosives. The other activities that are defined as illegal are very general and unclear, and can be used against any peoples' organisation, such as disturbing the public order, disturbing the peace, hindering or obstructing the working of the rule of law, its institutions and officials or which may have a tendency to do so etc. These are not extremist acts and any organisation trying to highlight the peoples' problems using non-violent or democratic means would fall within the scope of the proposed law. A number of organisations in Madhya Pradesh have announced their determination and declared they will fight the Bill.

Karnataka: Indigenous Peoples Victims of "Conservation" in Rajiv Gandhi National Park

After the brutal and forceful dislocation of 51 families carried out by the Forest Department and the Police at midnight on June 12th last year, on September 23rd 2000, a large troop of Forest Department personnel arrived at the Kolengere tribal settlement in Nagarhole to forcefully move the 30 tribal families from the settlement to a new "rehabilitation" site at Veeranahosalli, on the fringes of the National Park, and to demolish their existing dwellings. Local people tried to defend themselves from this attack, and were brutally repressed. Men and women were beaten by armed officers. Some very seriously injured individuals were admitted to hospitals at Gonikoppal and Kumara, while others were given first aid locally. Some local media, instigated by the Forest Department, falsely issued information that local people were the ones instigating the clash with the support of NGOs such as CORD, Kushalnagar and DEED, Hunsur.

The historical conflict between the Forest Department and the traditional inhabitants of the Park intensified over the last years with the Government of Karnataka's move to implement the controversial World Bank Eco-development Project in the area. The official plan went ahead, even violating the operational directives of the Bank itself with regard to the Indigenous/Tribal Peoples, as well as their constitutional rights. The Government of Karnataka has turned a blind eye to the report of the World Bank's Inspection Panel that visited the area and justified the tribals' position.

Tamil Nadu: Adivasi Reoccupy Their Traditional Land

In the state of Tamilnadu, the Adivasi Thannatchikkana Tamizhaga Munnani (Tamilnadu Front for Adivasi Self-Rule) - a loose forum of Adivasi organisations involved in the struggle for self-rule - has been quietly taking over patches of traditional lands in different parts of the state where it is active, despite the fact that unlike adjacent Kerala, there is no law here that either protects Adivasi lands from alienation or restores alienated lands. Tamilnadu Pazhangudi Makkal Sangam (Tamilnadu Indigenous Peoples Organisation) and Tamilnadu Pazhangudi Makkal Iyakkam (Tamilnadu Indigenous Peoples Movement) a breakaway group, have both formally declared self-rule and land struggle as the key to the future of Adivasis. These organisations were formed by activists of the former United Communist Party of India, which has merged with its parent body - the Communist Party of India. Efforts are on to forge joint action.

Kerala

Contempt Charges Against the Government for Failure to Restore Adivasi Land

On 6 December 2000, when the contempt of court petition filed by Dr. Nallathambi Thera came up for hearing, a Divisional Bench of the Kerala High Court, consisting of Justice P.K Balasubramaniam and Justice T.M Hassan Pillai, issued a directive to the Chief Secretary of the Government, M.Mohan Kumar, to appear in person on 18 December to frame contempt charges against him for the Government's failure to carry out the Bench's directives for restoring alienated lands to the tribals. The bench issued notices to all the District Collectors and Revenue Divisional Officers (RDOs) to show cause why proceedings under the Contempt of Court Act should not be initiated against them for violating the directives. They were asked to submit their reply before 8 January 2001. Earlier in 1993, the Court had directed the Collectors and RDOs to restore the alienated lands of tribals in cases where no appeals against the RDOs orders restoring land were pending and no compensation was payable. The directives were issued under the Kerala Scheduled Tribes (Restriction on Transfer of Lands and Restoration of Alienated Lands) Act 1975 on a petition filed by Dr. Thera to implement the Act whereby all alienated lands since 1960 were to be restored.

The High Court, where a case has been pending since 1988 for implementation of the 1975 Act, had come down heavily against the Government of Kerala for "lack of will" in implementing the 1975 Act but has repeatedly agreed to the Government's request for an extension of the deadline. As the government failed to implement it, he moved a contempt of court petition.

On 16 December 1999, the Division Bench consisting of Justice P.K. Balasubramaniam and Justice C.S. Rajan, hearing the contempt petition filed gave the ruling that the Government of Kerala had committed contempt of court and gave another five months to implement the 1975 Act. The Government was warned that if it failed to carry out the restoration of land to the Adivasis for which no compensation was payable and in which no appeals were pending within five months, the Chief Secretary would be punishable. The Bench also said that the 1999 Act could not override the 1975 Act that a contempt charge was "liable to be framed against" the Chief Secretary. The Bench had then observed that the contempt proceedings could not be dropped due to the mere fact that a new Act - the Kerala (Restriction on Transfer by and Restoration of Lands to Scheduled Tribes) Act 1999 (See *The Indigenous World* 1998-99) - had been passed repealing the 1975 Act and where alternate lands were promised instead of the original lands. In addition, the High Court had itself stayed the contentious provisions regarding alternate lands. Meanwhile on 7 October, the Government began distributing 225 acres of land to the 76 tribal families and another approximately 1,200 acres to nearly 400 tribal families in Attapady in Palakkad district. These lands are surplus lands, barren, uninhabitable and uncultivable. On 11 October 1999, the High Court issued an interim stay of operation of sections 5 and 6 of the 1999 Act, which permitted alternate land to be given instead of restoration of alienated lands. The Bench had given the government another opportunity to implement the directives. However, the Government appealed to the Supreme Court and a stay on the contempt proceedings was granted on 7 February 2000. Thereafter, the High Court Bench had disposed of the writ by a judgement on 24 August 2000, which struck down as unconstitutional Sections 5(1), 5(2) and 22 (discriminatory provisions against the tribals) of the 1999 Act.

Thus the 1999 order on the framing of contempt charges became final. The government has been granted more time for replying to the charges. Predictably, the Government of Kerala has now challenged both the High Court judgement overruling the anti-Adivasi clauses of the 1999 Act as well as the contempt of court charge in the Supreme Court.

Since the passing of the Act in 1975, only 5,445,602 hectares of the total claim for 99,094,522 hectares have been restored. Along with the struggles, the legal battle continues to drag on, with people naturally losing faith in the judiciary. The Adivasi leaders have once again begun the process of re-launching their struggle and this time they are organising the support of Dalit organisations.

Unwed Mothers - the Price of Development?

The women of Kerala in particular enjoy a higher social status than women elsewhere in the country. This is attributed in part to the matrilineal tradition. Adivasi women traditionally enjoyed a prominent position in their community. However, their experience - the increasing trauma they face - once again presents an entirely contrasting modern reality. The colonisation of Adivasi territory and consequent breakdown of the traditional self-governing system, along with enticement, cheating, rape and extreme poverty are the causes. Wayanad as well as Attapady have become the focal points of protest on the issue of atrocities against Adivasi women. They have also become infamous for what has come to be popularly referred to as "unwed mothers".

Attapady, with its 25,000 Adivasis in 174 hamlets, is second to Wayanad in terms of Adivasi population in the state. "Namu", an organisation of Adivasis in Attapady, in a recent survey identified 378 "unwed" mothers, most of whom are in the age group of 18 to 25 in just 52 hamlets. Way back in 1988, the Assembly Committee for Scheduled Caste/Scheduled Tribe Development was apprised of the problem. Although the then District Collector enquired about the allegation, no action was taken. Again in 1997, 25 cases were brought before the Assembly Committee but no action was forthcoming.

The estimate of unwed Adivasi mothers in Wayanad district ranges from 300 to 1000. In one year, 200 women were found missing in Wayanad alone, with about 20 of the sexually assaulted women committing suicide. Tragically, the total literacy campaign in Kerala, which mobilised the literate, primarily non-Adivasi youth to fan out to the villages, turned out to be another curse for many Adivasi women who fell prey to their sexual needs. Investigations in Thirunelly in Mananthavady Taluk of Wayanad show that many outsiders go there with false identities and marry the girls, stay for two or three years, supply them with children and leave the village as and when they like. The poor women become easy prey to sexual diseases. Sometimes money is promised or paid to hush up the matter. Another factor was the sexual assault of police camping in the area during anti-Naxalite (Marxist-Leninist revolutionary group) operations that started at the end of the 1960s.

The negligence and complicity of the police is an important factor contributing to the high degree of sexual exploitation of women, as the culprits know that they can get away with the crimes even if they are reported to the police - which in most cases does not happen - or even if the media make the incidents into sensational news. The women who approach the police station are softly advised or fiercely threatened to go home with their complaints. Cases are hushed up. Investigations are botched up to protect the culprits.

North East India

In 1991, 8.14 millions of India's 67.76 million tribals lived in the seven north eastern states. (Figures for 2001 are shortly to be published.) Most of these belong to six major Mongoloid groups. Some, like the Bodo, inhabit the plains but most live in the hills. Certain areas fall under the Sixth Schedule of the Constitution, which recognises rights such as community ownership of land and forests, autonomous district councils and customary law. The region also has more than 4 million indigenous peoples from mainland India, most of them from Jharkhand brought by the British to work in tea gardens or as punishment for the anti-colonial rebellions. They are mostly illiterate, landless and powerless in the North East but are not included among the Scheduled Tribes for reservations in education or jobs. Some features of this region cause conflicts and lead to the violation of tribal rights. Most tribes are ethnically and culturally different from the mainland Indian population. The Sixth Schedule helps some of them to protect their identity, but even they are not protected from the tendency of an important section of the Indian leadership to impose a single culture on them. In addition, their economy is controlled by outsiders. That, combined with massive immigration, raises the spectre of unemployment and adds to their sense of being different. In response, many try to protect their identity by proclaiming their sovereignty. The official reaction is to treat these economic and political issues as a "law and order problem". Repression follows and atrocities are committed. The year 2000 witnessed both atrocities and attempts at peace-making.

The Naga Peace Initiative
The cease-fire signed with the NSCN (I-M) - one of the two main Naga groups - three years ago gave hope of a just and lasting peace

since it came after 40 years of struggle including large-scale deployment of the Indian armed forces and the involvement of Burma. But the other major faction, the NSCN (K), was excluded from the cease-fire until April 2001. Many feel that, although some confrontation continues and the cease-fire has meant a cessation of hostilities between the two armies, civilian casualties have not declined but it has brought down violence considerably. (More on the recent developments in Nagalim, see chapter on Southeast Asia in this volume.)

The Bodo-Kachari

The Bodo in Western Assam and the Kachari, who are related to them, form a third of the three million tribals of Assam. One section of them demands sovereignty and the rest want an autonomous State within India. Until the arrival of the British, the Bodo were the dominant group throughout much of western Assam. But now they have been pushed into only two districts of the state. Even there they have to compete with others for land, among them immigrant Adivasi. The consequence has been severe killings, the best known being those of May 1996 when more than 500 were left dead on both sides and an estimated 300,000 homeless. There have been at least five incidents of stray killings in 2000.

The Bodo have two militant groups: the National Democratic Front of Bodoland, which began as the Bodo Security Force in the 1980s and became the NDFB in 1993, and the Bodo Liberation Tigers (BLT) formed in 1996 allegedly under the aegis of the Indian Government. It too has been waging a war whose cost has been high. In March 2000, a cease-fire was signed between the Government of India and the BLT. But despite public propaganda, one is not certain that it has been welcomed with the same enthusiasm as in Nagaland. There are no signs of the NDFB either being invited to it or joining it. Hence the struggle continues, with the accompanying atrocities.

The Kachari, their sister tribe - also known as the Dimasa - have their own armed group, the Dima Halam Daoga. Out of several encounters in 2000, the best known is that of 13th August when militants shot at the security forces in Taijungphang village. In retaliation, the Assam Police and the Assam Regiment attacked the village and raped two women at Dimaimur. Its *gaonbura* (village chief) was beaten up and killed. There was also large scale looting of jewellery and other valuables from Arulong village. After protests, Mr Tanu Singh, the District Collector, ordered an inquiry. Among other things, it revealed that after every raid the villagers are made to render free labour to the security forces for three days a week. His successor, Mr L. S. Changsang, has not taken any action on the report.

The Immigrant Issue

Immigrants also trouble the region. The biggest number come from Uttar Pradesh, Bihar and Jharkhand. Another important section is from Bangladesh. Most of the latter are Muslims, the former primarily Hindus. There is resentment against both. But official focus is on the latter. It gives the issue a religious colour. One wonders whether efforts are being made to divide the Bodo and others along religious lines. Another example is the controversy on whether the Bodos should accept Hindi or Roman script. Their literary convention held during the summer of 2000 accepted the Hindi script. Although the division is not a religious one, it is being presented as a Christian-Hindu divide. There are fears that the killings too will erupt along religious lines.

The Karbi in Karbi Anglong, Assam, bordering on Nagaland, are another tribe resisting all immigration, not merely that of Bangladeshis. About 70 persons, both immigrants and Karbi, were killed in their region between June and August 2000. The immigrants killed were mostly Bihari and Nepali.

The immigrant question is much more severe in Tripura, where the tribals were over 70% of the population at the beginning of the 20th century, 56% in 1951 and only around 28% today because of heavy immigration from Bangladesh. However, they are rarely referred to as immigrants because most are Hindus. The tribals have been resisting them and have formed a militant group, the National Liberation Front of Tripura. The media accuse them of being inspired by missionaries. Christians, however, form less than 2% of the State's population, and around 5% of the indigenous people. During 2000, the Bengalis formed a counter grouping. There have been several killings, and violence can be expected to continue.

The Manipur Massacre

A third of the population of Manipur is tribal, predominantly Naga but including others like the Kuki. The Naga-Kuki conflict has drawn the media's attention for many years. The Kuki are allegedly armed by the Indian army. The struggle was primarily for control of land and the border trade with Burma. The issue seems to have been decided and today there is relative peace. But Manipur is estimated to have 18 militant outfits belonging to different ethnic groups. So conflicts and atrocities continue. One example was the massacre on 28th December 2000, during which eight men in Tabanglong, a Naga village on the Tamenglong-Imphal Highway, were killed. The fact-finding team found out that a patrol party of 15 Jat Regiment was attacked by suspected militants at around 7 a.m. on 28th December

2000, about 200 metres from the bus stand of Tabanglong village. One soldier was killed and four were injured. At 11 a.m. the same day, personnel of the 15 Jat Regiment came to Tabanglong. When they reached the village, there were only ten men there and two Meitei chilli traders, who were hiding in the village after having heard the gunfire. The army forced the men to gather at the volley-ball court and beat them up. Then, forcing five of them to lie face down on the volleyball court, the soldiers opened fire and killed them. One man survived with a bullet wound. Two men were made to sit near a memorial stone and shot dead. A mentally retarded young man and another man were forced to sit at the road near the church and were shot at. Fortunately, the latter escaped by jumping down and running to the bushes nearby. Before and during the killings, women and children were kept in different houses and not allowed to come out. After the killings, the army took the women and children to the church and detained them for the rest of the day. At dusk, a police team came to the church and asked women and children about the incident and the identities of the dead. That was the first they had heard of the deaths. The villagers were then asked to accompany the police to locate the dead bodies and identify their family members.

All those killed by the army were aged persons, innocent villag-ers, chilli traders and a young mentally retarded person. There was no sign of an encounter at the village. So it was a one-sided assault by the army, 4 to 5 hours after the attack on the army by suspected armed militants. Neither the army nor the police recovered any incriminating documents, arms or ammunition from Tabanglong at the time of the incident.

Sources

Meeting held on July 4th 2000 at the Centre for Ecological Sciences, Bangalore
Kothari, Ashish 2000. An Exercise in Conservation. *Frontline*, Feb 2, 2001
World Rainforest Movement. *Bulletin* N° 38, September 2000
Newsletter, Issue 3 September 2000.
Contributions by Xavier Dias
Contributions by Bela
Contributions by Stan Swamy

On North East India:

Anon., N. D. *Peace Initiatives among the Nagas.*
Dubey, Amaresh and Shubhashis Gangopadhyay. 1998. "Turbulent Intelli-gence", *The Telegraph*, March 23.
Fernandes, Walter. 1999. "Conflict in North-East: A Historical Perspective", *Economic and Political Weekly*, 34 (n. 51, Dec. 18-24), pp. 3579-3582.
Datta Ray, B. et al. (eds). *Population, Poverty and Environment in North East India.* New Delhi: Concept Publishing Company.

Hazarika, Sanjoy. 1994. *Strangers of the Mist: Tales of War and Peace from India's North East*. Viking Penguin Books.

Mukerjee, Sanu et al. (eds). *Demographic Profile of North-East India*. New Delhi: Omsons Publications, pp. 1-7.

Pakem, D. (ed). *Insurgency in Northeast India*. New Delhi: Omsons Publications.

Report of the Joint Fact Finding Team on Tabanglong Massacre on 28th December 2000.

SRI LANKA

Wanniyala-Aetto Women Being Trafficked to Arab Oil Countries

The hunter/gatherer Wanniyala-Aetto people survived the Sinhalese, Tamil, Portuguese, Dutch and English colonizations by withdrawing into the *wanni*, the Dry Zone Tropical Forest. The most critical impact on their lives, however, is more recent. In 1983, they were moved from the forest to make way for a national park. Their traditional hunter/gatherer means of subsistence became prohibited. They were detained if they crossed the national park border. The park guards even killed some of them. The government placed the forest people in "System C" rehabilitation villages in a development area. With their forestland taken away from them and their way of life prohibited, their women are now being sold as laborers to other continents. Those targeted are mainly young women, the few (approximately only 380 women) of reproductive age on whom the survival of the Wanniyala-Aetto ultimately depends. The Wanniyala-Aetto are ill prepared to deal with this new threat. None of their myths, legends or narratives tells of trafficking, sexual abuse or the brothels the women contract laborers may end up in.

The first seven Wanniyala-Aetto women contract workers were delivered to their employers' houses at the beginning of February 2001. The girls were dispersed to different cities. The local recruiter is a Sinhalese daughter of an alcoholic shopkeeper from the area. She receives 7,000 Rupees (a little less than US$80) per woman. This is a considerable sum in Sri Lanka (compare this with a government school teacher's salary of 6,000 Rs.). The shopkeeper's daughter believes the job descriptions presented by the agents from the capital. The future of the girls in a society in disintegration seems unpromising compared to life in Kuwait, Bahrain, Riyadh or Dubai. Signing the two-year or, alternatively, five-year contract as a housemaid would allow them to wear silk saris with gold embroi-

Young mother and son cooking in an ordinary Wanniyala-Aetto home environment. Photos: Wiveca Stegeborn

dery, many gold bangles and jeweled necklaces every day - a tempting alternative for a girl from a government Rehabilitation Village.

Once the local recruiter has a group of five to six women, a minibus arrives to take them from their forest homes to the capital. The first minibus arrived at the village without prior notice at eleven o'clock at night. The girls had to depart instantaneously. Seven hours later they arrived in Colombo, the capital. There they had to wait for another vehicle that took them the last kilometer to a private house where the agents evaluate their human merchandise. This takes three to five days. No-one has yet had the chance to tell what happens inside.

According to Supreme Court Attorney, Mr. Tampoe, in Sri Lanka the exploitation, both sexual and labor, of women contract workers has been ongoing for many years. Their work is a "cornerstone" (Tampoe 2001a) of Sri Lanka's economy, he says and continues: "Women's Groups (private) have been crying out for reform of the system for decades" (Tampoe 2001 b). It is difficult, he says, to achieve statistical data on the illicit trade. Some documentation, however, has been retrieved that exposes the involvement of the Sri Lankan government. Insurance papers stamped with the seal of the Bureau of Foreign Employment (BFE) disclose "Recruitment Fees" of 5,000 Rupees per person to the same Bureau. Prior to employment, the young women are asked to sign a contract from a Recruiting Office in Saudi Arabia. They are signed with finger prints added with the written names in Roman orthography. The contract is written in poor English with an Arabic heading. The Wanniyala-Aetto cannot read or write in either English or Arabic. Quoting the last sentence:

> I hereby Agreed to Pay Rs 35,000:- for my Visa Charges, ticket and other relavant Expenses, also I have agreed not to Refuse for Working under any Circumstances and will bear total expenses if I do so (Sahman Recruiting Office 1999 [spelling mistakes in original doc.]).

Birth Control
Although the transactions appear arbitrary and sudden, they are well prepared. As soon as the girls are listed, they have to seek, *at their own initiative*, a hospital in Colombo to give them a physical health check and for a consultation with "Family Planning". "Family Planning" in India and Sri Lanka most commonly means sterilization. Nonetheless, today there are alternatives such as a hormone injection lasting five years or an artificial ampoule subcutaneously inserted into their upper arm. The ampoules emit hormones daily over five

years to prevent pregnancy. The reason for this "voluntary" action is said to prevent pregnancy when the girls come home on vacations.

From Cooking Fire to Microwave

Once the girls are dispersed to Africa or the Arabian peninsula, they cannot flee nor tell anyone at home where they are. Many cannot write in Sinhalese orthography, much less in other forms of writing. Even if women from the tropical monsoon forest become house-maids and nothing else, there are severe obstacles to their training. The Wanniyala-Aetto speak an almost extinct language that few outsiders understand in their own country, much less anyone in the Middle East. They can understand Sinhalese, as long as it is simple. The training and transmittance of household knowledge is problem-atic since the Wanniyala-Aetto women are brought up under very different living conditions. They cook on an open fire and collect food from the forest or their swidden fields. Compared to societies scoring the highest GNPs in the world, the transformation, albeit voluntary, must be hard. According to the Foreign Employment Bu-reau in Sri Lanka, some Sri Lankan women in the Middle East have been "subjected to harassment because they were not familiar with the work expected of them and lack training" (A. M. J. Perera, 2001).

An Investigation

The government of Sri Lanka was contacted through the Sri Lanka Embassy in Sweden at the beginning of February. Attached were the names of two recruiters, and the address of the travel agency used at the first delivery. The Sri Lanka Embassy replied with silence. The contact was renewed and an austere answer received that the matter had been forwarded to the Ministry of Foreign Affairs in Sri Lanka, which would conduct an investigation.

Meanwhile, Human Rights workers are investigating airlines with destinations in the Middle East, the Bureau of Foreign Em-ployment and the Office of Emigration. What they are trying to establish is whether the travel documents and the passports are legal. The Superintendent of Police and the Director of the Children and Women's Bureau, Ms. P. Diwakara, when asked about the police's possibility of detecting Wanniyala-Aetto women at the airport, replied that there were several incidents pointing towards forged documents and illegal trade (Pers. com. to Mr. M. Cardillo Feb. 20, 2001).

An Awareness Raising Campaign

The International Movement Against all Forms of Discrimination and Racism (IMADR), an NGO in Sri Lanka that works against women's exploitation abroad, has agreed to organise an awareness raising campaign in Mahaiyangana, the closest town to the Wanniyala-Aetto settlements. Visiting the town instead of the villages helps spread awareness on a broader level. By having the meeting there, the IMADR experience will reach local recruiters, the transporters of the indigenous women to the capital, hospital personnel, the local police and, not least, the Wanniyala-Aetto women themselves, who are being informed about the event. Once advice has been broadcast, a follow-up visit is planned for Dambana, the largest Wanniyala-Aetto village. Families that have lost their daughters can then ask for help in tracing them.

Meanwhile, unaware that the Golden Days may soon end, the female recruiter continues going from door to door in the Wanniyala-Aetto settlements. A new list is growing. This time even the granddaughter of the late legendary chief Uru Warige Tissahamy is awaiting the night-time vehicle.

References

Cardillo, Maurizio. 2001. February 20. E-mail in author's possession

Perera, A. M. J. 2001. February 7. "Lankan maids suffer abuse in Gulf." In *Hindustan Times.*

http://www.hindustantimes.com/nonfram/080201/detFOR13.asp

Sahman Recruiting Office. 1999. July 21. Contract from Saudi Arabia. Document in author's possession

Tampoe, Arun. 2001a. April 3. E-mail. Document in author's possession
2001b. April 4. E-mail. Document in author's possession

EAST AND SOUTHEAST ASIA

JAPAN

The Establishment of a Human Rights Victims Relief Agency and the Recognition of the Ainu People

The Japanese Ministry of Justice is currently preparing for the possible establishment of a human rights victims relief agency - which will be independent from the government - by setting up an advisory body, the so-called Round Table for Human Rights Promotion. The government has recognized that it is necessary to study the feasibility of establishing measures for the relief of the victims of human rights violations. According to the inquiry, two reasons were given for the establishment of the new agency:

The first is the realization by the ministry that, "there exist human rights violations such as irrational discrimination based on social status, family origin, race, belief, sex or so on even today." This reflects the actual fact that the existing system of the Civil Liberties Commissioners has not worked effectively to end discriminatory incidents.

The second reason given for the establishment of the agency is that, "various new factors have appeared, along with the development of a more internationalized, high aged, and information-oriented society." This can be understood as referring to the fact that, due to the Japanese society's inability to adjust itself to changes, new social problems have developed such as those connected to the rapid increase of foreigners staying in Japan, or the circulation of slander and discriminatory information like the List of Buraku Communities via the Internet. In addition, it can be said that Japan's government is afraid to be isolated from international community if it fails to create the legal systems needed to address human rights violations.

As stated by the Ministry, "Japan's government has implemented various arrangements such as ratifying several international covenants as a member of the international community." The government has ratified the International Covenant on Economic, Social and Cultural Rights (1979), the International Covenant on Civil and Political Rights (1979), the Convention on the Elimination of All Forms of Discrimination Against Women (1985), the Convention on the Rights of the Child (1994), and the International Convention on the Elimination of All Forms of Racial Discrimination (1996).

In response to the Convention on the Elimination of All Forms of Discrimination Against Women, the Law on Equal Employment Opportunity and Law on Prevention of Sexual Harassment, and in response to the International Convention on the Elimination of All Forms of Racial Discrimination the Ainu Culture Promotion Law were enacted. However, these laws were passed mainly to maintain the government's international image and, due to lack of domestic grass roots discussion and consultation within Japanese society, violations of those laws have continued.

Civil Liberties Commissioners, who are nominated by local assemblies, have the responsibility of responding to discriminatory incidents. The commissioners have, however, no power to investigate or make recommendations in response to a discriminatory incident without the voluntary cooperation of all parties involved. Rulings by the commissioners have no force under the law. In the 1999 survey on the situation of the Ainu people, the number of people reporting discriminatory incidents actually increased. The obsolescence of this system has been pointed out ever since its beginning.

Furthermore, the United Nations has stressed the necessity for an independent human rights agency because of increasing human rights violations in the government immigration offices, jails, and even among the police. It is highly appreciated that the Ministry of Justice made the decision to establish a new agency for human rights victims. However, many concerns have been expressed as to what kind of agency it will be and what powers it will have:

Firstly, a Human Rights Committee, which will accept complaints from victims and make decisions on recommendations, orders, or surveys, will be established only in Tokyo, not in the regions.

Secondly, it is not certain that the Human Rights Committee will include members from the victimized sectors.

Thirdly, the mandate of the Human Rights Committee has not yet been clearly defined, although the Committee needs to have strong enough powers to investigate internal governmental discrimination related to public power, for example, related to the police or immigration offices.

As for the Ainu people, the Round Table for Human Rights Promotion, like all government agencies, uses the Japanese term "Ainu no hitobito" (people of Ainu descent), avoiding the term "the Ainu people". In short, they are taking the position of not recognizing the existence of the Ainu as an indigenous people. Even though they have included people of Ainu descent as a category of victims of human rights violations, they have not addressed the roots of these violations as racial discrimination.

Now, the Ainu people have to examine cases of discrimination to find what this discrimination is based on, and what forms of discrimination they suffer. It is necessary to accurately analyze the discriminatory consciousness, which has been socially and historically formed, by which people see the conquered people as being "backward", "inferior", and "better to be assimilated". It is impossible to appropriately respond to the discrimination of the Ainu people if it is not recognized that this form of discrimination is a discrimination of a conquered indigenous people. As long as the government maintains this deceitful approach to ethnic groups like the Ainu of Hokkaido or the Ryukyu people of Okinawa, the response to discriminatory incidents will be far from adequate.

The Japanese government has already submitted the first and second report to the Committee on the Elimination of Racial Discrimination under the International Convention on the Elimination of All Forms of Racial Discrimination, and the report was considered in March of this year. The government has shown its duplicity in using different terms for the Ainu in the Japanese and English versions of the reports. All Japanese versions use the term "Ainu no hitobito", by which the Ainu are not recognized as a distinct people. In the earlier English reports, the government showed its uncertainty by using the term "the people of Ainu", which has a very unclear meaning.

In response to international pressure, the government now uses the term "the Ainu people" in the English version. However, the Japanese version still retains "Ainu no hitobito". In spite of the change of terminology in English reports, the refusal of the government to use "Ainu minzoku" (Ainu people) clearly shows its lack of political will to recognize the Ainu as an indigenous ethnic group, and thus to accept Ainu collective rights and self-determination.

The enactment of the so-called "Ainu Culture Promotion Law" in 1997 must also largely be seen as an attempt on the part of the Japanese government to maintain a positive image in the international community. The law is, however, very vague in its definition of Ainu culture. According to the government's concept, "culture" encompasses only aspects such as language, ceremonies or crafts, and does not include world view or lifestyles of indigenous peoples.

One positive aspect of the new law has been an increase in activities related to Ainu culture and a new awareness in Hokkaido of the Ainu as a distinct people with a unique and valued culture, despite its expression being limited to cultural activities and research. At a recent public hearing held in Sapporo by the Round Table for Human Rights Promotion, representatives from various NGOs representing discriminated groups came together to testify on the situation of discrimination in their areas. It is hoped that these groups, in a joint effort, will be able to pressure the Japanese government into making the proposed human rights relief agency an effective tool for safeguarding human rights in Japan.

CHINA

China's "Go West" Campaign

During the last two years, the Chinese government has introduced a strategic shift in the country's development. This strategy, which is termed "The great opening of the western regions" (*Xibu da kaifa*), or "Go West" for short, is of vital concern to many of China's minority peoples. However, their voice is hardly heard among the clamour emanating from the different interest groups that push for a development of China's western regions.

Historically speaking, China has oscillated between being predominantly land-oriented and sea-oriented. The opening up of the Silk Road more than two thousand years ago was followed by a prolonged period of developing maritime relations with Southeast Asia, before the grand Tang dynasty (618-907) once more redirected the country's main orientation towards the interior. This does not, however, mean that the Tang was inward-looking. On the contrary, it was China's first and only truly cosmopolitan period, and open-minded Chinese today appreciate the Tang period as precisely that. The Song and Yuan periods - the last one ruled by the Mongols - were once again rather sea-oriented. Then came the Ming (1378-1644) and the Qing (1644-1912), which were largely land-oriented. The notable exception was the spectacular Chinese expeditions into the South China Sea and the Indian Ocean all the way to the Arabian Peninsula and the East African Coast in the early fifteenth century. The commander of these expeditions, Zheng He, was a Muslim from Yunnan in south-western China.

Starting in the mid-nineteenth century, China once more became sea-oriented, but this time the condition was forced upon the ailing empire by the contending Western colonial powers and later also by Japan. During the period of the People's Republic, one may also say that China has changed orientation. In the first part of the period, the country "leaned" towards Russia, whereas the last twenty years have seen a continued orientation towards the sea, a shift that was initiated by the Chinese government itself, and not forced upon them, like in the 19th century. The present shift in strategy may not be seen as a dramatic shift in orientation in the sense that China is once more in the process of turning its back on the sea. Rather, it may be seen as an effort *to do both at the same time.*

However, there are wider implications that go beyond China's borders, namely the closer relations that have developed during the last ten years between China and four states that have common borders with China in Central Asia, namely Russia, Kazakhstan, Kyrgyzstan and Tajikistan, the so-called "Shanghai Five", so named after their first conference in Shanghai some years back. The situation in these regions is different from what it was back in the Soviet days, because the ruling elites in these countries all face ethnic unrest in their respective countries. These elites have therefore developed a common interest in quelling ethnic tensions, which in many cases would involve cross-border activities.

Furthermore, the improved relations between China and Russia, which have been characterized by the partners as a "strategic relationship", may contribute to pulling China once more towards a more continental orientation. But it remains to be seen to what extent this is based on real intentions and how much of it is based on tactical considerations in the global game between these two powers and the US. At any rate, it may just as easily contribute to pulling Russia towards China and not the other way around, which has been the established pattern.

The region which is considered to be a part of China's West is huge indeed. It covers ten of China's provinces and autonomous regions. In the north-west, we have Shaanxi, parts of Inner Mongolia, Gansu, Ningxia, Qinghai and Xinjiang, and in the south-west, we have Sichuan, Guizhou, Yunnan and Tibet. Some would also add the southern province of Guangxi. This region covers more than half of China's territory with a population of more than 300 million. It accounts for most of the country's mineral and oil reserves and is of great strategic importance, since it comprises most of China's border regions. Finally, it comprises almost all of China's minority regions, including all the five province-level autonomous regions: Xinjiang (Uighur, Hui, Kazakh, Kirgiz, etc.), Ningxia (Hui), Inner Mongolia (Mongols), Tibet (Tibetans) and Guangxi (Zhuang, etc.)

There has been a rush among the leading strata of these provinces to get their share of the public investments that are pouring into the region. Some are afraid that most of the resources will be tied up in the populous Han Chinese provinces like Sichuan and Shaanxi. Others are afraid that it will be no more than another chance for bureaucrats to enrich themselves through corruption, but the deciding point is that in most cases, it is the local Han Chinese who have a say in these matters, and not the indigenous peoples.

And the stakes are great indeed. The present phase is characterized by infrastructure projects, like a pipeline linking Xinjiang's natural gas fields to Shanghai. The railway from Ürümqi to Kashgar in Xjinjiang, which runs 1000 km, was completed in 1999, and a new railway running from Golmund in Qinghai to Lhasa is under construction. This will be the highest railway in the world, with a total length of about 1100 km.

A new road has been constructed running roughly north-south through the vast Taklamakan desert in Xinjiang and, from the Xinjiang capital Ürümqi, a new four-lane highway is under construction westwards towards Kazakstan, financed by the World Bank. The biggest engineering project takes place in the north-eastern part of Xinjiang, where water from the river Ertix is harnessed and redirected to supply water to hubs like Ürümqi and Karamay.

The Chinese authorities may thus have good reasons to develop these vast regions, in order to make their riches more accessible and to secure a more balanced development between the richer coastal provinces and China's vast hinterland. The ideological rationale for such a move is expressed in two typical Chinese catchwords. The first one is "the two no-leaving-each-other" (*Liangge libukai*), which simply means that the Han Chinese cannot do without the minority peoples, and the minority peoples cannot do without the Han Chinese. Mao Zedong himself, in his time, gave a more forthright version of the same idea when he said that the merits of the Han Chinese are their large population and skills, and the merits of the minority peoples are their large land and extensive resources.

The second catchword for the "Go West" campaign stems from Deng Xiaoping's thinking about the way China should develop, and is called "the two big general prospects" (*Liangge da ju*). The first one of these prospects refers to the Dengist strategy of letting the coastal regions go ahead and enrich themselves, and that these regions in turn should support the interior regions to do the same. This plan, which the central authorities are now trying to implement, is considered, in the words of party leader Jiang Zemin, as "a revitalization of the Chinese people".

However, besides this compulsory traditional sloganeering, the issue is mostly discussed in contexts that are void of ideological trappings. It has first and foremost kindled a kind of Chinese "pioneer" spirit, which plays on the traditional Chinese image of these western regions as inhospitable and forbidding while at the same time presenting them as the lands of golden opportunities. It is characteristic that the term "development" (*fazhan*) is not applied in this connection but rather the term "opening up" (*kaifa*). The Chinese press has discussed what one can learn from developments in other countries that are considered to be similar, like the Russian expansion into Siberia and the American westward expansion in the nineteenth century (sic).

The crucial point is that the minority peoples are hardly mentioned and hardly audible in this clamour for opening up of the west. A few voices of concern have been raised, for example, that the legal rights of the minority peoples in these regions have to be considered. But on the whole, the prospect of grand technological projects completely overshadows ethnic issues. The only area in which ethnic voices are heard is that of tourism and the prospect of presenting the minority regions as worthy caretakers of environmentally-friendly tourism. But for the rest, the plans seem to be drawn up to benefit the Hans both at the local and national level.

The thinking from the Han Chinese planners seems to be that development of the region will also contribute to developing the economies of the minority peoples. This aspect is certainly important because, if carried out well, it may result in tying an increasingly affluent political and economic elite among the minority peoples closer to these development plans. There has also been talk about making use of the Uighurs of Xinjiang, who are unsurpassed traders, as a pivotal developmental force in a regional Central Asian context.

There is no doubt that a campaign for developing China's western regions will lead to increased ethnic conflicts in the short run. The plans for opening up these regions are thus closely scrutinised by the regional military planners in Lanzhou in Gansu, which is the centre of the military command for the vast north-western regions.

In the last couple of years, there have been fewer armed clashes between Uighurs and Han Chinese, even if it seems clear that Uighurs have been given training for guerrilla warfare both among fundamentalist groups in Pakistan and among the Taleban in Afghanistan. The two incidents in Xinjiang that have aroused most concern recently are the arrest of the prominent Uighur woman, Rebiya Kadeer, and the death by torture of the political activist, Abduhelil Abdulmejit.

Kadeer, who is one of the *nouveau riche* among the Uighurs, was arrested in the spring of 2000 and sentenced to eight years in prison for allegedly revealing state secrets because she had mailed local newspapers to her husband, who is in exile in the United States. The arrest caused quite a stir, also among Uighur women in Kazakhstan and Kyrgyzstan, because Kadeer was known for her philanthropic projects and had served on high-level government commissions in Xinjiang. Abduhelil Abdulmejit was accused of being the brain behind the violent riot in Yili back in 1997 (see *The Indigenous World 1997-98*, pp. 187-88). On October 17, 2000, he died in prison as a result of torture by the Chinese police.

More recent reports claim that Moslem communities in Gansu, Ningxia and Shaanxi further east are getting more restive. The ethnic group in question is the Hui, who are often called "Chinese Moslems" due to the fact that they speak Chinese but are Moslems. Historically speaking, they are a result of intermarriage between Central Asian tradesmen and Chinese women. Their proximity to the Han Chinese regions has not made them more amenable to cultural assimilation. On the contrary, some of the most violent ethnic riots in China have originated in these areas, the last one in the 1930s, headed by the legendary Ma Zhongying.

Even the eastern province of Shandong has been the site of deadly clashes between Hui and Chinese police. In December 2000, the police fired at a crowd of about 2000 Hui demonstrators in the county centre, Yangxin, an incident that was reported in the Chinese press. Most of the Moslems involved were said to have come from Mengcun County in neighbouring Hebei province. The tensions had been building up after a Han shop owner in Yangxin advertised the sale of "Islamic pork", resulting in he and another Han being killed. Later, a pig's head was found hanging in front of the local mosque. The result of these incidents was that the communist party boss in Shandong, the head of the administration and the police chief of Yangxin County were sacked but many Moslems considered that the government should do more than just make these officials the scapegoats for the incidents.

TAIWAN

The Historical Ending of Indigenous Land?

The latest revision to the "Regulation on the Development and Management of Indigenous Reserve" was made at the end of the year 2000 by the Ministry of Internal Affairs. The revision again followed the theme of "the acquisition and development of indigenous reserve by non-indigenous people", and has now been sent to the Aboriginal Council for inquiry. On the key point deciding the future of indigenous reserve, we found exceptionally low concern regarding revision of the Regulation. This kind of abnormal silence might be a deliberate move on the part of those who stand to benefit from the revision.

The Regulation was first made in 1948. (It was then called "Regulation on the Development of the Mountainous Reserves in all Counties, Taiwan".) For the past 50 years, it has been revised six times. Every revision stressed that the reserve was to protect the livelihood of the indigenous population but it was actually through these revisions that the government failed to stop non-indigenous people from developing the mountain area, and sacrificed indigenous rights instead. Although the Regulation has formally insisted on the sole entitlement of the indigenous population to the reserve, there are numerous cases of illegal purchase of reserve land left unresolved. And we do not even know the exact number of cases according to official research. The six large-scale "clearances", which legitimized the illegal non-indigenous usufruct of reserve land, actually resulted in the indigenous peoples losing their land through the Regulation and government action.

From the very beginning, when the government claimed ownership of indigenous land, there was an assumption within the reserve policy that the government should take care of each and every indigenous individual. As a result, the reserve land became private property, and as such it was assumed that it would be cultivated in the best way possible, or used to its greatest efficiency. Such a biased perspective of efficiency under a system of privatized property underestimated the efficiency of sustainable development supported by a traditional system of land use, and ignored the cultural and societal benefit of the collective aspect of traditional indigenous land use. As a result of the government's "privatization policy", and due to the urgent need for cash, those who are entitled to the reserve often sell the land legally or illegally, and are left with nothing. Rather than securing the livelihood and the survival of the indigenous people, the "privatization" of the reserve policy, i.e. the entitlement of individual indigenous Taiwanese to reserve land, will ultimately cause the loss of a great deal of indigenous reserve land.

The "Regulation on the Development and Management of Indigenous Reserve Land" is a decree formed by means of Article 37 of the "Act on Conservation and Use of Mountainous Area" (the Act). The Act does clearly not incorporate the peculiarity of indigenous reserve land; Article 37 speaks only about the establishment of indigenous reserve land and the sole entitlement of the indigenous population to it. The right of the indigenous nations to collectively self-manage the reserve land and the obligation of the government to assist them in this is not included. Indigenous peoples have campaigned and demanded the revision of the Regulation or the enactment of separate legislation since the 1980s. On the other hand, the "Ping-quan-hui" (an interest group for the non-indigenous population inhabiting or investing in traditional indigenous areas), which has close connections to political powers and private enterprises, is also making an effort to have the Regulation revised or new legislation promulgated that would release the reserve from the sole entitlement of the indigenous peoples, "in order to promote the development of the area inhabited by indigenous people". Under such contention, the Ministry of Internal Affairs, the body in charge of the indigenous reserves, in fact began to draft the "Act on the Development and Management of Indigenous Reserve Land". In case Congress did not ratify the draft law rapidly, the Ministry also prepared a revision of the Regulation. From this draft revision of the Regulation, it is possible to understand the view of the Ministry in charge of the policy on indigenous reserve land, and one can therefore also get an idea of the possible direction of future legislation.

Article 15 & Article 18 of the Draft Revision of "Regulation on the Development and Management of Indigenous Reserve Land"
An important direction of the revision is to allow non-indigenous people to be entitled by inheritance. To prevent inconsistency between the Regulation and the Act, which it forms a part of and which legitimizes the validity of the Regulation, the Ministry of Internal Affairs at the same time proposes the revision of Article 37 of the Act. It is already questionable as to how a decree could decide the direction of legislation. The fact that the effort the Ministry made was in the interest of non-indigenous people is itself in contrast with existing law, and also inconsistent with the essence of the provisions governing reserve land as expressed in Article 3 of the Regulation, which states that the reserve land is to secure the livelihood of the indigenous population and is reserved for their use.

It might seem unreasonable or unfair to prohibit non-indigenous people from inheriting the reserve. However, the rationale is that indigenous land is embodied with social solidarity, and the distribution and use of commonly owned land is based on an individual's status within the nation he or she belongs to. Such connection between human beings and the land is more radical than the "common" ancestral heritage.

In the latest revision, the Ministry of Internal Affairs not only ignored the collective aspect of reserve land, but it also made no effort to put an end to the illegal purchase of reserve land. On the contrary, it tried to lift the barrier preventing non-indigenous people from being entitled to reserve land, which would make it easier for consortia and "Ping-quan-hui" to purchase indigenous reserve land.

Article 28-1 & Article 42-1 of the Draft Revision of "Regulation on the Development and Management of Indigenous Reserve Land"
In addition to the possibility that non-indigenous people could be legally entitled to indigenous reserve land, other articles are trying to legitimize the illegal transactions of the past. The "Investigation Program on the Use of Indigenous Reserve Resources 1995" in Article 28-1 of the revision is in fact the seventh "clearance", following the previous six, legitimizing even more illegal appropriations of indigenous reserve lands. The first two clauses of Article 28-1 indicate that: those who used the reserve illegally before the clearance could continue to use the land with a lease, and reserve used illegally after the clearance should be taken back by the government. The rhetoric is nothing new. In other words, all those illegal cultivators need not be too worried about the possibility of the land being "taken back" since the Ministry of Internal Affairs has always been indifferent to the offences, and there will always be another "clearance" to legitimize all the illegal transactions once there have been a certain number of further illegal appropriations.

Aftermath of the Earthquake

In recent years, it seems that disaster looms in indigenous areas whenever rains fall. Landslides, road collapses or mudflows have been common events. These disasters were usually connected to the so-called "921 earthquake" of September 1999. But it has become evident that not only natural forces have to be blamed but also the reckless and unrestricted profit-oriented mode of development. It reveals what the indigenous peoples have been forced to engage in for their economic survival, as well as the extent of cultivation in mountain areas by non-indigenous people, all in the name of the "development" of indigenous areas. Both sharply reflect the failure of the government to positively respond to the transitions taking place in indigenous societies.

After the earthquake, members of the indigenous peoples ranked, as usual, at the bottom of the priority list for rescue and rehabilitation. And the supplies often failed to cover the needs. The geographical and cultural distance between the indigenous peoples and the majority population left the latter either little concerned, or figuring out for themselves what the needs of the indigenous people could be. This has been the case no matter whether there was a disaster or not. Ironically, the autonomy of the tribes grew under such difficulties. The self-reconstruction of the Thao village of the Mihu community of Tayal is an example of the re-organization of indigenous social institutions that have been weakened over many decades. But the opportunity for indigenous tribes' autonomy to grow also carries with it potential dangers. The government still controls the usufruct of the land, the management of resources and development planning, and it is still ignorant of the increasingly destructive impact of the present mode of development in indigenous areas. The blueprint for its reconstruction efforts seems to be based on the principles of reconstruction to the "original style", which ultimately means to accommodate the needs of the majority. Instead of considering what kind of reconstruction the indigenous communities want, what is good for the economy of the tribe or what will help to solve their own problem, they are looking for "safer" spots to enjoy the scenery, building wider roads and thicker supporting walls, and trying to revive tourism to bring about economic growth.

The indigenous peoples fear that all the provisions of the "921 Earthquake Reconstruction Act" that are aimed at helping the earthquake area to recover, such as reduction in revenue, low-interest loans, simplified registration of real estate, simplified requirements for investigations on environmental effects, will ultimately help construction companies and enterprises who bear the same logic of "development" to gain easier entry to indigenous areas. Those budding movements in indigenous communities aimed at regaining more control over their affairs, of reconstructing the autonomy of the tribe, could be killed again if there is no special program to support them, if there are not enough funds, or if the legal requirements cannot be adjusted. The efforts of the tribes seeking autonomous development, to attract the urban migrant workers back to the communities, to solve the problem of unemployment, to become economically independent, and to recover their dignity may then not succeed.

PHILIPPINES

Constitutionality of Indigenous Peoples Rights Act Upheld

In its ruling of 28 November 2000, the Supreme Court of the Philippines upheld the Constitutionality of the IPRA by a 7 to 7 vote. The ruling of the Supreme Court on the Isagani-Cruz case had been anxiously awaited by indigenous organisations and their supporters. The case questioned the constitutionality of several provisions in the Indigenous Peoples Rights Act (IPRA), among them, and most important, the provision for communal ownership of land and resources (including sub-surface resources) on the part of indigenous peoples. It was argued that this provision violates the Regalian Doctrine, which established State ownership over public land and the resources therein (for a more detailed analysis of the arguments given, refer to the article "Constitutional Challenges on the Indigenous Rights Act" in *Philippine Natural Resources Law Journal* Vol. 10, No. 1, of June 2000).

It is considered that the decision, which was officially released on December 6, marks the first time in Asia that a national government has legally recognized indigenous peoples' territorial rights. However, although the battle may be won, the war is not yet over. The 7 to 7 vote of the Supreme Court was very close, and the petitioners submitted a Motion for Reconsideration. Since there was one vacancy in the SC, the new 15th judge appointed by ousted President Estrada shortly before he stepped down will determine the new majority. Holders of large vested interests (mostly in mining) behind the petition are putting heavy pressure on the end result.

National Commission on Indigenous Peoples Paralysed under Estrada

Throughout the time ex-President Estrada was in office, his administration showed a blatant lack of political will to implement the law. With reference to the pending court case, funds for the proper operation of the NCIP were withheld and the Secretary of the Department of Environment and Natural Resources (DENR) gave orders to stall the implementation of IPRA, meaning: not to sign any certificates of ancestral domain title (CADT).

The National Commission on Indigenous Peoples (NCIP), whose task it is to implement the IPRA, has therefore been virtually non-functioning ever since its creation. Furthermore, two other Indigenous Peoples "Task Forces" were created under Estrada and superimposed on the NCIP (the "Presidential Task Force on Ancestral Domains" in February 1999 and the "Presidential Task Force on Indigenous Peoples" in February 2000).

Like its predecessors, the NCIP was in danger of becoming a tool for protecting the interests of politicians and private enterprises rather than those of the indigenous peoples. Not a single ancestral

Mass demostrations against President Estrada in Baguio City, Cordilleras. Many indigenous of the Cordillera joined the countrywide mass protests that led to the ousting of Estrada in January 2001. Photos: Cordillera Peoples Alliance

domain title had been issued up to the time Estrada was ousted by the massive and peaceful popular protest that came to be known as "Peoples Power II" (in reference to the protests that forced Dictator Marcos out of office and country in 1986). While all of the 181 Ancestral Domain Claims had been left pending, the NCIP did issue 101 certifications to mining companies stating that the areas under certification were either not inhabited by indigenous peoples or outside any claims for ancestral domain/lands, even in the face of clear evidence that indigenous peoples lived in these areas.

After the ruling of the Supreme Court, the NCIP was put under pressure by NGOs and indigenous organisations to start issuing Certificates of Ancestral Domain Titles (CADTs) and, by the end of the term of its former chairman Dao-as on February 20 this year, a small number of CADTs had indeed been signed.

Commitment to IPRA Signalled by the New President Gloria Macapagal-Arroyo

There is reason to hope that the events will turn in favour of the IPRA under the newly installed president Gloria Macapagal-Arroyo. On February 20, 2001, President Arroyo signed Executive Order No. 1 creating the Office of the Presidential Adviser for Indigenous Peoples Affairs (OPAIPA) and appointed Ambassador Howard Dee as its head. Immediately after assuming his post, Dee organized a consultative forum on March 9 last, with representatives of indigenous peoples organizations, NGOs and Church groups, dealing with how to assist the government in fully implementing the Indigenous Peoples Rights Act. President Arroyo also appointed Edtami Mansayagan, a Manobo from Mindanao who has been involved in the indigenous movement for decades and who is known for his commitment and integrity, as Officer In Charge and Executive Director of NCIP pending the institutional and performance audit and appointment of its new commissioners.

During the forum, the participants reviewed and assessed the performance of the former officials of the NCIP and noted the public's negative perception of the organization. It criticised the selection process by which its officials and personnel were appointed and its failure to address and respond to issues affecting the indigenous peoples. It also stressed a number of issues that required government attention:

- A change in the government's position on the IPRA case at the Supreme Court to ensure a favourable ruling.

- A moratorium on the issuing of CADTs and CALTs and certification of free and prior informed consent (FPIC) pending review of its process.
- Stopping the practice of deputizing the security guards of business firms operating in ancestral domains as CAFGU or similar paramilitary units.
- A return of indigenous peoples displaced from their ancestral territories, such as the Quezon Manobo Tribes Association (QUEMTRAS).
- The creation of an Indigenous Peoples' Consultative Committee.
- The immediate release of the NCIP budget.

Cordillera Region

Mining

In June 2000, nine mining applications in the Cordillera, covering a total land area of 15,064 ha., were approved by the national government. These are located in the municipalities of Mankayan, Tuba and Itogon in Benguet Province, and Bucay and Licuan-Baay in Abra. The applications approved are those of Lepanto Consolidated Mining Company, Philex Mining Company, Crescent Mining and Development Company and Jobel Corporation, all registered as local companies. The mining areas applied for lie within the territories of the Tingguian, Kankanaey and Ibaloi indigenous peoples. The communities affected were never properly informed or consulted.

Another 126 mining applications in the Cordillera region are being processed for approval, covering a total land area of 711,965 ha. The Department of Environment and Natural Resources (DENR) said that they were fast-tracking the approval of these applications in order to encourage foreign investments in the country. Most of these applications are from multinational companies, such as Newmont based in the U.S., or Climax Arimco of Australia. Opposition in the areas covered by these applications remains firm.

Dams

Opposition to the San Roque Dam is becoming stronger with the formation of Timmawa, the Agno River Peasant Movement to Free the Agno River. Timmawa was launched on March 13 with more than 300 members from Itogon, Benguet, and San Manuel and San Nicolas of Pangasinan. This US$1.1 billion mega-dam project, funded by the Japanese Bank for International Cooperation (JBIC), is currently under construction and targeted to be completed by 2004. The continuing construction of this dam violates several laws, such as the Indigenous Peoples Rights Act, the Local Government Code and the Investment Code. JBIC has not fully released the loans because of the growing protest and since several legal requirements have yet to be met.

Aside from the San Roque Dam, two others are presently undergoing construction, the Agbulu Dam in Apayao and the Bakun Dam in Benguet. Foreign funding is furthermore being sought for two more mega-dam projects in the Cordillera: the Matuno Dam in Ifugao and the Palsuguan Dam in Abra. None of the mega-dam projects complied with the requirement for obtaining the free and informed prior consent of the affected indigenous peoples, as stipulated in the Indigenous Peoples Rights Act.

The New Administration
The leaders of the former "Erap Resign Movement" held a meeting with the new President Gloria Macapagal Arroyo on March 24, 2001. The CPA called the attention of the new president to the urgent issues of the Cordillera indigenous peoples in relation to the dams and mining projects in the region. The president promised that her administration would seek the consent of the indigenous peoples to projects implemented in the region.

Elections
Because of the success of the Peoples Power II in ousting the former President, there is now a strong movement among the indigenous peoples to participate in the local and national elections scheduled for May 2001. The CPA and its affiliate organizations are actively building alliances with progressive parties and candidates to hopefully influence the result of the elections towards a more democratic governance and legislation for the genuine recognition of indigenous peoples rights from local up to national level.

Death of Two Cordillera Indigenous Leaders
Mrs. Susan Longid, a member of the Regional Ecumenical Center in the Cordillera (RECCORD) and a member of the Regional Council of the Cordillera Peoples Alliance passed away on March 19. She was 55 years old and had been suffering from cancer. Mrs. Longid, a Bontoc from Bontoc town in Mountain Province, was at the forefront of the movement for the recognition and protection of indigenous peoples rights. She was one of the pioneers in developing educa-

tional modules on Cordillera issues and concerns during her time as Executive Director of the Cordillera Schools Group, a network of protestant schools in the Cordillera.

Mr. Eddie Daguitan, the Secretary-General of the Kalinga Chapter of the Cordillera Peoples Alliance also died of cancer on March 18, 2001. He was 42 years old. Eddie, a member of the Mangali Tribe of Kalinga was already an activist against the Chico Dams in the late seventies and became an organizer of indigenous students in Baguio. As an agriculturist, he was very much involved in the development of appropriate technology and socio-economic work for indigenous communities in Mountain Province and Kalinga.

The demise of Mother Susan Longid and Eddie Daguitan is a big loss for the Cordillera indigenous peoples' movement. Their lives will always be a source of inspiration and they will remain in the heart and struggle of the people.

Sources
   MGB-DENR Certified List of Approved and Pending Mining Applications in
      the Cordillera Region
   CPA press releases

Mindoro

Mining Permit in the Ancestral Domain of Mangyan on Mindoro Revoked

DENR Secretary, Heherson Alvarez, revoked the Mineral Production Sharing Agreement (MPSA) of Abglubang Mining Corporation on 11 April 2001.

On March 14, 1997, Mindex Resources Development, Inc., a Norwegian company engaged in exploration and development of mineral resources in Norway, Greenland, Ghana and Vietnam, was issued an exploration permit by the Mines and Geo-Sciences Bureau of DENR. The Mindex subsidiary in the Philippines is Aglubang Mining Corporation, which held a two-third share in the concession area. Mindex Resource Development was later renamed Crew Mineral Philippines (CMP) after Canadian investors bought into the company.

The MPSA acquired by Aglubang Mining Corp. (AMC) covered 9,720 hectares in Sablayan, Occidental Mindoro and Victoria, Oriental Mindoro for 25 years. The planned nickel mining project would have encroached upon the ancestral lands of the Samahan ng mga Nagkakaisang Mangyan Alangan (SANAMA) and Kapyan Agpaysarigan Mangyan Tadyawan of the Alangan and Tadyawan people. Both groups were awarded a certificate of ancestral domain claim by the DENR prior to the granting of the exploration permit.

The local government, church and civil society of Mindoro have opposed the mining project. At the forefront of the struggle were indigenous peoples' organizations, primarily the Kapulungan Para sa Lupaing Ninuno (KPLN), a provincial federation of Mangyan in Oriental Mindoro. The DENR found that there was sufficient grounds for revoking the MPSA of AMC, such as failure to obtain an environmental impact assessment (EIA) and prior approval from the relevant Local Government Units. It also noted that AMC had no "proven track record".

Palawan

Ancestral Domains Remain Unrecognised

Due to the NCIP's lack of implementation of the IPRA over the past years and the unsupportive attitude of local governments, especially in the Municipality of Rizal, the Ancestral Domains of the indigenous peoples of Palawan island remain unrecognised. The Palawan NGOs Network Inc. (PNNI) and other organizations are now trying to come up with alternative solutions to secure the indigenous peoples' rights to their Ancestral Domains by appealing to Republic Act No. 7611. This latter empowers the Palawan Council for Sustainable Development (PCSD) to govern, implement and give policy direction to the Strategic Environmental Plan for Palawan (SEP), and to provide for the recognition of tribal ancestral lands as a main component of the Environmentally Critical Areas Network (ECAN). Until now, the Palawan Special Committee on Tribal Ancestral Zones (PSCTAZ) has had very limited capacities and technical skills to perform tasks pertaining to the identification and delineation of tribal zones. In addition, there is very little communication between PSCTAZ and the DENR concerning the follow-up of pending CADC applications, such as those for the Pälawan communities of Rizal and the Batak of Tanabag. However, there is hope that pending CADC applications will be re-examined and processed through implementation of recent presidential Executive Order No.1 (see paragraph above).

During 2001, the zoning of Palawan according to the ECAN criteria has continued, and this represents a further threat to indigenous access and control over their territories. ECAN is the centrepiece strategy of the SEP law that places most of the province under controlled development. The areas covered by ECAN include three major components: Terrestrial, Coastal/Marine and Tribal Ancestral Lands. Some of these proposed zones (e.g. core zones) limit or exclude human access to natural resources, with predictable repercussions on indigenous livelihoods. ECAN zoning is now being completed for the whole province of Palawan without any form of coordination with the local indigenous communities. The result of the ECAN survey and related maps are expected to be presented to the Provincial government before or immediately after the national elections in May 2001.

Destruction of Natural Resources and Mining

During the year 2000, there was a resurgence of dynamite fishing, also in connection with the so-called "shark operations". Some of the fish that are generally used as bait for sharks cannot be easily captured by hook and line, and thus bombs are used to catch them. Gangs from Bancalaan, Mangsi and Balabac islands are not only directly involved in illegal fishing but also selling dynamite and cyanide to the local populations, especially in Rizal and Quezon municipalities. The relevant government agencies and military authorities are well aware of the situation but have no means (e.g. speed boats) to apprehend the illegal fishermen. Because of over-exploitation of marine resources, traditional fishing methods have become ineffective. As a result, indigenous peoples have been forced to refine their fishing technology, doubling the size of their nets, or even using dynamite.

Over the past year, threats from large-scale mining activities have increased exponentially. Surprisingly, the Palawan Council for Sustainable Development (PCSD) has endorsed the plan of Rio Tuba Nickel Mining Corp. (RTNMC) concerning the establishment of a nickel refinery, the establishment of a support hydrogen sulphide production plant and limestone quarrying operations. PCSD is a unique government body formed by Republic Act No. 7611 with a mandate to protect the environment within the province. In reality, indigenous interests are not represented on the council, whose members continue to entertain new mining applications. The risk posed by the Process Plant to the environment and local communities is very high. Local NGOs in Palawan are now requesting the assistance of international organizations to lobby the Philippine Government against the expansion of RTNMC in southern Palawan, and to stop all large-scale mining operations in Palawan.

Mindanao

New Cease Fire Between the Government and the MILF

Despite intermittent skirmishes and violations of the cease-fire forged on July 17, 1997 between the government and the Moro Islamic

Liberation Front (MILF), both parties decided to formally open peace talks on 25 October 1999. Four rounds of formal peace talks resulted in both sides agreeing to submit their formal position papers on the nine agenda items presented by the MILF. However, the military began a shooting war on 28 April 2000 for the purposes of clearing the Narciso Ramos Highway (a highway connecting Cotabato and Lanao del Sur) purportedly of MILF rebels who were setting up checkpoints. The war was pursued vigorously by the government despite calls for a cease-fire and a return to the negotiating table by groups such as the Catholic Bishops Conference of the Philippines, the Bishops-Businessmen's Conference or the Organization of Islamic Conference. Caught in between were the Lumad, the indigenous peoples of Mindanao. Thousands were forced to leave their homes and seek shelter in evacuation camps and elsewhere (see *The Indigenous World 1999-2000).* They have been left with no choice. Both of the opposing forces, the military and the Moro rebels suspect them to be supporters or sympathizers of their enemies. The Lumad communities living in the periphery of the Moro-controlled areas are accused by the military to be "spies" for the rebels and are receivers of the government's troop shelling and bombings. On the other hand, the rebels accuse the Lumads to be government's informers. Furthermore, the Lumad communities residing within the rebel-controlled areas are endlessly forced to pay "revolutionary contributions" and their young boys are recruited as fresh crop for the Moro guerilla.

Due to superior firepower and the use of aircraft, MILF camps fell one after the other. The MILF simply abandoned their camps. On 9 July 2000, the MILF main camp, Abubakre As-Siddque, fell to military hands. President Joseph E. Estrada himself raised the Philippine flag in a place considered holy by Muslims, it being the "capital" of their Islamic State and celebrated the "victory" with *lechon* (roasted pigs) and beer, a move that clearly demonstrated a lack of sensitivity to the religious feelings of Muslims. A few days later, a *jihad* (holy war) was declared by Chairman Hashim against the Philippine government and its armed forces.

In the midst of the government's "all-out-war" and the MILF's *jihad*, the government has announced a massive, 100 billion Peso (US$2.1 billion) relief and rehabilitation program. Some 600,000 refugees have to be returned and assisted by the government. The government also plans to rehabilitate damaged roads and bridges, buildings and mosques. However, refugees in many instances refused to return on account of the near daily ambuscades by the MILF on GRP positions.

During the turbulent times of the impeachment, the MILF decided to remain open to the peace process. The newly installed government of President Arroyo adopted and popularises "all-out-peace" in contrast to the former administration's "all-out-war" as the new policy of solving the conflict in Mindanao. The government halted all military operations against the Moro rebels as a gesture for the new peace negotiations. However, the government strongly declared not to give back all overtaken rebels camps.

To avoid sabotage, the government pushes backdoor negotiation with the Moro leaders. Last March 2001, the Presidential Adviser on Peace Process, Eduardo Ermita secretly met with the MILF representatives lead by Al Haj Murad, Vice-Chair for Military Affairs in Kuala Lumpur, Malaysia. They agreed to resume the thwarted peace negotiations. Moner Bajunaid, Chair of the MILF Technical panel and concurrently an independent senatorial candidate disclosed over a radio interview that MILF is consulting its constituencies all over Mindanao for the peace negotiation. However, the campaign for the 14 May 2001 national election has stalled the process on both sides.

EAST TIMOR

East Timor was a Portuguese colony for more than 400 years. In 1975, it was invaded by Indonesia. This was the start of a brutal and illegal occupation. In 1999, when Indonesia was temporarily weakened by a regional economic crisis, its government allowed a referendum in East Timor in order to determine the future of the territory. When the referendum took place in August 1999, an overwhelming majority voted for independence.

Pro-Indonesian militias, created and supported by the Indonesian military, tried to influence the outcome. In the months leading up to the referendum, independence supporters were harassed and intimidated. Several thousands were killed. When the result was announced, the militias and the Indonesian military went on a rampage, destroying property and killing more people.

In September 1999, an international military force (INTERFET) led by Australia arrived in East Timor and, in October, the last Indonesian soldiers left the territory. In February 2000, INTERFET was replaced by a regular UN peacekeeping force. Since 1999, East Timor has been administrated by UNTAET, the United Nations Transitional Administration in East Timor. Formal independence is expected to begin at the end of 2001 or the beginning of 2002. The country's official name will probably be Timor Loro Sa'e.

The people of East Timor are finally free. The Indonesian occupation is history but the future will not be easy. They face a number of serious problems, which they will have to solve to build their new nation.

Infrastructure and Economy

One problem is infrastructure. Many roads are in a poor condition, especially during the rainy season (November-March). In the coastal cities, harbours will need to be repaired and expanded so that the country can trade with the rest of the world.

A second problem is the economy. During the Indonesian occupation, all major economic assets were in the hands of Indonesian generals - the Suharto family and its cronies - who exploited East Timor for their personal profit. Now the East Timorese have to take control of these assets. Coffee is an important product but, during the year 2000, the international price of coffee dropped by 50 per cent, to the lowest level in the last 30 years. Wood was once an important product but too many trees have been cut down and there is a serious risk of deforestation.

The sea around East Timor is rich in fish but many fishing boats were destroyed by pro-Indonesian militias during the turbulent days of 1999. The East Timorese have to build a new fishing fleet. Traditionally, fishing was not a major activity in East Timor, as most people worked in agriculture. In the future this may well change.

Oil and natural gas can be found under the ocean bed between East Timor and Australia, in the area known as the Timor Gap. These natural resources will probably give the new nation a solid economic foundation. Australia, however, is reluctant to give up the rights it secured in a treaty concluded with Indonesia in 1989. The old treaty divides the revenue from energy taxes 50-50 between the two parties. Naturally, East Timor wants a larger share. The old treaty was illegal as Indonesia had no legal claim to East Timor and thus a new treaty is now being negotiated.

It is possible to develop tourism to a certain extent, but not until the infrastructure has been improved.

Education and Administration

A third problem is the education system. During the Indonesian occupation, everybody was forced to learn the Indonesian language

Bahasa Indonesia. This will not continue. There are several local languages in East Timor, but *tetum* is the *lingua franca*. Portuguese used to be the language of administration, and some people still speak it, mostly the older generation. The younger generation prefers English because it is the language of computers and of the internet. This does not, however, mean that they actually master this language. Because of recent history everybody knows *Bahasa Indonesia*, and this language will probably be used by many for a long time to come.

A fourth problem is a civilian administration. During the Indonesian occupation the territory was controlled by the military with a small civilian administration in a junior role. This will not continue. A new civilian administration will have to supervise infrastructure, the economy and the school system.

It will also have to deal with the problem of where the people are. Towards the end of the Indonesian occupation East Timor had about 800,000 inhabitants, of which some 100,000 lived in the capital Dili. Since Indonesia's departure, many people have moved from the countryside and the smaller towns to Dili. If this influx is not stopped, the capital will soon be full of poor and unemployed people. In a free country it is hardly possible to prohibit people from moving, so the new administration must make it attractive for people in the countryside or the smaller towns to stay where they are.

In September 1999, when the pro-Indonesian militias escaped across the border to West Timor, they forced some 200,000 people to go with them, and they all ended up in camps controlled by the militias or the Indonesian military. Since then, some of them have been allowed to return to East Timor but about 100,000 people are still living in camps in West Timor, waiting to return. Providing jobs, housing and education for 100,000 refugees (or hostages) will be a major task for the new administration.

Political System

A fifth problem is the political system. East Timor must have a constitution. In addition, it needs to elect a parliament and a president. It is widely expected that the constitution will be dominated by respect for human rights, democracy and respect for international law. The East Timorese know better than most people what may happen when these concepts are ignored and violated.

The first president of an independent East Timor will probably be Xanana Gusmao, who was the supreme commander of the armed resistance in the mountains (Falintil) until he was captured by the

Indonesians in 1992. The first foreign minister will probably be José Ramos-Horta, who represented the resistance movement in exile during the Indonesian occupation. Bishop Carlos Belo was an important figure in the humanitarian struggle against Indonesia but, being a man of the cloth, he is not likely to have political ambitions.

A new eight-member cabinet of the transitional government in East Timor was established on 15 July 2000. *Timor Link*, the newsletter of CIIR (Catholic Institute for International Relations), reported:

> *"The new body is regarded by both the United Nations Transitional Administration in East Timor (UNTAET) and the National Council of Timorese Resistance (CNRT) as a further step towards independence. With four East Timorese members, it is the first time that East Timorese leaders have participated as equal partners in the governance of their country."*[1]

Internal Divisions

In addition to the problems concerning institutions and organisations, the East Timorese also have to face the fact that they are divided among themselves. In the past, it was easy to unite against Indonesia. But now that Indonesia has left, they discover that they do not agree on everything.

There is a division between right and left-wing politics; between the old generation who lived under Portuguese colonialism and the young generation who knows only the Indonesian occupation; and maybe a division between the external group that went into exile and the internal group that remained in East Timor.

The role and influence of the Catholic Church may also be a source of conflict. During the occupation, many people turned to the Church because it was the only legal organisation that was not controlled by Indonesia, and this was a (relatively) safe way of expressing your opposition to the invader. Not all people who joined the church did so for purely religious reasons.

The same phenomenon could be seen in Poland during the Cold War, where many Poles joined the church to express their opposition to the communist government and Soviet influence. After the Cold War, however, many people came to see the Catholic Church as a reactionary force that demanded obedience and rejected divorce, birth control and abortion.

The Crimes of the Past

The Indonesian occupation of East Timor is history but the memories linger on. How to deal with the crimes against East Timor? In Latin America, several military dictatorships handed over power to civilian and democratic governments on the condition that the generals receive immunity from any criminal charges. They wanted to bury the past, and they were quite successful, at least until recently. For the victims, this approach was clearly unacceptable.

In South Africa, a Truth & Reconciliation Commission (TRC) was established to deal with the crimes committed during apartheid. The idea was that the truth should be told and thus make reconciliation possible. In South Africa, they did not want to use the Latin American approach where the past was buried and the criminals got away with murder. On the other hand, they also wished to avoid taking revenge. By taking revenge you merely produce new victims and the cycle of violence continues.

The South African approach has many advantages but it was also criticized. Some white people felt that it was a witch-hunt against them, while some non-white people felt that the TRC did not go far enough: the smaller fish became scapegoats while the bigger fish were allowed to escape. Those at the top in the system of apartheid were never touched.

With regard to East Timor, the superpowers never wanted a serious investigation of the past. The evidence would point not only to Suharto and his regime but also to the powers that supported him with money and arms.

East Timor cannot undertake an investigation by itself; Indonesia is not likely to do it. What is needed is an international investigation by the UN. The geographical scope should be not only East Timor and Indonesia but also the Western governments and private companies that supported the aggression against East Timor. The time frame should be not only the turbulent year of the referendum in 1999 but it should go all the way back to 1974 when the first plans for the invasion were being laid. Given the position of the superpowers, it is not very likely that the UN will ever undertake such a project in earnest.[2]

A Period of Transition

From 1999 to 2000, East Timor took a giant step from Indonesian occupation towards independence. At the moment, the former Portuguese colony is in a period of transition during which it is governed by the UN.[3] Although the UN administration was welcomed by many and is there to help, it may - paradoxically - be a problem in itself. One reason is the huge economic gap between the affluent UN personnel on the one hand and the poor people of East Timor on the other. A second reason is that the UN has been very slow to hand over management of local affairs to the East Timorese. The Scandinavian jurist, Christian Ranheim, who was a UN observer in East Timor before and after the August 1999 referendum, summarises the situation thus:

> "While the process to convict the guilty ones continues, international organisations are being accused of conducting a new colonisation of East Timor. Some observers have even claimed that the people are worse off under international administration than during the Indonesian occupation.

> "The East Timorese live in extreme poverty, but they see international aid workers living in floating hotels with prices of US $200 per night, drinking beer and having a good time in the newly established beach club in Dili. The coffee they produce is no longer exported due to a lack of infrastructure. The people who were prepared to make a national effort to rebuild their own country now feel a despondency and apathy which may endanger the whole transition process."[4]

Notes

[1] *Timor Link*, no. 50, August 2000. The transitional cabinet now has nine members: José Ramos-Horta was added as foreign minister in the autumn of 2000.

[2] *Timor Link*, no. 51, December 2000, contains a special supplement entitled "In search of justice: An international tribunal for East Timor".

[3] Damien Kingsbury, "East Timor at a cross-roads", *Jakarta Post*, 15 December 2000. Via internet. Se also James Traub, "Inventing East Timor", *Foreign Affairs*, July-August 2000, pp. 74-89.

[4] Christian Ranheim, "Øst-Timor: På vei mot selvstendighet", *Mennesker og rettigheter*, vol. 18, no. 3, 2000, pp. 231-240. Translated into English this is "East Timor on the road to independence". The title of the Norwegian journal is *Human Beings & Human Rights*.

East Timor on the Internet

East Timor Action Network / www.etan.org
East Timor Daily News / www.timor.com
Timor Aid / www.timoraid.org
Timor Today / www.easttimor.com

INDONESIA

Decentralization: New Autonomy Laws

With the overthrow of President Suharto in May 1998, the country's political structures and its centralist architecture were called into question. In the reform agenda with which the transition government of B. J. Habibie cast its lot, the devolution of political and fiscal powers from the center to the regions took a prominent place. Although the economy was in a shambles, some regions rich in natural resources demanded both a more equitable share of the profits from their exploitation as well as greater freedom to do with them as they pleased. Other regions asked for less central intervention in local politics. Most requested wider autonomy.

In an attempt to reverse this centralization, the Habibie government promulgated two new laws: Law 22/1999 on Regional Governance and Law 25/1999 on Fiscal Balance Between the State and the Regions. Law 22 decentralizes authority over all fields except foreign affairs, defence and security, justice, monetary and fiscal policy, religion and a number of broad economic issues. Significantly, it provides for the election of regional heads – provincial governors and district regents – who, during Suharto's time, had been appointed by the center. Law 25 gives regional governments more control over taxation and allows them to retain a substantial share of revenues produced in their realms. Provincial districts will now receive 80% of the income from most mining and forestry operations, 30% of earnings from natural gas and 15% from oil (if such resources relate to them). The laws became effective on January 1, 2001.

The implementation of Act No. 22/1999 and Act No. 25/1999 has drawn diverging perceptions in the eyes of the public. On the one hand, local governments and, indeed, a substantial proportion of citizens on the outlying islands, are excited about the promise of self-determination and self-government in terms of natural resource management, local governance, and investment planning contained in the laws (or, rather, the representation of their content in official discourse). It is widely recognized that centralized government, "New Order" style, has proven unsatisfactory in that it has failed to enhance people's living conditions economically, socio-politically or culturally. The concentration of political decision-making powers in Jakarta and the predatory economic relationship between the centre and the regions have generated disintegrative tendencies, especially with regard to provinces with rich natural resources who have received very little benefits in return, like some provinces in Sumatra (Aceh among them), East Kalimantan and West Papua (Irian Jaya).

Centralization has not only negatively impacted on the material aspects of people's lives but also created problems such as cultural disorientation among the peoples living on the outer islands. This disorientation has in turn fostered volatile relations between the different religious and ethnic communities that could be ignited at any time, with the result that violent "horizontal" conflicts (conflicts that are communal in nature) may explode all over the archipelago at ever shorter intervals. The empowerment of the districts and municipalities will go some way to quieting the discontent, at least of those local elites whose concerns can be answered by giving them a greater stake in the distribution of state revenues. Many locals, for their part, have been swayed by the rhetoric on "autonomy", clearly the buzzword of the year in official discourse.

On the other hand, for many people – critical academics and most NGOs among them – the two laws raised more questions than they answered. For them, firstly, the drafting process has taken place without proper consultation of the population in the regions. They criticize the schedule for implementation of the autonomy measures as being too tight, not allowing for proper awareness to be raised of the implications of "regional autonomy" among the general public in the regions. It would have been desirable, say the critics, to implement the process in a gradual way, starting by shifting some administrative powers to the provinces, followed by more financial powers.

Critics also caution, secondly, that while the law assigns far-reaching powers to the districts and municipalities, provincial governments are being bypassed, which will leave those movements unhappy that want to have more fundamental questions addressed, like the Acehnese and the West Papuans. Quite rightly so, activists in those regions suspect divide-and-rule tactics to be behind the laws' focus on sub-provincial entities, a suspicion fuelled in the case of West Papua by the plan decreed at the beginning of 2000 to carve up the province of West Papua into three separate provinces. Similar moves have been reported from Aceh where the central government suggested hiving off much of the centre, south and the west coast of the province, areas less affected by separatist activity, into a new province called "Galaksi", an abbreviation coined from its constituent parts. Clearly enough, these perennial flash-points in Outer Indonesia will most likely not find peace by tinkering around with administrative boundaries, while eschewing solutions based on addressing the basic grievances of large sectors of the local population. Special arrangements for Aceh and West Papua are said to be prepared but in the absence of an honest dialogue with the rebel movements active there (or, indeed, with any segment of civil society), "autonomy" is bound to remain a mere slogan.

A third concern is that while the laws give too little to independence-minded groups in resource-rich but politically oppressed regions, they are taking away too much from areas with little natural wealth and which have, in the past, indeed benefited from government subsidies to their provincial budgets. A study conducted by Bappenas (the National Development Planning Body) showed that some provinces would go bankrupt if the Acts were implemented as planned, based on the fact that so far 82 % of some provincial budgets has come from the central government, and the Acts maintain that provinces who are not self-supporting need to be liquidated or merged with other, more prosperous provinces. The Eastern Indonesian provinces of Nusa Tenggara Timur and Nusa Tenggara Barat, provinces with a predominantly indigenous population, are among the candidates for bankruptcy (as, by the way, are the Capital Region of Jakarta and the Special Region of Yogyakarta on Java).

Fourthly, and more generally, NGOs fear the vagaries of shifting responsibility for the provision of basic social services to local government. With no experience in shouldering vital responsibilities, they say, local governments could find themselves unable to provide health and education, or may allow costs to rise so sharply that ordinary citizens cannot meet them anymore. In addition, there is a danger that public services like education will, in the future, be delivered according to ethnic or even religious criteria, excluding minority groups (indigenous peoples among them), since the equalizing influence of central government policy no longer holds.

Inevitably, and fifthly, NGOs are questioning the autonomy of policy-makers in Jakarta in formulating the autonomy laws. The spirit of centralism, they argue, is still howling in the Acts as a result of the influence of the International Monetary Fund (IMF) and other foreign stakeholders that have given loans to Indonesia. In order to have a guarantee for the return of their loans, these players have ensured that the exploitation of high-earning natural resources is left under central government control, which is why separate Acts granting better conditions to Jakarta will be formulated for timber- and mineral-rich Irian Jaya (West Papua) as well as for Aceh where the number one foreign currency earner, natural gas, comes from.

Sixthly, NGOs have come to the conclusion that the present power-sharing scheme with the regions will - in all likelihood - not empower the broad population in the provinces but the provincial elites, thereby exacerbating rather than alleviating the lot of the rural masses. The empowerment of local government is widely expected to result in an increase in corruption, and environmentalists warn that money-hungry local politicians will encourage faster timber extraction and hence quicker deforestation. And instead of putting a lid on environmentally harmful mining operations, they maintain, local legislators have merely used their new clout to demand bigger payments from the firms.

Lastly, and seventhly, some Indonesian and foreign NGOs hold decentralization more or less directly responsible for some of the worse instances of communal clashes that have shaken the archipelago over the past two years. Since the beginning of 1999, a score of new districts and four new provinces have been set up in an attempt to accommodate the demands of local elites for the spoils of office and power. In many cases, this engendered intense struggles over the boundaries of the new units and entitlement to office, and often violence prior to assembly elections. The creation of the province of North Maluku in mid-1999 is a case in point, Poso in Central Sulawesi (see below) is another one: as the elites of the old sultanates of Ternate and Tidore fought for supremacy in the new province-to-be, and commoners tried to prevent the resurgence of aristocratic power, the domains of the sultanates, including North Halmahera, soon descended into communal strife as each side tried to weaken the power base of the other. As a result, fighting between Muslims and Christians since October 1999 has left about 3,000 dead and made over 100,000 more homeless. In the face of the pernicious effects of ill-planned decentralization efforts, therefore, foreign NGOs like the US-based Human Rights Watch have called for a "complete moratorium on any administrative boundary changes or local administration restructuring until a credible law and order presence is in place and the situation in Jakarta becomes more stable".

In sum, the critics of the laws on regional autonomy fear that they will only replace the exploitative and corrupt rule of the centre with that of local elites, that they prolong, if not worsen, the mismanagement of natural resources, and that they will fail to strengthen the bases of local communities in terms of self-governance and the enjoyment of the benefits from the extraction of the natural wealth of their ancestral domains. They also call into question the present capabilities of the component ethnic groups and their elites in the regions to devise feasible ways of living together and governing themselves, which makes the centre's rush to devolve power and reorder the administrative set-up of the country a sure recipe for disaster.

The Position of AMAN on Regional Autonomy

AMAN (Alyansi Masyarakat Adat Nusantara) was founded as the first and so-far only nation-wide umbrella organization of indigenous peoples in March, 1999. Its position on regional autonomy, submitted for this Yearbook, is rendered below:

"Given all these problems, there should be serious thought on how the Indonesian people could find its way out of the pervasive social, political and economic crisis the country finds itself in today. There is a danger that the implementation of an ill-conceived decentralization scheme and the power vacuum it creates will considerably worsen the problems of the Republic, especially in the short run. The outbreak of violent conflicts such as the one in Sampit, Central Kalimantan, in February and March, 2001, highlights the need for urgent political action. Legislative measures on autonomy and the agrarian question will have to be informed by the following basic needs to improve the well-being of indigenous peoples and the rural population in general:

- fair and equal access to resources, especially to land;
- sustainability of production, consumption, and distribution systems;
- sustainability of other systems and sub-systems of social reproduction;
- sustainability of autonomous local livelihood systems.

Throughout its history, the country has seen how the concentration of decision-making powers over land and natural resources in the central government has had negative impacts on ordinary people's lives. The haves are getting richer, while the have-nots are getting poorer. Without the empowerment of the local units of governance, we are faced with the prospect of never-ending exploitation by the State, i.e. the central government and its cronies, of indigenous rights, particularly the right to enjoy at least some of the fruits of the exploitation of natural resources in their ancestral territories. The problem is: is Local Autonomy, as it has been conceptualized now, a suitable way out of the crisis, and can it erase the roots of problems such as the break-up in Suharto times of autochthonous structures of local governance in favor of the creation of uniform *desa* (village) structures with its concomitant officials under government control? The continued reliance of Act No. 22/1999 on the concept of *desa* as a future locus of the powers of self-regulation and self-governance, albeit qualified as 'based on local customary systems and local history', bodes ill for the re-empowerment of customary systems of local governance. As long as they are premised on uniformity, the lowest administrative units and their officials will continue to lack real authority, which is so direly needed if ethnic and religious strife is to be effectively checked in the future. If it is to be successful, the administrative re-organization of the country has to be inspired by the structures developed by the local people (indigenous peoples among them) in accordance with their own culture and socio-political condition. Then, and only then, can we truly speak of self-government, of government by the people."

Not the Only Worrying Law

Over the past year, the impacts of another new law of crucial importance for indigenous peoples, the new Forestry Law, have begun to make themselves felt. The law, passed during the last week of the presidency of B.J. Habibie, in October 1999, recognizes – for the first time in Indonesian history – the existence of indigenous peoples and their customary rights to their territories. It does not, however, put indigenous land rights under any kind of automatic State protection by virtue of native title. The law also contains no provisions stipulating the need to include indigenous peoples in development planning processes concerning their land. Far from being offered permanent titles, local indigenous communities are obliged to form cooperatives in order to apply for use and management rights over their ancestral domains; in the process, they have to compete with commercial firms who are given the same right to apply for resource extraction permits over areas inhabited by indigenous peoples.

The new forestry law, moreover, in keeping with its general thrust towards "social forestry", provides for the re-classification of some parts of what was once exclusively classified as "State forests" as *Hutan Kerakyatan Adat* or "People's Customary Forest". Use rights over these parts of village territories are placed under the jurisdiction of the respective local communities who are free to retain exclusive rights over the exploitation of forest resources or else grant access to them to outside interests. Economically hard-pressed, many local communities have come to see this as an opportunity to make quick money, without realizing the dangers. Indonesian and Malaysian bosses (*cukong*) in their hundreds have tried to capitalize on this by acquiring so-called *Izin Pemanfaatan Kayu* (IPK) or *Izin Pemanfaatan Hasil Hutan* (IPHH) from indigenous communities. For the – often empty – promise of supplying valuable goods (like high-yield rice seeds or a community truck) to the communities or providing them with irrigated rice fields or a water supply once the forest has been removed, and generally in return for sums of cash, the *cukong* thus acquire the right to strip the forest. Since many companies disappear without fulfilling their promises, many indigenous communities have wound up frustrated and bitter which, however, does not prevent others from entering into the same fraudulent and environmentally destructive agreements.

It is therefore one of the cruel ironies of the age of "reform" in post-Suharto Indonesia that environmentalists and, belatedly, indigenous communities came to realize that, in some ways, the formula of "the forest for those who live in it" has backfired. An unintended but predictable consequence of democratizing access to the forest and its resources is that local communities are putting short-term benefits above long-term considerations and have thus become willing accomplices in the destruction of their forests.

Indigenous Peoples' Self-organization and Initiatives for Policy Reform

Nevertheless, some positive developments on the way to policy reform at the local level could be registered over the last year. Some indigenous communities have succeeded in drafting bills to be passed by local legislative assemblies (DPRD) at the district or provincial level. Some of these bills, if passed, will go a long way towards asserting the recognition of indigenous peoples' existence and their sovereignty over ancestral territory, including the rights to natural resource management and respect for local culture.

Sanggau in West Kalimantan, Bali and Lombok in West Nusa Tenggara, Southeastern Maluku, Toraja in South Sulawesi, are some districts of the Republic where indigenous communities have succeeded in drafting local legislation bills. While not all of them have yet been formally submitted to the local legislature, they have at least been proposed and discussed with local government, local legislative assemblies and other stakeholders.

Not surprisingly, some of these draft bills demand that the *desa*, as the lowest administrative unit of governance, tainted as it is by its function as a tool of government manipulation, be replaced by autochthonous structures of local self-government.

Sulawesi is perhaps the region where implementation of Local Autonomy has drawn the most lively response from NGOs, indigenous organizations and other stakeholders in natural resource management and agrarian reform. Except for West Kalimantan, Southeast Maluku and Lombok, there is probably no other region where indigenous peoples and local NGOs cooperate as smoothly in putting forward people's aspirations and launching policy initiatives to assert them. The Pakava, Toraja and Muna have framed their own draft bills concerning autonomy and natural resource management. Toraja has even developed into something of a pilot project for NGOs to explore the possibilities of attaining meaningful local autonomy through working with local legislatures.

According to reports from *East Nusa Tenggara* (*NTT*), there have been repeated meetings at kampung (village) level to discuss the revitalization of traditional political institutions and resource management systems within ancestral territories. The Kuan Hiun, in the districts of Soe and Kefa, succeeded in pushing the local government to revoke a regulation that denies the existence of adat (customary/ancestral) land. In the same districts, local communities have also successfully reclaimed ancestral land from an industrial tree plantation (HTI or Hutan Tanaman Industri).

In *Sumatra*, the indigenous movement has made significant progress with regard to the revitalization of customary natural resource management institutions. North Sumatra, West Sumatra, Jambi and Riau are just some of the provinces in which indigenous peoples' organisations, along with local NGOs, have worked hard to force local government and investors to recognize their sovereignty over ancestral domains and their right to the self-management of their natural resources.

In the context of AMAN's work, some new indigenous organizations have sprung up at community level. In East Kalimantan, for instance, AMA (Alyansi Masyarakat Adat) Paser, an organization of indigenous peoples living in Paser District, was founded.

Conflicts – Agrarian, Communal, Separatist

Still, on the ground, the land base of indigenous communities continues to be under severe pressure all over the archipelago.

In *North Sumatra*, conflicts between indigenous communities and government over land and other natural resources are rife. Over the past year, indigenous villagers have staged frequent mass actions (e.g. blocking the access to the operation sites of some companies) and called public hearings with the executive and legislative bodies to press for recognition of their sovereignty over land and natural resources. Generally, however, these efforts have been met with repression on the part of the police and military. Most cases are agrarian conflicts involving State-owned plantation companies (PTP) or else are over the planned development of public facilities in urban areas.

Although police repression is still a likely response from the State whenever indigenous communities become emboldened, many indigenous groups throughout the archipelago have grown more assertive in promoting their own systems of political governance and customary law. Some communities are also pointing proudly to the fact that by recalling and upholding traditional modes of conflict resolution, they have successfully prevented their communities from sliding into communal violence. For example, when the island of Kei Kecil was wrecked by rioting, *Raja* Johanes Rahail, the revered chief of a dozen Christian villages around Watlaar on the island of Kei Besar in Southeastern Maluku, succeeded in preventing people from resorting to arms, however frightening the rumours from outside. He reminded them that, according to customary law, communities would only go to war over boundary disputes and disputes involving the honour of women, and since no such grievances existed against the purported Muslim enemies, the people of Watlaar should stay out of the fray.

Unfortunately, no such remedies are available for *Aceh*, since 1989 the province that boasts the saddest human rights record and has suffered the highest number of conflict victims. While intellectuals, academics, political elites and foreign observers are debating autonomy, Aceh's insurgency problem is as far from a solution as ever. President Wahid initially took a far more moderate stance towards the province's separatists than his predecessors. He rejected the military's demands to once again impose martial law there and instructed his negotiators instead to agree to the renewal of a truce, which had been in force since May, 2000. The new truce, pathetically called a "moratorium on violence", became operative on January 15, 2001. Previously, he had already announced the government's willingness to let the province adopt *sharia* law, a widespread demand in Aceh. Late last year, his government had also rushed through a US$ 10.5 million aid package for the province to help alleviate the poverty caused by decades of government neglect.

Nevertheless, during the first five months of 2001, it has become obvious that the Wahid government has no real concept of how to solve the conflict in Aceh. Whilst last year he had come forward with an offer to hold a referendum on independence, he later rescinded it, stating that he had meant a referendum on the introduction of the *sharia*. His initial promises to right the wrongs of the past have been exposed as hollow, since he has consistently failed to deliver on them. In the meantime, the army has made it clear that it would oppose any East Timor-style independence vote, with force if need be. According to most outside observers, a fair referendum in Aceh would produce a resounding "yes" for independence.

The "moratorium" was supposed to be a chance for the government and the rebels of the Free Aceh Movement (Gerakan Aceh

Merdeka, GAM) to sit down on neutral ground in Europe and discuss the political issues separating them. That chance has passed largely unused, not only because neither side would move away from their initial political positions but also because on the ground, the truce was consistently violated by rebels and security forces alike. Simultaneously with the army's crackdown on West Papuan independence activists in October, 2000, the Indonesian Defense Minister, Mahfud M.D., had declared that it would end its "persuasive approach" to the insurgency in Aceh because, said Mahfud, the goodwill it had extended had been betrayed by GAM. Yet there is little evidence that the security forces themselves ever felt bound by the letter of the agreement. Throughout the present and the previous truce, the police continued to conduct sweeping operations, ostensibly to seize weapons and hunt down suspected GAM sympathizers. Under cover of the truce, mutual raids and the "disappearance" of suspected rebel sympathizers by army elements continued. During the year 2000, more than 1200 people – mostly civilians – were killed in Aceh, and throughout the first three months of this year alone, at least 250 more.

Maybe the conflict that was followed most closely abroad was the one that pitted indigenous Dayak against Madurese migrants in Sampit and other areas of *Central Kalimantan*. For more than a month, the area was brimming with the presence of camera teams and newspaper journalists when Dayak tribesmen, mostly Ngaju and Ot Danum, hunted down settlers from the barren island of Madura off the north-eastern tip of Java. The story they were after was the tale of the "new generation of head-hunters" (a *Washington Post* headline) whose swords were once again "eating people" and whose warriors were reviving that "disused tribal practice" in defense of their territories and "ethnic pride". European and American homes were flooded with the grisly images of marauding savages and their decapitated and disembowelled victims but, generally, the shock troops of war journalism bothered very little to back up their visual trophies with convincing inquiries into the economic and political reasons for the "atavistic" slaughter they had witnessed.

The Indonesian part of Borneo has, over the past years, witnessed several outbreaks of violence against migrants from Madura and the perpetrators were not always Dayak. Most noted are the bloody purges of Madurese from the interior of West Kalimantan by Dayak between January and March, 1997, killing some 500 – according to unofficial estimates even as many as 1 to 2,000 – migrants and driving 10,000 more from their homes. The same areas were partly the scene of another round of clashes exactly two years later when native Malay of Sambas, West Kalimantan, rose to drive out the

Madurese from their district, producing 200 casualties on the Madurese side and permanently displacing some 60,000 others, the vast majority of whom languish to this day in refugee camps in the provincial capital, Pontianak.

Central Kalimantan itself displays a rather long history of conflict between the native Dayak and the Madurese. The Dayak point to at least 16 instances of bloodshed and lesser clashes since 1972 which, they say, invariably had their origins in acts of violence – stabbings or rape – by the Madurese. The majority of these murders and the bloody skirmishes they sometimes occasioned were left to the two sides to mediate; the few instances that prompted police intervention were "settled" in a manner typical of "New Order" trouble-shooting: under the auspices of the security forces, the warring parties, represented by government-accredited leaders with little credibility in their respective communities, were forced to sign "peace agreements" that were not so much genuine efforts at reconciliation as rituals of submission to State authority, leaving the basic grievances of the two camps untouched. After two major clashes in Kotawaringin Timur in July and December 2000, it was clear that a time bomb was ticking but the authorities pretended not to notice it.

Tempers were still high when Dayak and Madurese high-school students got into a brawl around mid-January, 2001, in the logging port town of Sampit, Kotawaringin Timur. A Madurese settler, known, say the Dayak, for his criminal proclivities, drew the ire of the Dayak side when he intervened in the brawl. On February 18, the Dayak attacked his house and killed three of the man's family members, whereupon a large Madurese crowd tried to burn a Dayak house, together with 39 people who had taken refuge there. The town of Sampit quickly descended into all-out war between the two groups as both sides ransacked and burned houses and killed whoever they could get their hands on. For a day and a half, the Madurese, who outnumbered the Dayak in the town, gained the upper hand. Soon, however, fortunes turned, for in the evening of February 19, the Dayak returned, reinforced by thousands of men from the surrounding countryside. Now, hundreds of Madurese houses on the outskirts of the town went up in flames and their inhabitants, if they did not flee in time, were slaughtered. Madurese settlements in much of the hinterland were torched and hundreds of migrants were killed. Thousands of Madurese men, women and children used every available form of transportation to escape the mayhem, crowding into the town's police headquarters or trying to leave Sampit altogether. The government sent navy vessels to evacuate as many of the refugees as possible but, for hundreds of them, help came too late.

Within a matter of days, the violence had spread to Kuala Kayan, a subdistrict 110 km north of Sampit, and to Palangkaraya, the provincial capital, some 220 km away. While the killings in the epicenter of the riots ebbed once all Madurese had been wiped out or driven away, the purges went on in the hinterland. As late as April 21, there were reports that there were still manhunts for migrants in the southeastern district of Kuala Kapuas and the westernmost one, Pangkalanbun. Dayak leaders threatened that there would be killings as long as Madurese could still be found in the province. The official death toll of the riots was given as around 500 but local sources indicate that there could have been between 2,000 and 3,000 casualties. A total of 40,000 Madurese were evacuated to refugee centers in East Java and Madura where they will have to stay without any prospect of ever being able to return to Kalimantan. The majority were probably born in Borneo and have never seen the island from where their parents or grandparents hailed before in their lives.

The security forces were slow to react to the crisis in Central Kalimantan. Police as well as the army units who were called in to restore order were seen standing idly by while houses were torched and people killed. In fact, in a development that surprised foreign reporters more than domestic observers, on 27 February the police and army started shooting at each other in the docks of Sampit. As it turned out, the stakes were the hefty fees both police and army had started to ask from the refugees for the favour of rescuing them from the war zone. Instead of turning their guns on rioters and murderers, the security forces were using them to fight a turf war among racketeers. To insiders, the dismal performance of the soldiers and police comes as no surprise since "internal security is the last thing on their mind", as one Western diplomat put it. Rather, assignment in Central Kalimantan to the men in uniform means an opportunity to get rich on illegal logging, gambling and prostitution rackets. On top of this, there is a longstanding rivalry between the army and the police which probably compounded the difficulties of restoring law and order.

Just as the disastrous hands-off approach of the security forces was entirely predictable, so were the hapless attempts of the authorities in trying to identify the causes of the slaughter. Early on, officials presented the riots as the handiwork of two disgruntled Dayak civil servants who stood to lose their jobs in an administrative reshuffle.

However, neither the authorities' attempts to find scapegoats nor a foreign press pandering to images of the savage Dayak can hope to shed light on the real causes of the carnage. Far from having their origins in petty personal motives or in primordial ethnicity, the present killings in Central Kalimantan, like those in West Kalimantan in 1997 and 1999, reflect a sharp conflict over natural resources and the heritage of more than 30 years of political marginalization of the indigenous Dayak population by outsiders.

The Dayak of Kalimantan have long felt under-represented in the way their four provinces are governed. While in the pre-1965 period, there were Dayak governors in Central and West Kalimantan (who, by the way, enjoyed tremendous popularity among the provinces' indigenous population), ever since the top posts in provincial government had been the exclusive domain of Javanese army officers. As for Central Kalimantan, even Madurese leaders found it easier to ascend to powerful positions than the native Dayak, a fact that is all the more upsetting since, in the eyes of the indigenous population, the province of Central Kalimantan had once been granted by the country's first president, Sukarno, to the Dayak as mainly their preserve.

The seeds of economic conflict were planted more than 30 years ago when the Suharto government began shipping landless farmers from overcrowded Java, Madura and Bali to the less densely populated outer islands. Since the 1970s, and above all during the 1980s, the Indonesian Government resorted to allocating large tracts of primary forest as logging concessions and for palm oil and other plantations without regard for indigenous land ownership or use. Government-supported transmigrants and spontaneous migrants (the Madurese figure prominently among the latter) provided the work force for these schemes. Little was done to mitigate the shock of ethnically and religiously diverse groups suddenly being brought into competition for limited economic opportunities. The official transmigration program and the encouragement by the State of migration in general "built conflict into the genetic code of the provinces", as one Jakarta-based diplomat put it.

Local resentment of the Madurese has three specific factors. Although themselves poor, unskilled and socially dislocated, as newcomers, Madurese often occupy farmland owned by Dayaks. On top of this, they also dominate petty trading in the towns and provide the labour force that clears the vanishing timber stands, which are controlled by military and other business interests in Jakarta. Although the land areas and the job opportunities wrested from the Dayak by Madurese migrants may be insignificant compared with the acreage alienated by the Government as logging concessions or plantations, the Madurese provide an easier target for resentment than mighty corporations or rapacious army generals.

These economic factors are exacerbated by cultural differences. Madurese culture strongly emphasises personal honour, and Madurese men are heirs to a vigorous martial tradition. Borneans and other Indonesians characterise them as rough, violent and quarrelsome. They are known to resort to particularly uncanny methods of asserting themselves in the contest for the land that characterizes Kalimantan's "frontier", like when they harvest other people's crops and knowingly squat on land belonging to others.

Thus although on structural grounds the Dayaks and Madurese must both be seen as the victims of the economic and political policies of the Suharto regime and its corporate collaborators, from a local perspective there are grievances enough to explain why they had to turn against each other.

Sources

Kompas, 18, 19, 20, February 2001.

Kompas, 13 - 20, July 2000.

Media Indonesia, 18, 19, March 2001.

Far Eastern Economic Review.

The Economist, Christian Science Monitor.

Inside Indonesia.

Südostasien.

The Jakarta Post.

R. Yando Zakaria in *Pemulihan Kehidupan Desa dan UU*, No. 22 Tahun 1999, a paper presented in the workshop of "Penguatan Dewan Perwakilan Rakyat Daerah ..."

R. Yando Zakaria and Noer Fauzi in *Pembaruan Desa dan Agraria Dalam Konteks Otonomi Daerah*, a position paper of Badan Pembaruan Agraria.

Interview by phone with some of AMAN's National Council members and NGO activists at local level.

Draft bill from Bali, Pakava, Sanggau, Maluku Tenggara.

MALAYSIA

D evelopments in indigenous issues in Malaysia appear to be increasingly dictated by two main dynamics: the political landscape (especially as it affects the fate of the party in power) and the interventions of indigenous peoples themselves (to secure their own fate and to seek redress). Both have different motivations but both serve to further alter the political and social context of indigenous peoples in Malaysia today.

Politics and Indigenous Peoples

Unquestionably, the way national and local politics is structured, and the fast-changing political dynamic resulting from this (especially as it pertains to electoral politics), has had an impact on the way indigenous peoples in Malaysia have been perceived and treated.

For instance, given the split in the Malay vote in the peninsula and the accompanying political insecurity in the ruling National Front, the vote of the Orang Asli minority has become crucial in certain constituencies, especially in the timber-rich state of Pahang. For this reason, the ruling coalition has stepped up its rhetoric-filled programmes for the Orang Asli – dishing out (or at least announcing) development funds for the communities in the interior areas or repeating the promises of titled lots for them in new resettlement schemes.

Predictably also, given that women were found to be an important reservoir of votes in the last general election, the ruling coalition has also directed its attention at Orang Asli women (and their votes). In particular, it proposed increasing the number of its women development centres in Orang Asli areas from a mere three in 1998 to 27 in 2001. Ironically, none of the existing centres are led by Orang Asli women – apparently because there were no Orang Asli women who qualified for such positions. This bluff, however, was exposed in 2000 when, once word got round that two such positions were vacant, eight aptly-qualified Orang Asli women applied for the positions. Alas, none of them were considered, let alone accepted – perhaps in accordance with the trend to slowly decrease the number of Orang Asli holding positions in the very department that is supposed to administer them, the Department of Orang Asli Affairs (JHEOA).

In the east Malaysian state of Sabah, the continual political manoeuvrings among indigenous elites has effectively reduced indigenous participation and dominance in the political arena from its high in the mid-1980s to levels where individual self-interest now eclipses the motivation to do good for the indigenous population. The decline in indigenous autonomy in Sabah was further sealed with the unprecedented introduction of the peninsular-based Malay-Muslim party UMNO into the state a decade later. Its presence invariably changed the political climate of the state, to the great disadvantage of the indigenous majority. One early strategy to this effect was the polarisation of the electorate along religious lines – viz. into Muslim-indigenous, non-Muslim indigenous and non-indigenous (i.e. Chinese-dominated) constituencies. This effectively led to a rebuff of multi-racial parties, causing the non-Muslim indigenous groups in particular to be split into four political parties, none of which can ever hope to regain power on its own or even as a coalition if voting patterns follow religious lines.

In the other east Malaysian state of Sarawak, state elections are, however, expected in 2001. Despite the unevenness of the political playing field and the absence of a united and credible opposition, there is some potential for a disturbance of the status quo. This is because issues that the Orang Ulu and Dayak indigenous groups hold close to their hearts are coming to the fore again. Invariably, these are the long-standing issues that relate to their claim to native customary rights (NCR) over their lands – claims that are persistently being ignored by the government and its civil servants. However, it is without doubt that the subtle, yet greatest, challenge to indigenous rights in Sarawak recently was the speedy amendment to the Sarawak Land Code in 2000, adopted without sufficient consultation and consensus from the indigenous groups. In essence, the amendment sought to further restrict the indigenous communities to their claims for native customary rights over their land while at the same time enabling the state government to extinguish such customary rights with greater ease. When the Land Code was first introduced in 1958, it was clear that the boundaries of such NCR land were to be determined in accordance with the spirit and methods of the customary laws and practices of the affected indigenous communities. The 2000 amendments, however, effectively removed this provision, thereby placing an undue burden on the indigenous groups to stake their claim to NCR land.

Development and Encroachments

In the preceding year, indigenous lands continued to be encroached on by corporations and governments bent on viewing the indigenous peoples as a necessary nuisance in the pursuit of their own enrichment. Logging remains the major culprit. In January 2001, Penan from Long Sayan and Long Belok in Ulu Baram, Sarawak erected fresh blockades on logging roads constructed by Lajong Lumber, a subsidiary of Rimbunan Hijau, one of the major logging companies in Sarawak, which has also expanded its operations overseas. In Sabah, logging activities in Long Pasia, located within the 80,000 hectare biodiversity-rich Ulu Padas area, are threatening ancient burial sites, medicinal plants, fish and animal resources and the historic settlements of the Lun Dayeh people. The Orang Asli in Peninsular Malaysia have also had to contend with more and more logging concessions being given out that invariably encroach upon their traditional lands. In the Sungei Lepar area in Pahang, for example, the Jakuns set up blockades in early 2001 when logging trucks and activities posed a danger to the community's safety and threatened their livelihoods. However, in keeping with the political strategy of not upsetting the Orang Asli for fear of losing their vote, the State Minister of Orang Asli Affairs immediately went to the area and, amidst wide media publicity, gave out cash compensation to the villagers to placate them.

But logging is swiftly being replaced by mega-development projects as the single-most devastating factor affecting indigenous lands and their cultures. Unlike logging activities, mega-development projects (such as huge plantation schemes, dams and other industrial projects) not only cause environmental damage but also permanently seize the lands of indigenous peoples. The US$5.3 billion Sabah Pulp and Paper Mill to be set up in Kalabakan, Tawau for example, will involve the clearing of 220,000 hectares of forest close to the Maliau Basin and Danum Valley conservation areas. The proposed multi-million dollar steel mill near Kudat in northern Sabah is another example. In Peninsular Malaysia, the construction of dams is also affecting Orang Asli lives. The Sungei Selangor Dam, for example, for which construction began in 2000, ultimately encroached upon the traditional lands of two Temuan villages. Approval has also been given to construct another dam in Pahang state, which will also affect the Temuan of the Klau area.

In Sarawak, such mega-development projects have already been embarked upon and the effects on the indigenous population are evident. The giant Bakun Hydroelectric Dam project, discontinued twice in the past due to lack of funds, has now been revived once more. Nevertheless, for the 1,700 indigenous families who were resettled in 1997, the predicted hardship and consequences of resettlement are already being experienced. For example, not only is the soil in the resettlement area not fertile, it is also too sandy for subsistence agriculture. Further, the original resettled population (of approximately 10,000 persons) has now increased by about 40 per cent, thereby requiring additional housing units. The housing units themselves are the subject of complaint. Despite being poorly designed and built, they come with an unjustified and exorbitant price-tag, and are too far from their subsistence fields. The result of all this: frequent communal conflict, especially over depleting resources, increased alcoholism especially among the men-folk, a high dropout rate among students, women losing their independence as a result of the changing social relations, and food shortages.

Apart from logging companies and industrial investors, the indigenous peoples of Sarawak also face the threat of losing their customary lands to agribusiness corporations and land development agencies. In at least one case, the conflict had fatal consequences for the encroachers. This was in Ulu Niah, where Sarawak Oil Palm Berhad wanted to occupy the customary lands of two Iban communities, with the tacit backing of state authorities. The corporation employed armed thugs to instil fear in the native peoples in the hope that they would vacate their customary lands. These gangsters, seeing that the police were not acting on the numerous police reports made against them, became more aggressive until the inevitable clash between themselves and the villagers resulted in four of them being killed. Nineteen of the villagers were, however, charged with murder and were detained for 18 months before their case was heard in November 2000. Eight were eventually discharged in March 2001 but the remaining eleven are still in prison awaiting the conclusion of their court hearing.

Reasserting Identity and Indigenous Rights

The courts, however, seem to be the final recourse for several indigenous groups in their strive for land rights. One case involved the Borneo Pulp and Paper Mill mega-project and its constituent forest plantation, which has caused much distress and dislocation of the native population in Bintulu and Sibu, Sarawak. This is a project of the Sarawak State Government and the Sarawak Timber Industry Development Corporation (STIDC) and involves 606,200 hectares of land. Much of this land is native customary lands belonging to the Iban, Kenyah, Kayan, Buketan, Punan as well as the minority Tatau dan Lugat peoples. A total of 180 longhouses are affected. While some communities have agreed to be resettled, others decided to challenge the appropriation of their lands and sought redress in the courts. The case was heard at the end of 2000 and a decision is now awaited.

In Sabah, the Dusun community in Ulu Apin-Apin, Keningau are also using the courts to challenge the state's right to grant a logging concession in the protected forest-cum-water catchment area that the indigenous communities depend on for their subsistence. In Peninsular Malaysia, the case of seven Temuans (who lost part of their traditional lands when it was acquired in 1996 for the construction of the highway to the Kuala Lumpur International Airport) resumed its hearing in December 2000. The Orang Asli are seeking a declaration that they are the owners of the land by custom, the holders of native title to the land and the holders of usufructuary rights. They are also claiming that their customary and propriety rights over the land that they and their forefathers have occupied and cultivated for a long time were not extinguished by any law. The state and federal governments, for their part, are claiming that the right given to the Orang Asli was related to occupation and residence only and not to ownership. The hearing proper ended in March 2001 and a decision on this precedent-setting case is expected soon.

Apart from taking the government to court over their customary lands, indigenous peoples in Malaysia are also asserting their identity in various ways. For example, the Warriors' Day (*Bujang Berani*) Celebration in Sarawak, a grassroots event organised annually to commemorate the homecoming of the Dayak warriors who were wrongly detained by the police for putting up blockades to protect their customary lands eleven years ago, was again celebrated in October 2000 in the Upper Bakun area. In Sabah, local indigenous groups continue to organise Cultural Exchanges that not only serve to reassert their indigenous cultural identity but also act as a means to unite the various indigenous groups in the state on their own terms. Thus far, these *Pertemuan Budaya* gatherings have been held in the interior areas such as Terian and Kinabatangan.

In Peninsular Malaysia, arguing that unity in numbers and culture is one way to assert their presence – and consequently claim their rights – the Perak chapter of the Peninsular Malaysia Orang Asli Association (POASM) has embarked on a programme to "standardise" Orang Asli culture. It is, however, unclear how far the Semai-dominated chapter will be able to convince the other ethnic subgroups to give up their own traditions for that of the dominant group. Nevertheless, to a certain extent it has succeeded in getting some groups to accept the third Saturday of February as the *Hari Perayaan Orang Asli* or the Orang Asli Festival Day. The first such common celebration day was held on 24 February 2001 and was mainly celebrated by the lowland Semai of Perak. However, some other communities endorsed the proposal – such as the Temuans of Bukit Bangkung and the Mah Meris of Pulau Carey – and coincided their own annual celebration with this date.

Land rights and indigenous identity aside, the indigenous peoples of Malaysia have also concerned themselves with other issues. One of these is the threat to their biological resources and the theft of their indigenous knowledge for commercial gain. To this end, indigenous leaders and communities were involved in discussions relating to the certification of timber from their areas and in the drafting of laws pertaining to the extraction and use of biological resources. However, indigenous participation in these moves remained limited. In an attempt to address some of these issues, the Indigenous Peoples Network of Malaysia (JOAS), in collaboration with the Faculty of Law of the University of Malaya, organised a round table conference in March 2000 between government, academic and indigenous representatives on the issue of Biodiversity and Indigenous Knowledge. This round table conference represented yet another of the very varied means the indigenous peoples of Malaysia are using to assert their rights and cultural difference.

THAILAND

Over the past 50 years, highland communities[1] in Thailand have faced serious pressure from outside agencies, in particular the government, to adapt and accept development policies and activities modifying their way of life and their resource management practices. This has resulted in an attempted change to new agricultural systems and methods of production together with new technologies and equipment altering their traditional and distinct way of life. It is argued by representatives of the lowland Thai population[2] that highland communities are overexploiting the country's natural resources in the highlands, with the result that the lowland people lay claim over forest areas and reserve for themselves the right to convert such land into protected areas. This has, in turn, led to serious conflicts between the two groups. Ultimately, as one scholar writes, "Such conflict is a direct violation of the basic Human Rights of the Highland communities"[3].

Highland communities are not only subject to pressure through individual land encroachment but society as a whole fails to adequately respect and accept their right to traditional lands. This opinion is currently backed up by State and Federal law concerning the control and management of natural resources. Added to the idea that highland people are destroyers of the forest are stronger accusations, for example, that highland people are responsible for the spread of narcotics. Furthermore, highland people are often viewed as "non-Thai" or illegal aliens.

Highland Development Policy Conflicts

Current policies concerning the highland communities of northern Thailand focus on the problem of national security in border areas, the prevention of deforestation and the control of narcotics. These policies are implemented under the "Community and Environment Development Drug Control Highland Master Plan". However, highland community members were not directly involved in the decision-making or planning process relating to this Master Plan. With regard to policy development for highland community decision-making, the planning process remains highly centralized, ethnocentric and discriminatory. Little emphasis is placed on the participation of target populations. Even though the Thai government has vowed to focus on people's participation, freedom, the protection of basic rights and decentralized decision-making, highland communities remain the victim of ill-conceived and poorly planned development initiatives, and are subject to strict conditions and rules associated with these programs, running the risk of further restrictions on their land and further violations of their rights.

When analysing the situation of the highland peoples' rights in Thailand it must be viewed with respect to both previous and current government policies. On the 6th January 2001, the Kingdom of Thailand went to the polling booths and elected a new government under the leadership of Dr. Thaksin Shinawatra. To date, it is clear that the new government has returned to previous policy approaches concerning highland communities, focusing policy mechanisms on drug suppression and border conflict resolution. Thus far, no clear policy has been established by the new government pertaining to the rights and status of highland communities.

In sum, the concepts and policies of highland development from the past to the present have been implemented under the banner of national security, resulting in attempts to integrate and assimilate ethnic minority groups into the wider Thai society. No matter what development approach was used - whether the static approach focusing on social welfare and poverty relief or the dynamic development approach emphasizing resolution of the drug problem and national security - by concentrating primarily on natural resource management and improved agricultural technology, considerable change has been forced on highland communities along with the restrictions imposed through the protection of watershed areas and the creation of national parks.

Rights and Security Issues

Two main policies directly affect the way of life and survival of highland peoples, namely: 1. the highland forest management policy, and 2. the citizenship policy. These policies, although at first glance seemingly unrelated, are in fact closely linked.

Highland Forest Management Policy

Over the past decade, the government has created policy measures for conservation of natural resources, reforestation and watershed improvement in order to solve the problem of the decline in soil fertility in northern Thailand. However, these policies fail to recognize the fact that there are currently 873,713 people living in these protected areas[4]. Such policies not only lead to conflict and uncertainty over the management of these resources between government bodies and highland peoples but also create problems in terms of the social, economic and political climate in highland areas.

With respect to forestry, four Acts have been used by the government in the name of Natural Resource Management: the Forestry Act (2484 BE) 1941, the Forestry Conservation Act (2507 BE) 1964, the National Park Act (2504 BE) 1961 and the Wildlife Conservation and Protection Act (2535 BE) 1992. When considering the concept and detail of these laws, one discovers that these Acts were implemented and introduced during the period when the government increased measures to take control of natural resource management, distinguishing between two classes of land rights only: private land holding rights and government land rights. All land that was not privately owned was considered to be under the control of the State.

According to these Acts, those who live in such areas have no legal claim to the land, regardless of the length of time they have resided in the area. In some instances, these communities were living in these - now protected - areas before the law was created. It can be seen that there are certain loopholes in the current Forestry Law that have been exploited for individual capitalist purposes, resulting in greater pressure on natural resources. This in turn creates conflict between government departments, local people and people's organizations at the community level.

Ultimately, the problem is caused by land seizures in highland community areas and increasing in-migration to forests. This has proved to be the catalyst for continued friction between highland communities and those authorities that wish to take control over forestry management, conserve the watershed and try to force highland people off their traditional lands. This is done with reference to the incorrect but common belief that highland peoples cannot manage these resources in a sustainable manner.

Thai Citizenship Policy

The policy concerning citizenship is complex and is closely linked to policies on national security, deforestation and narcotics. Due to their alleged role in the narcotics trade, deforestation and national security, highland peoples are rarely granted full Thai citizenship under the Constitution of the Kingdom of Thailand. It has been recognized that this lack of citizenship is the most important issue facing highland people today. It directly affects their personal security and leads to the loss of other basic rights, such as the right to make a living, the right to use the forest in a sustainable manner, the right to participate in development activities and the right to have access to government facilities and services[5].

To date, the citizenship granting process has been slow and cumbersome and citizenship applications can be cancelled at any stage of the proceedings, whenever applicants are perceived as a threat to national security. Today, the number of eligible highland people yet to be granted citizenship by the government is 509,110 persons out of a total population of 873,713. This figure does not include other minority groups[6].

The Ministry of Interior recently introduced new regulations concerning the granting of citizenship, which classified highland peoples into different time periods depending on when they or past generations migrated to Thailand. Another classification focuses on the legal status of the parents. However, as explained above this, process remains complicated, slow and confusing.

According to the Ministry of Interior's classification of highland groups, those who have the opportunity to be granted Thai citizenship must meet the following criteria: highland people currently residing in Thailand who migrated to Thailand between 1913 and 1972. It is estimated that there are approximately 100,000 people who fall within this category.

Highland people currently residing in Thailand and who migrated to Thailand between 14th December 1972 and 3rd October 1985 are eligible for permanent resident status (approximately 90,000 people). Their children are eligible for Thai citizenship. It is currently estimated that there are approximately 120,000 people who fall within this category.

People who fall into a third classification of highland people are considered illegal residents and can be forcibly removed from the country. There are currently approximately 190,000 people who are considered to belong to this category. The government has opened a window for citizenship applications from 29th August 2000 up to 29th August 2001, during which time highland people can request that their status be reviewed and apply for citizenship of the Kingdom of Thailand. At the end of this period, the government and National Security Council will use tough measures to force unregistered highland people and other minorities out of the country. The problem for the majority of those people who are, in fact, eligible to receive Thai citizenship is that they cannot produce the appropriate documentation in proof and have therefore had there request and application denied. Such problems are compounded by the ever present hand of corruption at all levels in the citizenship granting process.

Highland Peoples' Civil Movements

The highland peoples' civil movement, supported by the National Hill Tribe Assembly Network and other NGOs, operates at two levels: policy and community levels.

At policy level, the goal of the National Hill Tribe Assembly Network, other NGOs and highland peoples as a whole is to focus on presenting a correct image of highland peoples to the wider society. Lack of information and understanding of the highland peoples in northern Thailand on the part of wider Thai society perpetuates stereotypes and discrimination. It is therefore considered important to reduce ethnocentrism, promote greater acceptance, mutual understanding and to eliminate inequalities through education and information dissemination. The image of highland peoples as destroyers of the forest, non-Thai, a threat to national security and causing the drug problem in Thailand must be changed if any real progress in the rights of highland people are to be made.

By basing the movement systematically on people's participation from the grassroots, dissemination to all other levels must involve a people's alliance working at all levels of society. The movement adopted the concept of decentralized decision-making, effective co-ordination and promotion of new and innovative ideas.

Work at the *community level* means coordination of highland peoples' networks and the strengthening of the National Hill Tribe Assembly so that it can move forward with powerful and clear objectives. The main strategy is to encourage learning and knowledge exchange between highland peoples' networks in order to increase their power of negotiation by speaking with a strong and unified voice. It is hoped that this will advance freedom of thinking, encourage and uphold dignity and pride and reduce suppression by administrators, politicians and the wider Thai society.

The success of any civil movement depends on the actors involved. It is therefore necessary that highland peoples promote such a movement at the community level. If highland peoples do not have a strong and unified voice, problems such as the right to land and citizenship cannot be solved. At stake is not only the right to land, forest and water but basic human rights and freedoms.

Notes

1   In this paper the term highland communities is used to refer to the peoples, often termed ethnic minorities, hill tribes or indigenous peoples, living in the mountainous regions of northern Thailand.

2   The term lowlanders and highlanders are used to differentiate between ethnic minorities who tend to reside in highland areas and the wider Thai population who live at lower levels.

3   Charernwong S. (2000). "Panha Khwam Kad Yang Lae Kan La Merd Sitti Bukkhon Bon Thee Soong, Amphur Chomg Thong Chiang Mai" (Conflicts and Violations of Highlanders' Rights: A Case of Conflict in Chom Thong District Chiang Mai).

4   Figure: Centre of Registration Office on the Issuing and Consideration of Person Status in the Household Registration of Highland People; 2543 BE (2000) p. 211.

5   It must be recognized that the problem of citizenship does not only apply to the highland ethnic communities but other ethnic minorities living in border areas throughout Thailand.

6   Figure: Centre of Registration Office on the Issuing and Consideration of Person Status in the Household Registration of Highland People; 2543 BE (2000) p. 211.

CAMBODIA

The majority of the people in Cambodia are ethnic Khmer who live mainly in the lowlands of the country. In addition, there are Lao, Cham and people of Chinese and Vietnamese origin. Cambodia is also home to different indigenous highland peoples who live in the hills of the provinces of Ratanakiri, Mondulkiri, Kratie, Stung Treng, Pursat, and Kompong Speu.[1]

Since the onset of peace in the 1990s, previously remote areas have become more accessible. As they are rich in natural resources such as timber, land and wildlife, they attract settlers, logging companies and poachers who encroach on the indigenous highlanders' communal lands and forests.

At the same time, a process of consultation to discuss and respond to indigenous peoples' needs and rights has developed between the Royal Government of Cambodia (RGC), Non-governmental Organisations (NGOs), International Organisations (IOs) and representatives of indigenous communities.

Changes in Access to Natural Resources during 2000-2001

In 2000, illegal logging continued, albeit at a lesser pace than in previous years. Timber is cut for private use or for export to Thailand and Vietnam. In Kon Mon, Bokeo, and Banlung districts in Ratanakiri province, local people are unhappy as the officials appointed to enforce the logging ban turn a blind eye to logging in the area. Indigenous people are also faced with double standards as police officers do not react to large-scale logging but clamp down on local villagers when they want to cut timber for house construction.

In Taveng district of Ratanakiri, the traditional fishery is threatened as people from outside the indigenous villages fish in the river using illegal nets and electric shocks. A fishing concession has been granted under which the whole river is blocked with a bamboo wall, depriving villagers downstream of their fish.

Villagers along the Se San River affected by the releases of water from the Yali Fall dam in Vietnam continue to demand more precise information about water releases, as accidents are still occurring. The Yali Fall dam director sends messages to Ratanakiri provincial authorities one or two days in advance of the planned water releases but communication with the affected villages is not effective.

Land Rights Issues

The New Land Law

In June 2000, the Minister of Land and Urbanisation and President of the Land Conflict Resolution Committee met with Asian Development Bank (ADB) representatives from Cambodia, the Philippines and Australia and NGO and IO representatives to discuss the proposed Khmer version of the draft land law in which some of the most crucial paragraphs from the chapter on indigenous peoples had been left out. It was agreed to maintain the content of the original English text, although slightly altered and not as strongly defending indigenous peoples' traditional land rights as NGOs and IOs had wanted. In July 2000, the Council of Ministers (CoM) approved the revised law. The law has now been sent to the National Assembly for approval, after which the Senate will also need to discuss and agree upon it.

King Norodom Sihanouk publicly backed the inclusion of the needs of the indigenous peoples in the land law and in July granted an audience to five representatives of indigenous peoples from Ratanakiri province who wanted to thank the King for his help and to ask for his support to get indigenous peoples' needs also reflected in the forest law presently being drafted. In addition to assuring his

A Hero logging truck blazes a new through a stretch of forest in Ratanakiri. Photo: IWGIA archive

support, the King promised to build a health clinic and a school in Poey commune in Taveng district of Ratanakiri, both of which were inaugurated on 29th December 2000.

Land Deals

On March 23, a Ratanakiri provincial judge ruled against the indigenous communities who have been fighting for two years to keep 1,250 hectares of their ancestral land out of the hands of Phnom Penh army general Noun Phea who has defrauded them. The land was "bought" from approximately 247 Jarai and Tampuan families from Chrong, Chet and Klik villages in Bokeo district. US$35,000 was paid to district officials but the villagers, aside from a package of salt, have received nothing from the land sale. The thumb printing on the agreement was done by only a handful of people and not by all families. And those who signed, most of whom cannot read, said they did not understand that the documents gave away their land. Villagers claim that district officials and a local soldier working on behalf of Noun Phea promised that a school, a new road and water wells would be built if they signed the documents.

The lawyers of the indigenous communities, Ea Sopheap and Yim Simene of Legal Aid of Cambodia, questioned the fairness of the trial, complaining that the judge refused to consider documents brought to the courtroom on the same day. The lawyers declared that they will appeal against the decision in a Phnom Penh court and it is expected that it will be heard within seven months.

This court case is considered a landmark case since its outcome will give a signal as to how developers can or have to behave in future land negotiations.

Forestry

Community Forestry

A number of community forestry management plans have received provincial endorsement all over the country. One example is the handing over of the protection and management of almost 5,000 hectares of semi-evergreen forest – officially within the 60,000 hectare Hero Taiwan timber concession – to the Ya Poey Community Forestry Association, comprised of representatives of six indigenous highlanders' villages in Ratanakiri province, who have lived in and used the forest for generations (*Phnom Penh Post*, 2001).

An ADB team, in consultation with NGO and IO representatives involved in community forestry, prepared National Guidelines for Community Forestry. These guidelines place the right for approval and facilitation of management plans at the provincial level. However, the Department of Forestry and Wildlife (DoFW) of the Ministry of Agriculture, Forestry and Fisheries (MAFF) insists that final decision-making power remains with the Ministry. This makes it much more difficult for indigenous communities to appeal should their request for community forestry management be rejected by the Ministry. The DoFW indicated that it did not intend to apply the community forestry sub-decree until the forest law in preparation was accepted.

The New Forest Law
The draft forest law was developed without significant public participation in order not to delay the process (as was earlier the case with the land law). The draft forest law, as presented by the MAFF, received much criticism from NGOs/IOs, both in relation to content and process.

NGOs/IOs and indigenous peoples have initiated an advocacy campaign to raise the awareness of the importance of forests for rural people's livelihoods and how they have managed the use of forest resources and protected the forests against overexploitation for centuries. The campaign also aims to raise awareness of the impacts and dangers industrial forestry poses to these local use and management systems. Attention is also drawn to the need for a multi-disciplinary approach by departments involved in land use planning (LUP) and that LUP should take place at the provincial level to allow people access to decision-making processes.

The NGO Forum monitors developments at the national level concerning forest law and forest policies development and keeps NGOs informed.

Forest Concessions
The forest concession sub-decree of February 2000 requires the formation of community consultative committees in the areas of forest concessions. These committees need government recognition but a pre-condition is that the committees have undergone training to be provided by the Provincial Forestry Office. In Ratanakiri province, this will be done in collaboration with the NGO "Non Timber Forest Products Project", but the content of the training is still unknown. No training has yet been offered and consultative committees, though formed already, are not yet recognised.

The Cambodian Timber Industry Association, based in the DoFW, is developing concession management guidelines. By November 2001, all concessions need to have an implementation plan for producing a management plan. Social and environmental impact assessments (S/EIA) have to be included. NGOs are informing communities of the S/EIA requirements so that they can prepare themselves.

Access to Governance and Decision-Making

Indigenous people are heavily under-represented in the national and provincial governments. They are mainly represented at the commune and village level. Also, within NGOs and IOs, only a few indigenous people are employed and, of these, only a small number work at programme and management level. This has now caught the attention of the organizations and the governor of Ratanakiri, and several strategies have been identified to give indigenous people more access to institutional processes. These include employment of and capacity building among indigenous people within NGO and government programs, or the introduction of indigenous people's advisory boards for the preparation of important workshops, conferences and similar activities.

However, only a small number of indigenous people complete primary school and very few continue on to secondary or higher education. This limited access to education is due to a lack of schools and teachers and because, previously, parents did not see much value in the education offered as it did not relate to their day-to-day lives. Now attitudes are changing as they see education as important in being able to deal with today's social and economic changes.

The lobbying for inclusion of specific indigenous peoples' needs into the land law at national level was, although based on discussions with indigenous communities at the village and provincial level, done by NGO and IO staff on behalf of the indigenous peoples. Over the past few years, the indigenous highlanders in Ratanakiri province have become more familiar with meetings, workshops and negotiating and their direct involvement in lobbying for indigenous highlanders' issues at the national level could enhance their voice. There are plans to support an indigenous peoples' advocacy group to build relationships and understanding between indigenous communities, government officials and members of parliament by explaining their living situation, culture and specific needs.

Women's Involvement in Decision-Making

Traditionally, village governance consists of the male-dominated village elders' council established by the villagers themselves. In addition to the traditional and government leadership systems, development agencies have introduced a variety of development committees. Although all these committees have female and male representatives, women are in the minority.

Women's input in the traditional and government leadership systems, as well as in development committees, is limited. One of the biggest reasons for women's lack of confidence is that often they do not know the Khmer language very well. This also excludes many women from information and gaining knowledge. The heavy workload of women is an additional and serious constraint to their participation in both meetings and training sessions.

Although there are still important gaps and disparities, workload reduction activities, gender training, confidence and capacity-building activities, along with non-formal education, have resulted in tangible progress in building more equal gender relations in decision-making and in the sharing of the workload. There is also a significant strengthening of women's confidence and capacity to participate in public and economic life.

Indigenous Women's Network Ratanakiri

The Indigenous Women's Network Ratanakiri (IWNR) was created in 1998. The members are now clear on what they want and they plan to develop a strategic plan and to clarify objectives and strategies, as well as the roles and responsibilities of network members. One member attended the International Conference on "Conflict Resolution, Peace Building, Sustainable Development and Indigenous People" in Manila in December 2000. Two members participated as researchers in the UNDP/CARERE gender study to develop a gender strategy for the Community Natural Resources Project.

Indigenous Highlanders Association

In 1993, indigenous individuals in high-level government positions living in the capital of Ratanakiri took the initiative to form an Indigenous Highlanders Association (IHA). In 1995, the IHA was officially registered as an NGO with the Ministry of Interior, although the National Assembly still needs to give its authorization. This initial initiative was not very successful as there was too little communication with the people in the indigenous communities themselves. Recently, one of the initiators requested advice from other indigenous senior level government officials and NGO/IO staff in order to set up a more active and lively association. It was decided to hand over the leadership to "ordinary" indigenous people and to first consult widely with each ethnic group in order to determine the level of support for the creation of an IHA as well as to assess people's opinion, with special attention given to the views of women, young people and the elderly, as to what the goals and functions of such an association should be.

Indigenous Youth

Over the past year, young people also received some attention. NTFP organised a "summer school" for indigenous students on participatory and sustainable development work. In December 2000, a NORAD-funded workshop for indigenous adolescents in Ratanakiri focussed on children's rights.

Note
[1] For more background information, see the chapter on Cambodia in *The Indigenous World, 1999-2000*. Examples come primarily from Ratanakiri province as the author is most familiar with this province.

Sources
    Resource persons:
    Graeme Brown, Department of Environment, Ratanakiri, Community Forestry Advisor.
    Tiann Monie, UNDP/CARERE Land Advocacy Assistant and member Indigenous Women's Network Ratanakiri
    Gordon Patterson, Non Timber Forest Products Project, Ratanakiri, Co-ordinator.
    Sang Polrith, UNDP/CARERE Provincial Project Manager, Ratanakiri.

References
    "Community forest gives hope to hill tribes." *Phnom Penh Post*, January 5-18, 2001.
    Minutes of the CAC meeting, Ratanakiri, 02 February 2001
    "Court Rules Against Hill Tribes in Ratanakkiri." *The Cambodia Daily*, March 24-25, 2001.
    "Hill Tribe's Lawyer To File Appeal Next Month." *The Cambodia Daily*, March 27, 2001.

VIETNAM

Ethnic minorities in Vietnam are mainly indigenous highland peoples. There are 53 recognised minority groups in Vietnam, representing approximately 9.9 million people (13.6% of the population). Of this, almost 8 million reside in the highlands. Only the Chinese (Hoa), Khmer and some Cham minorities live in the lowlands. The 53 recognised minorities do not represent the actual number of cultures and languages in Vietnam. Some groups have been 'amalgamated' into government ethnologies, so the actual number may be 60 or more. Some of the groups live in only one or two villages, and number less than 200 people.

Highland Development and Forest Conservation Policies

The government of Vietnam has many policies and programmes to promote highland development, including infrastructure, forestry, education and health care. But many of these programmes have recorded only limited results. One government policy that has had little success is the resettlement of minority communities and promotion of sedentary farming based on wet rice. Most highland peoples have relied on swidden agriculture systems for hundreds of years but rather than look closely at how these systems work, the government decided they were wasteful or inefficient, and programmes were designed to stop shifting agriculture. In some areas, ethnic minorities have stopped shifting agriculture but this has not always resulted in higher incomes or a better quality of life. In some cases, resettlement involved major lifestyle changes, which the minority groups were not prepared for. Traditional cultural and community structures were damaged, and in many areas this has resulted in social problems such as alcohol abuse, gambling, and so on.

Blaming highland peoples for deforestation through shifting agriculture has also turned attention away from the true causes of deforestation in Vietnam: logging companies, major infrastructure projects like dams, and large-scale cultivation of cash crops such as coffee. Other industrial crops, like eucalyptus, have had negative impacts as well. The root cause of deforestation is the opening up of the country's economy to the market. Logging companies hire local people to cut down the forest, and they offer very high incomes. For example, in one Hmong village in Son La province, a company from Hanoi told the villagers they would build a road for them, so they could sell their corn. The company said they only wanted to cut a few trees in return. Luckily, a local NGO was able to find funds so that the villagers could build a road themselves.

But, in general, even if the government has a policy of protecting the forest, the attraction of money is too great. In most cases, it is lowland Kinh (Vietnamese) people who have the resources to go to the highlands and cut down large numbers of trees.

Another source of deforestation is cash cropping. In the Central Highlands, coffee is now a major crop and it brings in high incomes. In this case, again it is Kinh people from the lowlands who find ways of persuading minority communities to sell land or cut down forest to open up new fields. Some of the areas are protected but people pay off those who are supposed to protect the forest. Only lowland Kinh have enough money to make these types of payments.

Eucalyptus was brought into the country in the early 1990s. It was promoted as a solution for the entire country and it was planted everywhere. In many cases, the villagers stated clearly that they did not want to grow eucalyptus — and some scientists agreed with them. But they had no choice, and the influence of eucalyptus on local knowledge systems was very severe. Eucalyptus releases toxins into the soil preventing other trees or plants from growing. The tree soaks up so much water that agricultural production is affected. In some cases, existing forest was cut down so that this imported tree could be grown. This is what happened near the Swedish-funded Bai Bang paper mill in northern Vietnam. Now, the mistake with eucalyptus has largely been recognised and accepted by the government. But the push for industrial cash crops is still very strong and shows no signs of slowing down.

The resulting impact on biodiversity and indigenous knowledge is very severe. The government approach has been similar to that of many other countries – protected areas and nature reservations are established with the goal of preserving rare species and forested areas. Unfortunately, implementation of these programmes often ignores or completely excludes local people. Indigenous communities have been resettled from protected areas in the belief that they cut down or damage the forest. As mentioned, this often leaves them worse off, and in danger of losing their culture. In general, there is little acceptance of the idea that indigenous people are the best able and most willing to protect forests.

Another government policy is the "five-million acre" reforestation program. This involves a substantial amount of government money for reforestation. But there is no real focus on who is responsible for managing and protecting existing forests. The result is that villagers are planting new trees but existing forest is still being cut at a fast rate. Forest enterprises hired villagers to plant trees, but

Houses of Kinh settlers in Daklak province, Central Highland of Vietnam. Photo: IWGIA archive

In a village of the Mnong Ralam, one of the indigenous peoples of Daklak province. Photo: IWGIA archive

that was all. So the villagers do not have any really sense of responsibility for protecting the areas after they have planted them. They just think they are growing trees for the government, not for themselves.

Gradually, however, some old approaches are being replaced by new programmes that offer greater participation at the local level, and the opportunity for highland people to protect their land. After the period of collective agriculture ended in the 1980s, privatisation of landholdings spread across Vietnam. This has now made its way to the highlands, and often includes forest land. Villagers in many areas are now receiving land use rights certificates for cultivation and forest land certificates, which offer all of the rights associated with full ownership.

Some social forestry programmes, such as a large project funded by the German government's development agency GTZ in Son La province, even offer the chance for villagers to create legally-recognised community forests. Many NGO staff and government forestry officials recognise that this is perhaps the best way to manage and protect forests. However, progress is slow and often not enough attention is paid to working closely with minority people – many of whom are illiterate – in order to make sure they understand laws and policies related to the land. There is insufficient effort to ensure that farmers understand their legal rights once they have obtained land use certificates. Also, apart from a few pilot projects, land certificates are issued only in the name of the male head of household, so women are excluded from the process.

The result is that villagers, particularly women, never really feel that they are responsible for the land, or they think they are powerless to protect forests from outsiders who want to cut down trees.

Education Policy

At the root of this problem are the many limitations in education programmes for highland ethnic minorities. The national policy is to promote the use of the Vietnamese (Kinh) language so that minorities can integrate into surrounding lowland communities. In practice, this means that minority pupils study in a foreign language, so they learn very slowly. Also, the curriculum is not related to their everyday lives, so pupils often lose interest. This is especially the case with female children, many of whom remain illiterate. This has a serious impact on their ability to learn new skills later in life, as participation in most development programmes requires an ability to understand Vietnamese. As it stands, there are only a few pilot education programmes where pupils are taught in their native languages for one or two years, before moving on to Vietnamese instruction.

Political Representation

As Vietnam's ethnic minorities struggle with issues such as cash cropping, land rights and education, one factor that works in their favour is a respectable degree of political representation at the local, provincial and national level. Although many Vietnamese policy-makers do not understand highland issues very well, many com-mune and district level staff members are drawn from minority groups. There is also representation of ethnic minorities at the provincial and national level. The newly-elected General Secretary of the Communist Party – the highest political office in Vietnam – is a member of the Tay ethnic group, from the north east.

This political representation helps many NGOs, including some local organisations, to focus their efforts on ethnic minority issues. There are many projects in areas such as social forestry and educa-tion that offer promising new models for involving minority people in society. However, positive change is limited by the top-down approach of many government officials, and a lack of awareness of highland issues among the majority population.

Massive Protests by Indigenous Peoples in the Central Highlands

In early February 2001, Vietnam's Central Highlands were swept by massive protests on the part of its indigenous peoples. The appar-ently well-coordinated protests took place in several major towns of Dak Lak and Gia Lai province but were concentrated in Pleiku, the capital of Gia Lai, where an estimated 5,000 protesters took to the streets from February 2 to 6. According to news agency reports, some of the protests turned violent. Government buildings were surrounded, roadblocks set up and telephone lines cut. The govern-ment reacted immediately with the deployment of troops, riot police and helicopters. Twenty people were allegedly arrested but no casualties were reported. According to the State-run media, some police were injured and hospitalised.

Only once were foreign journalists allowed to enter the area and phone contact was curtailed in order to prevent local officials, jour-nalists and members of local organizations from talking to the for-eign press. The whole Central Highlands has remained completely sealed off ever since.

The government acknowledged in late March that protests had actually started months earlier, in October 2000, when hundreds of young indigenous set up no-go zones to which outsiders were refused entry. The government also admitted that the unrest had actually continued into March, contrary to their earlier proclamations that the demonstrations ceased right after the government intervention. According to other reports, there were already isolated clashes between indigenous people and settlers back in August when about 150 members of the Ede indigenous people attacked Vietnamese settlers in Ea H'leo district of Daklak province.

It has been suggested that the immediate reason for the large protests were fears of increased migration, which spread in late January. According to the rumours, Daklak and Gia Lai province were destined to receive 100,000 of the 300,000 people to be resettled because of the US$ 3 billion Son La hydropower project in North Vietnam. The Central Highlands has already experienced heavy immigration, both State planned and, in recent years, spontaneous which has profoundly changed its demographic composition. At the turn of the century, the plateau and surrounding mountains of the Central Highlands had a population of about 240,000, almost all of them indigenous. Due to the massive immigration of Kinh and indigenous peoples of the North, the number has risen to nearly 3 million, the indigenous accounting for less than one third. Formerly covered by extensive forests, the Central Highlands has become the country's largest coffee-growing area. Most of the good land is now in the hands of migrants.

An additional reason for the protest has allegedly been the government's repression of the Protestant Church, which most indigenous people in the region belong to. According to some reports, the Protestant underground church played a crucial role in organising the protests.

The Vietnamese authorities have accused anti-Communist exiles in the United States of being behind the protests. According to the Public Security Ministry newspaper, the disturbances were caused by agitators working for ex-members of the United Front for the Liberation of Oppressed Races (FULRO, the acronym for its name in French). FULRO is an armed resistance group of the indigenous of the Central Highlands that has fought for self-determination against successive Vietnamese governments from the late 1950s until the early 1990s.

Sources
Agence France-Presse, March 23, 27 2001
BBC News, February 7, 8, 9, 2001
Far Eastern Economic Review, March 1, 2001
Reuters, February 7, 2001
South China Morning Post, March 28, 2001

LAOS

Laos harbours one of the most ethnically diverse populations in Southeast Asia. The largest ethnic group, the Lao, comprise approximately 30% of the 4.8 million inhabitants of Laos (far more Lao live in the Northeast of present-day Thailand than in Laos), while the remaining 70% encompass more than 230 different ethno-linguistic groups belonging to four ethno-linguistic super-stocks: the Tai-Kadai, Austro-Asiatic (Mon-Khmer family), Hmong-Mien and Sino-Tibetan (Tibeto-Burman family) (ILO 2000: 3). There are 80 Mon-Khmer groups alone, and 10 new Vietic groups have been identified only recently. The 47 groups used for classification in the last government census are therefore far too crude.

It is these small, non-Lao ethnic groups that are usually referred to as the indigenous peoples of Laos. Officially, these peoples are today called "ethnic groups", "ethnic peoples" or "Lao son phau" ("non-ethnic Lao"). The government has dropped the formerly - among some government officials and other people, however, still very common – geo-morphological classification of Laos' population into "Lowland Lao" (Lao Loum), "Midland/upland Lao" (Lao Thoeng) and "Highland Lao" (Lao Soung).

The Present Ethnic Minority Policy of the Lao Government

The 1991 Constitution provides the general framework of Laos' policy with respect to the different ethnic groups. It provides for equal rights to culture and customs for all ethnic groups, forbids discrimination between ethnic groups and mandates the State to promote unity and equality among them and to implement measures that provide for the economic and social development of all ethnic groups.

The present indigenous peoples or ethnic minority policy was formulated in the "Resolution of the Party Central Organization Concerning Ethnic Minority Affairs in the New Era" of 1992. In a recent ILO report the authors conclude that: "It is in fact difficult to identify specific articles in ILO Convention No. 169 with which Lao policy is in conflict. At a recent consultative meeting convened by the LFNC [Lao Front for National Construction] in September, 1999, where the Convention was introduced to key decision-makers from line ministries and agencies including the Ethnic Minorities Committee of the National Assembly, the attendees voiced their agreement with the contents of the Convention" (ILO 2000: 40). The positive response of the government officials at the consultative meeting organized by the ILO gives reason for hope that the government of Laos will eventually even consider ratifying Convention 169.

The present policy of the Party as outlined in the 1992 Resolution was summarized by the authors of the ILO report as follows (ILO 2000: 23):

1. Build national sentiment (national identity).
2. Realize equality between ethnic minorities.
3. Increase the level of solidarity among ethnic minorities as members of the greater Lao family.
4. Resolve problems of inflexible and vengeful thinking, as well as economic and cultural inequality.
5. Improve the living conditions of the ethnic minorities step by step.
6. Expand, to the greatest extent possible, the good and beautiful heritage and ethnic identity of each group as well as their capacity to participate in the affairs of the nation.

The Resolution goes on to identify essential tasks through which the policy may be achieved. Among others, it calls for, "the resolution of disagreements between members of the same ethnic minority, between ethnic minorities, between ethnic minorities and government officials, soldiers and other citizens" and "states that whenever violations of the policy on ethnic minorities occur these must be immediately resolved by the relevant authority and the offenders punished" (ibid.).

The Resolution further demands "concentration on the expansion of education, culture, health, and other social benefits" through, among other things, expansion of formal primary education, teacher training, researching the writing systems of the Hmong and Khmou, enlarging the health care network "by joining modern and traditional medicine", dissemination of information in remote areas, especially through radio broadcasting in indigenous languages, the appointment of specialist officials who speak minority languages etc.

Somewhat worrying is that while the Resolution calls for the promotion and expansion of the traditional cultural heritage of each ethnic group, it also calls for reducing and eradicating "backward traditions" without specifying what is considered as "backward" (ILO 2000: 24).

Another rather problematic paragraph is the one calling for "increased production and open [channels of] distribution in order to change the 'natural' or 'semi-natural' economic system towards one of production of goods" and its emphasis on the need to reduce shifting cultivation (ILO 2000: 23).

Heuny woman in Ban Chat San resettlement site. Photo: IWGIA archive

Heuny women on a visit to their old village from where they have been forcibly relocated. Photo: IWGIA archive

The Resolution provides for a certain degree of recognition of land rights of indigenous communities by calling for a strict and clear policy of land allocation for every family (ibid.). Unfortunately, there is evidence that land allocation has so far been used rather as a means to reduce shifting cultivation than to provide indigenous communities with security of tenure over their traditional agricultural and forest lands.

In order to increase "the level of Party leadership in ethnic minority affairs", the Resolution identifies the need to (a) increase national identity and solidarity among ethnic minorities and to train civil servants, Party members, and soldiers to understand the content of the policy; and (b) to improve the personnel mechanism responsible for ethnic affairs and, at the central and provincial levels, establish a mechanism responsible specifically for ethnic affairs under the Lao Front for National Construction (LFNC). Its central administration was designated advisor to the Party Central Organization and the Government, while at the local level the Party committee should assist the LFNC in carrying out its duties (ibid.: 25).

The LFNC is also given the crucial mandate of coordinating and ensuring the implementation of the policy laid out in the Resolution through:

- researching policies affecting ethnic minorities and disseminating the resolution to the "Political Bureau in order to coordinate with various departments for true implementation";
- following up, evaluating and reporting regularly to the Party Central organization and the government on the process of the policy's implementation.
- The request to all central level agencies to coordinate with the LFNC.

The Resolution is very clear in its critique of past failures and its commitment to an improved policy and a more determined implementation. A few aspects have already been highlighted as being potentially problematic. These are partially linked to already existing government programs, which will be briefly discussed below:

Reduction of Shifting Cultivation and Relocation

In spite of the potentially favourable policy laid out in the party resolution of 1992, some of the current government programs carried out in indigenous areas have proved to have serious consequences for indigenous communities. One of them is the relocation and village consolidation program, which is the program with the most severe impact on indigenous peoples. Contrary to a ministerial statement on 28th April 1992, relocation is still a policy. This was reconfirmed at the 5th party congress in 1996, although it was stated that no "forced relocation" should occur.

The relocation program has existed since the early 1980s and was originally initiated for security reasons (i.e. to relocate former "allies" of the USA, above all, Hmong communities). Since the drawing up of the Tropical Forestry Action Plan (TFAP) of 1990, environmental (forest) conservation is the official underlying rationale. It is suspected that the TFAP made the government realise that it was more profitable for the State to use forests for logging than for shifting cultivation. The consequence is that relocation now targets shifting cultivators.

The aim to reduce shifting cultivation is clearly stated in the Forestry Law of 1996. On the other hand, the Forestry Law provides for a decentralized forest management and, to a certain degree, recognizes customary rights (to small-scale domestic use of forest products, including timber, hunting and fishing). Villages are given the authority to develop their own rules and regulations for forest management, provided that they comply with the general aim of conserving forests. While customary laws, land tenure systems and resource management practices are explicitly recognized (Ministerial Agreement on Customary Rights and Use of Forest Resources, see ILO 2000), they are still subordinate to the national legislation. Activities considered as contradicting the law are non-sustainable activities, which include, among others, some forms of swidden farming.

A total of 300,000 families are considered to be shifting cultivators, which is more than 40% of the rural population (Goudineau, Y.,1997: 15), most of them belonging to indigenous peoples. Since the government has planned to eradicate shifting cultivation by the year 2000, these people are all targeted for relocation. But unlike elsewhere in Asia, the government is not very aggressive in the implementation of this program. Nevertheless, many tens of thousands have already been relocated. Some observers have pointed out that if the program is fully carried out, it will be the world's biggest relocation program. People are supported to make a living from coffee cultivation etc. Wet rice cultivation is, in most cases, not an option simply because there is very little additional land left that is suitable for paddy cultivation.

ORSTOM (Institut Français de Recherche Scientifique pour le Développement en Coopération) on behalf of UNDP and UNESCO has undertaken a study on "Resettlement and Social Characteristics of New Villages" (Goudineau, Y.,1997) covering 67 villages in six provinces of North and South Laos. The report shows that in some villages, up to 30% of the people died from malaria and other illnesses within the first years.

While the government has now acknowledged that relocation programs are highly problematic, and although the official policy is that no forced relocations should take place anymore, it still honestly believes (or tries to appear to believe) that relocation and village consolidation (i.e. grouping small villages together to form a larger settlement) is ultimately good for the people. The argument given is that only in this way can the people be provided with education, health and other government services. The government also sees it as a way of "civilizing" the ethnic minorities, an attitude also reflected in parts of the 1992 Resolution.

Observers in Laos are of the opinion that the government is slowly moving away from the relocation policy. But the situation remains unclear; the government is vacillating on the issue. At present, the problem is that, while central government has a clearer and more cautious policy, the provinces often just ignore it. The "uncontrollability" of remote communities in the thinly populated southern provinces has been mentioned as a possible reason for the ongoing relocation, as in Attapeu province. Another possible reason for ongoing relocation in some provinces could be the interest in having unimpeded access for logging.

On the other hand, no communities have so far been relocated due to the establishment of protected areas. In that respect, the government has a more pro-people approach than in many other countries.

In sum, relocation of indigenous communities for "environmental reasons" is still an option – and a reality - in Laos. It remains the most problematic government program with regard to the rights of indigenous peoples. While there are good reasons to believe that the government is moving away from this policy, still more pressure – from within or by ODAs and international organisations – will be needed to ensure complete abandonment of the program, as well as proper implementation of a non-relocation policy.

Land Rights and the Land and Forest Allocation Program

The Land Law of 1997 provides the legal framework for the allocation of land under the land and forest allocation program. Permanent land use rights (land titles) for land under permanent use (e.g. paddy land or orchards) and temporary land certificates for farming in upland (forest areas), i.e. for shifting cultivation, are given to individuals and households. The management rights over community forests are given to villages.

The actual land allocation takes place at district level. The District Office of Agriculture and Forestry, under the Ministry of Agriculture and Forestry, is responsible for its implementation. As a precondition for getting village land allocated, a land use plan has to be drawn up and submitted to the district government for approval.

The point of departure for land allocation are the existing customary rights. This means that these rights are clearly recognized by the government. Unfortunately, there are several weaknesses and potential dangers in the land allocation program as it is currently practiced.

The problem is that, firstly, people do not know about it and, secondly, the financial means to implement the program is lacking. In many areas, no official village boundaries exist, and therefore in some areas a great deal of encroachment onto indigenous communities' land is taking place.

The most problematic aspect, however, is that the land allocation program also explicitly states the reduction of shifting cultivation as one of its main aims. It is mentioned second out of the three major objectives of the program, which are: 1. Sustainable management and use of natural resources; 2. Reduction and gradual elimination of shifting cultivation; 3. Promotion of commercial production (ILO 2000: 96).

In fact, land allocation is currently the government's main instrument for reducing shifting cultivation. This is done by confining the land area allocated for swidden farming in the uplands. While a total land area of up to 22 ha. (including land for fruit gardens, grazing etc.) per head is possible, the land that can be used for swidden farming is limited and therefore leads to a shortening of the swidden cycle. In the long run, this policy may backfire when, after only a few cycles, people (if not given viable alternatives) will simply be forced to open up new land for cultivation and move on to the now "protected" forest land.

The Lao government has, on the other hand, clearly stated its commitment to a decentralized and participatory approach to resource management and biodiversity conservation. Several decrees and ministerial orders recognize customary rights over land and forests and provide for decentralized, community management of forests. As part of the land and forest allocation process, agricultural land is allocated to households (or private investors for commercial tree plantations) while some forests (three types: water source forest, village forest reserve and utility forest) are allocated for village management (ibid. 2000: 86f).

But the government imposes specific forms of land use determined through zoning (into Resource Management Areas). Community rights over, e.g. "production forests" (forests other than the ones mentioned above) are very limited. They can be opened up for logging and community rights are only recognized to the extent that an agreement has to be made with the respective communities who will receive "community development" aid in return.

In sum: while individual and community rights over land and forests do exist, restrictions on their use are imposed, and "control is wrested away from individuals and communities" (Chamberlain 1995: 41). Which means that the government can grant access to community land to logging companies, for plantations etc.

Hydropower Development

With the opening up of Laos to foreign investment under its New Economic Policy initiated in the 1980s, numerous foreign consultants and multinational corporations came to Laos to investigate the potential for developing large hydropower dam projects. Foreign engineers have long viewed southern Laos, including the Sekong Basin, as an area with considerable potential for large-scale hydropower development. However, the first foreign consultants to conduct detailed field surveys regarding the potential for hydropower in the area since the American War in Vietnam were the Japanese government's bilateral aid agency, JICA. JICA has undertaken a number of hydropower studies in the Sekong, including the recently completed "Sekong Basin Hydropower Master Plan", which envisages building 12 large dams in the Sekong Basin in Laos.

However, no hydropower projects were yet under construction by 1993, when the governments of Laos and Thailand signed an agreement in which the Laotians agreed to sell power-hungry Thailand 1,500 MW of electricity per annum by the year 2000.

Heuny and J'rou Communities Relocated

Since then, the construction of several dams has commenced. Some have been completed, some are still under construction and several others are planned. Due to the construction of the Houay Ho reservoir on the Bolaven Plateau in southern Laos, ten villages in total - including nine Heuny communities (out of a total of 20 communities of the Heuny people) and one J'rou village - have been forcibly relocated to the resettlement site at Ban Chat San. 1,598 people in 421 families have been moved there so far (*pers. comm.*, Lao government officials, July 2000).

It is ironic that, of the ten villages that have been relocated, only one (Ban Nam Han) was situated within the reservoir areas for the Houay Ho and the planned Xe Pian-Xe Nam Noy dams. It is therefore incorrect to assume that the communities had to be relocated to make way for the dams. The reason given for the relocation of the other communities was the conservation of the catchment area. However, the Environmental Impact Assessment for the Xe Pian - Xe Nam Noy dam specifically recommended that the communities should not be relocated to Ban Chat San. Instead, it was suggested that they either be left in their previous locations or moved a little up the mountain to avoid being flooded by the dam reservoirs (Electrowatt, 1996). The project developers and the government, however, did not follow this advice (for more on the relocation of the Heuny communities, see *Indigenous Affairs* 4/2000).

Nakai Plateau to be Flooded
The Nakai Plateau and the adjacent forested mountain in central Laos have been identified as one of the biodiversity hotspots in Indochina. Not only is the area home to a bewildering diversity of plant and animal life but also to indigenous communities speaking 28 different languages. Three of them are hunter-gatherer groups previously unknown to the outside world and who speak languages that are not related to any of the five major language groups found in the area but to Vietnamese spoken across the Annamite chain.

For approximately the last ten years, a logging company run by the Lao military has been logging in an area of 450 square kilometres on the Plateau to make way for the reservoir of the proposed 1,069 megawatt Nam Theun 2 hydroelectric dam.

Contrary to all expectations, the World Bank-funded Panel of Experts, who were hired to provide advice on the proposed US$1.1 billion dam, found the current situation "encouraging" and proposed that the project should be carried out as planned and the World Bank remain involved. Otherwise, they conclude, rural poverty will increase rather than decrease, and the globally recognized biodiversity of the Nakai-Nam Theun National Biodiversity Conservation Area (NBCA) will be degraded or entirely lost. The large reservoir, it is assumed, will represent a barrier that prevents easy access and therefore the further degradation of the NBCA. For the members of the Panel, like Thayer Scudder, a Professor of Anthropology at the California Institute of Technology, known to be an "expert on resettlement", logging and flooding 450 square kilometers of land and relocating 6,000 people is apparently a price worth paying for the conservation of the Nakai-Nam Theun NBCA.

According to Scudder, the 6,000 people to be relocated are "incredibly poor to start with". He believes that they are going to be moved anyway but prefers "to try to improve that resettlement rather than just sit back and criticize it".

Problems connected with the proposed dam have already arisen. The military-run logging company, Bholisat Phattana Khed Phou Doi (BPKP - the Mountain Region Development Company), has already logged several areas outside of the proposed reservoir area, including a proposed community forest area that was supposed to provide an income for evicted villagers. Since a sizeable industry has already been developed to process the timber, the Panel of Experts fear that this industry "may exert strong political pressure to be allowed to log inside conservation areas when their existing log sources are exhausted and before plantation grown timber becomes ready to harvest." This does not, however, diminish the Panel's support for the project. BPKP has also already moved families out of the proposed reservoir area, independently of any planned World Bank resettlement program.

Whether the dam will be built remains uncertain, however, since the Nam Theun 2 Electricity Consortium (NTEC) says it depends on a World Bank US$100 million "partial risk guarantee" covering the commercial loans. Without such a guarantee, commercial banks will not put money into a financially risky scheme. NTEC hopes that the World Bank will agree to the loan-guarantee in the next few months.

Sources

Chamberlain, James R., Charles Alton, Arthur G. Crisfield. 1995. *Indigenous Peoples Profile. Lao People's Democratic Republic.* Prepared for the World Bank. Care International, Vientiane.

Goudineau, Yves. 1997. *Resettlement and Social Characteristics of New Villages. Basic needs for resettlement communities in the Lao PDR.* An Orstom Survey. Vientiane: UNDP.

Khamin, Nok. 2000. "More Trouble for the Heuny." *Indigenous Affairs 4/2000.* Copenhagen: IWGIA

Lang, Chris. 2001. "Cutting the Trees to Save the Forest." *World Rainforest Movement Bulletin* Number 4, 2001. Montevideo

ILO 2000. *Policy Study on Ethnic Minority Issues in Rural Development. Project to Promote ILO Policy on Indigenous and Tribal Peoples.* Geneva: International Labour Office.

BURMA

Steps Towards a Political Dialogue?

On January 9, a UN spokesperson announced after the visit of United Nations special envoy on Burma, Razali Ismail, that Lt. General Khin Nyunt and National League for Democracy (NLD) leader Daw Aung San Suu Kyi had been engaged in a direct 'dialogue' since October. On the following day the NLD confirmed that it was engaged in talks with the State Peace and Development Council (SPDC) and that some progress had been achieved. Prior to this, Lt. General Khin Nyunt met NLD Chairperson Li Aung Shwe on September 14.

While the talks have been described by certain quarters as a "dialogue", it is important to note that the current circumstances give no indication that these talks fulfill the conditions needed for a genuine 'dialogue'.

The talks raised expectations, but very little is known about their nature, extent and content. There are many reasons for caution about the outcomes and the time frame for change. Comments have been made by a number of important players who have indicated that change will come slowly and the outcome will not be a "Western-style democracy".

It is yet to be seen if the SPDC is attempting to manipulate the international community for the removal of sanctions and the resumption of aid and loans or if they are actually willing to engage in a sincere discussion about the future welfare of the peoples of Burma.

While some exiled activists have hailed the talks as "historic", the NLD's position appears to be one of cautious optimism. The NLD has refrained from making public statements about the content or progress of the talks apparently in order to build up goodwill and avoid offending the regime. However, it is speculated that the NLD leadership has its own timetable for outcomes, possibly focused on the release of political prisoners, the ability to exercise its rights as a legally registered political party, the cessation of human rights violations against ethnic nationalities and joint cooperation for development projects.

Despite the hype and excitement, the 6-month long talks at this stage have not delivered any substantive outcomes apart from the release of a limited number of political prisoners, all arrested shortly before the dialogue process. The Central Executive Committee of the NLD (CEC) have received particular attention being twice released from house arrest and detention in government 'guesthouses'.

The talks are presently not official and many believe that only the Khinn Nyunt faction is represented. There have been a number of unconfirmed rumours that Senior General Than Shwe and General Maung Aye were involved in some of the talks at the early stages. Later rumours suggest a split between the factions, with Maung Ave opposed to the dialogue. These rumours increased after the February 19 helicopter crash that killed Secretary No. 2, Lt. General Tin Oo who was in the Maung Aye faction, with many seeing the death as an assassination by the Khin Nyunt faction. There have even been speculations of a coup and arrests of high ranking military officers including Maung Aye. The veracity of these reports or their relationship to the talks is presently unknown. However, Khin Nyunt has publicly denied rumours of a split in the military. There is not just the issue of splits in the upper echelons of the military, but increasing discontent in the lower ranks.

It is not clear at this stage, which NLD representatives have been involved in the dialogue. There was at least one meeting between U Aung Shwe (then under arrest in a 'guest-house') and Lt. General Khin Nyunt. Accompanying Khin Nyunt at the September 14 meeting was U Khin Maung Win, Deputy Foreign Minister. Aung San Suu Kyi is one of the key protagonists in the talks, with perhaps NLD chairperson U Aung Shwe and NLD Secretary U Lwin. The SPDC-imposed house arrests on NLD leaders they are supposed to be in dialogue with has aroused suspicions of the true intentions of the regime. While the NLD leaders have been allowed a few appointments with visiting diplomats, free access to other democracy leaders and ethnic nationality groups has yet to happen.

Participation of Indigenous Peoples' Representatives not Confirmed

Information is scant about the possibility of other representatives involved in the talks. Comments from a range of exiled groups suggest that 'representatives' of minority ethnic groups [Burma's indigenous peoples] are not involved at this stage. The perceived main initiator of the 'dialogue', United Nations special envoy on Burma Razali Ismail, has met with some SPDC-endorsed 'representatives' of minority ethnic groups during his visits to Burma.

Rumors exist that some 'representatives' have been involved in discussions with SPDC officials outside of Burma, but this has not been confirmed. Phado Mahn Sha, the Karen National Union (KNU) Secretary said that there was a meeting between the liaison officers of the KNU and SPDC but that there is no possibility of a dialogue at the moment. A representative of the Karenni National Progressive

Party (KNPP) stated that a letter from the SPDC asked them to join with the SPDC and engage in development activities and in talks. The non-inclusion of 'representatives' from ethnic nationality groups will be a source of continuing conflict if the 'dialogue' brings about some 'resolutions' between the SPDC and the NLD.

This report has been adopted from ALTSEAN Burma Report Card Sept. 00 - Jan. 01 "Burma: Tentative Steps", which we herewith gratefully acknowledge.

Continuing Military Operations:
Tens of Thousands of Indigenous People Displaced

Throughout 2000, the Burmese army continued its crackdown on the pro-democracy movement. Government counter-insurgency operations, forced labour, forced relocation, extra-judicial executions, and other gross human rights abuses continued against several indigenous opposition groups. People have been relocated on a large scale, homes were frequently burned, crops destroyed, and belongings looted. At the relocation sites, villagers had to contribute up to 15 days a month of forced labour. So far, ceasefires have been signed with 13 of the 28 indigenous resistance groups. The Karen guerrilla has experienced heavy losses during the past years.

According to the *Human Rights World Report 2000*, tens of thousands of indigenous people in the conflict areas of central Shan state, Karenni state, Karen state, Mon state, and eastern Tenasserim division are being kept in forced relocation sites. They faced curfews, looting, and restrictions on movement at the hands of the Burmese army. Shan refugees escaping to Thailand reported that strict curfews had been implemented in Burmese government relocation sites forbidding Shan villagers from leaving their homes between dusk and dawn and, in some instances, prohibiting speaking and imposing a strict lights-out policy. Tens of thousands of other villagers in eastern and southeastern Burma remained displaced in the forests or in areas contested by the army and insurgent groups.

More than 2000 indigenous people have been displaced by army persecution in Kler Lwe Tu district since November 2000 alone. They fled to the east of Mu Traw district in Karen state. Some of them continued and sought shelter across the border in Thailand. The "Scorched Earth" operations of the Burmese Army was directed against those villagers hiding in the jungle with the intention to eliminate all those found in the military declared free fire zone. They were shooting anyone on sight and destroyed all crops and food supplies found.
Sources
Human Rights Watch World Report 2000.

Internally Displaced peoples News. Issue 6, February 2001.
Institute of Peace and Conflict Studies: *Armed Conflicts Report 2000.*
(www.ploughshares.ca/ CONTENT/ACR/ACR00/ACR00.html).

Massive Transmigration of Wa to Shan State

In an attempt to take control of narcotic production centres along the
Thai-Burma border, the Burmese-backed United Wa State Army
(UWSA) moved thousands of soldiers and civilians into areas formerly controlled by the Shan people. The SDPC reported the relocation of tens of thousands of mostly Wa poppy farmers to the Thai
border as a "drug eradication effort". Thai and international anti-
narcotic officials believe that the military junta is covertly supporting
drug production by the Wa and Kokang ethnic groups. There are
reportedly plans to relocate 50,000 households from the Wa region
in the north to the Thai-Burma border in Shan State. At the end of
December it was estimated that between 15,000 and 25,000 households have been relocated. In addition to the Wa, eight hundred
Kokang families, neighbours of the Wa, have been reported to be
relocated from northern Shan state near the China border to the
South.

Sources
> ALTSEAN *Burma Report Card* Sept. 00-Jan. 01 "Burma: Tentative Steps".
> *Burma Alert, Vol 12:5.*
> *Human Rights Watch World Report 2000.*

ILO Criticized Continuing Practice of Forced Labour

The SPDC failed to put a stop to its use of forced labour for infrastructure development, the construction of Buddhist structures,
maintenance of military camps, and portering for army patrols. A
delegation from the International Labour Organization (ILO), visited
Rangoon and other areas at the SPDC's invitation from May 23-27,
shortly before the June annual conference of the ILO. In its report on
the visit, the ILO again called for the SPDC to cease the use of forced
labour, repeal or amend legal provisions for forced labour in the Village
and Towns acts, monitor compliance, and penalize those who employed
forced labor. Burmese Minister for Labour Maj. Gen. Tin Ngwe wrote
a letter dated May 27 to the ILO's director-general, stating that the
SPDC leaders "have taken and are taking the necessary measures to
ensure that there are not instances of forced labor in Myanmar." The
ILO conference, however, concluded that the SPDC had failed to end

the practice and gave the SPDC until November 2000 to institute reforms or suffer possible sanctions. On October 19, an ILO delegation travelled to Rangoon to assess whether forced labour was still in use.

Source
> *Human Rights Watch World Report 2000.*
> (www.ploughshares.ca/ CONTENT/ACR/ACR00/ACR00.html).

NAGALIM

Civil Society Initiative

In March 2001, at a two-day Convention in Kohima, in the present Nagaland State of India, civil groups from India, Kashmir and Nagalim called for the restoration of basic human rights in the Naga areas. Declaring that they were "convinced that the overwhelming desire of the Naga people is to live in dignity and freedom, which has been denied them for over 53 years", the delegates reiterated the call for a peacefully negotiated settlement.

In preparation for this historic Convention, the delegates toured the Naga areas extensively, meeting a cross-section of the people including Indian military and civilian officers. After a careful study of the information gathered from the tour, the Convention concluded that all the draconian laws, including the Armed Forces Special Powers Act, National Security Act, Nagaland Security Regulation, 1962, and Unlawful Activities Prevention Act, should be withdrawn. Furthermore, the government of India should ensure withdrawal of all cases against members of the Naga National Movement. They urged the government of India to fulfil, without further ado, its commitment to hold unconditional talks at the highest level. Expressing concern over the partial observance of the cease-fire, the Convention called on the NSCN (IM) and the Indian government to honour the cease-fire to the letter and the spirit.

The Kohima Convention marks a turning point in the civil society initiative for a just peace in South Asia. It firmly sets the ground for extending the role of civil society in peace processes. The civil groups are now in the process of constituting a "People's Commission", comprising eminent persons from Naga areas and from India to look into all violations of the democratic rights of the Naga people as well as to investigate how scarce resources meant for the State of Nagaland have been squandered by various agencies.

India's "Peace Offensive"

Naga villages and towns are swarming with Indian soldiers carrying "development projects" in their rucksacks. The mission, code named "Operation Good Samaritan" includes anything from building schools, churches, playgrounds, to health care and education tours. Coming from a country with chronic poverty, corruption and caste segregation, this sounds profoundly revolutionary, apart from a number of cruel facts:

a) The proponents are part of the Occupation Army that continues to suppress the fundamental human rights of the local people;
b) The Army is taking over the few remaining State functions handled by the civil administration, which is a clear violation of the Indian Constitution;
c) The government has shown little concern for the homeless millions crowding the city streets and railway platforms in India. "At least a third of India's people live in the direst of poverty, with millions sleeping on city streets. Delhi just announced it will acquire a nuclear submarine and deploy sea-launched ballistic missiles to complement its air and missile-delivered nuclear forces" (Eric Margolis, *The Ottawa Sun*, March 26, 2001).

Indian leaders and military officers are proudly speaking of this operation as a "peace offensive". However, other intentions may stand behind the initiative. Through "Operation Good Samaritan", the army is actually able to freely interfere in people's lives, to disorient them and then co-opt and assimilate them. The Indian authorities fully understand that the Naga sense of dignity, self-respect and responsibility is rooted in their traditional self-sufficient community-based way of life. The "peace offensive", it appears, is an attempt to cripple this.

Operation Good Samaritan goes hand in hand with raising more roadblocks and military posts inside the villages. People passing by the army post or roadblocks are stopped, searched and made to explain their reason for passing the place. Harassment at the roadblocks and army posts makes people reluctant to move around. In this way, the Indian soldiers intentionally disrupt the daily activities of the people and the flow of essential goods between the villages. The Indian security forces have killed about 20 cadres of the Naga resistance army over the past twelve months. Most of these Nagas

Indian army camp in the middle of Kohima, capital of "Nagaland State". Photo: IWGIA archive

The aftermath of an Indian army operation. Photo: IWGIA archive

were killed while travelling unarmed.

At the political level, Indian leaders continue their tactics of ambiguity and self-contradiction. In the beginning, Naga elders gave them the benefit of the doubt. However, it has now become clear that the Indian leaders have merely been playing for time.

After all this, it should not be difficult to understand that the Indian State has taken a very dim view of civil society's initiative at strengthening the peace process and time and again it has attempted to put it down. The security forces and undercover agents have stepped up harassment of civil society members in the north east of India. This includes frequent checks by the military aimed at restricting their movements, constant disruption of communication lines and maintaining secret files on the activists.

This was confirmed by the Indian Minister of State for Home Affairs on April 24, 2001 when he told Parliament that his Ministry had blacklisted six NGOs in the north east for having links with militant outfits and that a close watch was being kept on their activities (*The Assam Tribune*, April 25, 2001). Several Members of Parliament from the Hindu Militant Party of the Home Affairs Minister used the occasion to further attack NGOs in the north east, even accusing them of channelling funds to the "insurgents". Two of the Naga civil organizations spearheading the human rights movement, the Naga Peoples Movement for Human Rights (NPMHR) and the Naga Student Federation (NSF), topped the blacklist. Other NGOs listed alongside them are: the Manad Adhikar Sangram Samiti (MASS) based in Assam, the North East Co-ordination Committee on Human Rights, the North East Indigenous Peoples Forum, and the All Manipur Students Union (AMSU), based in Imphal.

The Minister admitted that these NGOs were not themselves directly engaged in activities of open support or promotion of militant groups but he emphasised that some of these NGOs had been seen to be championing the cause of self-determination for the indigenous peoples, and organising protest actions to condemn the alleged harassment and atrocities against militants and the public on the part of the security forces.

Naga Leader Muivah Excluded from UNHCR Protection

One of the longest serving leaders of the freedom movement, Th. Muivah, has been excluded from UNHCR protection. Th. Muivah's application for protection was rejected by the UNHCR on the basis of a "report" that he had committed "war crimes and serious non-political crimes" (the UNHCR has failed to provide the source of this "report", let alone the details). This has caused concern in human rights circles in South Asia. They have urged the UNHCR to review its decision. The NSCN (I-M), the main national resistance organisation of the Naga people, of which Th. Muivah is the General Secretary, has never been accused of terrorist crime by any recognised NGO. In a letter addressed to the Director, Bureau of Asia Pacific, UNHCR, Geneva, the General Secretary of the South Asia Forum for Human Rights (SAFHR), Mr.Tapan K.Bose has conveyed that "the decision of the UNHCR to 'exclude' Mr. Muivah on grounds of 'war crimes' came as a rude shock to many of us in the human rights movement in South Asia; many of us feel that the decision to 'exclude' Mr.Muivah on the grounds of 'war crimes' was taken on the basis of insufficient information and inadequate evidence". In order to assist the UNHCR, the General Secretary of SAFHR gave the following information in his letter: "The late Jaiprakash Narayan, the respected Gandhian leader of India, had led a Peace Mission to Nagaland in the sixties. He is on record having described the Naga movement as 'most certainly a struggle for national freedom'. Lt. General F.A. Vyas of the Indian Army, who was in charge of the counter insurgency operations in Nagaland, has said, 'Naga insurgents never adopted terror tactics'. (1989, *The Search for Security*, Dehra Dun, Natraj Publishers, P.126.) Mr.Murkot Ramuny, an Indian security expert, in his reports had admitted that, 'The Nagas do not kill civilians'. Nagaland's former Director General of Police, Mr. Chaman Lal in an interview with the Kohima based newspaper *Naga Banner* on November 26, 1994 had commented, 'In Punjab it was terrorism while in Nagaland it is insurgency. And we have to distinguish between the two. We are here not to end insurgency. Nagaland's is a political problem and it has to be solved politically'. In the mid nineties General Shankar Roy Chaudhury, then Chief of the Indian Army had urged the government of India to hold political dialogue with the Nagas."

The legal restriction on Muivah's movement (he is on bail in Thailand) and the threat of his deportation to India have gravely hampered the peace process in the region. The peace talks between India and Nagalim have been stalled since the arrest and detention of Muivah in Thailand in January 2000.

PART II

INDIGENOUS RIGHTS

UNITED NATIONS

REPORT ON THE 6ᵀᴴ SESSION OF THE COMMISSION ON HUMAN RIGHTS WORKING GROUP ON THE DECLARATION ON THE RIGHTS OF INDIGENOUS PEOPLES

On 3 March 1995, the Commission on Human Rights (CHR) decided to establish an open-ended inter-sessional working group with the purpose of elaborating a draft Declaration *"considering the draft contained in the annex to resolution 1994/45 of 26 August 1994 of the Sub-Commission on Prevention of Discrimination and Protection of Minorities entitled 'Draft United Nations declaration on the rights of indigenous peoples'"* (CHR resolution 1995/32). The 6th session of the CHR Working Group (CHRWG) was held in Geneva from 20 November to 1 December 2000. This report seeks to describe the debate at the 6th session (CHRWG6), to evaluate movement in positions of particular delegations, and to assess the progress, if any, in building consensus in relation to the Declaration.

Meetings and Attendance

At its 6th session, the CHRWG held 8 formal and 8 informal plenary meetings, and one informal meeting. The session was attended by more than 300 people, including representatives of 71 indigenous and non-governmental organisations, and 43 governments.

The following United Nations member States were represented at the session: Argentina, Australia, Bangladesh, Belarus, Brazil, Canada, Chile, China, Colombia, Costa Rica, Cuba, Denmark, Ecuador, Egypt, Estonia, Finland, France, Germany, Guatemala, India, Indonesia, Japan, Latvia, Malaysia, Mauritius, Mexico, Morocco, Nepal, New Zealand, Norway, Pakistan, Panama, Peru, Philippines, Russian Federation, South Africa, Spain, Sweden, Togo, Ukraine, United Kingdom of Great Britain and Northern Ireland, USA, Uruguay, Venezuela. In addition, the non-UN members Holy See and Switzerland were represented.

Chairperson

For the second year, Mr Luis-Enrique Chavez of the Peruvian Mission to the United Nations at Geneva was elected Chairperson-Rapporteur of the CHRWG. In a joint statement made on 20 November 2000 at the commencement of the 6th session, the Indigenous Caucus proposed the appointment of Mr Wilton Littlechild of the International Organization for Indigenous Resource Development as indigenous Co-Chair. On 23 November, Chairperson Chavez responded to the proposal, stating that indigenous co-chairpersonship would be allowed only in informal sessions. Chairperson Chavez referred to a memorandum produced by the Office of Legal Affairs at UN Headquarters in 1999 in response to a request for a legal opinion as to whether the rules of procedure allowed the CHR's ad hoc working group on a permanent forum for indigenous people to nominate a representative of an indigenous organisation as co-chairperson. That memorandum provided:

> *"Pursuant to rule 24 of the rules of procedure of the functional commissions of the Economic and Social Council, the rules of procedure of the Commission shall apply to the proceedings of its subsidiary organs in so far as they are applicable. In its relevant part, rule 15 provides 'the Commission shall elect, from among the representatives of its members, a Chairman, one or more Vice-Chairmen and such other officers as may be required'.*
>
> *As the Bureau must be elected from among the representatives of the members of the Commission, rule 15 therefore precludes the possibility of nominating a representative of an indigenous organization as a chairman, vice-chairman or any other officer. Moreover, it should be noted that rule 15 explicitly provides for a Chairman. The rules of procedure therefore also preclude the possibility of co-chairmen."* (E/CN 4/1999/83, par. 9)

Report

As with reports of previous sessions of the CHRWG, the report of the 6th session contains a record of the general debate and the debate which took place in formal plenary meetings. The debate which took place in the informal plenary meetings is reflected in summaries of the Chairperson-Rapporteur. As with reports of previous sessions, paragraph 4 of the report of the 6th session explains that the expressions "indigenous peoples" and "indigenous people" are used without prejudice to the positions of particular delegations, where divergence of approach remains. As with the report of the 5th session, paragraph 5 of the report of the 6th session provides:

> *"It is noted by indigenous representatives that all indigenous representatives and some Governments could accept the expression "indigenous peoples" as used in the current text of the draft declaration."*

As at previous sessions, the CHRWG was suspended for two meetings to enable preparation of the report for adoption at the final meeting. There were significant technical problems with the draft report. For example, Mexico complained that paragraphs 21 and 54 of the draft report did not properly reflect the statements made on behalf of the Mexican delegation. This was of particular concern in relation to the detailed Mexican statement on the core concept and sensitive subject of self-determination. Argentina, Bangladesh, China, Cuba and Pakistan expressed concern that particular interventions on self-determination and/or process were either nowhere to be seen or inaccurately and incompletely reflected in the draft report. Brazil commented on the many technical errors in Annex 1, consisting of amendments proposed by Governments for future discussion. The Chairperson asked that proposals to improve the text be submitted to the Secretariat within 14 days. As at 15 April 2001, there is no evidence that any such improvements have been reflected in the report posted on the web-site of the Office of the High Commissioner for Human Rights.

During the adoption of the draft report, several States made procedural interventions which made clear how they are generally disposed towards the Declaration. For example, several proposals by indigenous participants to recast particular words to reflect more accurately the debate which actually took place were opposed by the UK. One such instance related to paragraph 5, which is cited above.

After the UK opposed the proposal of an indigenous representative to replace "some Governments" with "most Governments", the Chairperson agreed to retain the language of "some Governments". Another instance concerned paragraph 103 which records indigenous perceptions of the discussion on article 1. The UK again opposed an indigenous proposal to introduce into this paragraph the following language: "They further noted that most States said they could accept the original language of article 1." On this occasion, the Chairperson commented that such language reflected the perception of indigenous participants, as well as his own perception, that such perception was not unjustified, and that it was reasonable that it be reflected in the report. After hearing an intervention by the USA against the indigenous proposal, and an intervention by Denmark in support, the Chairperson accepted the Danish proposal as most accurately reflecting the correct nature of the debate. Numerous technical points were taken during the adoption of the report by Australia and the USA.

Organisation of Work

At the first meeting of the 6th session, the Chairperson-Rapporteur gave a brief summary of his consultations on the organisation of work. It was proposed to conduct a general debate on the different aspects of the process in which the CHRWG is involved, followed by a general debate on substantive aspects of the Declaration, such as self-determination, land rights and natural resources. It was proposed then to focus on articles 1, 2, 12, 13, 14, 44 and 45.

Working Methods

The 6th session saw the continuation of the practice, begun at the 5th session, of regular meetings amongst States in an effort to narrow their differences on text. This practice was again the subject of trenchant criticism by indigenous participants. In a joint statement made on 20 November 2000, the Indigenous Caucus stated:

> *"The closed meetings which have resulted in governments providing alternative texts are in violation of the principles established in the Commission on Human Rights resolution 1995/32, which provides for the full and equal participation of Indigenous Peoples."*

Accordingly, the Caucus proposed the revision of the provisional programme to allocate time for discussion of process, in particular the full and equal participation of indigenous peoples. Despite a lengthy debate on process, summarised below, indigenous participants did succeed in preventing the institutionalisation of inter-governmental meetings and proposals for alternative text. The result is evident in Annex 1 to the report of the session (UN Doc E/CN 4/WG 15/CRP 4), entitled "Amendments proposed by Governments for Future Discussion". Annex 1 reproduces proposals in relation to articles 1, 2, 12, 14, 44 and 45, tabled at the 6th session, as well as proposals in relation to articles 15, 16, 17 and 18, tabled in 1999 at the 5th session.

At the same time, it was apparent that States are participating in the intergovernmental meetings with varying degrees of enthusiasm, and accordingly identify with the outcomes to varying degrees. For example, each of the working papers on articles 1, 2, 12, 13, 44 and 45 contains the comment *"Some states can accept the article as originally drafted."* In the course of informal plenary discussion, numerous State delegations stated that they could accept a particular article as drafted, but in the interest of reaching consensus were willing to consider proposals to alter the text.

Throughout the 6th session there were problems with discussion papers not being ready in sufficient time to enable participants to consider their often detailed and complex content, to consult in relation to them, and to prepare statements in response. For example, valuable meeting time was wasted as the Chairperson declined to open the debate on article 2 as there was no working paper before the CHRWG. Indigenous representatives saw no reason why there could not be a debate on article 2 as drafted. However, the Chairperson adjourned the meeting, stating that debate would be premature in the absence of concrete proposals.

Particular problems arose as discussion papers, drafted in English, were not immediately translated into Spanish, French, Russian and the other languages spoken by participants. All discussion papers appeared first in English and only subsequently in Spanish and French. Discussion of article 14 was disrupted because the discussion paper was available only in English. Similarly, the discussion paper on article 13 was produced only in English. These difficulties not only emphasised that the redrafting process is being principally driven by the Anglophone CANZUS bloc (Canada, Australia, New Zealand, USA), but also placed non-Anglophone participants at a considerable disadvantage. The difficulties faced by non-Anglophone indigenous delegations in undertaking a considered analysis of proposals was manifest.

General Debate

Process: Interventions of State delegations
The general debate began with interventions on process in the CHRWG. In this general debate, Switzerland stated that participants should avoid a text without any substance, and that the final text must not represent any weakening of the current text. It was also important to avoid a sterile debate on the alleged need for a definition of indigenous peoples. New Zealand referred to the importance of genuine dialogue and open and inclusive deliberations. At the same time, New Zealand recognised the importance of indigenous peoples and States meeting separately in informal sessions, with all

participants continuing to negotiate in good faith. The Russian Federation remarked that the present text was unacceptable to virtually all State delegations, and that States were unable to work to reach agreement on text in informal plenary sessions. It was time to get down to drafting text, starting with easy articles and moving to more difficult concepts.

Canada expressed concern that half way through the International Decade for the World's Indigenous Peoples little progress had been made in the CHRWG. The purpose of the closed meetings was to bring governmental positions closer together so that indigenous representatives were not confronted with a wide variety of proposals. According to Canada, the time had come to ask indigenous peoples to look at alternative texts to see whether agreement might be reached. Cuba noted that it had never previously attended a meeting at which there were so many separate meetings of governments and NGOs. Cuba did not want a Declaration which reflects the status quo, and urged greater flexibility in the negotiations. Australia referred to the "significant changes" needed in order to arrive at a document which could go forward.

Norway maintained the belief that adoption of the Declaration by consensus would still be possible. This would most likely not be as currently drafted, although agreement should be possible in relation to the structure and most articles as currently drafted, or with minor amendments. Mexico referred to dialogue as the *sine qua non* of success, noting that a critical point had been reached in the process with many States worried that dialogue is not occurring and that sperate blocs have emerged. According to Mexico, the negotiations in relation to the Permanent Forum demonstrated that progress was possible where negotiations were conducted in good faith and with transparency. Guatemala stated that many State delegations considered the text a good text to which they could subscribe without any change. Denmark proposed that indigenous representatives be invited to be present during intergovernmental meetings.

Process: Interventions of indigenous delegations
In their contributions to the general debate on process, numerous indigenous representatives commented upon the lack of transparency resulting from separate meetings of States. Indigenous participants were presented with drafts without any information as to the origins of, or extent of support for particular proposals. As a result, they were unable to identify which States had particular problems with the text, and there was no opportunity to engage in direct dialogue with those States. Numerous representatives stressed that

any such meetings should not be held behind closed doors nor in authorised meeting time. Work behind closed doors was not conducive to dialogue and took participants further away from the understanding and consensus which are necessary if the Declaration is to be proclaimed by the General Assembly and make any difference in the lives of indigenous peoples.

Many representatives stressed the need for the full and equal participation of indigenous peoples in all aspects of the CHRWG's work, including in developing the work plan, during sessions, in decision-making, in the right to vote, in preparation of the report, and at all inter-governmental meetings. Indigenous representatives had consistently emphasised the importance of flexible, frank and consensual methods of work. Accordingly, they had watched with dismay the development of adversarial methods of work, and the polarisation of indigenous and State delegations into separate and opposed blocs.

Several indigenous delegations, including that of the Saami Council, stressed the need for an approach to consensus in accordance with standard UN practice. Reference was made to ECOSOC resolution 1835 (LVI) of 14 May 1974 which defines consensus as general agreement without a vote, not necessarily with the agreement of all. Reference was also made to a 1976 UN Legal Opinion which defines consensus as every effort to achieve unanimous agreement but with those dissenting placing their concerns on the record (UN Doc ST/LEG/12 1976). It was said that if normal UN practice in relation to consensus were applied in the CHRWG, numerous articles would already have been adopted by consensus. Several delegations suggested that the impasse in relation to consensus might be overcome if the Chairperson were to ask those States which must dissent from the general trend to note their reservations, but not to block the consensus needed to move forward with the adoption of particular provisions of the Declaration.

Several indigenous participants commented upon the failure of States to respond to indigenous representatives' arguments in defence of the Declaration in terms of international law and theory, and consistency with standards articulated in other instruments. State delegations had largely ignored this analysis of international norms and practice. Several indigenous speakers commented on the disappointing failure of States to acknowledge the work of the UN's independent human rights treaty bodies which provides an important line of defence in efforts to advance support for the Declaration.

A representative of African indigenous peoples regretted the lack of African governments in the meeting. Indigenous delegations from

Australia had *"registered with grave concern the statement by the Austral-ian Government concerning the 'significant changes' needed to arrive at a document which can go forward. Such statements surely justify the very real fears of Indigenous participants in relation to States' intentions to dismember completely the existing text."*

Numerous delegations, including the Inuit Circumpolar Confer-ence (ICC), the Saami Council, the Indian Law Resource Center, the Aboriginal and Torres Strait Islander Commission (ATSIC), National Secretariat of Torres Strait Islander Organisations, National Aborigi-nal and Islander Legal Services Secretariat, Indigenous Woman Abo-riginal Corporation and the Foundation for Aboriginal and Islander Research Action reiterated their preparedness to consider changes which strengthen the text and are consistent with the principles of equality and non-discrimination, subject to unqualified recognition of the right of self-determination and collective rights and use of language of indigenous peoples in the Declaration. The representa-tive of ATSIC noted that since those criteria were first proposed, changes had been put forward, without any justification, which had obscured the clarity of and, weakened the existing text. There had also been the retrograde bracketing of the term indigenous peoples at the insistence of only a few State delegations.

Self-determination, land rights, natural resources: Interventions of indigenous delegations

In their interventions in the general debate on self-determination, indigenous representatives again affirmed the right of self-determi-nation, as formulated in article 3, as the fundamental provision in the Declaration. Numerous indigenous representatives expressed con-cern about initiatives to develop alternative wording for article 3. It was stated that the CHRWG had no mandate to lower international standards as applied to indigenous peoples. The right of self-deter-mination was said to be firmly established in international law, including in the Charter of the United Nations, common article 1 of the International Covenant on Civil and Political Rights (ICCPR) and International Covenant on Economic, Social and Cultural Rights (ICESCR), and the Vienna Declaration and Programme of Action, adopted by the 1993 World Conference on Human Rights ("the Vienna Declaration"), as well as having attained the status of ius cogens, or a peremptory norm of international law from which no derogation is permitted. The representative of the International Organization of Indigenous Resource Development stated that to negotiate alternate text for article 3 irrespective of indigenous peo-ples' views was contrary to General Recommendation XXIII(51) of the Committee on the Elimination of Racial Discrimination, adopted on 18 August 1997, which provides that *"no decisions directly relating to the... rights and interests [of indigenous peoples] are taken without their informed consent"*.

Indigenous speakers variously described self-determination as a way to strengthen the capacity of indigenous peoples to chart their economic, social, cultural and political destinies, to lessen conflict between indigenous peoples and States, to promote peaceful co-existence, and to enable indigenous peoples to bring about sustainable development. An indigenous representative from the Philippines noted that in the end, recognition of self-determination would strengthen the UN as a global body dedicated to defending the rights of the weakest and most vulnerable.

Several indigenous speakers urged States, in continuing the dialogue on self-determination, to have regard to the jurisprudence of the UN's human rights treaty bodies. Not only is it accepted practice in the treaty bodies to use language of "indigenous peoples". It is also general practice in the Human Rights Committee and the Committee on Economic, Social and Cultural Rights, the bodies responsible for supervising implementation of the two Covenants, to inquire in relation to common article 1 as to indigenous peoples' right of self-determination. Particular reference was made to the concluding observations of the Human Rights Committee on Canada (UN Doc CCPR/C/79/Add 105/1999, para 7) and Norway (UN Doc CCPR/C/79/Add 112/1999, para 17). In this regard, the representative of the Saami Council noted that Finland, Norway and the Russian Federation, by referring to internal self-determination, sought to impose a qualification not imposed by the Human Rights Committee.

Several indigenous representatives commented that States' concerns in relation to territorial integrity are taken care of by article 45 of the Declaration, which provides *"Nothing in this Declaration may be interpreted as implying for any State, group or person any right to engage in any activity or to perform any act contrary to the Charter of the United Nations."* Other indigenous representatives suggested that States' concerns in relation to territorial integrity were also protected by the General Assembly's 1970 *Friendly Relations Declaration* (resolution 2625). The *Friendly Relations Declaration* clarified the relationship between the principle of self-determination and those of territorial integrity and national unity, establishing that the right of self-determination as articulated in the UN Charter did not normally entail a right of secession from independent States. The *Friendly Relations Declaration* suggested a criterion of "effectively representative" to determine when indigenous peoples are no longer bound to exercise their right of self-determination by seeking to reach agreement on sharing power within existing States. This approach promoted the negotiation of agreements. The representative of Na Koa Ikaika O Ka Lahui Hawaii noted that as expressed in *Friendly Relations Declaration* and the *Vienna Declaration*, the principle of territorial integrity imposes a requirement of legitimacy on States.

Several indigenous speakers commented that international law does not impose any one form of exercise of self-determination. Others commented that in the exercise of self-determination, few, if any, indigenous peoples seek to dismember existing States. Instead, most take a functional approach, expressing a preference for recognition and constitutional reform within States in order to develop indigenous political institutions and determine their development in accordance with their own values.

Those indigenous organisations such as the ICC and Saami Council which have expressed a willingness to engage in a dialogue about changes that strengthen or clarify the existing text stated clearly that there can be no qualification of self-determination, and that it would be unacceptable and discriminatory to restrict indigenous peoples' self-determination to internal self-determination. Although the vast majority of indigenous peoples would chose to implement their right of self-determination through autonomy and self-government arrangements, the right could not be limited a priori to such arrangements.

Numerous indigenous speakers vigorously opposed attempts by some States to introduce a distinction between internal and external self-determination. For example, the representative of ATSIC stated that:

> "[T]he distinction suggested by some States between internal and external self-determination is **ahistorical** and **artificial**. It is **ahistorical** because it ignores the inherent nature of our right of self-determination. The equation of external self-determination with secession is **artificial** because it confines the right and cuts off choices. The right of self-determination requires States to recognise our human rights internally. It also requires recognition of our human rights at the international level. Our participation in UN fora is one external expression of self-determination which does not involve secession or independence. There may well be others."

The representative of ATSIC also referred to the proposal by the Chairperson at the 5th session in 1999 that future debate on self-determination be based on three premises, including that *"the universally accepted International Covenants, which contain the right to self-determination"* be taken as a basis for future discussion. The representative commented that in reaffirming its inability to accept inclusion of the term self-determination in the Declaration, Australia had apparently chosen to ignore the Chairperson's request.

Significant interventions on self-determination were made by representatives of the indigenous peoples of Africa and, for the first time, the Solomon Islands. It was stated that in Africa, democratic States are in a nascent state of development and that the rights of indigenous peoples must be tailored in. Mr Ian Aujare described self-determination as a fundamental issue in the Solomon Islands, referring to current social unrest inherited from colonisation, and the many problems not addressed in the decolonisation process.

Much less debate was devoted by indigenous speakers to the Declaration's provisions concerning land and resources. Indigenous speakers again urged States to have regard to developments in the jurisprudence of the Human Rights Committee and the Committee on the Elimination of Racial Discrimination. Numerous interventions referred to the CERD Committee's General Recommendation on the Rights of Indigenous Peoples, which calls on States to:

> "recognise and protect the rights of indigenous peoples to own, develop, control and use their communal lands and territories and resources and, where they have been deprived of their lands and territories traditionally used or otherwise inhabited or used without their free and informed consent, to take steps to return these land and territories. Only where this is for factual reasons not possible, the right to restitution should be substituted by the right to just, fair and prompt compensation. Such compensation should as far as possible take the form of lands and territories."

In relation to land and resource rights, several indigenous representatives urged States not to be limited by domestic constitutions, legislation or policy. It was said that such an approach would conflict fundamentally with the purpose of international human rights standard-setting. The representative of the African Indigenous and Minorities Peoples' Organisation noted that the Batwa people of the Great Lakes Area had been deprived of the enjoyment of the natural resources which constitute the basis of their survival. The Batwa people continued to be dispossessed through development initiatives including resettlement schemes, the creation of national parks and reallocation of land to private developers. An indigenous representative from the Philippines stated that throughout the world, indigenous peoples are losing control of their land and resources.

Self-determination, land rights, natural resources: Interventions of State delegations

In the general debate on self-determination, Norway referred to the critical stage of negotiations which have been reached in the CHRWG, and to the need to reach consensus on core principles in the Declaration. Norway remained convinced that the success of the CHRWG's efforts will depend on its ability again to consider self-determination. According to Norway, self-determination exercised within States included the right of indigenous peoples to participate at all levels of decision-making in legislative and administrative matters and in the maintenance and development of their political and economic systems. The Declaration contained various provisions concerned with the implementation of self-determination, including the right of indigenous peoples to maintain and develop their own economic and social systems, to control their own affairs, and to develop and make use of their own institutions if they so chose. It was crucial to find ways so that indigenous peoples can live within existing States through power sharing arrangements. In relation to land and resources, the Norwegian Government was currently preparing legislation concerning the use, management and ownership of land in Finnmark. A committee was being formed to consider Saami rights in other parts of Norway.

Finland expressed support for the term indigenous peoples because it makes meaningful the great number of collective number rights contained in the Declaration. Some features of collective rights were essential when seeking to preserve the identities of indigenous peoples. Finland supported self-determination in the Declaration provided that article 31 concerning self-government remained formulated in the manner proposed, that is, to refer to internal and local affairs. Self-determination contained two dimensions, internal and external. Finland considered the Declaration's land and resource provisions to require revision. They should be flexible in order to make possible a number of fair and just national solutions.

Canada commented that the issue raised by the Declaration was whether the right of self-determination applied to indigenous peoples living within existing States and, if so, what this right consisted of. As stated at previous sessions, Canada accepted a right to self-determination for indigenous peoples which respected the political, constitutional and territorial integrity of democratic States. Exercise of the right involved negotiations between States and the various indigenous peoples within those States to determine the political status of the peoples involved and the means of pursuing their economic, social and cultural development. Canada could accept many of the principles contained in Declaration's land and resource provisions. In particular, Canada recognised the right of indigenous peoples to own, control, develop and use their resources, as well as the right to determine and develop priorities, and the importance of adequate process. In order to ensure their universal application, however, the provisions had to be flexible enough to take account of many different national situations. For example, according to Canada the current text did not address the situation of indigenous peoples who had left their traditional lands and no longer lived in traditional communities.

Australia remained unable to accept the language of self-determination since this implies for many peoples the establishment of separate States. In relation to land and resource rights, Australia accepted that the relationship of indigenous peoples and their traditional lands is special and important, but was unable to accept the provisions of the Declaration in their present form. Venezuela stated that the new Constitution of Venezuela recognised the existence of indigenous peoples and communities, as well as their collective rights, and guaranteed direct representation of indigenous peoples through their representatives in the national assembly. In Venezuela, the original rights of collective ownership of ancestral lands were recognised. Denmark confirmed the support of Denmark and the Greenland Home Rule Government for the right of self-determination for indigenous peoples and for the inclusion of such right in the Declaration. During the last two to three decades, new forms of relationships between indigenous peoples and states had evolved. The establishment of the CHRWG and a Permanent Forum were examples of such evolution. Whilst Denmark could accept article 3 in its current wording, one way of accommodating the concerns of some States would be to retain the language of article 3 but expand upon article 45 as proposed by Finland.

Guatemala considered it unnecessary to redefine or restrict the right of self-determination. During the decolonisation period, the right to self-determination resulted in the birth of nations. Today, exercised within States, self determination enabled peoples and national groups to define their political status through processes of decentralisation and autonomy and to pursue their economic, social and cultural development. It was a contradiction to believe, on the one hand, in a pluralistic and participatory democratic system and, at the same time, to deny or restrict the right of self-determination. France confirmed its recognition of the right of indigenous peoples to self-determination, however not to the detriment of other populations in the territories concerned. The principle should be applied through negotiation and dialogue, and adapted to the circumstances of each case. France noted that the right of self-determination also contains a territorial aspect relating to land and resources.

The Russian Federation proposed the reformulation of the Declaration's provisions dealing with self-determination in order to reflect broad autonomy of indigenous peoples within State boundaries, without posing any detriment to the territorial integrity of the State. The Russian Constitution took into account the principles contained in the Declaration's land and resource provisions concerning the particular link of indigenous peoples with their land. New Zealand accepted a right of self-determination for indigenous peoples in the Declaration, if the meaning of the term was clearly elaborated in a manner consistent with New Zealand domestic understanding of the relationship between Maori and the Crown. Some of the present language of the Declaration (for example, references to autonomy, self-government and separate legal, taxation and judicial systems) were inconsistent with New Zealand policy, and more appropriate to the situation of indigenous people living on reservations than those integrated into the wider society as in New Zealand. The language of the Declaration would need to be clarified to ensure consistency with the Treaty of Waitangi settlement processes and policies, international understandings and domestic New Zealand law.

Ecuador expressed a commitment to work with indigenous representatives to find a fair and balanced solution in relation to the issue of self-determination. The Constitution of Ecuador recognised the diversity of cultures and languages, establishing Ecuador as a pluri-cultural and multi-ethnic state. Since the transition to democracy in 1979, political participation of indigenous peoples and Afro-Ecuadorian peoples had been guaranteed, and political participation processes further consolidated to guarantee collective rights to maintain, develop and strengthen indigenous traditions. In particular, Ecuador recognised the right of ownership of communal lands, the right to participate in the use, administration and conservation of renewable natural resources, an entitlement to be consulted in relation to the exploitation of non-renewable natural resources as well as to benefit from the proceeds of the exploitation of such resources, where possible to receive compensation for any harm caused, as well as collective intellectual property rights in ancestral knowledge. This positive approach led Ecuador to appeal to States with difficulties with the concept of self-determination to reach agreement in order to bring indigenous rights into line with existing international law and the UN Charter.

Spain supported the right of indigenous peoples to self determination, it being understood as an internal process of political, geographical and administrative decentralisation allowing indigenous peoples to participate at all levels of decision making, but not impacting upon the territorial integrity of democratic States. Spain supported an initiative of Denmark to hold seminars at which States and indigenous peoples might seek to achieve some common understanding in relation to self-determination. The representative of the World Bank referred to issues concerning land tenure and the control over natural resources as essential conditions for the eradication of poverty. Discussion of land and resource rights are normative aspects of development which should be respected and cultivated.

Cuba supported the inclusion of the right of self-determination in the Declaration, referring to the UN Charter and the General Assembly's *Friendly Relations Declaration*. The concerns of some States were not fully founded as the *Friendly Relations Declaration* adequately protected the political unity and territorial integrity of States. Japan stated that there were no international instruments within the UN system which refer to collective rights. According to Japan, the human person is the central subject of human rights, and such human rights can be exercised in community with others (article 3 of the UN Declaration on the Rights of Minorities). It was important not to take a discriminatory approach in the Declaration and to provide to indigenous peoples collective rights which no other groups enjoy.

Pakistan considered the concerns of some States in relation to territorial integrity to be ill founded. According to Pakistan, there was no contradiction between self-determination and territorial integrity, rather these were mutually reinforcing principles which strengthened democratic values at the national and international levels. Pakistan referred, as well, to the *Friendly Relations Declaration*. According to Pakistan, it was wrong to associate self-determination with the historical process of decolonisation: It was not colonisation which led to the emergence of self-determination, rather self-determination which required the process of decolonisation. The Mexican Constitution recognised particular forms of self-determination, including control, to the extent possible, by indigenous peoples of their own development. In addition, local constitutions in Mexico addressed self-determination in different ways. Bangladesh referred to global acceptance of self-determination as a right which includes the right to respect and preserve the identities of indigenous communities. However, the indigenous/non-indigenous dichotomy did not apply in Bangladesh where one was still grappling with questions of definition. As part of the Asian group, however, Bangladesh had decided to put aside the debate on the definition of indigenous peoples at the present time.

In his summary at the conclusion of the general debate, the Chairperson commented that most of the debate had involved repetition of previous positions without providing any new material. Nevertheless, he stressed some positive aspects including greater flexibility, willingness to listen and to take into account positions of other participants, as well as recognition that formal, rigid dialogue will not enable progress in the CHRWG. He expressed support for an approach which focussed both on the most difficult articles and intensified dialogue on crucial themes, whilst also considering the easiest articles in order to reach agreement and generate sufficient trust in order, at an appropriate time, to deal with the more sensitive issues in the Declaration.

Articles 1, 2, 12, 13, 14, 44 and 45:
The general approach of State delegations

In 1998 at the 4th session of CHRWG, then Chairperson Urrutia received an informal paper setting out concrete proposals of a number of State delegations, especially Australia, Canada and the USA, in relation to articles 15 to 18 of the Declaration. Indigenous representatives expressed grave concern that they had not participated in the elaboration of this non-consensual paper, and emphasised that the CHRWG had no mandate to engage in a drafting or negotiating exercise. In response, then Chairperson Urrutia confirmed that the paper was not a Chairperson's nor a Secretariat document, and that the CHRWG was not engaged in a drafting or negotiating exercise.

At the 5th and 6th sessions, Chairperson Chavez requested State delegations to continue their informal consultations with a view to bringing closer together various positions. Thus, the Chairperson actively encouraged the efforts of States to negotiate alternate language to the current text. At the 6th session, consultations focussed on articles 1, 2, 12, 13, 14, 44 and 45 and produced 7 documents for discussion in informal plenary sessions. In the first such plenary session, Chairperson Chavez referred participants to the summary of the general debate on these provisions at previous sessions, in particular at the 2nd and 5th sessions in 1996 and 1999 respectively (UN Doc E/CN 4/1997/102 and E/CN 4/2000/84).

Introducing the agenda item, Chairperson Chavez emphasised the need to demonstrate concrete progress to the CHR. Whilst he did not anticipate that consensus would be possible on any one proposal, he proposed to allow specific proposals and to hear comments upon them. In particular, he encouraged collective proposals. Paragraph 97 of the report of the 6th session provides that in all the

7 discussion documents, the term peoples appeared between brackets. The paragraph continues:

> *"Annex 1 of this report contains an explanatory note where the different positions of governmental delegations are reflected in connection with the use of the term 'peoples' in the proposals they have presented. It was noted that all indigenous delegations and some governmental delegations can accept use of the term indigenous peoples.*

98. *Indigenous representatives opposed the inclusion of the proposals made by governments in Annex 1 of this report as well as the explanatory note on the term 'peoples' because they were presented for discussion purposes and the content of the discussion paper appears in the report. They also requested the inclusion of a statement on the use of the term 'peoples' in annex 2 of this report, which contains indigenous representatives proposals. The Chair decided that both the proposals and the note would be included in Annex 1."*

Articles 1, 2, 12, 13, 14, 44 and 45:
The approach of indigenous delegations

Many indigenous delegations maintained strong opposition to commenting upon anything other than the original text of the Declaration, as approved by the Sub-Commission. These delegations considered the States' discussion papers to reflect an unacceptable departure from the consensual working methods agreed upon at the earliest sessions of the CHRWG. The agreed working methods had been to focus upon the original text as a basis for all discussion. Any comments addressed to the States' discussion papers amounted to tacit endorsement of the inevitability of textual change, and legitimised the approach of those States most aggressively pursuing such change.

Other indigenous participants, including the Saami Council, ICC, Assembly of First Nations, Indian Law Resource Center, Navajo Nation, the Aboriginal and Torres Strait Islander Commission and other indigenous delegations from Australia, and many indigenous delegations from Asia, analysed the States' proposals to determine whether they succeeded in rebutting the very high presumption as to the integrity of the current text. They considered whether the proposed changes were reasonable, necessary, improved and strengthened the existing text, and conformed with the principle of equality and the prohibition of racial discrimination. These participants concluded that the majority of proposed changes lacked any justification, and frequently obscured the clarity of or weakened the existing text.

Paul Chartrand on behalf of the Metis National Council proposed a test of functional clarity, according to which "*a thing is good enough if it does what it is designed to do*". In order to rebut the presumption of the validity of the current text, the test was whether the language was so ambiguous, its meaning so opaque that it failed to identify the subject matter the concern of the article. In accordance with this test, in asking whether the language of the Declaration was clear enough, States should consult with indigenous peoples because of: (i) their obligations as Members of the United Nations in relation to self-determination; and (ii) fundamental values of democracy which required the design and implementation of State policy in consultation with the intended beneficiaries.

Article 45

Article 45 of the Declaration, as drafted, provides:

> "*Nothing in this Declaration may be interpreted as implying for any State, group or person any right to engage in any activity or to perform any act contrary to the Charter of the United Nations.*"

The States' discussion paper on article 45 proposed no alternate text, however commented that:

> "*Although no alternate language is being proposed, this article is not yet ready for adoption, because it qualifies the entire Declaration and will have to be reviewed at a later stage.*"

Numerous indigenous delegations called on States to demonstrate tangible progress in consideration of the Declaration by the adoption, at first reading, of article 45. Several representatives commented that without the adoption of article 45, the suggestion that the absence of alternate language constituted progress was illusory. They referred to the CHRWG's commitment to securing concrete outcomes and emphasised the importance of solid confidence-building gestures on the part of States. Numerous indigenous representatives reminded participants that the CHRWG was currently engaged in a first reading of the Declaration. It was stated that the purpose of a first reading was to reach broad agreement on the language of provisions. At first reading, any matters requiring review at a later stage were noted. The purpose of a second reading was to address any matters identified at first reading for review at a later stage. The purpose of a second reading was to consider fine tuning said to be required as a result of the adoption, at first reading, of a draft text as a whole. Several indigenous representative reminded participants that article 45 of the Declaration is based upon article 30 of the Universal Declaration of Human Rights (UDHR).

States which spoke against adoption of article 45 included Australia and the USA. Argentina stated that the provision was not important, that it was "almost a standard, marginal text" which had precedents and could be adopted in its present form. Denmark commented that the provision dealt with a procedural issue, a technicality, and should be dealt with at a later stage. The representative of Denmark emphasised the interrelatedness of all provisions of the Declaration.

The Chairperson resisted calls to seek provisional adoption of article 45, stating that the consensus amongst States was to postpone its adoption, as stated in the discussion paper which had been tabled.

Article 44

Article 44 of the Declaration, as drafted, provides:

> "Nothing in this Declaration may be construed as diminishing or extinguishing existing or future rights indigenous peoples may have or acquire."

The alternate language proposed in the States' discussion paper places square brackets around the word peoples. Under the heading "Items for further Discussion", the discussion paper provides:

> "The term 'existing or future' in the English version is redundant; it si not consistent with the Spanish and French texts, which are clearer. We suggest that the English version be reviewed to make it consistent with the Spanish and French versions. Improved language may be developed through consideration of other international instruments, however the current language serves the purpose."

Ecuador and Sweden supported article 44 as drafted. Switzerland supported the article as it stands, and commented that it should also be possible to delete the square brackets around indigenous peoples and conduct the debate concerning the term indigenous peoples in connection with article 3. Guatemala stated that there should be no qualification, limitation or restriction on the word peoples. According to Guatemala, the concept of self-determination made no sense if used in connection with language of people, rather than peoples.

Spain could similarly support article 44 as it stands, noting that the reference to indigenous peoples presented no difficulties. France was able to accept the language as it stands, in particular the term peoples, even though France would prefer the expression "peoples or individuals". Numerous States, including Australia, Canada, Denmark, Finland, New Zealand, Norway and the Russian Federation, indicated that they could accept article 44 as drafted, but opined that the text might be improved, in particular by bringing into line the different language versions. The USA supported the Chairperson's approach to bracketing the term peoples.

In numerous interventions, indigenous representatives stated that in consideration of the Declaration, they could not accept, now or at any future time, any bracketing of the term indigenous peoples. Indigenous speakers urged those few States which oppose use of the term indigenous peoples to consider that their resistance had become the main stumbling block to progress in the CHRWG, and to reflect upon the destabilising effect that such intransigence was having on confidence-building. The representative of ATSIC appealed to those States which have no problems with the term indigenous peoples *"to assist us in ensuring that the UN applies its own standards universally and equally, that it acts without prejudice and without discrimination. We would appreciate your support in finding a way to continue our discussion of the Declaration without any bracketing of the 's' in indigenous peoples."* Several indigenous speakers called on those States which dissent from the general trend to note their reservations, in language along the lines of that contained in paragraph 4 of the reports of the CHRWG, but not to insist on square brackets and hence impede movement forward in discussion of the Declaration.

Article 1

Article 1 of the Declaration, as drafted, provides:

> *"Indigenous peoples have the right to the full and effective enjoyment of all human rights and fundamental freedoms recognized in the Charter of the United Nations, the Universal Declaration of Human Rights and international human rights law."*

The alternate language proposed in the States' discussion paper (i) places square brackets around the word peoples; (ii) introduces a reference to indigenous individuals; (iii) introduces before the phrase "international human rights law" the adjective "applicable"; (iv) replaces the term "law" with "instruments"; and (v) introduces a new second paragraph which provides:

"[2. Indigenous individuals may exercise their rights, including those set forth in this Declaration, individually as well as in community with other members of their group, without any discrimination.]"

Guatemala and Mexico supported the original text of article 1. Denmark, Ecuador, Finland and Switzerland similarly had no difficulties with the original text. Norway accepted the text as drafted but was open to improving and strengthening the text, and accommodating reasonable concerns of other delegations.

Australia, Canada, Japan, Norway, Spain, Sweden and the USA supported the introduction of the adjective "applicable" to qualify "international human rights law". Denmark, Finland and Switzerland could accept a reference to "applicable", even if, according to Switzerland, such a reference added little. Guatemala did not consider such a reference to be appropriate, nor did Denmark see any need for such a reference. Ecuador similarly considered the current text to be quite clear.

Canada emphasised the importance of a reference to indigenous individuals in the first article of the Declaration. To similar effect Japan, New Zealand, the Russian Federation and Spain. Ecuador considered that such a reference might be quite useful, provided that the reference to collective rights was maintained. Finland could accept such a reference. As a compromise, Switzerland could also accept a reference to individuals.

Canada rejected the proposed restriction to "international human rights instruments", rather than "international human rights law", as such restriction excluded the body of customary international law. To similar effect Denmark, Guatemala, Norway, Spain and Switzerland. The USA advocated use of the term "instruments", which term, it said, included customary international law.

Japan and the USA supported the proposed second paragraph of article 1. Sweden also supported the paragraph, the wording of which is drawn from article 27 of the ICCPR and the 1992 UN Declaration on the Rights of Persons belonging to National or Ethnic, Religious and Linguistic Minorities. Canada, Denmark, Finland, Guatemala, Norway, Spain and Switzerland opposed the proposed second paragraph, with Norway commenting that it added no value to the current text.

Indigenous representatives commented that the proposed introduction of a reference to indigenous individuals was unnecessary, referring to the protection conferred upon indigenous individuals by, amongst others, articles 2, 5, 6, 7, 8, 9, 18, 22, 32, 33, 43 and 45 of the Declaration. It was stated that indigenous individuals already enjoy, in theory though not in practice, the whole body of international human rights law concerning the rights of the individual. As at previous sessions of the CHRWG, indigenous speakers rejected the proposed introduction of a reference to "applicable" as unnecessary to improve the clarity of the text, or for any other reason. The representative of ATSIC posed the question: *"Surely, no State delegation is suggesting that the text, as drafted, can be construed to refer to inapplicable international human rights law?"*

Indigenous speakers consistently rejected the proposed limitation to international human rights instruments, rather than law as an unacceptable weakening of the text, the effect of which was to exclude the body of customary international law. In relation to the US intervention, one indigenous delegation was at a loss to understand how the term "instruments" could possibly be construed to include customary international law.

Like many States, indigenous representatives rejected the proposed second paragraph as contributing nothing by way of strengthening or clarifying the text. The representative of ATSIC, for example, stated that the rights of indigenous individuals and the concept of non-discrimination are already adequately dealt with elsewhere in the Declaration. The ATSIC representative continued: *"And with respect to the reference to the exercise of rights 'individually as well as in community with other members of the group', we vigorously oppose any attempt – unintended or surreptitious – to introduce into the Declaration language which is associated with international standards on the rights of minorities. It is well settled that indigenous peoples and ethnic minorities are conceptually distinct groups. This working group must not be used as a forum to reagitate questions which have been settled elsewhere."*

Article 2

Article 2 of the Declaration, as drafted, provides:

> *"Indigenous individuals and peoples are free and equal to all other individuals and peoples in dignity and rights, and have the right to be free from any kind of adverse discrimination, in particular that based on their indigenous origin or identity."*

The alternate language proposed in the States' discussion paper (i) places square brackets around the words "and peoples"; (ii) places square brackets around the adjective "adverse"; and (iii) introduces a new second sentence which provides:

> *"This does not preclude special measures as contemplated in article 1.4 of the International Convention for the Elimination of All Forms of Racial Discrimination."*

Finland, Norway and Switzerland could accept article 2 as drafted.

The USA and UK supported language for article 2 closer to that contained in article 2 of the UDHR. Australia and Guatemala commented that the adjective "adverse" could be eliminated. Ecuador, Guatemala and Norway could also support the deletion of "adverse".

Australia and Guatemala supported the introduction of the second sentence. Canada considered an explicit reference to "special measures" preferable in order to avoid any doubt. Ecuador and Finland could support such a proposal. Norway considered that the proposal required further discussion.

Indigenous representatives stated that the States' proposals concerning article 2 neither strengthened nor clarified the text, and were therefore neither necessary nor acceptable. It was stated that the adjective "adverse" was usefully employed in article 2 to distinguish between adverse discrimination and positive discrimination or affirmative action. Similarly, indigenous representatives stated that the proposed second sentence, with its reference to special measures, was superfluous. It was noted, for example, that the General Comments of the Human Rights Committee and the CERD Committee confirmed that the guarantee of equality and non-discrimination comprehends special measures. That is, international jurisprudence already established that special measures were consistent with the guarantee of equality and non-discrimination.

Article 12
Article 12 of the Declaration, as drafted, provides:

> "Indigenous peoples have the right to practise and revitalize their cultural traditions and customs. This includes the right to maintain, protect and develop the past, present and future manifestations of their cultures, such as archaeological and historical sites, artifacts, designs, ceremonies, technologies and visual and performing arts and literature, as well as the right to the restitution of cultural, intellectual, religious and spiritual property taken without their free and informed consent or in violation of their laws, traditions and customs."

The alternate language proposed in the States' discussion paper contains numerous square brackets and proposals in relation to article 12. Without setting out each proposal, the principal thrust of the alternate language is (i) to place square brackets around the word peoples; (ii) to introduce at the end of the first sentence a reference in square brackets to "in conformity with domestic laws";

(iii) to treat in separate paragraphs recognition of a right to practice and revitalise cultural traditions and the issue of return of cultural property; (iv) to place square brackets around "intellectual"; and (v) to introduce in connection with property taken without consent a temporal limitation to property taken "after the present Declaration comes into effect". The accompanying comments provide that whilst some States are concerned with the potential retroactive application of this part of article 12, "*[o]ther states accept that this paragraph could apply to property taken in the past*". The comments also provide several proposals for a new general paragraph on third party rights.

Finland considered the provisions of Part III of the Declaration, to which article 12 belongs, to be the least controversial in the Declaration. Accordingly, Finland could accept article 12 as drafted. Guatemala could also accept the language as drafted, but was prepared to discuss alternate language in order to make consensus possible. Brazil had no particular difficulties with the first part of article 12. However, Brazil had concerns in relation to the potential retroactive application of the 2nd part of the article to property taken in the past. For this reason, Brazil preferred language of "best possible efforts". Australia commented upon the need to have regard to the rights of others, and considered that the issue of intellectual property would be better dealt with in article 29. Australia had no difficulty with the retroactive application of article 12. Denmark could accept the first 2/3 of article 12 as drafted, but proposed the treatment of the words after "literature" dealing with restitution in a separate paragraph. Denmark also saw merit in the insertion of a separate article dealing with 3rd party rights, although expressed no preference for particular language at the present time.

New Zealand considered that the 2nd sentence needed to be tempered by an appropriate reference to the public interest, possibly through language of "as far as practicable". New Zealand preferred clarification of the part of article 12 dealing with restitution to ensure consistency with existing intellectual property conventions and NZ domestic law, and saw merit in moving this part of the article to the end of article 29. In relation to the first sentence of article 12, Japan supported the introduction of language "to the same extent as other nationals". In relation to the 2nd part of article 12, Japan considered that any restitution should be based upon appropriate national laws equally applied to all other persons, and should refer to property taken in "violation of relevant laws and regulations", rather than in "violation of their laws, traditions and customs".

Sweden supported the first sentence as drafted. In relation to the 2nd sentence, Sweden supported 2 paragraphs, the 2nd of which would commence "States shall make best efforts to promote the return to indigenous peoples of ...". Canada similarly supported the insertion of 2 paragraphs. In relation to the issue of third party rights, Canada supported the use of language consistent with article 18(3) of the ICCPR. Canada also commented that the issue of intellectual property was substantially dealt with in article 29, and therefore proposed the deletion of "intellectual" in the proposed new paragraph dealing with the return of property. The language proposed by Canada included the mandatory "shall" rather than "should", as proposed by some other State delegations.

France considered the present wording of article 12 to be too vague, especially in relation to restitution, and shared the concerns of some delegations in relation to 3rd party rights. France supported a separate article dealing with restitution. Switzerland supported the first half of article 12, and in relation to the 2nd half supported the deletion of the reference to intellectual property.

Indigenous representatives expressed alarm at the large number of brackets and qualifications proposed by States. Indigenous delegations also protested against the manner in which the discussion paper on article 12 had been presented. It was stated that the paper proposed a total of 25 changes to the text of article 12. It was presented in English only. And, on the spot, indigenous delegations were expected to analyse the 25 proposals, consult in relation to them, and prepare interventions in response. It was asked whether any State could seriously suggest that the process ensured equal and effective participation by indigenous delegations.

In their interventions on article 12, indigenous representatives again referred to the unacceptable bracketing of peoples. Numerous representatives commented on the unacceptable weakening of the current text wrought by the proposed reference to "in conformity with domestic laws". The effect of limiting article 12 or any other article to operate in conformity with existing domestic laws would be to render nugatory the rights contained in the Declaration and allow the Declaration to become an instrument to protect the status quo in States.

Similarly, indigenous delegations stated that the proposal to introduce the expression "as far as practicable" to qualify the rights referred to in article 12 represented an unacceptable weakening of the text. One delegation commented that in the implementation of all the rights in the Declaration, considerations of availability of resources and other practical issues would play a role. However, it was stated, these are issues which relate to all guarantees of human rights, and not just those in this Declaration. They were no reason to qualify any of the rights recognised in the Declaration. Moreover, it was said, issues of implementation were adequately addressed in article 37. For similar reasons, indigenous speakers also opposed the introduction of any language of "best" or "appropriate" efforts to qualify the minimum standards contained in the Declaration.

Consistently with previous interventions, indigenous speakers vigorously opposed the introduction of language of "should" in the second paragraph of the proposed alternate language. Several speakers referred to the statement of the delegation of Switzerland at previous sessions of the CHRWG that the Declaration must be drafted consistently with the UDHR. Indigenous speakers voiced particular opposition to the proposed redrafting of paragraph 2 to destroy the concept of a right to restitution of cultural, intellectual, religious and spiritual property. It was stated that the effect of the redrafting was to remove any obligation of States. The paragraph's non-retroactive application brought it into direct conflict with the international prohibition of racial discrimination. The States' proposals made the right conditional upon relevant laws and regulations, and thus dependent upon the whims of domestic law and policy makers. It was stated that the removal of the reference to intellectual property severely eroded the protection provided in the current text. Whilst article 29 dealt with the issue of intellectual property, it did not address the issue of restitution dealt with in article 12, as drafted.

Finally, with respect to the concerns of some States in relation to 3rd party rights, it was noted that the drafters of ILO Convention No 169 had not considered such a limitation to be necessary in that instrument. Accordingly, it should have no place in the UN Declaration.

Article 14
Article 14 of the Declaration, as drafted, provides:

> *"Indigenous peoples have the right to revitalize, use, develop and transmit to future generations their histories, languages, oral traditions, philosophies, writing systems and literatures, and to designate and retain their own names for communities, places and persons.*
>
> *States shall take effective measures, whenever any right of indigenous peoples may be threatened, to ensure this right is protected and also to ensure that they can understand and be understood in political, legal and administrative proceedings, where necessary through the provision of interpretation or by other appropriate means."*

The alternate language proposed in the States' discussion paper (i) places square brackets around the word peoples; and (ii) places square brackets around the second paragraph, with the commentary that the issues contained in the paragraph should be addressed in the context of other articles of the Declaration, in particular:

- *"States shall take effective measures, whenever any right of indigenous peoples may be threatened, to ensure this right is protected" should be considered in the context of articles 37 and 39; and*

- *"to ensure that they can understand and be understood in political, legal and administrative proceedings, where necessary through the provisions of interpretation or by other appropriate means" should be considered in the context of article 19.*

Ecuador had no difficulty accepting both paragraphs of article 14 as drafted, as these were simply the application of universally recognised human rights principles to indigenous peoples. Denmark, Finland, Norway, the Russian Federation, Spain, Sweden and Switzerland could accept article 14 as drafted, but agreed that it might be more appropriate to deal with the 2nd part of article 14 elsewhere in the Declaration. Denmark and the Philippines did not support the limiting language in the 2nd paragraph "whenever any right of indigenous peoples may be threatened". In a move applauded by numerous indigenous delegations, Mexico declined to associate itself with any square bracketing of the 2nd paragraph of article 14. In relation to the 2nd paragraph, Mexico proposed the removal of the qualification "where necessary" and the insertion of "and effective" after the adjective appropriate.

Ukraine supported the alternative version of article 14. Australia, Canada, France and New Zealand supported the first paragraph of article 14 as drafted (with France preferring to see a reference to individual rights), but considered the issues in the 2nd paragraph better dealt with elsewhere in the Declaration. If the 2nd part were dealt with elsewhere in the Declaration, Canada, Denmark and Sweden would wish to see a reference in article 14 to the obligation of States to take effective measures to ensure these rights are protected. Brazil sought clarification from indigenous peoples' organisations of the reference to "political" and "administrative" proceedings in the 2nd paragraph, and of the costs implications in particular circumstances. Argentina was similarly concerned at the costs implications of this aspect of the 2nd paragraph.

Indigenous representatives again expressed their concern at the lack of time to prepare for discussion of the States' discussion paper on article 14. Those few indigenous representatives who were in a position to participate in the discussion on article 14 urged the

CHRWG to adopt article 14 in its original text, as there were no proposals for alternate text.

Article 13

Article 13 of the Declaration, as drafted, provides:

> *"Indigenous peoples have the right to manifest, practice, develop and teach their spiritual and religious traditions, customs and ceremonies; the right to maintain, protect, and have access in privacy to their religious and cultural sites; the right to the use and control of ceremonial objects; and the right to the repatriation of human remains.*
>
> *States shall take effective measures, in conjunction with the indigenous peoples concerned, to ensure that indigenous sacred places, including burial sites, be preserved, respected and protected."*

The alternate language proposed in the States' discussion paper (i) places square brackets around the word peoples; (ii) inserts the expression "in accordance with human rights standards" after "ceremonies" in the 2nd line; (iii) recasts the remainder of paragraph 1 as an obligation of States to take reasonable measures; (iv) qualifies the reference to States'' obligation with the expression "[s]ubject to domestic laws"; (v) replaces every reference to "shall" in the current text with the expression "shall/should"; (vi) introduces the adjective "reasonable" before "access" in the first paragraph; (vii) places square brackets around "use and control of ceremonial objects" in the 1st paragraph and moves this language, with the qualification "where necessary" to the end of the 2nd paragraph; (viii) inserts in square brackets after "repatriation of human remains" a reference to "and associated funerary objects"; (ix) replaces the obligation in the 2nd paragraph to "take effective measures" with language of "make best efforts"; and (x) inserts in square brackets next to "in conjunction" in the first line of the 2nd paragraph the term "consultation".

The discussion paper on article 13 was again presented only in English. It was not made available until the final informal meeting of the Working Group, thus preventing its discussion at the 6th session. The Chairperson initially proposed including the paper in the report of the session so that it could be translated and made available in the official languages of the UN. Indigenous representatives voiced strong opposition to the inclusion of the proposal in Annex 1 of the report, as the annex only contains proposals already discussed in the working group. Its inclusion, it was said, would misrepresent the discussion in relation to it. The Chairperson acceded to the protest of indigenous participants, noting that there was no consensus in relation to the inclusion of the paper on article 13 in annex I.

Annex 1:
Amendments proposed by Governments for future discussion

As at CHRWG5 in 1999, again at CHRWG6 the annexes to the report were the subject of much controversy. Annex I, entitled "AMEND-MENTS PROPOSED BY GOVERNMENTS FOR FUTURE DISCUS-SION", contains the alternate texts for articles 1, 2, 12, 14, 44 and 45 proposed by States at the 6th session, as well as texts for articles 15, 16, 17 and 18 proposed at the 5th session. In addition, the Annex contains an Explanatory Note on the bracketed use of the term indigenous peoples in the Declaration.

In this way, States have set up their own text, rather than that of the Declaration, as the basis for future discussions. Annex 1 does not reproduce the comments found in the original discussion papers, which reflect that some States could accept the text as drafted, or opposed particular changes proposed. Nor does Annex 1 reflect the actual debate in informal plenary sessions during which a significant number of States indicated that they supported the text as drafted, and opposed changes proposed.

States have also formalised their own closed inter-governmental sessions as the de facto mechanism for redrafting the Declaration. In this way, the are seeking to piece together a Declaration, the text of which is presented to indigenous representatives in plenary sessions as a fait accompli. This is tolerably clear from the fact that the States' proposals reproduced in Annex 1 are settled before indigenous representatives have any opportunity to comment upon them in an informal plenary session. Again, Annex 1 fails to reveal the varying degrees of enthusiasm amongst States for this process.

During the course of the 6th session, indigenous representatives expressed particular concern in relation to what was said to be the provocative nature of the "Explanatory Note" on the term indigenous peoples. This "Explanatory Note" is worded in language more specific and restrictive than that contained in Annex 1 to the report of the 5th session (UN Doc E/CN 4/200/WG 15/CRP 4) and in paragraph 4 of the reports of the CHRWG. In particular, it introduces a new reference to article 1(3) of ILO Convention No 169, as well as new possible expressions "indigenous populations" and "individuals in community with others". The Explanatory Note provides:

> *"There is no consensus on the use of the term 'indigenous peoples' at the Working Group on the Draft Declaration (WGDD). Some States*

can accept the use of the term 'indigenous peoples'. Some States can accept the sue of the term "indigenous peoples" pending consideration of the issue in the context of discussions on the right of self-determination. Other States cannot accept the use of the term 'indigenous peoples', in part because of the implications this term may have in international law including with respect to self-determination and individual and collective rights. Some delegations have suggested other terms in the Declaration, such as 'indigenous individuals', 'persons belonging to an indigenous group', 'indigenous populations', 'individuals in community with others' or 'persons belonging to indigenous peoples'. In addition, the terms used in individual articles may vary, depending on the context. Some delegations have suggested that if the term 'indigenous peoples' is used, we should also refer to Article 1.3 of ILO 169. Hence, the bracketed use of the term 'indigenous peoples' in the draft Declaration is without prejudice to an eventual agreement on terminology."

Annex 2:
Proposals by Indigenous Representatives

At the 5th session in 1999, in response to the use of square bracketing in the discussion papers of States, the Indigenous Caucus proposed an "Annex on the term indigenous peoples" for inclusion in the final report. That annex was not included in the final report. At the 6th session, however, the Chairperson agreed to include in Annex II, entitled "PROPOSALS BY INDIGENOUS REPRESENTATIVES", an "Explanatory note on the use of the term indigenous peoples" prepared by the Indigenous Caucus. That Explanatory Note sets out the position of indigenous peoples' representatives in relation to the term indigenous peoples, providing *inter alia*:

"There can be no doubt that we are peoples with distinct historical, political and cultural identities. We are united by our histories as distinct societies, by our languages, laws, traditions. In addition, the profound social, cultural, economic and spiritual relationships of indigenous peoples with our lands, territories and resources are unique. Indigenous peoples are unquestionably peoples in every legal, political, social, cultural and ethnological meaning of the term. It would be discriminatory, illogical and unscientific to identify us in the United Nations Declaration on the Rights of Indigenous peoples as anything less than peoples. ...

We continue to insist that the United Nations apply its own standards universally and equally, that it accord us the same rights as other peoples in the world, that it act without prejudice and without discrimination. We cannot agree, now or at any future time in consideration of the Declaration, to any qualification, explanation, definition, bracketing, parenthesizing or footnoting of the term indigenous peoples or peoples.

The term indigenous peoples is well-established in international and national legal practice and ahs been consistently employed by the United Nations own expert human rights treaty bodies. Finally, since the establishment of the CHR working group on the Declaration in 1995, numerous States have accepted the usage of the term indigenous peoples."

Outcomes

The 6th session of the CHRWG did not see the adoption of a single article of the Declaration. Instead, it saw the inclusion in Annex 1 to its report of alternate language proposed by States for articles 1, 2, 12, 14, 44 and 45. With the proposals in relation to articles 15, 16, 17 and 18 annexed to the report of the 5th session, this brings to ten the articles of the Declaration in relation to which States have proposed alternate text. After 6 sessions of the CHRWG, only two articles of the Declaration have been adopted, and these in 1998: article 5 which provides *"Every indigenous individual has the right to a nationality"*; and article 43 which provides *"All the rights and freedoms recognized herein are equally guaranteed to male and female indigenous individuals"*.

In their approaches to the Declaration, State delegations can be divided into the following three blocs:

1. Those which support the adoption of some or all of the articles under discussion as drafted: The Nordics (Denmark, Finland, Norway, Sweden); Latin Americans (Brazil, Cuba, Ecuador, Guatemala, Mexico), Spain and Switzerland; Pakistan.

2. Those which support the principles contained in particular articles but insist on amendments to the current text. More flexible: France, New Zealand, Peru, the Philippines, Russian Federation, Ukraine, Venezuela. Less flexible: Argentina, Bangladesh, Canada, China.

3. Those which challenge fundamental principles underlying the Declaration, in particular, the concept of self-determination, language of indigenous peoples and/or the recognition of collective rights: Australia, Japan, the United Kingdom and the USA.

In assessing the relative influence of each of these positions, it is noteworthy that two members of the Security Council, the UK and the USA, belong to the bloc which raises fundamental, conceptual objections. Three other members of the Security Council, China, France and the Russian Federation, are closer to the compromise bloc. Generally speaking, the 6th session saw reasonably strong support for the Declaration from Asian Governments (with the exception of Japan), the Latin Americans (especially Ecuador and Guatemala), the Nordics (especially Denmark), Spain and Switzerland; a silence on the part of African governments; continuing obstructionist interventions by the UK; continuing positive shifts by Brazil and France; the entrenchment of a division in the CANZUS bloc (Canada, Australia, New Zealand and the USA), with Canada and New Zealand acting as independent brokers, and Australia and the USA consolidating their position as hard-liners.

The activity of States during the 6th session can be evaluated as follows:

1. Most active: Argentina, Australia, Bolivia, Brazil, Canada, Denmark, Ecuador, Finland, France, Guatemala, Japan, Mexico, New Zealand, Norway, Russian Federation, Spain, Sweden, Switzerland, Venezuela, UK and the USA.

2. Largely silent: Bangladesh, Chile, China, Cuba, Mauritius, Pakistan, Peru, Philippines, Ukraine.

3. Silent: Belarus, Colombia, Costa Rica, Egypt, Estonia, Germany, Holy See, India, Indonesia, Latvia, Malaysia, Nepal, Panama, South Africa, Togo, Uruguay.

4. Previously attended CHRWG but did not attend the 6th session: Algeria, Angola, Austria, Belgium, Bolivia, El Salvador, Ethiopia, Fiji, Honduras, Iran, Iraq, Italy, Jordan, Kenya, Libya, Morocco, Netherlands, Nicaragua, Nigeria, Paraguay, Poland, Portugal, Saudi Arabia, South Korea, Sudan, Thailand, Vietnam.

It is noteworthy that the number of active State participants has decreased since the first session of the CHRWG in 1995, with an increasing number of States registering as participants and remaining absent, silent or largely silent throughout the 6th session. It is also tolerably clear that after six sessions, the consensual working methods agreed upon in relation to all aspects of the CHRWG's work have broken down. Despite much rhetoric about inclusive, transparent processes, it is evident that States have opened up the text adopted by the WGIP and Sub-Commission for redrafting. The general debate on process which took place during the first week failed to secure any change to the formalisation of closed inter-governmental sessions as the de facto mechanism for redrafting the Declaration. Despite differing degrees of keenness amongst States about the inter-governmental redrafting exercise, no State has been willing openly to challenge the approach nor to propose alternative working methods.

Notwithstanding frequent affirmations by States of the importance of maintaining a general dialogue on the fundamental issues and concepts underlying the Declaration, the value of such dialogue is not immediately apparent. Despite such formal dialogue, many questions which indigenous representatives have raised remain unanswered. Similarly, numerous attempts by indigenous representatives to address issues raised by States have met with no response. Virtually every change proposed in the States' discussion papers on articles 1, 2, 12, 14, 44 and 45 has been proposed at a previous session. Similarly, almost every point made in an indigenous intervention in defence of those articles has been made at a previous session. As at previous sessions, numerous State delegations had expressed an ability to live with the text of these articles as drafted. As a result of their participation in the informal inter-governmental drafting sessions, however, supportive States found themselves shifting to accommodate the most inflexible of State positions in an effort to build consensus.

Nor is it clear that informal attempts to progress dialogue have yielded better results. For example, in the middle of the second week of the 6th session, an informal informal meeting was held, attended by indigenous and State representatives and co-chaired by a representative of the Indigenous Caucus and a representative of States. The meeting provided a less formal setting in which to exchange views on issues such as self-determination, the term indigenous peoples, collective rights, the use of the expression shall/should, references to domestic law. The exchange of views saw the recitation by delegations of well-rehearsed and known positions. There was no principled explanation, for example, by Australia of why it no longer supports self-determination, despite having been the first State in the WGIP to support its unqualified inclusion in the Declaration. Nor was there any credible justification by the UK and USA for their insistence on language of "should" rather than "shall", as found in the UDHR. Nor did the USA make any attempt to account for the apparent inconsistency between the recognition of collective rights and self-determination in USA domestic law, and the USA's steadfast refusal to countenance their recognition internationally.

If States are genuine in their desire to ensure meaningful participation of indigenous representatives, they must address as a matter of priority the inequalities in resources available to indigenous representatives and States in terms of preparation for and participation in the CHRWG. In relation to the States discussion papers, there was insufficient time adequately to analyse the proposals, to caucus and to respond to proposed textual changes. A particular difficulty arose as the Anglophone instigators of the process had failed to make adequate provision for translation. This placed many indigenous representatives at a considerable disadvantage in their ability to analyse and respond to proposed changes. Such an off-handed approach can only exacerbate the increasing sense of alienation and frustration amongst indigenous delegations.

Within the Indigenous Caucus, formal unanimity again prevailed. However, there was at times more activity within the regions and across the regions than within caucus. As reported previously, there has from the outset been tension within the Caucus as to whether the Declaration, as drafted, ought be defended to the end, or whether changes which improve or strengthen the text might be countenanced. Proponents of the latter view accept the reality of States' insistence on involvement in shaping the final version. It may well be that such differences of approach are fruitful, and lead to the deployment of a range of different, not inconsistent strategies for engagement in defence of the Declaration.

On a more encouraging note, there continues to be movement in the positions of States in the debate on self-determination and indigenous peoples. As reported last year, France now accepts language of indigenous peoples and a concept of self-determination, however qualified. At the 6th session, the Federation of Amerindian people of Guyana congratulated France on taking a step forward and making a major effort towards recognition of rights of indigenous peoples. Similar positive shifts were evident in the interventions of Brazil. It is unmistakable that the Nordic States, the Latin Americans, Spain and Switzerland remain generally sympathetically disposed towards the Declaration. Such sympathy has ensured that after 6 sessions of the CHRWG, the basic principles in each provision have been respected and the basic structure of the Declaration remains intact. It is also apparent that these States, at least, are listening to the interventions of indigenous delegations. The result has been a tempering of the impact of the redrafting zeal of some States and a thwarting, as yet, of efforts to wreak irremediable harm upon the Declaration.

THE UNITED NATIONS PERMANENT FORUM ON INDIGENOUS ISSUES

The Economic and Social Council (ECOSOC) of the United Nations made a historic decision on 28 July 2000, when the Council adopted a resolution to establish a "Permanent Forum on Indigenous Issues".

This decision is a significant milestone in the decades-long struggle of indigenous peoples to gain standing within the global community. The new UN body will formally integrate indigenous peoples and their representatives into the structure of the United Nations. It marks the first time that representatives of states and non-state actors have been accorded parity in a permanent representative body within the United Nations.

The Permanent Forum contains unique opportunities for enhancing the human rights, as well as the economic, cultural and social rights, of indigenous peoples. However, to what extent its establishment will cut an edge and make a difference to the world's indigenous peoples still remains to be seen. It is IWGIA's firm opinion that a Permanent Forum *might* have the potential of becoming a catalyst for the improvement of the rights of indigenous peoples worldwide. Under the umbrella of the United Nations system the Permanent Forum is the most promising institutional mechanism to which indigenous peoples will have access in order to enhance their social, economic and human rights; its establishment will hopefully consolidate and make more fiscally efficient the work of the UN regarding indigenous peoples.

In the year 2000, by establishing the Permanent Forum on Indigenous Issues the United Nations has come closer to fulfilling one of the goals of the International Decade of the World's Indigenous People. Another important but still outstanding goal is the adoption of a universal declaration on the rights of indigenous peoples.

Historical Facts about the Process Leading to the Establishment of the Permanent Forum on Indigenous Issues

The discussion concerning the establishment of a Permanent Forum for Indigenous Peoples within the United Nations system has been going on for nearly a decade.

The idea of establishing a permanent forum dealing with indigenous issues was derived from the realisation amongst the indigenous representatives, members of the Sub-Commission's Working

Group on Indigenous Populations and many member states of the UN that there was no permanent mechanism within the United Nations system to address the problems of the indigenous peoples of the world.

Though mention of the idea for a permanent forum can be found in several UN documents, it was not until the World Conference on Human Rights in Vienna in 1993 that the concept was seriously considered on the United Nations Agenda. The Vienna Declaration and Program of Action recommended the establishment of a Permanent Forum. The same year, when the General Assembly adopted the program of activities for the International Decade of the World's Indigenous People (1995-2004), it identified the establishment of the Forum as one of the main objectives of the Decade.

Since then the issue of establishing a Permanent Forum for indigenous peoples within the UN system has been the subject of many deliberations and resolutions by the Working Group on Indigenous Populations, the Sub-commission on Discrimination and Protection of Minorities, the Commission on Human Rights, ECOSOC and the General Assembly. Two workshops of experts on the subject have been organised, in Copenhagen, Denmark (June 1995) and in Santiago de Chile (June to July 1997), respectively. In between the two workshops a "Review of the existing mechanisms, procedures and programs within the United Nations concerning Indigenous Peoples" was published. This Review made by the Secretary General clearly illustrated the need for an integrative and coordinating mechanism within the United Nations for indigenous peoples.

Moreover, since the first workshop took place, indigenous organisations have expressed the need to initiate indigenous activities focusing on information, discussion and strategy development with regard to the establishment of the Forum, between indigenous organisations themselves at regional level. Five indigenous international conferences have been held in Temuco (Chile), Kuna Yala (Panama), Indore (India), Arusha (Tanzania) and Chiang Mai (Thailand). The indigenous declarations resulting from those conferences and the Arctic Indigenous Peoples Declaration on the establishment of the Permanent Forum have been included both as official UN documentation and as annexes in some of the UN meetings reports.

The indigenous declarations resulting from those conferences have been included both as official UN documentation and as annexes in some of the UN meetings reports.

Based on the recommendations from the workshops the Commission on Human Rights in 1998 adopted a resolution that opened the way for a new stage in the process towards the establishment of the Permanent Forum. This resolution decided to establish an Ad Hoc

Working Group to elaborate and consider further proposals for the possible establishment of the Permanent Forum. With regard to indigenous participation, the resolution stated that they would benefit from the same procedures as those established for the Working Group on the Draft Declaration.

The Working Group met for the first time in 1999, and the most significant advance made in this session was that the idea of establishing a Permanent Forum was consolidated and progress was achieved in discussions on fundamental issues such as mandate, level and composition.

Based on the results of this session, the Commission on Human Rights in 1999 decided to renew the Working Group's mandate in order for it to finalise its work. The second and last meeting of the Ad Hoc Working Group was held in February 2000, when governments achieved a long awaited consensus on the establishment the Permanent Forum for Indigenous Peoples. Based on the agreements reached in the 2nd Ad Hoc Working Group, the Danish Government sponsored a resolution for the establishment of the Permanent Forum on Indigenous Issues for the 56th session of the UN Commission on Human Rights. On the 27th of April 2000, the resolution to establish a Permanent Forum on Indigenous Issues was adopted in its entirety by a roll call vote of 43 in favour to none against it, with nine abstentions.

In July 2000, the United Nations Economic and Social Council considered the UN Commission on Human rights resolution and adopted by consensus the establishment a Permanent Forum for Indigenous Issues – an unprecedented event in the international community. The General Assembly endorsed ECOSOC's decision in its Millennium Session in December 2000.

Short Description of the Permanent Forum

The Permanent Forum on Indigenous Issues will be a **subsidiary organ of the Economic and Social Council**. It will consist of **16 members**, eight members are to be nominated by governments and elected by the Council, and eight are to be appointed by the President of the Council following formal consultations with the bureau on the basis of broad consultations with indigenous organisations and groups. The selection process is to take into account principles of representation and the diversity and geographical distribution of indigenous peoples.

All members of the Forum are to serve in their personal capacity as independent experts on indigenous issues for a period of three years with the possibility of re-election or reappointment for one further period.

The Forum shall hold an annual session of ten working days at the United Nations Office at Geneva or at the United Nations Headquarters in New York or at such other place as the Permanent Forum may decide in accordance with existing financial rules and regulations of the United Nations.

The meetings will be open in the same sense as the Working Group on Indigenous Populations (WGIP). Governments, intergovernmental organisations, NGOs as well as organisations of indigenous peoples may participate in the Forum as observers. Although the WGIP has only five government-appointed members, hundreds of indigenous persons and others have over the years participated in its meetings.

The Permanent Forum shall submit an annual report to the ECOSOC Council on its activities, including any recommendations for approval; the report shall be distributed to the relevant United Nations organs, funds, programmes and agencies.

The financing of the Permanent Forum shall be provided from within existing resources through the regular budget of the United Nations and its specialised agencies and through such voluntary contributions as may be donated.

Five years after its establishment, an evaluation of the functioning of the Permanent Forum, including the method for selection of its members, shall be carried out by ECOSOC.

Finally, the continuing role, even the existence, of the UN Working Group on Indigenous Populations after the establishment of the Forum is being questioned. The ECOSOC resolution states on this point that once the Permanent Forum has been established and has held its first annual session, the Council will review all existing mechanisms, procedures and programmes within the United Nations concerning indigenous issues, including the Working Group on Indigenous Populations, with a view to rationalizing activities, avoiding duplication and overlap and promoting effectiveness.

The Regional Division

The issue regarding the manner in which the eight indigenous members shall be geographically distributed has been an issue that indigenous peoples have been successful in achieving consensus on in 2000.

In an indigenous caucus held in Geneva on Sunday, 26 November 2000 during the 6th Session of the Open Ended Inter-Sessional Working Group on the Draft United Nations Declaration on the Rights of

Indigenous Peoples, participants thoroughly discussed the issue of the geographic distribution of the indigenous members of the Forum and agreed that eight indigenous representatives be selected from the following regions:

1. Arctic/Europe
2. Africa
3. Asia
4. North America
5. Central/South America and the Caribbean
6. Pacific
7. Former USSR and Eastern Europe
8. Rotating an additional seat between three regions – Asia, Africa and Central/South America and the Caribbean.

The Caucus also agreed that Central/South America and the Caribbean would be the first region to hold the 8th seat.

This regional division has since then been endorsed by several indigenous meetings where the issue of the Permanent Forum was discussed.

Remaining Challenges

Yet, many challenges remain before the Permanent Forum is finally established and can start its work in 2002 as planned.

One is the nomination of the eight indigenous members of the Forum. Indigenous peoples, unlike the member states of the United Nations, do not have approved organisational structures at regional level to enable them to nominate their representatives. While the resolution refers to broad consultations of the ECOSOC President with the indigenous organisations, there are no criteria to define what constitutes broad consultation.

The first nomination process of indigenous peoples is important in many ways, and indigenous peoples have emphasised that regional consultations being organised by indigenous peoples for the nomination of indigenous members is the best process "to ensure broad consultation with indigenous organisations" as enshrined in the resolution on the Permanent Forum on Indigenous Issues.

Unless indigenous peoples are able to nominate their representatives after the widest consultations possible, many governments may propose or nominate the indigenous peoples' representative instead. This would obviously be done without the participation and consent of the indigenous peoples, and it would be contrary to the spirit for establishing the Permanent Forum.

Moreover, indigenous peoples have also expressed their concern about the circular sent by the High Commissioner for Human Rights on the 26th of February 2001 inviting indigenous peoples' organisations to submit their nominations. Indigenous peoples believe that although calling for nominations from different indigenous peoples' organisations facilitates participation by all indigenous peoples, it excludes indigenous organisations' own regional consultation processes for the nomination of indigenous members. If the UNHCHR or the Secretariat of the Permanent Forum receives a large number of nominations from individual indigenous peoples organisations, indigenous peoples will effectively be denied the opportunity to nominate members through a their own consultation processes. In such a scenario, the Secretariat would effectively be screening the indigenous members, contrary to the resolution on the Permanent Forum.

From IWGIA's point of view the Forum will only be able to play an important role if it is closely linked to indigenous peoples' organisations and communities; if this sort of connection does not exist, the Forum will risk merely becoming an entity that is detached from reality.

Another remaining problem is the location of the Forum Secretariat. Indigenous peoples representatives have consistently demanded that the Permanent Forum should have its own secretariat staffed by indigenous persons. Since the Forum is established directly under ECOSOC and concerns itself with many other issues than human rights, indigenous peoples have strongly emphasised that it should be independent and not located under the High Commissioner for Human Rights (HCHR). Indigenous peoples have repeatedly expressed that the lack of a separate secretariat for the Permanent Forum will seriously hamper fulfilling the mandate of the Permanent Forum. They have also stressed the relevance of giving "preference to equally qualified indigenous candidates" for the staffing of the Secretariat of the Permanent Forum. At present it is still unclear whether the Secretariat of the Permanent Forum will be placed in the United Nations Headquarters in New York or in UN quarters in Geneva.

To what extent some governments and the UN bureaucracy will use the opportunity, maybe under cover of saving money, to have the Secretariat of the Permanent Forum located under the HCHR, and thus indirectly try to restrict its competence, still remains to be seen.

Final remarks

Now six years into the "International Decade of the World Indig-enous People" the establishment of the Permanent Forum on Indig-enous Issues is the most significant and concrete step so far taken by the United Nations system to address the unique issues faced by indigenous peoples. IWGIA sees this as the first indication of a political intent to put into practice the goals of the Decade, which the UN outlined as the strengthening of international cooperation for the solution of the problems faced by the indigenous peoples of the world.

However, IWGIA is fully aware of some of the pitfalls of the Permanent Forum in its current form. The Permanent Forum on Indigenous Issues as established does not meet the entirety of aspi-rations of indigenous peoples, but in our view, although the Perma-nent Forum is not an ideal construction, it is a compromise that after all is the first body within the UN system where indigenous peoples are being represented. It can never be perfect or ideal, and all interested parties must make every attempt to make it as ideal as possible. Furthermore, it is not to be forgotten that the effectiveness of the Permanent Forum in the end not only depends on the indi-vidual members of the Forum but also on the competence, credibility and legitimacy of those who want to make an impact on its work. Finally, the workings and doings of the Permanent Forum constitute a process continuously to be improved.

TOWARDS INTEGRATION OF NON-INDEPENDENT COUNTRIES IN THE UNITED NATIONS SYSTEM

The integration of non-independent countries (NICs) in programmes and activities of the United Nations system is an important element in the promotion of the self-determination process for those NICs which are *non*-self-governing, and for the overall development process of the *self-governing* NICs as well. As defined by the United Nations, legitimate models of governance are achieved through independence, free association, or integration with full political rights.[1] Independent states have full access to the U.N. system, while the non-independent countries, including the non-self-governing and self-governing territories, have partial and often inconsistent access.

Table 1. Non-Independent Countries as defined by United Nations Principles

Non-Self-Governing	Self-Governing Territories	Former Territories that were integrated (for comparison purposes only)
Caribbean: Anguilla Bermuda Netherlands British Virgin Islands Cayman Islands Montserrat Turks & Caicos Islands U.S. Virgin Islands	Aruba Antilles Puerto Rico	Guadeloupe & dependencies Martinique French Guiana
Pacific: American Samoa Guam New Caledonia Tokelau	Northern Mariana Islands Cook Islands Micronesia (Fed. States) Marshall Islands Belau (Palau) French Polynesia Wallis and Futuna	Hawaii

The self-governing nature of Puerto Rico and the Northern Mariana Islands vis a vis their respective 'commonwealth' arrangements with the United States has sparked increased interest from scholars due to the continual unilateral authority of the U.S. Congress to legislate for those 'self-governing' territories. The limitations of sovereignty exercised in the Federated States of Micronesia, Marshall Islands and Belau, pursuant to their free association agreement with the U.S., are also being reviewed in the academic community. The unilateral removal of French Polynesia and Wallis and Futuna from U.N. non-self-governing status without U.N. review is a further area of debate. Further, some territories like Easter Island, administered by Chile, are not even considered as appropriate for discussion in the self-government debate.[2]

Legislative Authority

Regarding the participation of non-independent countries in the United Nations system, it is important to recognise that the U.N. General Assembly has had the issue on its agenda (especially as related to the non-self-governing territories) since 1950.[3] Of special note was Resolution 566 of 1952 which recognised that the direct association of non-independent countries in the U.N. was an effective means of promoting the progress of the people of those territories. Throughout the decades of the 1960s through the 1980s, the General Assembly continued to address the question.

In the 1990s, the General Assembly, and the Economic and Social Council (ECOSOC), approved a series of resolutions in favour of a closer association between the non-self-governing territories and the U.N. system. In this connection, both the Assembly and ECOSOC repeated throughout the period the need for the formulation of assistance programmes to the non-self-governing territories - similar language used in previous decades in relation to liberation groups. The U.N. continued to expand its perspective during this period by requesting the various U.N. bodies to work toward the acceleration of progress in the economic and social sectors of the territories. It also requested the U.N. bodies to facilitate the participation of the representatives of the elected governments in relevant meetings and conferences of U.N. agencies and organisations "so that they might draw maximum benefits from the related activities of the specialised agencies and other organisations of the U.N. system."

Toward Integration in the U.N. System

A number of U.N. organisations have sought to implement this mandate. In the case of the specialised agencies, accommodations were made for the non-independent countries in general to achieve associate membership or observer status, depending on the terms of reference and rules of procedure of the specific U.N. body concerned. In the 2000 *Statement of the Government of the U.S. Virgin Islands to the U.N. Fourth Committee*, the representative revealed that "only seven of 14 specialised agencies have the necessary provisions within their rules of procedure for direct participation (of the non-independent countries)." [4] The specific bodies listed were the Food and Agriculture Organisation (FAO); the International Maritime Organisation (IMO); the International Civil Aviation Organisation (ICAO); the U.N. Educational, Scientific, and Cultural Organisation (UNESCO); the Universal Postal Union (UPU); the Pan American Health Organisation (PAHO) and the World Meteorological Organisation (WMO). Unfortunately, the number of territories directly participating in the programmes of these and other U.N. bodies remains insufficient, and it is only through the active implementation of the longstanding mandate on assistance to the non-independent countries contained in the resolutions on the issue for almost half a century that this participation deficit can be remedied.

U.N. Regional Commissions

Perhaps the most successful implementation of the mandate on participation by non-independent countries has been undertaken by the U.N. regional commissions - albeit with deliberate caution and passivity. The Economic Commission for Latin America and the Caribbean (ECLAC) and the Economic and Social Commission for Asia and the Pacific (ESCAP) have been especially active in extending associate membership to the countries and territories "within the geographic scope" of the work of the commission. In this case, with the notable exception of Tokelau, nine of the ten Non-Independent Pacific Countries (NIPCs) maintain associate membership in ESCAP, while seven of the ten Non-Independent Caribbean Countries (NICCs) enjoy the same status in ECLAC.

Table 2. Current Associate Members of the Economic Commission for Latin America and the Caribbean

Country	Date of Admission	Resolution of Admission
Montserrat [a]	23 April 1968	283 (AC.61) [b]
Netherlands Antilles	14 May 1981	445 (XIX)
British Virgin Islands	6 April 1984	453(XX)
U.S. Virgin Islands	6 April 1984	454(XX)
Aruba	22 April 1988	490(XXII)
Puerto Rico	10 May 1990	505(XXIII)
Anguilla	20 April 1996	561(XXVI)

[a] The West Indies Associated States, including Montserrat, were admitted as a single associate member.
[b] Committee of the Whole Resolution.
Source: *Working Group of Non-Independent Caribbean Countries, Caribbean Development and Cooperation Committee.*

The involvement of associate members in ECLAC, for example, had been bolstered by the existence of the sub regional Caribbean Development and Cooperation Committee (CDCC) as a separate intergovernmental body of small island Caribbean countries, serviced by the ECLAC Secretariat. Within the CDCC was formed the Working Group of NICCs in 1990 which led the effort within the wider U.N. system for increased inclusion and participation for Caribbean and Pacific non-independent countries. The decline and virtual demise of the CDCC by the beginning of the last quarter of the 1990s as a functioning ministerial body with the concomitant political support from regional governments, and the CDCC Secretariat's efforts to re-direct the Group's work programme away from anything considered the least bit controversial, made the efforts of the Working Group more difficult to sustain.

U.N. World Conferences and General Assembly Special Sessions

Despite the lack of support from the remnants of the CDCC, the momentum of the Working Group continued, in conjunction with other intergovernmental bodies such as the Offshore Governors' Forum, comprised of the Caribbean and Pacific territories of the U.S., namely American Samoa, Guam, Northern Mariana Islands, Puerto Rico, and the U.S. Virgin Islands. For strategic and practical reasons, a shift in focus was made to concentrate on the participation of the associate member countries - the non-independent countries that were already associate members of ECLAC and ESCAP - in the world conferences of the United Nations. Under the leadership of the founding chairman of the Working Group, the Government of the U.S. Virgin Islands, efforts had been initiated at the beginning of the 1990s for associate member participation in the upcoming U.N. world conferences in the economic and social sphere. The first move to expand the participation in U.N. world conferences to associate members of the regional economic commissions was made in relation to the 1992 U.N. Conference on Environment and Development (UNCED). Supported by the newly formed Alliance of Small Island States (AOSIS) at the U.N., a resolution was adopted at the preparatory committee to grant observer status to UNCED to the associate members of the regional economic commissions.

This objective was not easily attained because of curious objections raised by the representative of one developed country that administered territories - other 'administering powers' were not politically threatened by the inclusion of the non-independent countries in a conference on environment. The isolated objection was ultimately withdrawn - after several days of informal debate - resulting in the new rule for associate member participation at the Earth Summit held in Brazil in 1992, which set forth that:

> *"Representatives designated by associate members of regional commissions may participate as observers, without the right to vote, in the deliberations of the conference, the Main Committee and, as appropriate, any other committee or working group."*

Ironically, the chairman of the Working Group who facilitated this historic observer status category could not attend the Rio Conference due to the unavailability of resources from within or outside the U.N. system. ESCAP associate members benefited from this effort. The UNCED decision paved the way for similar approvals for the participation of the associate members of ECLAC and ESCAP in subsequent U.N. world conferences between 1992 and 1996. These included the U.N. Conference on Straddling and Highly Migratory Fish Stocks (1993-95, New York), the Global Conference on the Sustainable Development of Small Island Developing States (1994, Barbados), the International Conference on Population and Development (1994, Cairo), the International Conference on Natural Disaster Reduction (1994, Yokohama), the World Summit for Social Development (1995, Copenhagen), the Fourth World Conference on Women (1995, Beijing), and the U.N. Conference on Human Settlements (1996, Istanbul).

Recent Developments

Recent activities on behalf of the associate member non-independent countries have focused o the participation in the special sessions of the U.N. General Assembly - another step in the direction of integration in the U.N. system. On the premise that these countries had participated in the world conferences in the 1990's, it only stood to reason that they should be eligible for participation in the special sessions of the General Assembly which were organised to "review and assess the implementation of the programme of action" of these world conferences.

Accordingly, decisions were taken, following the advocacy of the Chairman of the Working Group of Non-independent Caribbean Countries, for the inclusion of these countries to participate as observers in the U.N. special session to Review and Assess the Implementation of the Programme of Action of the Global Conference on the Sustainable Development of Small Island States (1999, New York), and to review the Cairo Plan of Action on Population and Development (1999, New York). Recent efforts were successful in gaining the identical observer status in the June 2001 General Assembly review of the 1996 U.N. Conference on Human Settlements, while present efforts are underway with respect to participation in the General Assembly Special Session on HIV/AIDS scheduled for June, 2001. Additionally, the associate members were granted observer status in the upcoming U.N. World Conference Against Racism, Racial Discrimination, Xenophobia, and Related Intolerance scheduled for September 2001, while efforts are underway to gain the same status in the ten-year review by the General Assembly of the 1992 Earth Summit. Most recently, the rules of procedure of the 2002 Second World Assembly on Ageing have included the observer status provision for the associate members.

After over ten years of work, the category of participation for the associate member countries in relevant world conferences and special sessions of the General Assembly seems somewhat established, although special consideration still must be sought for each conference to ensure the inclusion of the observer status category.

In order for the non-self-governing territories to achieve their full measure of self-government, and for the self-governing territories to progress economically as well as constitutionally, they must have direct access to the wide range of programmes and institutions of the U.N. system. And the U.N. system must continue its widening approach to embrace the development concerns of all small island developing countries irrespective of political status.

Notes and references

1   See Annex to U.N. General Assembly Resolution 1541 (XV) of 1960.
2   United Nations Association of the Virgin Islands, St. Thomas, USVI, 1999.
3   See U.N. General Assembly Resolution 66-1 of 1950 which recognised the value to non-self-governing territories of participation in U.N. specialised agencies. In 1950, the present-day small island self-governing territories were non-self-governing.
4   See Statement of Dr. Carlyle Corbin, Minister of State for External Affairs, Government of the U.S. Virgin Islands, to the United Nations Fourth Committee, on the agenda item "Implementation of the Decolonisation Declaration by the Specialised Agencies and the international institutions associated with the United Nations", 28th September 2000.

PART III

IWGIA PUBLICATIONS

IN ENGLISH

No. 104: Kathrin Wessendorf (ed.): *Challenging Politics: Indigenous Peoples' Experiences with Political Parties and Elections* (2001), 291 pages
US$ 19.00; GBP 13.00; DKK 150.00
ISBN: 87-90730-45-3

No. 103: Rosalva Aída Hernández Castillo (ed.): *The Other Word: Women and Violence in Chiapas Before and After Acteal* (2001), 151 pages
US$ 13.50; GBP 9.20; DKK 108.00
ISBN 87-907730-43-7

No. 102: Jens Dahl, Jack Hicks, Peter Jull (eds.): *Nunavut: Inuit Regain Control of their Lands and their Lives* (2000), 223 pages
US $ 16.00; GBP 11.20; DKK 120.00
ISBN: 87-90730-34-8

No. 101: Albert Kwokwo Barume: *Heading Towards Extinction? Indigenous Rights in Africa: The Case of the TWA of the Kahuzi-Biega National Park, Democratic Republic of Congo* (2000), 142 pages
US$ 14.00; GBP 9.80; DKK 105.00
ISBN: 87-90730-31-3

Update Report 4, *"Life is not ours": Land and Human Rights in the Chittagong Hill Tracts, Bangladesh* (2000), 101 pages
US$ 10.00, GBP 7.00; DKK 75.00
ISBN: 87-90730-42-7

No. 99: Rajkumari Chandra Roy: *Land Rights of the Indigenous Peoples of the Chittagong Hill Tracts, Bangladesh* (2000), 231 pages
US$ 16.00; GBP 11.20; DKK 120.00
ISBN: 87-90730-29-1

No. 98: Andrew Madsen: *The Hadzabe of Tanzania. Land and Human Rights for a Hunter-Gatherer Community* (2000), 96 pages
US$ 11.00; GBP 7.70; DKK 90.00
ISBN: 87-90730-26-7

No. 97: Marcus Colchester and Christian Erni: *Indigenous Peoples and Protected Areas in South and Southeast Asia: From Principles to Practice* (2000), 334 pages
US$ 20.00; GBP 14.00; DKK 150.00
ISBN: 87-90730-18-6

Indigenous Affairs 2000

1/2000 The Pacific
2/2000 Hunters & Gatherers
3/2000 Indigenous Women
4/2000 Indochina

Indigenous Affairs 2001

1/2001 Racism
2/2001 Military Training
3/2001 China
4/2001 International Processes

IN SPANISH

Jens Dahl & Alejandro Parellada: *Pueblos Indígenas* (2000) 125 pages,
US$ 15.00, GBP 10.50; DKK 115.00
ISBN: 87-90730-30-5

No. 30: Morita Carrasco: *Los Derechos de los pueblos indígenas en Argentina* (2000), 354 pages,
US$18.00; GBP 12.60; DKK 135.00
ISBN 950-843-429-5

No. 29: Claudia Briones, Morita Carrasco: *Pacta sunt Servanda. Capitulaciones, Convenios y Tratados con Indígenas en Pampa y Patagonia, Argentina* (2000), 211 pages,
US$ 13.00; GBP 9.10; DKK 97.00
ISBN 950-843-423-6

Asuntos Indígenas 2000

1/2000 Latinamérica - El Pacífico
2/2000 Cazadores & Recolectores
3/2000 Mujeres Indígenas
4/2000 Indochina

Asuntos Indígenas 2001

1/2001 Racismo
2/2001 Entrenamiento Militar
3/2001 China
4/2001 Procesos Internacionales

IN FRENCH

Voix africaines. Pasteurs nomades et chasseurs-cueilleurs en Afrique subsaharienne (2001) (Translation of *Indigenous Affairs* no. 2/99 on Hunter-Gatherers and Pastoralists in Africa), 121 pages,
US$ 10.50; FRF 75.00; DKK 85.00
ISBN 2-912114-04-7

IN SWAHILI

Marianne Jensen and Greta M. Maganga (eds.) *Wenyeji Asilia Katika Afrika Mashariki, Kati Na Kusini* (Translation of *Indigenous Affairs* no. 2/99 on Hunter-Gatherers and Pastoralists in Africa) 2001, 148 pages,
US$ 10.50; GBP 7.30; DKK 85.00
ISBN 87-90730-44-5

IN TAGALOG (PHILIPPINES)

Katutubong Mamamayan
(Translation of the Spanish book *Pueblos Indígenas*) 2001,
131 pages.

IN BAHASA (INDONESIA)

Masyarakat Adat di Dunia - Eksistensi Dan Perjuangannya
(Translation of the Spanish book *Pueblos Indígenas*) 2001,
139 pages.

IN DANISH

Hvem er de indfødte folk?

2. *Van Gujar – Et skovfolk i indisk Himalaya,* Sille Stidsen & IWGIA
3. *De Indfødte Australiere,* Hanne Miriam Larsen & IWGIA
4. *Buskmennesker - Et folk i Kalahari Ørkenen,* Arthur Krasilnikoff & IWGIA
5. *Indianer i Danmark – Shuar i Ecuador,* Birgitte Feiring & IWGIA
6. *Indianske folk i Perus Andesbjerge,* Karsten Pærregaard & IWGIA
7. *Naga - Et folk mellem Indien og Burma,* Shimreichon Luithui & IWGIA

DKK 25.00, IWGIA 2000, ISSN 1399-9540

SUBSCRIPTION RATES 2001

INDIGENOUS AFFAIRS & THE INDIGENOUS WORLD

Individuals: 40.00 US$ / 310.00 DKK
Institutions: 70.00 US$ / 545.00 DKK

INDIGENOUS AFFAIRS & THE INDIGENOUS WORLD & BOOKS

Individuals: 95.00 US$ / 740.00 DKK
Institutions: 135.00 US$ / 1,050.00 DKK

ASUNTOS INDÍGENAS & El MUNDO INDÍGENA

Individuals: 40.00 US$ / 310.00 DKK
Institutions: 70.00 US$ / 545.00 DKK

ASUNTOS INDÍGENAS & El MUNDO INDÍGENA & LIBROS

Individuals: 75.00 US$ / 585.00 DKK
Institutions: 110.00 US$ / 860.00 DKK

IWGIA's publications are published on a non-profit basis.
Your subscription to our publications is a direct contribution to the
continuing production of IWGIA's documentation and analysis of the
situation of indigenous peoples worldwide.

For subscription - contact IWGIA by

e-mail: iwgia@iwgia.org
website: www.iwgia.org
or fax: +45 35 27 05 07

International Secretariat

Classensgade 11 E, DK-2100 Copenhagen, Denmark
Tel. (+45) 35 27 05 00 – Fax (+45) 35 27 05 07
E-mail: iwgia@iwgia.org - Web: www.iwgia.org

Local Groups

Denmark, Copenhagen
Classensgade 11 E, DK-2100 Copenhagen, Denmark
E-mail: wiinstedt@mail.tele.dk

Sweden, Gothenburg
c/o Inst. of Social Anthropology,
Brogatan 4, S-41 301 Gothenburg, Sweden
E-mail: iwgia@goteborg@sant.gu.se

Norway, Tromsø
c/o Sidsel Saugestad
Institut for Socialantropologi
Universitetet i Tromsø
9037 Tromsø, Norway
E-mail: sidsels@isv.uit.no

Switzerland, Zürich
c/o Ethnologisches Seminar
der Universität Zürich
Freienstrasse 5, CH-8032 Zürich, Switzerland
E-mail: daniwgia@ethno.unizh.ch

Switzerland, Basel
c/o Ethnologisches Seminar
Münsterplatz 19
CH-4051 Basel, Switzerland
E-mail: iwgia@kali.urz.unibas.ch

Russia, Moscow
Olga A. Murashko
117574, Odoevskogo, st.7-5-595, Moskow, Russia
E-mail:olga@murkre.aha.ru